THE FALL OF MAN AND THE FOUNDATIONS OF SCIENCE

Peter Harrison provides a new account of the religious foundations of scientific knowledge. He shows how the new approaches to the study of nature that emerged in the sixteenth and seventeenth centuries were directly informed by theological discussions about the Fall of Man and the extent to which the mind and the senses had been damaged by that primeval event. Scientific methods, he suggests, were originally devised as techniques for ameliorating the cognitive damage wrought by human sin. At its inception, modern science was conceptualised as a means of recapturing the knowledge of nature that Adam had once possessed. Contrary to a widespread view which sees science emerging in conflict with religion, Harrison argues that theological considerations were of vital importance in the framing of the new scientific method.

PETER HARRISON is the Andreas Idreos Professor of Science and Religion, University of Oxford. He is author of *'Religion' and the Religions in the English Enlightenment* (1990, 2002) and *The Bible, Protestantism and the Rise of Natural Science* (1998, 2001).

D1564741

THE FALL OF MAN AND THE FOUNDATIONS OF SCIENCE

PETER HARRISON

University of Oxford

CAMBRIDGE UNIVERSITY PRESS
Cambridge, New York, Melbourne, Madrid, Cape Town, Singapore, São Paulo, Delhi

Cambridge University Press
The Edinburgh Building, Cambridge CB2 8RU, UK

Published in the United States of America by Cambridge University Press, New York

www.cambridge.org
Information on this title: www.cambridge.org/9780521117296

First published 2007
Reprinted 2008
This digitally printed version 2009

A catalogue record for this publication is available from the British Library

ISBN 978-0-521-87559-2 hardback
ISBN 978-0-521-11729-6 paperback

For Grace

We desire truth, and find within ourselves only uncertainty . . .
This desire is left to us, partly to punish us, partly to make us perceive from whence we have fallen.

Blaise Pascal, *Pensées,* §401

Contents

Contents

Acknowledgements

This book has been some eight years in the making. That it has been completed at all is owing to the generosity of several institutions and numerous individuals. I must acknowledge first of all the support of the Australian Research Council which provided funds for teaching relief during the years 2000–3. I am also grateful to the Institute for Advanced Study, Princeton, where an Elizabeth and J. Richardson Dilworth Fellowship for the first six months of 2005 made it possible for me to complete the first draft of this book. It is difficult to imagine an environment more conducive to scholarly endeavour than that provided by the Institute and the School of Historical Studies. I should also express my gratitude to a second Princeton Institution, the Center of Theological Inquiry. A membership during 2001 was devoted to another project which will be the subject of a forthcoming book. However, my time there afforded me the opportunity to conduct research that has found its way into this volume, and I should thank the members and staff of the Center, in particular Wallace Alston, Robert Jensen, and Kathi Morley. Last, but not least, Bond University, until recently my home institution, was always supportive of my research both financially and in its willingness to allow me to take leave from teaching duties from time to time.

I have benefited greatly from the assistance of numerous individuals. Special thanks are owed to David Lindberg, who kindly read a complete draft of the book and offered invaluable advice. Various chapters were read by other colleagues and friends – Peter Anstey, Rhodri Lewis, and Will Poole. Their comments and observations have also been enormously helpful. Jonathan Israel's congenial early modern group at the Institute for Advanced Study also read drafts of some of the earlier material and I would specifically like to thank Jonathan himself, along with Kinch Hoekstra, Noah Efron, Karl Appuhn, and Wijnand Mijnhard. Kinch Hoekstra also offered helpful suggestions for the title. Heinrich von Staden's history of science seminar was also a source of valuable feedback. Over the years many others have provided suggestions, advice and encouragement – Philip Almond, Stephen Gaukroger, Richard Yeo, Michael Lattke, Ed Conrad, Marina Bollinger, Stephen Snobelen, Ron Numbers, Jon Roberts, Conal Condren, Ian Hunter, Peter Barker, Raoul Mortley, and Bill Krebs. My greatest debt, as always, is to my wife Carol. She has supported me in this endeavour from the start, has happily accompanied me on extended sojourns away from our home in Australia and now here, to Oxford. In what could only have been a labour of love, she has read numerous drafts of each of the chapters. Grace and Thomas, both of whom arrived during the gestation of this book, have also been a source of great joy, providing wonderful distractions from the writing process and keeping me firmly grounded in the mundane realities of life. This book is for Grace.

Abbreviations

ANF	*The Ante-Nicene Fathers*, 9 vols. (Edinburgh, 1990)
AT	*Œuvres de Descartes*, ed. Charles Adam and Paul Tannery, 13 vols. (Paris, 1897–1913)
BJHS	*British Journal for the History of Science*
CHLMP	*The Cambridge History of Later Medieval Philosophy*, ed. Norman Kretzmann, Anthony Kenny, and Jan Pinborg (Cambridge, 1982)
CHMP	*The Cambridge History of Later Greek and Early Medieval Philosophy*, ed. A. H. Armstrong (Cambridge, 1970)
CHRP	*The Cambridge History of Renaissance Philosophy*, ed. Charles B. Schmitt and Quentin Skinner (Cambridge, 1988)
CSM	*The Philosophical Writings of Descartes*, tr. John Cottingham, Robert Stoothoff, and Dugald Murdoch, 2 vols. (Cambridge, 1985)
FaCh	Fathers of the Church, Washington DC, 1932–
JHI	*Journal of the History of Ideas*
LW	*Luther's Works*, ed. Jaroslav Pelikan and Helmut Lehmann, 55 vols. (Philadelphia, 1957)
NPNF I	*Nicene and Post-Nicene Fathers, Series I*, ed. Philip Schaff and Henry Wace, 14 vols. (Peabody, MA, 1994)
NPNF II	*Nicene and Post-Nicene Fathers, Series II*, ed. Philip Schaff and Henry Wace, 14 vols. (Peabody, MA, 1994)
PG	*Patrologiae cursus completus*, Series Graeca, ed. Jacques-Paul Migne, 162 vols. (Paris, 1857–1912)
PL	*Patrologiae cursus completus*, Series Latina, ed. Jacques-Paul Migne, 217 vols. (Paris, 1844–1905)
SCG	Thomas Aquinas, *Summa contra gentiles*, tr. English Dominican Fathers (New York, 1924)
ST	Thomas Aquinas, *Summa theologiae*, Blackfriars edn, (London, 1964–76)

Introduction

He came into the World a Philosopher, which sufficiently appeared by his writing the Nature of things upon their Names: he could view Essences in themselves, and read Forms with the comment of their respective Properties; he could see Consequents yet dormant in their principles, and effects yet unborn in the Womb of their Causes; his understanding could almost pierce into future contingents, his conjectures improving even to Prophesy, or the certainties of Prediction; till his fall it was ignorant of nothing but of Sin, or at least rested in the notion without the smart of Experiment . . . I confess 'tis difficult for us who date our ignorance from our first Being, & were still bred up with the same infirmities about us, with which we were born, to raise our thoughts, and imaginations to those intellectual perfections that attended our nature in its time of Innocence . . . [1]

These effusive estimates of Adam's abilities were delivered by Robert South in a sermon to worshippers at St Paul's Cathedral, London on a Sunday morning in November 1662. While this description of Adam's philosophical acumen was notable for its eloquence – South was widely acknowledged as the most gifted preacher of his generation – there was nothing unusual in its substance. From quite early in the Christian era, patristic writers had commented on the unique intellectual capacities of our first father, on the vast extent of his knowledge, and on the magnitude of his losses at the Fall. These ideas were further elaborated during the Middle Ages and were commonplace in the early modern period. For many champions of the new learning in the seventeenth century the encyclopaedic knowledge of Adam was the benchmark against which their own aspirations were gauged. Francis Bacon's project to reform philosophy was motivated by an attempt to determine whether the human mind 'might by any means be restored to its perfect and original condition, or if that may not be, yet reduced to a better condition than that in which it now is'.[2] In 1662, the year in

[1] Robert South, 'Man was made in God's Image', *Sermons Preached upon Several Occasions* (Oxford, 1679), pp. 127, 128.
[2] Francis Bacon, *The Great Instauration*, in *The Works of Francis Bacon*, ed. James Spedding, Robert Ellis, and Douglas Heath, 14 vols. (London, 1857–74), IV, 7.

which South delivered his sermon, Bacon's intellectual heirs formed the Royal Society, the goals of which were also expressed by the apologist for the Society, Thomas Sprat, in terms of a regaining of the knowledge that Adam had once possessed.[3]

Such sanguine expectations, it must be said, were not shared by all. Robert South himself, while clearly impressed by the scope of Adam's original knowledge, entertained serious doubts about the prospects for its contemporary recovery, and he could be scathing of those who cherished such proud ambitions. In his capacity as the Public Orator at Oxford, he had presided at the opening of the Sheldonian Theatre in 1669. In a long speech on that occasion he had observed that Fellows of the fledgling Royal Society 'can admire nothing except fleas, lice, and themselves', no doubt causing acute embarrassment to the Fellows present, including Christopher Wren, architect of the theatre. South's reservations about the programme of the Royal Society were owing to his scepticism about the extent to which Adamic knowledge could be re-established in the modern age and to his concerns about the links between such projects and a discredited Puritan utopianism. Indeed one of the major themes of South's sermon was the vast disparity between the ease with which Adam had acquired knowledge and the difficulties encountered by his latter-day progeny: 'Study was not then a Duty, night-watchings were needless; the light of Reason wanted not the assistance of a Candle.' For Adam's fallen issue, however, it was a very different matter: 'This is the doom of faln man to labour in the fire, to seek truth in *profundo*, to exhaust his time and impair his health, and perhaps to spin out his dayes, and himself into one pittiful, controverted, Conclusion.'[4] Adam's knowledge, on this more sober account, would not be easily reacquired. Yet, whatever the differences between South and the Fellows of the Royal Society, it was agreed on all sides that those seeking to determine the rightful course for the advancement of knowledge needed to reckon with Adam and what befell him as a consequence of his sin.

The narrative of the Fall has always exercised a particular fascination over Western minds. It has been described in recent times as 'the anthropological myth *par excellence*', 'the most elemental of myths', and 'the central myth of Western culture'.[5] During the seventeenth century, this myth assumed

[3] Thomas Sprat, *History of the Royal Society of London* (London, 1667), pp. 349f. The Society had met informally from 1660, but was officially incorporated on 15 July 1662.
[4] South, *Sermons*, pp. 127f.
[5] Paul Ricoeur, *The Symbolism of Evil* (Boston, 1967), p. 281; T. Otten, *After Innocence: Visions of the Fall in Modern Literature* (Pittsburgh, 1982); Philip Almond, *Adam and Eve in Seventeenth-Century Thought* (Cambridge, 1999), p. 1.

a particular importance. At this time, the bible came to oc
tion of unparalleled authority, informing discussions about the na.
the state, the rights of the individual, private property, education, inte.
national sovereignty, the status of indigenous peoples, work and leisure,
agriculture and gardening, anthropology and moral psychology. In each of
these spheres, the story of Adam had a significant place. According to historian Christopher Hill, 'The Fall then was central to seventeenth-century
debates about the nature of the state and its laws, as well as about the
justification of private property, social inequality and the subordination of
women.'[6] This was particularly so in England, where Calvinist understandings of the doctrine of original sin predominated. It is no exaggeration to
say that this dogma dominated the theological agenda and became a crucial
point of reference in broader social and intellectual discussions.[7]

The central concern of this book is to illustrate the ways in which the
myth of the Fall informed discussions about the foundations of knowledge
and influenced methodological developments in the nascent natural sciences. While the first half of the book will be devoted to making this general
case, the second half will focus on the more specific example of experimental science in seventeenth-century England. What should become apparent
from the more general discussion is that the differences between competing strategies for the advancement of knowledge put forward during the
sixteenth and seventeenth centuries can be accounted for largely in terms
of different assessments of the Fall and of its impact on the human mind.
The renewed focus on the Fall and original sin that is characteristic of the
early modern period was occasioned by the religious upheavals of the sixteenth century. These events not only precipitated a crisis of confidence
in the traditional sources of knowledge, but also coincided with a revival
of an Augustinian anthropology that emphasised the corruption of human
nature and the limitations of the intellect. Four aspects of this development
will be examined.

First, the early modern preoccupation with sin meant that in the realm
of epistemology error was often equated with sin, and the human propensity to invest false claims with the character of truth was attributed to
Adam's fall. Considerations such as these explain why philosophers of the
seventeenth century tend to be preoccupied with error and its prevention,
and commonly assume that avoidance of error is not merely a necessary

---

[6] Christopher Hill, 'Sin and Society', *The Collected Essays of Christopher Hill*, 3 vols. (Amherst, 1986),
II, 117–40 (125).
[7] *Ibid.*, p. 132; W. M. Spellman, *John Locke and the Problem of Depravity* (Oxford, 1988), pp. 8, 9;
William Poole, *Milton and the Idea of the Fall* (Cambridge, 2005), pp. 4f., 21–39.

condition for knowledge, it is in fact sufficient for it.[8] The tradition according to which Adam was in possession of the perfect philosophy implies that human minds had originally been designed to know the truth, and that if those impediments that arose as a consequence of the Fall could be identified and neutralized, the mind would once again, of its own nature, arrive at truth or at least be better equipped to do so. Francis Bacon, as is well known, saw in the sciences the prospect of restoring, or at least repairing, the losses to knowledge that had resulted from the Fall.[9] His emphasis lay on purging the mind of those flaws introduced by Adam's defection. Describing his goal as 'the true end and termination of error', he suggested that this could only be accomplished if knowledge was 'discharged of that venom which the serpent infused into it'.[10] Later in the century a number of those involved in the establishment and running of the Royal Society set out a similar strategy. Joseph Glanvill, an early and influential fellow of the Society, explained that knowledge could not be set on a sure foundation until a full account had been given of the causes of ignorance: 'And therefore besides the general reason I gave of our intellectual disabilities, The *Fall*; it will be worth our labor to descend to a more particular account: since it is a good degree of *Knowledge* to be acquainted with the *causes* of our *Ignorance*.'[11] Even opponents of the experimental method of the Royal Society adopted this approach. John Sergeant, a champion of Aristotelianism who opposed both English experimentalism and Cartesianism, observed in his *Method to Science* (1696) that even the greatest minds 'still miss of Reasoning rightly, and so fall short of True Knowledge, which is their Natural Perfection'. Once again, the proposed solution involved an analysis of the primordial cause of error: 'Whence, our First Enquiry ought to be, how Man's Nature came to be so Disabled from performing its Primary Operation, or from Reasoning rightly.'[12]

This preoccupation with error and its causes was by no means the sole preserve of English philosophers, although admittedly it was they who most enthusiastically focused their attentions on the history of Adam. An important feature of Descartes' programme to establish new foundations

---

[8] On the avoidance of error as sufficient for truth, see Thomas Lennon's introduction to Nicolas Malebranche, *The Search after Truth*, tr. and ed. Thomas Lennon and Paul Olscamp (Cambridge, 1997), p. xii.

[9] Bacon, *Novum Organum* II.lii (*Works* IV, 247–8). Cf. *Valerius Terminus* (*Works* III, 222).

[10] Bacon, *Great Instauration*, (*Works* IV, 20–21).

[11] Joseph Glanvill, *The Vanity of Dogmatizing. or, Confidence in opinions manifested in a discourse of the shortness and uncertainty of our knowledge, and its causes: with some reflexions on peripateticism, and an apology for philosophy* (London, 1661), p. 63; cf. *Scepsis Scientifica, or, Confest ignorance, the way to science* (London, 1665), p. 48.

[12] John Sergeant, *The Method to Science* (London, 1696), Preface, sig. a1v–a2r.

for knowledge was 'to investigate the origin and causes of our errors and to learn to guard against them'.[13] While Descartes makes no mention of the Fall in this context – indeed he is typically silent on matters relating to sacred history – his compatriots were less reticent. The subtitle of Nicolas Malebranche's *Search after Truth* (1674–5) reads: 'Wherein are treated the nature of man's mind and the use he must make of it to avoid error in the sciences'. Malebranche went on to explain that this approach called for a specific investigation into 'how we might conceive the order found in the faculties and passions of our first father in his original state, as well as the changes and disorder that befell him after his sin'.[14] Blaise Pascal went further, castigating Descartes for not having taken the Fall seriously enough. Had he done so he might not have spoken so confidently about attaining certain knowledge. Pascal allowed that 'if man had never been corrupted, he would, in his innocence, confidently enjoy both truth and felicity'. The present situation, however, was rather different: 'We perceive an image of truth and possess nothing but falsehood, being equally incapable of absolute ignorance and certain knowledge; so obvious is it that we once enjoyed a degree of perfection from which we have unhappily fallen.'[15]

For all the attention directed towards sin and error, the ultimate aim was to determine the conditions under which knowledge would be possible and, more particularly, what kinds of things could be known and by what methods. Writing in the Preface of *Micrographia* (1665) Robert Hooke, curator of experiments at the Royal Society, declared that 'every man, both from a deriv'd corruption, innate and born with him, and from his breeding and converse with men, is very subject to slip into all sorts of errors . . . These being the dangers in the process of humane Reason, the remedies of them all can only proceed from the real, the mechanical, the experimental Philosophy.'[16] Hooke's statement neatly encapsulates the positive aspect of proposals to advance knowledge in the seventeenth century. Having identified the specific privations suffered by the mind on account of Adam's lapse, an argument could be made as to how they could be most successfully redressed by the suggested procedures. The 'mechanical and experimental philosophy', while it will be a major focus of this book,

---

[13] Descartes, *Principles of Philosophy* I, §31, CSM I, 203–4. It is also significant that one of Spinoza's chief criticisms of both Descartes and Bacon was that 'they never grasped the true cause of error'. Letter to Henry Oldenburg, September 1661, *The Collected Works of Spinoza*, ed. and tr. Edwin Curley (Princeton, 1985) I, 167.

[14] Malebranche, *Search after Truth*, 1.5 (p. 19).

[15] Blaise Pascal, *Pensées*, L 131, tr. A. J. Krailsheimer (London, 1966), p. 65. This edition uses the Lafuma (L) numbering. Cf. L 45, L 199, L 401.

[16] Robert Hooke, *Micrographia* (London, 1665), Preface.

was not the only solution proposed to overcome the inherent incapacity of fallen minds. Despite a general consensus about the limitations of the intellect and the need to overcome its deficiencies, projects to address these shortcomings varied considerably. The priority accorded to proposed sources of knowledge – be it reason and innate principles; the senses, observation, and experimentation; or divine revelation through the scriptures or personal inspiration – were intimately related to analyses of the specific effects of original sin. Similar considerations apply to the certitude with which various forms of knowledge could be held.

The second aspect of the thesis of this book, then, is that the various solutions offered to the problem of knowledge in the early modern period are closely related to assessments of exactly what physical and cognitive depredations were suffered by the human race as a consequence of Adam's original infraction. If, for example, the Fall were understood as having resulted in the triumph of the passions over reason, the restoration of Adamic knowledge would be accomplished through re-establishing control of the passions, thus enabling reason once again to discharge its proper function. If the Fall had dulled Adam's senses, this deficiency might be overcome through the use of artificial instruments capable of restoring to weakened human senses some of their original acuity. If the Fall had altered nature itself, rendering its operations less obvious and less intelligible, intrusive investigative techniques would be required to make manifest what had once been plain. Varying estimates of the severity of the Fall, moreover, gave rise to different assessments of the prospects of a full recovery of Adam's knowledge. Those who regarded the Fall as a relatively minor event were generally far more optimistic about the possibility of constructing a complete and certain science than were those for whom the Fall was an unmitigated catastrophe. As will become apparent, the contrasting experimental, speculative, and illuminative solutions to the early modern problem of knowledge were informed by varying conceptions of the nature and severity of the Fall. To express it in more familiar (but historically more problematic) terms, advocates of 'rationalism' and 'empiricism' largely fall out along lines related to an underlying theological anthropology. Descartes' confident assertion that the 'natural light' of reason could provide the basis of a complete and certain science presupposed the persistence of the natural light and the divine image even in fallen human beings. This was strongly contested by those who believed that the Fall had effaced the divine image and all but extinguished the natural light. On this latter view, if knowledge were possible at all, it would be painstakingly accumulated through much labour, through trials and the testing of nature, and would give rise to a modest knowledge that did not penetrate to the essences of things and was at best probable rather than certain. Such mitigated scepticism characterised the experimental approach commonly associated with such figures as Francis Bacon and Robert Boyle.

The third element of this argument concerns the religious background of these early modern discussions of the Fall and its impact on knowledge. One event that led to a renewed interest in the human condition and its inherent fallibility was the Protestant Reformation and the resurgence of Augustinian thought that accompanied it. The reformers' focus on human depravity, originally articulated in the context of a particular view of justi-fication, was also to set the agenda for the epistemological debates of the following two centuries. In general, those influenced by the anthropology of Luther and Calvin were to adopt the position of mitigated scepticism characteristic of empiricism and the experimental philosophy. Those who took a more positive view of human nature were more inclined to assert the reliability of human reason, the possibility of *a priori* knowledge, and the perfectibility of the sciences. To a degree, then, the methodological prescriptions offered by philosophers in the seventeenth century mirror their confessional allegiances. Hence, the Catholic Descartes held fast to a relatively optimistic Thomist account of human nature and aspired to attain, in his own words, a 'perfect knowledge of all things that mankind is capable of knowing'.[17] By way of contrast, Francis Bacon, raised as he was in a Calvinist environment, thought that knowledge would be accumulated gradually and only with meticulous care. The work of many unexceptional minds, science would ultimately amount to 'judgment and opinion, not knowledge and certainty', as John Locke would later express it.[18] These confessional correlations are, admittedly, far from perfect, partly because of the emergence of a Protestant scholasticism that reverted to the optimistic Thomist/Aristotelian view of knowledge and human nature, and partly because early modern Catholicism witnessed its own Augustinian revival, most conspicuously in the Jansenist movement that exercised such a pro-found influence over Blaise Pascal and Antoine Arnauld. Nevertheless, it is possible to establish significant links between particular thinkers' commit-ments in the sphere of theological anthropology and their methodological prescriptions in the realm of the sciences.

Finally, and following directly from the previous point, the trajectories of the major philosophical projects of the seventeenth centuries can be

---

[17] Descartes, *Principles*, CSM I, 179.
[18] John Locke, *Essay concerning Human Understanding* IV.xii.10, ed. A. C. Fraser, 2 vols. (New York, 1959), II, 349.

understood to some extent as developments of different aspects of Augustinianism. While Augustine's influence on early modern philosophy has long been taken for granted by French authors, Anglophone writers are now increasingly aware of the significance of aspects of Augustine's thought for this period.[19] In keeping with the received version of the history of philosophy, according to which the chief concern of modern philosophy is epistemology, Augustine's theories of knowledge have been the primary focus of attention. Accordingly, Augustine is seen to have had most impact in the rationalist epistemologies of Descartes and Malebranche. While not wishing to deny the significance of this line of investigation, I shall trace an alternative avenue of Augustinian influence in the early modern period, namely, his views on human nature and his doctrine of original sin. While these are not unrelated to his epistemological views, Augustine's understanding of the Fall and original sin, as already indicated, was to play a vital role in traditions of investigation rather different from that of the Cartesians. The experimental approach, I shall argue, was deeply indebted to Augustinian views about the limitations of human knowledge in the wake of the Fall, and thus inductive experimentalism can also lay claim to a filial relationship with the tradition of Augustinianism. In much the same way that both Protestantism and early modern Catholicism can quite legitimately be regarded as heirs of Augustine, so too can both of the chief sects of seventeenth-century philosophy.

The claims set out in this book represent a significant challenge to some common assumptions about the origins of modern philosophy and science, and about the onset of modernity generally. At this point it is worth giving a preliminary indication of where the thesis stands in relation to a number of standard positions. At the most general level, the book seeks to challenge the idea that early modern philosophy, including natural philosophy, is concerned largely with issues of method and epistemology *per se*. The primary focus, I shall suggest, was rather human nature – 'anthropology' in its broadest sense – and epistemological concerns, while undoubtedly present,

---

[19] See, e.g., Etienne Gilson, 'The Future of Augustinian Metaphysics', in *A Monument to St. Augustine* (London, 1934); Jean Laporte, *Le cœur et la raison selon Pascal* (Paris, 1950); Jean Delumeau, *Le Péché et la peur: La culpabilisation en Occident XIIIe–XVIIIe siècles* (Paris, 1983); G. B. Matthews, *Thought's Ego in Augustine and Descartes* (Ithaca, 1992); 'Post-medieval Augustinianism', in Eleonore Stump and Norman Kretzmann (eds.), *The Cambridge Companion to Augustine* (Cambridge, 2001), pp. 267–79; Stephen Menn, *Descartes and Augustine* (Cambridge, 1998); Zbigniew Janowski, *Cartesian Theodicy* (Dordrecht, 2000); Michael Moriarty, *Early Modern French Thought* (Oxford, 2003), pp. 41–9 and passim. See also Louis-Paul Du Vaucel, 'Observations sur la philosophie de Descartes', in E. J. Dijksterhuis (ed.), *Descartes et le Cartésianisme Hollandais* (Paris, 1950), pp. 113–30; Michael Hanby, *Augustine and Modernity* (London, 2003), esp. pp. 134–77.

were secondary to this.[20] This contrasts with a widespread view that regards
the seventeenth century as preoccupied with the foundations of knowledge
and which characterises the transition from the medieval to the modern in
terms of a shift from metaphysics to epistemology. On this account, it is
Descartes who inaugurates the modern age by issuing a sceptical challenge
and then solving it with his own radical foundationalism. The agenda thus
set, the British empiricists react against Descartes' rationalism, leaving it
to Immanuel Kant (or possibly Hegel, depending on one's philosophical
predilections) to offer the definitive solution to the problem of knowledge. This version of the history of modern philosophy can be found, for
example, in the influential writings of Kuno Fischer (1824–1907).[21] Fischer
secured the place of Descartes' *Meditations* as the founding document of
modernity, and enshrined the view that modern philosophy was characterised by a split between rationalists and empiricists that was healed by the
critical philosophy of Immanuel Kant. Many introductions to modern philosophy still follow this line, and undergraduates are typically introduced
to the subject through the *Meditations*. Integral to this received view is the
assumption that the modern epistemological project is essentially a secular
one, representing the ascendancy of reason over faith, and setting up the
conditions for the age of Enlightenment to follow. Descartes' reliance on
God as the guarantor for his foundational project is thus often dismissed
as window dressing designed to placate potential ecclesiastical critics. Certainly, it is true that Descartes avoids making reference to the revealed
truths of Christianity, including the doctrine of original sin, and he is quite
forthcoming about his reluctance to engage in 'theological' discussions. In
this respect, however, he is rather atypical and thus a poor exemplar for
seventeenth-century philosophy generally. Very few discussions of knowledge in the seventeenth century are devoid of references to the problem
of sin in relation to knowledge. Indeed, surprising as it may seem, what
distinguishes seventeenth-century discussions of knowledge from scholasticism is not their secular character but rather the fact that they tend to
be more explicit in their reliance on the resources of revealed theology
than their medieval equivalents. Hence, as we shall see, one of the most

---

[20] Wilhelm Dilthey observed, at the close of the nineteenth century, that the advent of modernity can
be characterised as a turn from metaphysics to anthropology. 'Die Funktion der Anthropologie in
der Kultur des 16. und 17. Jahrhunderts', in *Weltanschauung und Analyse des Menschen seit Renaissance
und Reformation. Wilhelm Diltheys Gesammelte Schriften* II (Leipzig, 1914).

[21] Kuno Fischer, *Metaphysik oder Wissenschaftslehre* (Stuttgart, 1852); *Geschichte der neueren Philosophie*,
6 vols. (Mannheim, 1860). See Knud Haakonssen, 'The History of Early Modern Philosophy: The
Construction of a Useful Past', in C. Condren, S. Gaukroger and I. Hunter (eds.), *The Philosopher
in Early Modern Europe: The Nature of a Contested Identity* (Cambridge, 2006).

common seventeenth-century objections to scholastic philosophy was that it was 'pagan' in character.

A variation on this thesis, and one closer to that set out in this book, is that the Protestant Reformation precipitated an intellectual crisis by challenging traditional sources of authority. Because this challenge extended to the very criteria for what counted as true belief, the problem of knowledge became particularly acute. The rediscovery of ancient scepticism, which coincided with the Reformation, greatly exacerbated the problem, providing an impressive range of arguments to the effect that nothing could be known with certainty.[22] Michel de Montaigne, whose *Apology for Raymond Sebonde* masterfully rehearses the sceptical arguments of Pyrrho of Elis, played a major role in the revival of the ideas of these ancient schools and, along with his disciples, made scepticism a fashionable philosophical option in the seventeenth century. To a degree, sceptical arguments proved useful to the Counter-Reformation because they could be deployed against Protestant claims to doctrinal certainty. Moreover, one of the standard sceptical prescriptions – in the face of our ignorance it is best simply to follow the customs and traditions of one's own country – counselled against the adoption of novel religious views (such as those of the Protestants). Again Descartes is the key figure. The sceptical intellectual atmosphere that flourished in the early seventeenth century provided the point of departure for Descartes' *Meditations*, which begins with a radical scepticism, but concludes by triumphantly dispelling all doubts with clear and distinct ideas. These provide the indubitable foundations for knowledge. Richard Popkin, who has done most to highlight the role of scepticism in early modern philosophy, thus considers Montaigne's *Apologie* to be 'the womb of modern thought, in that it led to the attempt either to refute the new Pyrrhonism, or to find a way of living with it'.[23] Descartes provided just such a refutation, and in doing so inaugurated the era of modern philosophy.

[22] L. Floridi, 'The Diffusion of Sextus Empiricus's works in the Renaissance', *JHI* 56 (1995), 63–85; and 'The Rediscovery of Ancient Scepticism in Modern Times', in M. Burnyeat (ed.), *The Skeptical Tradition* (Berkeley, 1983), pp. 225–51; Charles B. Schmitt, *Cicero Scepticus: A Study of the Influence of the 'Academica' in the Renaissance* (The Hague, 1972).

[23] Richard H. Popkin, *The History of Scepticism from Erasmus to Spinoza* (Berkeley, 1979), p. 54. Cf. Ernst Cassirer, *Das Erkenntnisproblem in der Philosophie und Wissenschaft der neueren Zeit*, 2 vols. (Berlin, 1906–7), I, 162, 181. Popkin's work appeared in three successively expanded editions, the earlier work being *The History of Scepticism from Erasmus to Descartes* (Van Gorcum, 1960), the later, *The History of Scepticism from Savonarola to Bayle* (Oxford, 2003). Also see Popkin's 'Scepticism and Modernity' in T. Sorell (ed.), *The Rise of Modern Philosophy: The Tension between the New and Traditional Philosophies from Machiavelli to Leibniz* (Oxford, 1993), pp. 15–32; 'Theories of Knowledge', in *CHRP*, pp. 668–84. For discussions or developments of this important thesis see Richard A. Watson and James E. Force, (eds.), *The High Road to Pyrrhonism* (San Diego, 1980); R. Popkin and Arjo Vanderjagt (eds.), *Scepticism and Irreligion in the Seventeenth and Eighteenth Centuries* (Leiden,

This is a persuasive argument and one that has been justifiably influential. My own view is that while there is some truth in the idea of a 'sceptical crisis', that crisis was precipitated not only by the reformers' challenge to traditional authorities and the revival of ancient scepticism, but also by a renewed emphasis on an Augustinian anthropology that stressed the Fall and its epistemic consequences. This was particularly so in England, although varieties of Augustinianism had strong support on the Continent as well. It is true that both scepticism and Augustinian anthropology lead to doubts about the reliability of human knowledge, but they offer quite different prescriptions. For the sceptics, our ignorance is not the consequence of a cosmic catastrophe precipitated by human disobedience; rather it is intrinsic to human nature and is thus to be accepted with equanimity. Accordingly, the appropriate response lies not in attempting to remedy the operations of the mind (which were naturally limited), but in accepting the inevitable, suspending judgement, and cultivating an inner peace.[24] For those who attributed our current state of ignorance to the Fall, the figure of Adam had a dual significance. On the one hand, the Fall provided an explanation for human misery and proneness to error; on the other, Adam's prelapsarian perfections, including his encyclopaedic knowledge, were regarded as a symbol of unfulfilled human potential. It is this hopeful, forward-looking element that is absent from scepticism in either its ancient or its modern formulations. The sceptical prescription, moreover, is consistent with the classical ideal of the philosopher as one who adopts a life of contemplation. Those who took seriously the reality of the Fall, by way of contrast, were often motivated to reverse, or partially reverse, its unfortunate effects, and this required a commitment to the active life and an energetic engagement with both social and natural realms. There will be further discussion of the Popkin thesis in chapter 2.

Turning to more specific theories about religion and the origins of science, and experimental science in particular, there is a long-established thesis that posits a connection between theological voluntarism and the

---

1993); José Maia Neto, 'Academic Skepticism in Early Modern Philosophy, *JHI* 58 (1997), 199–220; Brendan Dooley, *The Social History of Skepticism: Experience and Doubt in Early Modern Culture* (Baltimore, 1999); Petr Lom, *The Limits of Doubt: The Moral and Political Implications of Skepticism* (Albany, NY, 2001); Gianni Paganini (ed.), *The Return of Scepticism from Hobbes and Descartes to Bayle* (Dordrecht, 2003); Richard Popkin and José Maria Neto (eds.), *Skepticism in Renaissance and Post-Renaissance Thought: New Interpretations* (Amherst, NY, 2003); Charles Larmore, 'Scepticism', in Daniel Garber and Michael Ayers (eds.), *The Cambridge History of Seventeenth-Century Philosophy*, 2 vols. (Cambridge, 1998), II, 1145–92; Michael Ayers, 'Popkin's Revised Scepticism', *BJHS* 12 (2004), 319–32.

[24] The Pyrrhonic sceptics thus aimed at the suspension of judgement (*epoche*), which led to a state of imperturbability (*ataraxia*).

emergence of an empirical approach to the investigation of nature. On most versions of this argument, the late Middle Ages saw the development of a theological voluntarism that asserted the radical freedom of God's will. The Protestant reformers took up this view and served as the agents for its propagation in the modern period. Because, on the voluntarist view, God was not constrained by any prior rational considerations in his creation of the world, the argument goes, human minds cannot know *a priori*, through the exercise of reason alone, what specific order God will instantiate in the world. Instead recourse must be had to empirical investigation.[25] While this position is not without merit and provides a plausible account of the origins of the modern conception of laws of nature, it has a number of deficiencies – not least the fact that Descartes was a radical voluntarist.[26] If my analysis is correct, it is not so much that God could have ordered nature in any way he chose which is significant for the development of an experimental approach to nature, but rather the fact that the Fall separated human beings from God and corrupted their minds. Nature itself had fallen, moreover, deviating from the original divine plan and becoming less intelligible. The empirical and experimental approach was thus not necessitated because of the in-principle unpredictability of the divine will. Rather the inconveniences and limitations of experimental natural philosophy are the inevitable outcome of a realisation of the fallen condition of humanity.

---

[25] M. B. Foster, 'The Christian Doctrine of Creation and the Rise of Modern Natural Science', *Mind* 43 (1934), 446–68; Francis Oakley, 'Christian Theology and the Newtonian Science: The Rise of the Concept of Laws of Nature', *Church History* 30 (1961), 433–57; J. E. McGuire, 'Boyle's Conception of Nature', *JHI* 33 (1972), 523–42; Eugene Klaaren, *Religious Origins of Modern Science* (Grand Rapids, 1977); Peter Heimann, 'Voluntarism and Immanence: Conceptions of Nature in Eighteenth-century Thought', *JHI* 39 (1978), 271–83; Betty Jo Teeter Dobbs, *The Janus Faces of Genius: The Role of Alchemy in Newton's Thought* (Cambridge, 1991); Margaret Osler, *Divine Will and the Mechanical Philosophy: Gassendi and Descartes on Contingency and Necessity in the Created World* (Cambridge, 1994); Henry Guerlac, 'Theological Voluntarism and Biological Analogies in Newton's Physical Thought', *JHI* 44 (1983), 219–29. See also Amos Funkenstein, *Theology and the Scientific Imagination* (Princeton, 1986), ch. 3; John Henry, 'Henry More versus Robert Boyle', in Sarah Hutton (ed.), *Henry More (1614–87): Tercentenary Essays* (Dordrecht, 1990), pp. 55–76; James E. Force and Richard H. Popkin, *Essays on the Context, Nature, and Influence of Isaac Newton's Theology* (Dordrecht, 1990); Antoni Malet, 'Isaac Barrow on the Mathematization of Nature: Theological Voluntarism and the Rise of Geometrical Optics', *JHI* 58 (1997), 265–87; Margaret Osler, 'Fortune, Fate, and Divination: Gassendi's Voluntarist Theology and the Baptism of Epicureanism', in Margaret Osler (ed.), *Atoms, Pneuma, and Tranquillity: Epicurean and Stoic Themes in European Thought* (Cambridge, 1991), 'The Intellectual Sources of Robert Boyle's Philosophy of Nature', in Richard Ashcroft, Richard Kroll, and Perez Zagorin (eds.), *Philosophy, Science, and Religion, 1640–1700* (Cambridge, 1991); 'Divine Will and Mathematical Truths: Gassendi and Descartes on the Status of Eternal Truths', in R. Ariew and M. Grene (eds.), *Descartes and his Contemporaries* (Chicago, 1995), pp. 145–58.

[26] For a broader critique see Peter Harrison, 'Voluntarism and Early Modern Science', *History of Science* 40 (2002), 63–89; 'Was Newton a Voluntarist?', in James E. Force and Sarah Hutton (eds.), *Newton and Newtonianism: New Studies* (Dordrecht, 2004), pp. 39–64.

If the manner of God's direction of the operations of nature is inscrutable to human minds, this is on account of the limitations of the latter, rather than the irrationality of the former.

Another important line of argument points to the significance of Puritan millenarianism, particularly in the context of seventeenth-century English natural philosophy. It is the misfortune of every historian who chooses to address the question of theological influences on the development of experimental science in England to stand in the great shadow cast by Charles Webster's magisterial and encyclopaedic *Great Instauration* (1975, 2002).[27] Inasmuch as a significant proportion of the present book deals with Adamic science and the prospects for its recovery, it bears an important relation to this earlier work. Webster has argued that one of the most significant periods in the development of English science took place during the period between 1640 and 1660, when Puritan millenarianism provided the inspiration for a range of revolutionary scientific projects. This millenarianism was inspired in part by the prospect of restoring to humanity the perfections once enjoyed by Adam in Eden, including his vast scientific knowledge, thus establishing a state of affairs that was thought to be a necessary precondition for the onset of the millennium. Following the restoration of the monarchy in 1660, the radical aspects of this vision were viewed with disfavour, but significant elements of it were taken up by the Royal Society and the Royal College of Physicians. My thesis is not a challenge to Webster's, but rather presupposes many of the basic contentions set out there and attempts to place them within a broader context, both temporally and geographically. Rather than emphasising the discontinuities between revolutionary and Restoration science, and indeed between Puritan science and the science associated with other confessional groupings, it seeks to show how their differences are to be understood in terms of varying assessments of the Fall, and of the extent to which prelapsarian conditions might be re-established in the present world. Moreover, while Webster's treatment of the theme of the Fall is primarily in the context of Puritan millenarianism, the emphasis of this work is the implications of the Fall for theological anthropology.[28] There will be further discussion of these issues in chapter 4.

Because a major focus of this book is the development of experimentalism in the English context, some of the themes of another classic work in the history of early modern science are also relevant. In *Leviathan and the Air*

---

[27] Charles Webster, *The Great Instauration: Science, Medicine, and Reform, 1626–1660* (London, 1975); 2nd edn (Bern, 2002).

[28] For Webster's emphasis, see *Great Instauration* (1975), p. xvi.

Pump (1985), Steven Shapin and Simon Schaffer pose fundamental questions about why one does experiments in order to arrive at scientific truth, and why experimentation has come to be regarded as superior to alternative ways of establishing knowledge.[29] They rightly argue that such questions are often overlooked by modern historians because the presuppositions of contemporary cultural practices – such as science – are rarely regarded as problematic. This is less true now than when Shapin and Schaffer first wrote, but it remains the case that historians are embedded within a culture in which the virtues of experimentation seem self-evident. From the present perspective, then, it can be difficult to understand the extent to which in the seventeenth century the new experimental approach of such figures as Francis Bacon and Robert Boyle was controversial and counter-intuitive. It is also easy to overlook the strength of the arguments raised against it. Key objections to 'the experimental philosophy' were that it did not count as genuine knowledge because it failed to establish the causes of phenomena, and that it fell short of the certainty that characterised genuine science, the goal of which was the kind of demonstration found in logic or geometry. I shall suggest that the new 'probabilistic and fallibilistic conception of man's natural knowledge', that according to Shapin and Schaffer distinguished the approach of the experimentalists, was inspired by a new theological emphasis on the inherent weakness of fallen human minds.[30] By the same token, many opponents of the experimental programme who retained elements of a more traditional Aristotelian approach or who emphasised the possibility of mathematical certainties subscribed to a more optimistic view of human capabilities. The role of theological anthropology in these various positions becomes more apparent the more we are able to enter into the cultural milieu of the seventeenth century and recapture something of the strangeness of the prescriptions of the experimental approach.

Another relevant contention of Shapin and Schaffer is that there was a close relation between the problem of knowledge and the problem of social order in the seventeenth century. One of the reasons for this, I shall suggest, is that ignorance and unsociability were numbered together among the more serious consequences of the Fall. As we shall see, those arguing for particular political arrangements typically supported their views by invoking, in various ways, the original sovereignty exercised by Adam. The coercive

---

[29] Steven Shapin and Simon Schaffer, *Leviathan and the Air Pump: Hobbes, Boyle, and the Experimental Life* (Princeton, 1985), p. 1.

[30] *Ibid.*, p. 23. For the new emphasis on probability, see Barbara Shapiro, *Probability and Certainty in Seventeenth Century England* (Princeton, 1983), ch. 2; Ian Hacking, *The Emergence of Probability* (Cambridge, 1975), chs. 3–5.

powers of the state, moreover, were justified as necessary evils designed to curb the aggressive and selfish impulses of sinful subjects. By analogy, the methodological strictures of particular programmes of natural philosophy – experimental method being perhaps the best example – were understood as applying necessary external constraints to fallen minds which, left to their own devices, would simply fail to accumulate any useful knowledge of the natural world.

Finally, the biblical elements of the present work also represent an extension of my own previous book on the bible and the rise of science.[31] In essence, that work suggested that when in the sixteenth century the book of scripture began to be read in a literal, historical sense, it had a major impact on the way in which the book of nature was interpreted. Medieval allegorical readings of scripture had assumed a natural world in which objects symbolised spiritual truths. The demise of the allegory and its replacement by a literal and historical approach called for a reconfiguring of the natural order, the intelligibility of which was no longer seen to reside in symbolic meanings. While the major focus of that previous work was a consideration of the consequences of the turn to the literal sense of the scripture, the present book looks at one consequence of that literal turn – the way in which the account of Adam's Fall, now read almost exclusively as an historical narrative rather than an allegory – influenced both theological anthropology and early modern science.

It remains to say something about the structure of the book. The first chapter offers a description of the biblical, patristic, and medieval interpretations of the story of Adam's fall, along with an account of the development of the doctrine of original sin. It is not intended as a history of the 'unit idea' of the Fall, but provides background without which it would be difficult to make sense of the arguments advanced by various early modern figures.[32] The second chapter deals with the anthropology of the Protestant reformers, their rejection of scholastic Aristotelianism, and their revisiting of the Augustinian position on original sin. Consideration is also given to the re-emergence of scepticism and the Catholic revival of

---

[31] Peter Harrison, *The Bible, Protestantism and the Rise of Natural Science* (Cambridge, 1998).

[32] This is not the appropriate place for a discussion of the relative merits of various styles of intellectual history. However it may be a relevant consideration that seventeenth-century thinkers, lacking the sophistication of Cambridge School intellectual historians, assumed that theological doctrines did have a chronological history. For a recent discussion of some of these historiographical issues, and for a specific justification of a chronological treatment of the idea of 'the Fall', see John Patrick Diggins, 'Arthur O. Lovejoy and the Challenge of Intellectual History', *JHI* 67 (2006), 181–209. In any case, readers can decide for themselves whether this chronological approach helpfully contributes to an understanding of later developments and forms part of a coherent historical account.

Augustinianism. In the chapter that follows, brief examples are provided of some of the ways in which Reformation anthropology influenced the development of natural philosophy in the sixteenth century – Philipp Melanchthon and his revision of the doctrine of 'natural light', subsequently adopted by Johannes Kepler; the attempts of Lambert Daneau and others to ground natural philosophy in the authority of scripture; 'enthusiastic' proposals to rely on personal inspiration for knowledge of nature. This chapter does not set out a comprehensive catalogue of those individuals who subscribed to these various positions, but rather provides examples of the possible range of views. The last two chapters bear the main burden of establishing the importance of the Fall in the genealogy of experimental science in the English context. The chief subject of chapter 4 is the 'anthropological turn' in seventeenth-century England, and the manner in which Francis Bacon's proposed instauration of natural philosophy was conceived of as a recovery of knowledge lost as a consequence of the Fall. The final chapter continues this story into the middle and later decades of the seventeenth century, giving consideration to how the methodological prescriptions of the English experimentalists, and Fellows of the Royal Society in particular, were shaped by the narrative of the Fall. Here the development of the experimental philosophy is closely linked with a particular understanding of original sin. The last two sections of the chapter deal with Boyle, Locke, and Newton, and show how the narrative of the Fall was gradually written out of justifications of scientific practice, leaving the impression that experiment was self-evidently the proper way to pursue scientific investigation. A conclusion and references follow.

CHAPTER I

Adam's Encyclopaedia

And out of the ground the Lord God formed every beast of the field, and every fowl of the air; and brought them unto Adam to see what he would call them: and whatsoever Adam called every living creature, that was the name thereof.   Gen. 2:19–20

And that their inventions might not be lost before they were sufficiently known, upon Adam's prediction that the world was to be destroyed at one time by the force of fire, and at another time by the violence and quantity of water, they made two pillars; the one of brick, the other of stone: they inscribed their discoveries on them both, that in case the pillar of brick should be destroyed by the flood, the pillar of stone might remain, and exhibit those discoveries to mankind; and also inform them that there was another pillar of brick erected by them.   Josephus, *The Antiquities of the Jews* 1.2

God, the Creator of Heaven and Earth, at the beginning when he created Adam, inspired him with the knowledge of all natural things (which successfully descended to Noah afterwardes, and to his Posterity: for as he was able to giue names to all the liuing Creatures, according to their seuerall natures); so no doubt but hee had also the knowledge, both what Herbes and Fruits were fit, eyther for Meate or Medicine, for Vse or for Delight. And that Adam might exercise this knowledge, God planted a Garden for him to liue in.
          John Parkinson, *Paradisi in Sole* (London, 1629), Epistle to the Reader

Hermetically sealed in the six-storey glass book tower of Yale University's Beinecke Library is a manuscript copy of what purports to be the oldest book in the world. The inauspicious label 'Osborn MS fa.7' and its prosaic description as an 'astrological treatise' give little indication of the nature of its contents.[1] On opening the soft vellum binding, however, the reader is confronted with a neat cursive script that reveals the true import of the work – its claim to contain a record of a book of secret knowledge

---

[1] Beinecke Rare Books Library, Osborn MS fa.7.

originally entrusted to Adam by God. This work thus presents itself as a copy of the first encyclopaedia – indeed, of the very first book in human history. Its contents include sundry cures, knowledge of the sun, moon, and stars, of the powers of the vegetable world, of precious stones, fishes, fowls, wild beasts, and the secrets of astrological prognostication. This last category, presumably, suggested itself to an unknown cataloguer as the best way to characterise the contents of this strange work. The manuscript is rare, but not unique. Other copies, a number of which date from the seventeenth century, are housed in the British Library.[2] While there are variations amongst the extant versions, all claim to contain the knowledge that God originally gave to Adam.

These manuscripts are versions of the *Sepher Raziel*, so named for the angel Raziel whom tradition identifies as the intermediary between God and Adam. Some of these sources suggest that this ancient knowledge was vouchsafed to Adam during his brief tenure in paradise; others that Raziel communicated the secret wisdom shortly after Adam's expulsion from Eden, or later, after a long period – 130 years is the specified duration – of repentance. In the first instance the book might have been the source of Adam's legendary wisdom; in the latter instances, a consolation for knowledge lost. In any event, this original deposit of knowledge was said to have become the source of the wisdom of the sages of antiquity. One version relates how Noah enclosed the tome in a casket of gold and took it with him aboard the Ark. After his disembarkation it was handed down from generation to generation, serving as a textbook for the biblical patriarchs and prophets. Solomon's much-vaunted wisdom was attributed to his knowledge of its contents, and indeed the Beinecke manuscript boasts that in addition to the original divine communication it contains the Hebrew annotations of Solomon.

The true provenance of these manuscripts, and of the original book of which they claim to be copies, is rather more commonplace. Most probably they derive from a twelfth-century compilation of Jewish cabbalistic writings, although the oral traditions on which the text is based may well be much older. The contents of the *Sepher Raziel*, moreover, are bound to disappoint the modern reader, for they appear to be more an eccentric collection of alchemical and astrological observations than an ancient and authentic record of truths about the world presented in the authoritative manner of, say, the *Encyclopaedia Britannica*. What is of enduring

[2] British Library MSS Sloane 3826, 3846, 3847; MS Additional 15299. There is now also a modern English translation of the 1701 Hebrew edition published in Amsterdam – *Sepher Rezial Hemelach: The Book of the Angel Rezial*, tr. Steve Savedow (Weiser, 2000).

significance in these documents, however, is that they bear witness to a long-standing Western tradition that accorded to Adam a God-given encyclopaedic knowledge of the natural world. That such manuscripts could still be accorded credibility in certain quarters during the sixteenth and seventeenth centuries provides an indication of how powerful and pervasive was the tradition of Adamic wisdom.

SCIENCE IN PARADISE

In Jewish and Christian canonical texts there is little explicit information on the extent of Adam's intellectual acuity or on the compass of his learning. Neither is there extensive comment on the impoverishment of his knowledge after the Fall. Certain passages, however, provided the foundation for the subsequent exegetical traditions. In Genesis we are told that man was created in God's image and that he exercised dominion over other living things. Most important for later justifications of a primitive science, Adam had given names to all of the beasts in an episode traditionally taken to mean that Adam had been possessed of a knowledge of their essential natures.[3] The prophetic book of Ezekiel records how the first inhabitant of Eden was 'full of wisdom and perfect in beauty', that he was clothed in jewels, immune to pain, and capable of walking 'in the midst of fiery stones'. In the Jewish wisdom literature, Adam is said to have been created by a personified 'Wisdom', who guarded him and gave him the strength to exercise his dominion over things.[4]

These scattered references may seem to provide a somewhat fragile foundation upon which to construct an influential tradition about Adam's great knowledge. Yet the agendas of later interpreters led them to gloss these texts in ways that reflected their own theological and philosophical interests. Moreover, because the Genesis narratives are silent on many issues that are of interest to the curious reader – how long Adam and Eve were in the garden before they fell, whether there was sexual congress in paradise, the fate of the first humans following their expulsion from Eden, where the children of Adam and Eve found their mates – later traditions developed to fill these lacunae in the bare biblical narratives and many of these subsequently found their way into non-canonical writings.

[3] Gen. 1:26, 28; 2:19.
[4] Ezek. 28:13–15; Wisdom 10:1–2. Cf. II Enoch 31; Job 15:7–8. See Clement of Rome, *Homilies* III, 28; Anthony Burgesse, *The Doctrine of Original Sin: Asserted and Vindicated against the Old and New Adversaries Thereof* (London, 1658), p. 406.

One influential account of the early history of the first family was compiled in the first century by Flavius Josephus (37–c. 100), the Jewish historian to whose work *The Jewish Wars* we are indebted for a contemporary account of the fall of Masada. In a later work, *The Antiquities of the Jews*, Josephus provided an account of the history of the Jews from the creation of the world to the time of the Roman occupation of Palestine. Here he recounted how Seth, the son born to Adam and Eve following the murder of Abel by his brother Cain, had preserved for posterity the knowledge of this first generation of human beings. According to this account, Adam had prophesied the destruction of the world by water and by fire. The prudent Seth had constructed two pillars, of brick and of stone, on which he inscribed the traditions of ancient knowledge in order to preserve them in the face of the impending catastrophe. These were, in essence, the first encyclopaedia. One of the pillars was still extant in the first century, according to Josephus, and could be seen in the land of Siriad.[5]

The history of Josephus was corroborated in a second version of events that appears in the apocryphal writings known as the *Apocalypse of Moses* and the *Vita Adae et Evae*.[6] These related works were probably composed between the first and third centuries of the Christian era, and provide an account of the history of the first couple and their progeny following the expulsion from paradise. Again, the main protagonist is Seth, who in this story embarks on a quest to obtain the 'Oil of Mercy' – a balm with properties similar to the fabled elixir later sought by alchemists – that will relieve the suffering of his ailing father. It is also Seth who plays the central role in transmitting the 'secrets' or 'mysteries' known to his parents, to posterity. On her deathbed, Eve summons Seth and his thirty brothers and thirty sisters, instructing them to make 'tables of stone and clay' that they might record upon them 'all that ye have seen and heard from us'. The stone would survive the earth's destruction by water; the clay would not be destroyed by fire. Thereupon, we are informed, 'Seth made the tables'.[7]

[5] Josephus, *Antiquities* 1.70–1. Cf. Michael Glycas, *Annales* 228–33 (Basel, 1572). The identity of the land of Siriad is unknown. On the basis of the spelling, some have thought Assyria, others Egypt.

[6] For the background of these works see Michael Stone, *The Literature of Adam and Eve* (Atlanta, 1992). Cf. John Levison, *Portraits of Adam in Early Judaism: From Sirach to 2 Baruch* (Sheffield, 1988). See also *The Gospel of Nicodemus* II, 3.

[7] *Vitae Adae et Evae* xxix. 1–3; xlix–li, *The Apocrypha and Pseudepigrapha of the Old Testament*, ed. R. H. Charles, 2 vols. (Oxford, 1977), II, 140, 152f. See also Johannes Tromp, 'Cain and Abel in the Greek and Armenian/Georgian Recensions of the *Life of Adam and Eve*', in Gary Anderson, Michael Stone, and Johannes Tromp (eds.), *Literature on Adam and Eve* (Leiden, 2000), p. 287; Louis Ginzberg, *The Legends of the Jews*, tr. Henrietta Szold, 7 vols. (Philadelphia, 1937–66) I, 93f. On Adam's knowledge see D. A. Bertrand, 'Adam prophète', in *Figures de l'Ancien Testament chez les Pères*, ed. P. Maraval, Cahiers de Biblia patristica 2 (Strasbourg, 1989), pp. 61–81.

These stories circulated widely in the medieval and early modern periods.[8] Indeed, as late as the nineteenth century, in histories of the world, Seth was identified as the medium through which Adam's knowledge was passed on to succeeding generations.[9]

These Jewish elaborations on the early history of the human race are relatively constrained in their assessment both of Adam's abilities and of what was lost as a consequence of the Fall. Subsequent Christian readings of the event, and in particular those informed by Platonic philosophy, differ in significant respects. The perfections of the prelapsarian Adam were magnified, as was the extent of the tragedy that befell him with the Fall. The introduction by the Church Fathers of the idea of original sin – that Adam's guilt was transmitted to his progeny – further emphasised the culpability of Adam and the impoverishment of the human condition. The combined effect of new Platonic and Christian readings of Genesis was thus a somewhat more negative anthropology that emphasized in an unprecedented way the moral and epistemological losses that accompanied the Fall.

FALLING INTO IGNORANCE

The idea of a fall from original perfection is not exclusive to the Judaeo-Christian tradition. Platonic philosophy makes reference to a 'fall' and to the need to recover lost knowledge. Plato had suggested that human souls, in a pre-existent, disembodied state, possessed direct knowledge of the 'Forms' or 'Ideas', those eternal realities of which base material things were but pale reflections. This ideal knowledge, on the Platonic account, had been 'forgotten' when spiritual souls were born into material bodies. The confusion that followed the birth of human souls in the fleshly prisons that housed them persisted throughout life, although those with a love of wisdom had the capacity to turn away from the distractions of the material

[8] Theodore Ziolkowski, *The Sin of Knowledge: Ancient Themes and Modern Variations* (Princeton, 2000), pp. 11f.; Walter Stephens, '*Livres de Haulte gresse*: Bibliographic Myth from Rabelais to Du Bartas', *MLN* 120, Supplement (2005), 60–83.

[9] See, e.g., J. A. Wylie, *History of the Scottish Nation*, 3 vols. (Edinburgh, 1886), I, ch. 6. Other ancient sources provide different trajectories for Adamic knowledge. The mysterious figure of Enoch is said to have authored three antediluvian books from which Noah was taught. 2 Enoch 33, Jubilees, 4:17–26; cf. I Enoch 8:1–4. See Pieter van Der Horst, *Japheth in the Tents of Shem: Studies on Jewish Hellenism in Antiquity* (Leuven, 2002), pp. 139–58. The Samaritan chronicle, *The Book of Asatir* (published as *The Asatir: The Samaritan Book of the "Secrets of Moses"* (London, 1927)), repeats this account. See Michael Stone, *Selected Studies in Pseudepigrapha and Apocrypha with Special Reference to the Armenian Tradition* (Leiden, 1991), pp. 220f.

world and gradually to reorient themselves towards the universal truths found in the realm of the Forms.[10]

In Plato's *Statesman* these ideas about human proneness to error were reinforced by a mythological account of a golden age in which humans led an idyllic existence under the direct governance of God. This age came to a close when a 'cosmic crisis' precipitated changes in the physical world similar to those wrought by the Fall of Adam and Eve: humans became weak and helpless, they were ravaged by wild beasts that had once been tame, and the earth no longer spontaneously provided sustenance for its human tenants. In this chaotic and disordered world, the survival of humanity was secured only by divine gifts of knowledge. Fire was the gift of Prometheus, the crafts were made known by Hephaestus, and the knowledge of agriculture was communicated by other gods. 'From these gifts', Plato explained, 'everything has come which has furnished human life since the divine guardianship of men ceased.'[11] The parallels with the biblical account of the Fall are far from precise, but the similarities were sufficient for significant elements of the Platonic myth to be incorporated into the Judaeo-Christian tradition. For Christian thinkers through the ages they also provided a degree of independent corroboration of the biblical account of human beginnings and of the divine origins of useful knowledge.

Subsequently in the Christian era, the mystical Platonist philosopher Plotinus (*c.* 204–270) had spoken explicitly of a Fall and a loss of an original image. Escape from the evils of our present condition, Plotinus wrote, was to be effected by 'attaining likeness to God' – the same formula that was to be employed by the Church Fathers.[12] This Platonic Fall, moreover, is directly related to epistemological questions, and our present attachment to the senses and sensory knowledge was directly attributed to it. For Plotinus, the whole realm of the senses is the fallen realm.[13] He could therefore argue that the empirically oriented philosophies of the Epicureans and Stoics typified the kind of enterprise to be expected in a fallen world since both relied excessively on knowledge derived from the senses.[14] In the Jewish sources, by way of contrast, the loss of original knowledge occurs within the span of human history and is only indirectly related to the Fall. It is not the consequence of a radical corruption of the human mind caused by birth in a material body, but takes place as the result

---

[10] Plato, *Phaedo* 73–7; *Phaedrus* 249, *Statesman* 273b.
[11] Plato, *Statesman* 272d–274d, *Collected Dialogues*, ed. Edith Hamilton and Huntington Cairns (New York, 1961), p. 1039.
[12] Plotinus, *Enneads* I.i.12; I.ii.1; IV.iii.12. Cf. Origen, *De principiis* III.vii.1.
[13] Plotinus, *Enneads* VI.vii.5.   [14] *Ibid.*, VI. Also see Menn, *Descartes and Augustine*, p. 371.

of historical contingencies – the disruption of the Deluge and the confusion of tongues at Babel. It was these historical events rather than a cosmic catastrophe that had severed the links to the original sources of knowledge.

There is no evidence that Plotinus was familiar with Jewish or Christian notions of the Fall, although there is an ancient tradition that his teacher Ammonius Saccas had been a Christian.[15] Certainly, there is no explicit reference in his *Enneads* to the Genesis narrative. But others – and most notably the Alexandrian writer Philo Judaeus (*c.* 20 BC–*c.* AD 50) – had already attempted to combine the two traditions of the human fall. Philo was eclectic in outlook, like a number of first-century Alexandrian thinkers, and he sought to bring together elements of Judaism and Greek philosophy. In order to do this he brought a powerful allegorical method of interpretation to bear on the text of the Old Testament, arguing that in the creation narratives Adam represented reason, and Eve the senses. At first, reason and the senses worked in harmony giving Adam an unparalleled philosophical superiority:

the first created men, as they received bodies of vast size reaching to a gigantic height, must also of necessity have received more accurate senses, and, what is more excellent still a power of examining into and hearing things in a philosophical manner. For some people think, and perhaps with some reason, that they were endowed with such eyes as enabled them to behold even those natures, and essences, and operations, which exist in heaven, as also ears by which they could comprehend every kind of voice and language.[16]

These superhuman abilities were demonstrated in the episode in which God parades the animals past Adam to be named (Gen. 2:19). Plato's *Cratylus* – a dialogue that deals with the origin of language – was no doubt of central importance in informing Philo's reading, and indeed the subsequent exegetical tradition.[17] In the dialogue it is established that 'the giver of the first names had also a knowledge of the things which he named' and that 'a power more than human gave things their first names, and that the names which are thus given are necessarily their true names'. Later the giver of names is identified as 'an inspired being or god'.[18] Read in conjunction

[15] Eusebius, *Ecclesiastical History* vi.9. For doubts about this tradition see R. T. Wallis, *Neoplatonism* (New York, 1972), p. 38.
[16] Philo of Alexandria, *Questions and Answers on Genesis*, 1.32, *The Works of Philo*, tr. C. D. Younge (Peabody, 1992), pp. 797f.
[17] J. Dillon, 'Philo Judaeus and the Cratylus', *Liverpool Classic Monthly* 3 (1978), 37–42. Antiochus of Ascalon was possibly a more immediate source of these ideas for both Philo and Varro. See P. Boyancé, 'Etymologie et théologie chez Varron', *Revue des Etudes Latines* 53 (1975), 99–115.
[18] Plato, *Cratylus* 438a–438c, *Collected Dialogues*, p. 472.

with the episode in which Adam names the beasts, Plato's contentions about naming lead to the conclusion that Adam, the giver of names, was imbued with a knowledge of the true essences of all living things. And it is precisely this conclusion that Philo draws: in assigning a 'natural nomenclature' to the beasts Adam shows himself to be 'a man of wisdom and pre-eminent knowledge'.[19] In the West, right up to the nineteenth century, virtually all subsequent readings of this passage make reference to Adam's exceptional natural knowledge. The early modern preoccupation with universal language schemes and the conviction that a natural language would lead to the establishment of the true science and genuine religion were similarly inspired by this passage in Genesis.

In spite of the suggestion that Adam and Eve might have enjoyed the advantages of superior organs of sense, Philo was nonetheless committed to a Platonism that elevated reason over the senses. At the same time he was ambivalent about the necessity of sensory knowledge, suggesting on occasion that the mind is utterly dependent on the senses and incomplete without them. In his account of the Fall, however, he seems thoroughly Platonic. Establishing an exegetical tradition that was again to remain in place until the early modern period, he explained that Adam is to be understood as the rational mind and Eve the senses. As Adam needed Eve as a help-meet, he pointed out, so the mind needs the senses.[20] Elsewhere, however, he opposes the feminine senses to reason, and credits them with being the source of ignorance and error: 'the rational part belongs to the male sex, being the inheritance of intellect and reason; but the irrational part belongs to the sex of woman, which is the lot also of the outward senses'.[21] Woman was also identified with the passions. 'But the passions are female by nature', he observed, 'and we must study to quit them, showing our preference for the masculine characters of the good disposition.'[22] If reason was opposed to the deceiving senses, action was opposed to passion. In each set of oppositions, the male principle was identified with the desirable trait: 'for as the man is seen in action, and the woman in being the subject of action, so also is the mind seen in action, and the external sense, like the woman, is discerned by suffering or being the subject of action'.[23] On account of

[19] Philo, *Questions and Answers on Genesis* I.20 (*Works*, p. 795); Cf. *On the Creation* LII, 148 (*Works*, p. 21).
[20] 'In human beings the mind occupies the rank of man, and the sensations that of the woman.' Philo, *De Opificio Mundi* LIX.165 (*Works*, p. 23).
[21] Philo, *De specialibus legibus I*, XXXVII (*Works*, p. 553).
[22] Philo, *Quod deterius potiori insidiari soleat* IX (*Works*, p. 115).
[23] Philo, *Legum allegoriae* II, XI (*Works*, p. 42). This analysis is reinforced by the etymological sense of *pascho* – 'to be acted upon'.

this supposed cognitive weakness the woman was the obvious target for the deceptions of the serpent, and she became the conduit through which the perverted hierarchy of her own mental faculties became forever the lot of the human race. Henceforth, reason will be subjugated to the senses, to the passions, and to pleasure.[24]

The central features of Philo's exegesis of the first chapters of Genesis strongly influenced later Rabbinical and Christian readings. Rabbinical theology became extravagant in its praise of Adam, who was said to exhibit perfection of body and mind. Some authors conferred upon Adam gigantic dimensions – some to the extent that he might have filled the whole world.[25] Adam's intellect, it was generally held, matched his stature. Thus the first man was also virtually omniscient, had vision that could encompass the whole of the earth at once (which, in the instance that he was as large as the whole earth, was probably not as impressive as it sounds).[26] Adam's knowledge extended not only to the natural world but to the contingent events of history, for at the moment of creation, God had revealed to him all the generations of men and their deeds. Adam was also the author of human arts and, most importantly, of the craft of writing.[27]

In the New Testament Adam receives comparatively little attention. In support of the contention that women should be silent and not exercise authority over men, St Paul points out that Adam was formed first and, unlike Eve, was not deceived by the serpent.[28] In another of Paul's writings, however – one that was to assume unparalleled authority in subsequent discussions of original sin – Adam becomes a 'type' of Christ. Typology was one of the methods used by Christian writers to invest characters from the Hebrew Bible with Christian meanings. Just as Philo had exploited allegory to render various Old Testament themes consistent with aspects of Greek philosophy, Christian writers resorted to non-literal readings to bring contemporary significance to narrative in the Hebrew Bible. In this instance, Adam was said to have been the conduit through which sin and death had entered the world. This paralleled Christ's redemptive act, through which life and salvation were universally offered to all: 'Adam . . . is a type of Him who was to come . . . For as by one man's disobedience many were made

---

[24] Philo, *De opificio mundi*, LIX (*Works*, p. 23). Cf. *Legum allegoriae II*, v; *Quaestiones et solutiones in Genesin I.*

[25] *Leviticus Rabba* 18.

[26] See, e.g., Ginzberg, *Legends*, I, 59; V, 79; Williams, *The Ideas of the Fall and of Original Sin* (London, 1927), pp. 71f.; F. Weber, *System der Altsynagogalen Palästinischen Theologie* (Leipzig, 1880), pp. 214f. In some Gnostic writings, however, Adam was a gigantic monster, bereft of intelligence. See, e.g., Hippolytus, *Philosophumena* 5.2.

[27] Ginzberg, *Legends*, I, 61f.   [28] I Tim. 2:13.

sinners, so also by one Man's obedience many will be made righteous.'[29]
Read in conjunction with other passages of scripture this could be taken
to mean that Adam's sin conferred personal guilt on all of his descendants,
who are born already bearing the stigma of sin.[30] Certainly this was the
influential interpretation of Augustine. Other passages in St Paul are suggestive of the epistemological consequences of sin. The 'unrighteous', he
suggests, 'suppress the truth' and do not 'retain God in their knowledge'.
As a consequence, they 'became futile in their thoughts, and their foolish hearts were darkened'. 'Professing to be wise', he adds, 'they became
fools.'[31]

    The writings of the Church Fathers bear the impress of the ideas of both
Philo and St Paul. The tradition that Adam's naming of the beasts gave
evidence of his great wisdom is widespread in patristic literature.[32] Gregory
of Nyssa (*c.* 330–*c.* 395) thus wrote that 'the intellectual faculty, made as it
was originally by God, acts thenceforward by itself when it looks out upon
realities and . . . there can be no confusion in its knowledge'. This was made
clear by the manner in which Adam attached 'some verbal note to each
several thing as a stamp to indicate its meaning'.[33] But the ability to name
the beasts and the exercise of a natural dominion over them was forfeited
when Adam lost the control of his own rational powers. For a number
of the Fathers, the Fall had wrought a dramatic inversion of the natural
hierarchical relationships. At a cosmic level Adam had rebelled against
God. This insurrection was mirrored in the newly created world where
animals became wild and no longer acknowledged Adam's authority. Even
the earth itself became barren and no longer provided abundant food. At
a psychological level, Adam's passions rebelled against his reason, resulting
in a loss of self-control, and the forfeiting of that encyclopaedic knowledge
that had made possible the naming and subduing of his erstwhile subjects.
'Man, when he has cast away the dominion of reason, and torn himself
into a commonwealth of God's devising', wrote John Chrysostom in the
fourth century, 'gives himself up to all the passions, is no longer merely a
beast, but a kind of many-formed motley monster.'[34] The rigorous practice

---

[29] Rom. 5:14, 19.   [30] Gen. 3; Ps. 51:5.   [31] Rom. 1:18–22.

[32] See, e.g., Clement of Rome, *Homilies* 3.18; Clement of Alexandria, *Stromata* I.21; Origen, *De principiis*
I, 3.7; Tertullian, *Adversus Marcionem* II, *De Virginibus velandis* 4; Jerome, *Gen.* 2.21. Cf. Aquinas,
Quaestiones disputatae de veritate 18, 4; Suarez, *De opere sex dierum* III.ix.14. For later traditions about
the naming of the beasts see *A Dictionary of Biblical Tradition in English Literature*, ed. David L.
Geoffrey (Grand Rapids, 1992), p. 537.

[33] Gregory of Nyssa, *Answer to Eunomius' Second Book* (NPNF II, v, 290). Cf. Origen, *Contra Celsum*
V, 43.

[34] Chrysostom, *Homilies on the Gospel of St John* II (NPNF I, XIV, 7). Cf. *Homilies on Genesis* VIII.14,
IX.7. For these associations and their medieval and early modern incarnations see Peter Harrison,

of ascetic disciplines of self-mastery gave hints of the dominion that Adam had once enjoyed, witnessed in the association of the saints with wild beasts – Jerome and his lion, Helenus and the crocodile, St Macarius and the hyena, St Columba and the beasts of the Vosges.[35] The thirteenth-century Franciscan Bonaventure was to praise the piety of Francis of Assisi, whose moral authority 'had such remarkable power that it subdued ferocious beasts, tamed the wild, trained the tame, and bent to his obedience the brute beasts that had rebelled against fallen mankind'.[36] It was a similar image of self-mastery and purity of mind that Francis Bacon drew upon in the seventeenth century in his quest to restore 'the sovereignty and power' that Adam had enjoyed 'in his first state of creation'. In his equating of knowledge and power Bacon observed that 'whensoever he shall be able to call the creatures by their true names he shall again command them'.[37]

If the Fathers could read the Fall as a rebellion of the passions against reason, this event could also be associated with the imprisonment of the soul in a fleshly body. Some of the Fathers went so far as to embrace a Platonic account of the Fall, attributing human misery to a fall into human bodies. The Alexandrian theologian and biblical commentator Origen (*c.* 185–*c.* 254), said to have been taught by the teacher of Plotinus, suggested that all souls were created equal but some, through the misuse of their free choice, had fallen into human bodies.[38] The association of the Fall with embodiment received some support from the Genesis narrative, for after the expulsion from the Garden, Adam and Eve are for the first time clothed by God in 'skin(s)' (Gen. 3:21).[39] Following Plato, Origen had compared the Fall of the human race to an individual who had once possessed a perfect mastery of an art or science such as geometry or medicine, who was subsequently reduced to a state of complete ignorance.[40] For a

---

'Reading the Passions: The Fall, the Passions, and Dominion over Nature', in S. Gaukroger (ed.), *The Soft Underbelly of Reason: The Passions in the Seventeenth Century* (London, 1998), pp. 49–78.

[35] Helen Waddell, *Beasts and Saints* (London, 1949), pp. 25–9; David Bell, *Wholly Animals: A Book of Beastly Tales* (Kalamazoo, 1992), p. 17; Joyce Salisbury, *The Beast Within: Animals in the Middle Ages* (London, 1994), pp. 168f.

[36] Bonaventure, *The Life of St Francis*, in *Bonaventure: The Soul's Journey into God, The Tree of Life and The Life of St Francis*, tr. Ewert Cousins (London, 1978), p. 261.

[37] Bacon, *Valerius Terminus* (*Works* III, 220).   [38] Origen, *De principiis* I.vii.3, I.viii.2.

[39] See, e.g., Philo, *Quaestiones in Genesin* 1.4; Ginzberg, *Legends of the Jews*, v, 93. The Hebrew can be rendered 'garments of skin(s)' or 'garments for the skin'. Clement of Rome interpreted the consciousness of nakedness that followed the Fall as an awareness of knowledge being stripped away. *Epistle to Diognetus*, xii. In the seventeenth century the Cambridge Platonist Henry More rehearsed this reading, *Conjectura Cabbalistica. Or, a Conjectural Essay of Interpreting the Mind of Moses* (London, 1653), pp. 50f.

[40] Origen, *De principiis* I.iv.1.

time, Augustine also seems to have entertained a view of the Fall in which a pre-existing soul descends into a corporeal body.[41]

Also associated with the Fall were the beginnings of sensory knowledge. The serpent had promised Eve that when she ate of the tree of knowledge her eyes would be opened. And so it transpired, for following Adam and Eve's transgression, 'the eyes of both of them were opened' (Gen. 3:5–7). Origen interpreted this to mean that sensory perception began with the first sin. Prior to this the primal parents had kept their eyes closed, so that they would not be distracted from perceiving with the eye of the soul. The postlapsarian 'senses of the flesh' and the 'eyes of the earth' were thus contrasted with the inner light of the rational soul.[42] Some of these ideas skirted dangerously close to a gnosticism that called into question the value of the material creation and of human embodiment, and indeed many of Origen's ideas were subsequently condemned at the Second Council of Constantinople (553). Yet if the Judaeo-Christian doctrine of creation asserted the positive value of the material realm, including the human body, the residual influence of Platonism remained strong. Plato's claim that the imprisonment of the soul in a material body is the cause of our present ignorance informed Christian understandings of the Fall and its epistemological consequences until well into the modern period. The associated view, according to which reliance on untrustworthy sensory knowledge is a consequence of the Fall, was also to have a long career in the West.

INHERITING ERROR

In Western Christianity the idea that Adam and Eve fell from their original perfection is invariably associated with the doctrine of original sin. The latter doctrine, however, was a relatively late development in the Christian West, not receiving its definitive form until the fifth century. Even then, subsequent Councils of the Church were to ameliorate the severity of its first formulation. Calvin, writing from the vantage point of the sixteenth century, was to observe that 'all ancient theologians, with the exception of Augustine, are so confused, vacillating, and contradictory on this subject,

---

[41] R. J. O'Connell, 'The Plotinian Fall of the Soul in St. Augustine', *Traditio* 19 (1963), 1–35; R. Penaskovic, 'The Fall of the Soul in Saint Augustine: A *Quaestio Disputata*', *Augustinian Studies* 17 (1986), 135–45; R. Teske, 'St. Augustine's view of the Original Human Condition in *De Genesi contra Manichaeos*', *Augustinian Studies* 22 (1991), 141–55.

[42] Origen, *Contra Celsum* VII.39; *Homily on Numbers* XVII.3. Cf. Philo, *Quaestiones in Genesin* 1.39. For these themes see C. P. Bammel, 'Adam in Origen', in Rowan Williams (ed.), *The Making of Orthodoxy: Essays in Honour of Henry Chadwick* (Cambridge, 1989), pp. 62–93.

that no certainty can be obtained from their writings'.[43] This is overstated, perhaps, and betrays Calvin's concern to rehabilitate the more severe Augustinian form of the doctrine. But it is certainly true that the earliest Church Fathers, and indeed the Greek orthodox tradition thereafter, tended to take a relatively mild view of Adam's transgression and of its impact on his progeny.[44]

Irenaeus of Lyons (*c.* 130–*c.* 202) had suggested that Adam and Eve were in an essentially childlike state when they fell, and that their lapse was more a consequence of immaturity than wilful disobedience.[45] In this respect Adam symbolised the human race which, although mired in error and sin in its infancy, retained a capability for moral maturity. Other earlier Christian writers expressed similar views, in part as a reaction against the deeply pessimistic anthropology of the Gnostics.[46] On the authority of St Paul, most held that the state of sinfulness was inherited, although Clement of Alexandria (d. *c.* 220) and Gregory Nazianzus (329–89) expressed the view that the universal deficiencies of the human condition were socially acquired.[47] But whether nature or nurture was regarded as the source of sinfulness, the fallen condition of humanity was generally held to be cause for regret rather than extravagant self-condemnation.

As for what was lost to human cognitive powers as a consequence of the Fall, this was often expressed in terms of some loss or disfigurement of the 'image of God', in which was thought to rest human uniqueness (Gen. 1:26f.). While this image was understood in different ways – and was sometimes contrasted with the 'likeness of God' – it was thought to encompass the capacity for a relationship with God, along with moral

---

[43] Calvin, *Institutes* II.ii.4 (Beveridge, I, 226); cf. *Institutes* II.i.5.

[44] Jacques Liébaert, 'La Tradition Patristique jusqu'au Ve siècle', in *La Culpabilité fondamentale: Péché originel et anthropologie moderne* (Lille, 1975), pp. 35–43; Gerald Bray, 'Original Sin in Patristic Thought', *Churchman* 108 (1994), 1–37; David Weaver, 'From Paul to Augustine: Romans 5:12 in Early Christian Exegesis', *St Vladimir's Theological Quarterly* 27 (1983), 187–206; Henri Rondet, 'Le péché originel dans la tradition: Tertullien, Clément, Origène', *Bulletin de Littérature Ecclésiastique* 67 (1966), 115–48; Julius Gross, *Entstehungsgeschichte des Erbsündendogmas: Von der Bibel bis Augustinus* (Munich, 1960), 69–255; Christina Gschwandtner, 'Threads of Fallenness according to the Fathers of the First Four Centuries', *European Explorations in Christian Holiness* 2 (2001), 19–40; F. R. Tennant, *The Sources of the Doctrine of the Fall and Original Sin* (New York, 1903), pp. 273–345.

[45] Irenaeus, *Adversus haereses* IV.xxxviii–xxxix, II.xxii. For a statement of the Irenaean position see John Hick, *Evil and the God of Love* (London, 1985), pp. 211–15; Chadwick, *The Early Church*, pp. 80f.; Henri Rondet, *Original Sin: The Patristic and Theological Background*, tr. C. Finegan (New York, 1972), pp. 37f. For its influence in the early modern period see Poole, *Milton and the Fall*, pp. 16f.

[46] Theophilus, *To Autolycus* II.xxv; Methodius, *Banquet of the Ten Virgins* III.5; Origen, *Commentary on John* XIII.37; Gregory Nazianzus, *Oration* 45.7–8.

[47] Romans 5:12–21; Gregory Nazianzus, *Oration* 45.8. For Clement's view see Williams, *Ideas of the Fall*, p. 206.

and rational abilities.[48] Irenaeus had suggested that after the Fall human beings had lost the image and likeness of God.[49] Carthaginian apologist Tertullian (*c.* 160–*c.* 225) agreed that Satan had overthrown the image of God and had entirely 'changed man's nature'.[50] For Athanasius (298–373), Bishop of Alexandria, the divine image was effaced as a result of the Fall, setting in place an ongoing process of corruption: 'the rational man made in God's image was disappearing, and the handiwork of God was in process of dissolution'.[51]

None, however, went so far as to suggest the complete destruction of the divine image. After all, if the image of God had been totally lost human beings would have become indistinguishable from the brute beasts. Irenaeus was to qualify his earlier claim that both image and likeness to God had been lost as a consequence of Adam's sin, suggesting that while the divine *likeness* was lost, the *image* remained.[52] The end of human existence, on this understanding, was gradually to reacquire likeness to God, a task made possible by the latent potential of the divine image. Origen similarly suggested that 'the possibility of attaining to perfection [was] granted him at the beginning through the dignity of the divine image'. The perfection of the divine likeness was to be reached 'in the end by the fulfilment of the necessary works'.[53] Later Greek Fathers were to express similar views.[54]

Stoic notions of an all-pervading *logos* or reason also played a role in these discussions. Philo had already linked the Stoic idea with the Hebrew concept of the divine image, and a number of early Christian writers were to follow suit.[55] Justin Martyr had spoken of the 'seed of reason' (*logos spermatikos*) lodged in all human minds. This spark of the divine had enabled noble pagans to inquire into the rational order of the cosmos and to have presentiments of Christian truths.[56] Tertullian, in spite of a reputation

---

[48] 'Then God said, "Let us make man in our image, according to our likeness; let them have dominion . . ."' Gen. 1:26.

[49] Irenaeus, *Adversus haereses* III.xviii.1.   [50] Tertullian, *De spectaculis* ii (ANF III, 80).

[51] Athanasius, *De Incarnatione verbi dei* VI.i (NPNF II, IV, 39).

[52] Irenaeus, *Adversus haereses* V.vi.1. Cf. Cyprian, *Treatises* IX.5; Clement of Alexandria, *Stromata* II.22. On the difference between likeness and image see Hick, *Evil and the God of Love*, pp. 217–21.

[53] Origen, *De principiis* III.vii.1 (ANF IV, 345). The use of two distinct terms in Genesis is more likely the consequence of a typical Hebrew parallelism than an intention to express two distinct kinds of resemblance.

[54] See, e.g., Gregory of Nyssa, *On Virginity* xii; *On the Making of Man* XVIII.8; Gregory Nazianzus, *On his Father's Silence* XVI.8, XVI.15; *Against the Arians* 33.12.

[55] W. Kelber, *Die Logoslehre von Heraklit bis Origenes*, 2nd edn (Stuttgart, 1958), pp. 92–132; C. Colpe, 'Von der Logoslehre des Philon zu der des Clemens von Alexandrien', in *Kerygma und Logos*, ed. A. M. Ritter (Göttingen, 1979), pp. 68–88; S. V. McCasland, '"The Image of God" according to Paul', *Journal of Biblical Literature* 69 (1950), 363–5.

[56] Justin Martyr, *II Apology* VIII, XIII. Cf. Origen, *Contra Celsum* V.34. For patristic views of pagan thought see Jaroslav Pelikan, *The Emergence of the Catholic Tradition (100–600)* (Chicago, 1971),

for being an implacable opponent of the pagan philosophers, believed that a primordial moral 'law' had been bequeathed to Adam and Eve. This law of nature provided the basis for the moral precepts of the various nations and thus accounted for what was noble and good amongst the pagans.[57] Origen also invoked the notion of a universal natural law, which he contrasted in typical Stoic fashion with the written law of nations. Christians, he argued, could legitimately resist the legal compulsion to engage in idolatrous acts on account of their duty to a higher natural law. This was an important anticipation of later justifications of civil disobedience through appeals to natural law.[58]

The early Church Fathers thus tended to be hesitant about elevating the original abilities of Adam to too high a degree, and were equally restrained in their assessments of the damage wrought as a consequence of his fall. By the fourth century, however, there was a growing tendency amongst the Latin fathers to emphasise the mythological perfections of Adam in paradise and to maximise the tragedy of his loss. The terminology describing this primeval catastrophe also underwent a significant change during this period. No longer was the Fall understood primarily as *deprivatio* – the loss of something good. Instead it came to be explained as *depravatio* – a perverse corruption.[59] The tendency to stress the corruption of the human condition and the magnitude of its losses is usually associated with the teachings of Augustine of Hippo (354–430). Augustine, who coined the expression 'original sin' (*peccatum originis*), insisted that with the Fall human nature was 'wounded, hurt, damaged, destroyed'.[60] This incapacity was transmitted to all of Adam's progeny. Thus we do not become sinners on account of our own actions, rather all of our actions result from the sinful condition in which we are born.[61] In Augustine's theology there could be no question of individual soul's meriting redemption, for the complete

pp. 27–41; Henry Chadwick, *Early Christian Thought and the Classical Tradition: Studies in Justin, Clement, and Origen* (New York, 1966).

[57] Tertullian, *Answer to the Jews* II; *De Corona* VI; Cf. *De anima* ii. Tertullian appealed to the Pauline contention that 'the heathens do by nature what the law requires'. Romans 2:14. Ambrose of Milan assumed what was to become the Augustinian position, arguing that 'through disobedience the privileges of natural law were corrupted and nullified' *Epistolarum classis* II, 73.5 (PL 16, 1306).

[58] Origen, *Contra Celsum* v.37 (ANF IV, 559f.). See *Origen: Contra Celsum*, ed. Henry Chadwick (Cambridge, 1953), p. 7. For Origen and the Fathers on natural law, see W. A. Banner, 'Origen and the Tradition of Natural Law Concepts', *Dumbarton Oaks Papers* 8 (1954), 51–92.

[59] Hick, *Evil and the God of Love*, p. 213.

[60] Augustine, *De natura et gratia* 62.53 (NPNF I, v, 442).

[61] Augustine, *City of God*, books 11–14; *Enchiridion* XXV–XXVII, XLV. For the difference between this position and that of the Eastern Fathers see P. Papageorgiou, 'Chrysostom and Augustine on the Sin of Adam and its Consequences', *St Vladimir's Theological Quarterly* 39 (1995), 361–78.

initiative for salvation lay with the prevenient grace of a sovereign and predestining Deity.

The apparent severity of the Augustinian position is to be accounted for in part by the fact that his doctrine was forged in a climate of theological controversy. In the prelude to one of the most celebrated polemics in the history of Christian thought, the Irish monk Pelagius had taken exception to some of Augustine's more extreme remarks about the moral incapacity of human beings.[62] Pelagius believed that Augustine's insistence on the irrelevance of personal righteousness for salvation was a formula for licentiousness and the abrogation of personal moral responsibility. Neither was Pelagius convinced by Augustine's insistence that all human beings were born into a state of sin. From Augustine's perspective, Pelagius seemed to espouse a doctrine of the perfectibility of man, and of the capacity of each individual to achieve sinless perfection in the present life without the assistance of divine grace. Adam's guilt was imputed to him alone, and did not descend to his progeny. For much of this, Pelagius would have had the support of contemporary Eastern theologians.[63] In the Western Church, however, the Augustinian view prevailed, at least for a time.

As for knowledge in a fallen world, Augustine emphasised the fact that Adam's lapse was not merely a moral loss but one that had plunged the human race into an irremediable epistemological confusion. As a consequence of original sin, individuals not only habitually make wrong moral choices but consistently confuse error for truth. All are thus condemned to spend their earthly lives in a state of perpetual ignorance. It pleased God, Augustine wrote, 'that we should be born of that first couple into ignorance and difficulty and mortality, since they, when they sinned, were precipitated into error and hardship and death'. There are two penalties for every sinful soul, he went on to point out, 'ignorance and difficulty'.[64] This association of the condition of ignorance with the Fall possibly owes something to Plotinus's Platonic conception of the Fall.[65] Augustine also relied on the same gendered images that Philo had employed: the passions and appetites are the feminine aspects of the mind which, in the ordained order of things,

[62] For concise accounts of the controversy see Friedrick Loofs, 'Pelagius und der pelagianische Streit', in *Realencyklopädie für protestantische Theologie and Kirche*, ed. Albert Hauck, 3rd edn, 22 vols. (Leipzig, 1896–1908), xv, 747–74; G. Bonner, 'Augustine and Pelagianism', *Augustinian Studies* 23 (1992), 33–52; 24 (1993), 27–47.

[63] Pelikan, *Emergence of the Catholic Tradition*, p. 316.

[64] Augustine, *De Libero Arbitrio* III.xx.55. Aquinas expanded the list to four – ignorance, malice, weakness, concupiscence: ST Ia2ae. 61, 2; ST Ia2ae. 85, 3.

[65] O'Connell, 'The Plotinian Fall of the Soul'.

are to be governed by a masculine reason.[66] As the Fall was occasioned by the wrongful submission of the rational (Adam) to the sensory (Eve), so in the proper conduct of life, 'the masculine part in the watch tower of Counsel' must constantly check sensory impulses and restrain actions guided by appetite. Our habitual reliance on the senses is a sign of our fallen condition.[67]

Part of Augustine's concern in his discussions of the Fall was to show that the misery of the human condition was not to be attributed to the Creator. Ignorance and error were not the natural condition of the human race as formed by the hand of God: 'to approve false things as true, so as to err unwillingly . . . is not the nature of man as established [by God], but the penalty of man as condemned'.[68] God thus bore no responsibility for the inherent tendency of humans to err. This attribution of error to the disorientation of the human will was part of a more comprehensive response to the problem of evil. One of Augustine's enduring theological achievements was a robust defence of the goodness of God in the face of the evils of the present world. The Augustinian theodicy, or 'free-will defence', remains one of two standard philosophical responses to the problem of evil.[69] Although it drew upon certain features of Neoplatonic philosophy, it represented a powerful refutation of both the Platonic notion that evil was a metaphysical necessity and the Manichaean dualistic idea of warring cosmic powers of good and evil. According to Augustine's 'free-will defence', the evils of the world are attributable to the abuse of free will, on the part first of the angels, and then of Adam. An 'evil will', as Augustine put it, 'is the cause of all evils'.[70] In individuals (who in their own actions rehearse the sinful choice of Adam) the errors of the intellect are consequent upon the errors of the will, and in particular the turning of the will away from the higher spiritual goods to lesser material goods. Yet the freedom of the will is held to be an intrinsic good that outweighs the evils that result from its abuse.

---

[66] Augustine, *Confessions* XIII.32 (Chadwick tr., p. 302). But Augustine does not thereby demote women's intelligence: 'In mental power she has an equal capacity of rational intelligence, but by the sex of her body she is submissive to the masculine sex.' See also *The Trinity* XII.IV13; Ambrose of Milan, *Paradiso* 2.11. For the views of the Alexandrian Fathers see Sarah Petersen, 'The Fall and Misogyny in Justin and Clement of Alexandria', in D. Foster and P. Mozjes (eds.), *Society and Original Sin* (New York, 1985), pp. 37–51.

[67] Augustine, *The Trinity* XII.IV.13 (Mackenna tr., p. 356). Augustine, *Letters* 55, v.8 (NPNF I, 1, 306). Cf. Athanasius, *Against the Heathen* I.iii.2. A number of medieval thinkers were also to argue that our enslavement to imperfect sensory knowledge was a consequence of the Fall. See Richard of St Victor, *Benjamin major* 2.4, 2.17 (PL 196, 82CD). For William of Auvergne's views, see Steven P. Marrone, *William of Auvergne and Robert Grosseteste* (Princeton, 1983), pp. 67f.

[68] Augustine, *De Libero Arbitrio* III.xviii.52. Cf. *Enchiridion* XXIV; Plotinus, *Enneads* II.ix.

[69] The definitive account is given in Hick, *Evil and the God of Love*, part II.

[70] Augustine, *De Libero Arbitrio* III.xvii.48. Cf. *Enchiridion* XXIII; *On Nature and Grace* III.iii.

In short, the risk of the possibility of sin is the price paid for the possession of free will. In the seventeenth century Descartes and Malebranche were to utilise different features of Augustine's free-will defence in their analysis of mental errors and in their explanations of why human proneness to error should not count against the goodness of God.[71]

CARNAL KNOWLEDGE AND THE DIVINE LIGHT

If, for Augustine, the Fall accounted for the human propensity for error, it also explained an unhealthy preoccupation with the 'lower goods' of the sensory realm. Not only are lapsed human beings condemned to perpetual ignorance in the Augustinian scheme of things – their very motivations in seeking knowledge of the natural world are tainted by sin. Hence the seemingly innocent quest for knowledge becomes a culpable curiosity, which is itself an expression of the lustful concupiscence that tainted all human activity in a fallen world. 'Curiosity' is now identified as the intellectual vice that had made its first appearance in the Garden of Eden, and subsequently infected the investigations of the Greek natural philosophers.

Augustine's theological forebears had already expressed reservations about the value of philosophical and scientific knowledge, and had wondered whether the motives of those engaged in the philosophical quest were entirely pure. To be sure, they had acknowledged the personal piety and philosophical acumen of such noble pagans as Socrates and Plato. Justin Martyr (*c.* 100–163), the first of the Christian apologists, went so far as to suggest that 'Christ was partially known, even by Socrates'. Clement of Alexandria thought that Greek philosophy had served the Greeks, as had the law of Moses for the Jews, as a tutor to bring the Greeks to Christ. Philosophy was 'a handmaid of theology', and 'a kind of preparatory training for those who attain faith'. Origen agreed that Greek philosophy was 'ancillary to Christianity'.[72] Yet these occasional confluences of Christian and pagan thought were often attributed to Greek plagiarism from the Old Testament. Ironically, the plagiarism thesis was itself not entirely original, for it had been first deployed by Jewish apologists living in Alexandria. Aristobulus of Paneus (*fl.* 160 BC) argued that a considerable portion of

[71] Descartes, *Meditations* (CSM II, 58); *Principles of Philosophy* (CSM I, 203f.). Malebranche, *Search after Truth* II.i.5 (pp. 122f.); *Elucidations* VII.x–xii (pp. 583f.). For an overview of Descartes' position see Janowski, *Cartesian Theodicy.*
[72] Justin, II *Apology* 10 (ANF I, 191); Clement of Alexandria, *Stromata* I.v (ANF II, 305); cf. *Stromata* I.xix–xx; *The Instructor* I.xi.; Origen, *Letter to Gregory* I (ANF X, 295).

Greek philosophy had been derived from the Hebrew scriptures.[73] Philo
and Josephus subsequently took up the idea, and Christian writers in turn
adapted it to their purposes.[74] Justin and Clement thus believed that the
Timaeus – Plato's profoundly influential account of the creation – had
been inspired by Genesis, while Origen thought that Plato's *Phaedrus* was
similarly derivative.[75] Latin writers, too, subscribed to the thesis, although
perhaps not with the same degree of enthusiasm. Tertullian thought that
the Greek philosophers had probably been familiar with the Jewish scriptures, while the North African Minucius Felix regarded pagan notions of
the earth's final conflagration as evidence of the originality and prescience
of the Judaeo-Christian prophets.[76]

But even these qualified concessions to pagan authors extended primarily
to their theology and moral philosophy. Works devoted to the study of the
natural world met with less enthusiasm. Drawing on the Genesis narratives,
the world-weary scepticism of the Old Testament wisdom literature, and St
Paul's cautions against commerce with 'the wisdom of this world', a number
of patristic writers had suggested that knowledge of nature was of little use to
Christians, and that the scientific quest was more often motivated by pride
and illicit curiosity than by a genuine desire for truth.[77] While certain pagan
achievements were admirable, if not entirely original, for the most part the
ceaseless quest after knowledge of nature was judged to have resulted only in
the accumulation of 'vain' and 'useless' opinions.[78] By the fourth and fifth
centuries there had begun to develop a formal understanding of curiosity
as an intellectual vice. Human curiosity was now distinguished both by
its objects and by its underlying motivations. The curious mind aimed at
that knowledge that surpassed human capacities or which was forbidden,
'worldly', or useless. As to its motivations, curiosity was prompted by pride,
vanity, or the desire to be like God. Again, it was Augustine who drew these
various threads together. In a lucid passage in *The Confessions* he set out the

[73] Eusebius, *Praeparatio Evangelica* 13.12; Clement, *Stromata* I.xxii. On Aristobulus see E. Schrer, *The History of the Jewish People in the Age of Jesus Christ*, tr. G. Vermes et al. (Edinburgh, 1986), pp. 579–87.
[74] Philo, *Quod omnis probis liber sit* 8.57; Josephus, *Against Apion* II.37.257. On the plagiarism thesis see Pelikan, *Emergence of the Catholic Tradition*, pp. 33–6.
[75] Justin, *I Apology* 59; Clement of Alexandria, *Protrepicus* VI; cf. *Stromata* I.xxv; Origen, *Contra Celsum*, VI.19.
[76] Tertullian, *Ad nationes* II.ii.5; Minucius Felix, *Octavius* 34.1–4.
[77] See, e.g., Gen. 3:1–7; Eccl. 1:18, 12:12, and passim; Esdras 4:23, 13:52; Ecclesiasticus, 3:21–3; 1 Cor. 1:19–27; 2:1f.; 8.1; Col. 2:8; 1 Tim. 6:20; 2 Tim. 3:13–16. For typical patristic and medieval commentary see Ambrose, *Hexameron* 1.7, 1.9, 1.24; Gregory, *Moralia in Iob* 27.1; Gregory [attr.], *Dialogorum Gregorii Papae Libri Quatuor* 2, preface 1; Bernard of Clairvaux, *Epistola* 190, *In Die Pentecostes* 3.5, and *In Solemnitate Apostolorum Petri et Pauli*, 1.3.
[78] Tertullian, *De anima* ii; Basil, *Hexaemeron* 1.8–11; Peter Chrysologus, *Collectio Sermonum* 11; Jerome, *Commentarius in Epistolam ad Ephesios* 4.17; John Cassian, *Colationes* XIV.xvi.

phenomenology of curiosity, identifying it as the intellectual expression of that universal lust that had blighted human nature since the Fall: 'Beside the lust of the flesh which inheres in the delight given by all the pleasures of the senses . . . there exists in the soul, through the medium of the same bodily sense, a cupidity which does not take delight in carnal pleasure but in perceptions acquired through the flesh'. Augustine thus furnished curiosity with a genealogy, placing it amongst sins of the first rank, and linking it back to the malefaction of the primal parents. Curiosity was nothing more than an original concupiscence refracted through the mind rather than the body – *concupiscentia oculorum* in Augustine's vivid turn of phrase, the lust of the eyes. As it represented the corruption of something more noble than the body, this species of lust was particularly contemptible. Most damning of all, curiosity was associated with the greatest and first of all sins – pride.[79] For Augustine, then, the fall of the mind meant not only that the human sciences were radically compromised, but also that the very quest for natural knowledge, in particular knowledge of the sensory world, exemplified the corruption of human nature. It was a curiosity to taste of the tree of knowledge that had precipitated the Fall, and all subsequent attempts to acquire knowledge represented, in varying degrees, rehearsals of that first sin. Natural philosophy, then, was best left well alone. 'It is not necessary to probe into the nature of things, as was done by those whom the Greeks call *physici* . . . even their boasted discoveries are oftener mere guesses than certain knowledge'.[80]

Yet even for Augustine 'secular wisdom' had a place. Knowledge of mathematics and astronomy, for example, had helped him to extricate himself from the cosmological fantasies of his erstwhile co-religionists, the Manichaeans. Aspects of natural history were also endorsed because, in his own words, the discipline was 'serviceable in solving the difficulties of Scripture'.[81] History, the mechanical arts, and dialectic also had their place, again primarily in relation to the business of biblical exegesis. And of course Neoplatonic philosophy was treated with guarded approval, as representing a distillate of all that was good in pagan philosophy.[82] Given

---

[79] Augustine, *Confessions* x.xxxv; *Sermons* 313A (*Works*, iii/9, 92). For the link with pride, see *De moribus Ecclesiae Catholicae et de moribus Manichaeorum* 1.21.38; *De agone Christiano* 4.4; *The Trinity* xii.9; *City of God* xiv.28; *Supra Genesi contra Manichaeos* 11.18.27.

[80] Augustine, *Enchiridion* ix (NPNF i, iii, 239f.); cf. *Confessions* iv.iii.3–v.iv.7; *The Trinity* iv.iv.

[81] Augustine, *Confessions* v.iii.3–v.vi.10; *Christian Doctrine* ii.16.24, ii.29.45. For the link between natural history and allegorical interpretation in Augustine's thought see Harrison, *Bible and the Rise of Science*, esp. pp. 23–33.

[82] Augustine, *Christian Doctrine* ii.40.60; chs. xxviii–xxxi; cf. *City of God* viii.5, viii.10. For positive features of Augustine's attitude to knowledge of nature see David C. Lindberg, 'The Medieval

the pivotal role played by Neoplatonism in liberating Augustine from his materialistic metaphysical commitments, this lingering fondness is hardly surprising. The limited achievements of the pagan authors, however, were attributed not to their own abilities, but rather to divine goodness and mercy. To be sure, human nature had been corrupted, but certain 'gifts' had remained to fallen man after the expulsion from paradise: 'Now God has never withdrawn from corrupted and depraved nature His own mercy and goodness, so as to deprive man of fruitfulness, vivacity, and health, as well as the very substance of his mind and body, his senses also and reason, as well as food, and nourishment, and growth.'[83] Moreover, the image of God, which Augustine associates with human reason, was not completely destroyed, but rather weakened. Hence some part of the image of God remains inasmuch as humans possess 'a rational mind by which we know God'.[84]

The retention of these 'gifts' provided Augustine with the confidence to refute scepticism. To entertain the thought that no knowledge was possible was to go too far. While scepticism could perform the useful role of humbling the pride of the pagan philosophers, it also had the potential to cause collateral damage to Christian faith. Augustine had himself once veered towards Academic scepticism in the wake of his earlier flirtation with Manichaeism. It is significant that the first work he wrote after his conversion was *Against the Academics*. In the more mature work, *The Trinity*, he again sought to refute the claims of the sceptics, outlining a number of propositions that cannot be doubted:

let us put aside all consideration of things we know outwardly through the senses of the body, and concentrate our attention on what we have stated that all minds know for certain about themselves . . . Nobody surely doubts, however, that he lives and remembers and understands and wills and thinks and knows and judges. At least, even if he doubts, he lives; if he doubts, he remembers why he is doubting; if he doubts, he understands he is doubting; if he doubts, he has a will to be certain; if he doubts, he thinks; if he doubts, he knows he does not know; if he doubts, he judges he ought not to give a hasty assent. You may have your doubts about

Church Encounters the Classical Tradition', in David C. Lindberg and Ronald L. Numbers (eds.), *When Science and Christianity Meet* (Chicago, 2003), pp. 7–32. See also K. Pollmann and M. Vessey (eds.), *Augustine and the Disciplines: From Cassiciacum to Confessions* (Oxford, 2005).

[83] Augustine, *De nuptiis et concupiscentia* ii.ix (NPNF i, v, 291).

[84] Augustine, *Reply to Faustus the Manichean* xxv.2 (NPNF i, iv, 318). Cf. *City of God* xxii, 24; *De spiritu et littera* 28.49. This concession represented a mitigation of an earlier and more severe view, informed by the ideas of Plotinus, that the image of God had been destroyed at the Fall. See *Retractions* 2.24. The mature Augustine asserted rather that the 'likeness' to God had been lost, but that the image remained. *The Trinity* xiv.xvi.22.

anything else, but you should have no doubts about these; if they were not certain, you would not be able to doubt anything.[85]

The Cartesian cadences of this passage are quite remarkable, and there are further parallels in other works of Augustine. Most striking of all, perhaps, is the proposition in *The City of God* – *Si fallor sum* (If I am deceived, I exist) – which has unmistakable similarities to Descartes' *cogito ergo sum* (I think, therefore I am). [86] For the moment, however, it is important to understand that Augustine's principal concern was not to establish indubitable foundations for knowledge, but rather to point to the manner in which vestiges of the divine image still remain in the fallen human mind. Augustine's position here is that through introspection the mind can discover with certainty that there are three basic mental acts – memory, understanding, and will. This triad is a dim reflection of the luminous image of the triune God.[87] The image of God thus remains after the Fall, and if the mind can successfully disregard the sensory images of the material world, it may discover within itself an image of the divine.

Augustine also believed that the created world, like the human soul, bears a *vestigium* of the image of its creator, and one that remains faintly visible even after the disorder wrought by the Fall. While the world ought to have descended into utter chaos after the Fall, the mathematical patterns of God's original plan were preserved.[88] Augustine's thoughts on this issue were inspired by a verse in the apocryphal Book of Wisdom according to which 'God disposed all things in measure and number and weight' (11:21).[89] The triune pattern was thus repeated in the human soul and in the material creation. In places, Augustine suggests that it is the correspondence between these divine vestiges – in the mind and in the world – that makes knowledge possible. Hence, 'the memory contains the innumerable principles and laws of numbers and dimensions. None of them has been impressed on the

---

[85] Augustine, *The Trinity* x.iii, in *The Works of Saint Augustine*, ed. John Rotelle, 20 vols. (New York, 1991–), 1/5, 296f.

[86] Augustine, *City of God* xi.26.   [87] Augustine, *The Trinity* x.iii.

[88] In a discussion of 'the injuries inflicted by Adam's Fall', Augustine notes: 'Nor does he repay to each individual the whole of what the fallen creature merits. Rather, he arranges all things in measure and number and weight and he allows no one to suffer any evil which one does not deserve, although each individual does not suffer as much as the whole mass deserves.' *Answer to the Pelagians* iii (*Unfinished Answer to Julian*) ii, 87 (*Works* 1/25, 199).

[89] Augustine, *The Trinity* xi.iv. For other uses of this passage – a favourite of Augustine's – see *The Literal Meaning of Genesis* iv, 3, 7–12; *Confessions* v.iv.7; *Answer to an Enemy of the Law and the Prophets* i, 6, 8; *Free Will*, iii, 12, 35. See also W. Bierwaltes, 'Augustins Interpretation von Sapientia 11,21', *Revue des études augustiniennes* 15 (1969), 51–61; A.-M. La Bonnardière, *Biblia augustiniana. Le livre de la sagesse* (Paris, 1970), 90–8.

memory through any bodily sense perception.'[90] Together the vestiges in the human mind and in the material order are the conditions that make possible human knowledge of the divine origins of the creation.[91]

It must be said, finally, however, that without direct divine assistance, human beings can know nothing. As Augustine explains,

Man's nature, indeed, was created at first faultless and without any sin; but that nature of man in which every one is born from Adam, now wants the Physician, because it is not sound. All good qualities, no doubt, which it still possesses in its make, life, senses, intellect, it has of the Most High God, its Creator and Maker. But the flaw . . . darkens and weakens all those natural goods, so that it has need of illumination and healing.[92]

Augustine's reference here to the need for illumination and healing refers to the utter dependence of Adam's offspring on divine grace, not merely for their salvation (healing), but also for knowledge (illumination). The epistemological corollary of Augustine's view that divine grace was required for all human acts of virtue was that all acts of knowing similarly required the direct activity of God. Drawing on an extended visual metaphor borrowed from Plotinus, Augustine suggested that the mind is like an eye that can see only when its ideas are illuminated by the divine light: 'For the senses of the soul are as it were the eyes of the mind; but all the certainties of the sciences are like those things which are brought to light by the sun, that they may be seen, the earth, for instance, and the things upon it: while God is Himself the Illuminator.'[93] In its dependence on God, the mind was thus a *lumen luminatum* (illuminated light) not a *lumen illuminans* (illuminating light).[94]

If the illumination of ideas called for God's immediate activity, the soul's ability to see was to some extent dependent on its own purity and clarity.

[90] Augustine, *Confessions* x.xii.9 (Chadwick, p. 190).
[91] 'The Lord our God, whom we worship, is praised somewhere in the scriptures with the words, You have arranged all things in measure and number and weight (Wis. 11:20). Furthermore, we are clearly instructed in the teaching of the apostle to perceive the invisible things of God through our understanding of the things that have been made, and to search out hidden things through those that are plain. So question creation, so to speak, on all sides, and it replies by its very appearance, as if it were its voice, that it has the Lord God as its designer and builder.' Augustine, 'On the Plagues of Egypt' (410), *Sermons* 8.1 (*Works* iii/1, 240).
[92] Augustine, *On Nature and Grace* 3.iii (NPNF i, v, 122).
[93] Augustine, *Soliloquies* 1.12 (NPNF i, vii, 541). Cf. *Confessions* iv.xv.25; *De magistro* 12.40; *Sermons* 88.6. Cf. Plotinus, *Enneads* ii.iv.5; ii.ix.3.
[94] Augustine, *Tractates on John* xiv.i. For Augustine's discussion of various 'lights', see *De Gen. ad lit. Imperf.* v, 20–5. The metaphor also reflected Augustine's theory of vision according to which although light was emitted from our eyes, it was insufficient for vision and needed to be supplemented by a more powerful external source of light. See David C. Lindberg, *Theories of Vision from Al-Kindi to Kepler* (Chicago, 1976), pp. 89f.

For Augustine this meant that certain knowledge was possible only for a 'mind pure from all stain of the body, that is, now remote and purged from the lusts of mortal things'.[95] The gifts of faith, hope, and love could 'cure' a mind of the inherited malady of sin, and enable it to see God.[96] But it also followed that true and certain knowledge (*scientia*) would only be possible when the human mind participated in the source of truth, God. This called for a turning away from the unstable and fallen realm of the senses, a repudiation of the vice of curiosity, and a renewed reliance upon the 'inner eye' rather than the corrupt and corrupting 'outer eye'.[97]

The writings of Augustine, considered as a whole, betray a deep-seated ambivalence towards the natural world and human nature. Some of this is derived directly from the Platonism that informed his theological views, but much of it is also a consequence of the fact that so many of his works were forged in a climate of controversy. If in his dispute with Pelagius he seemed to denigrate the human condition, in his dealings with the dualistic Manichaeans he found it necessary to insist that the embodied condition of human beings was, of itself, good. Thus, while the influence of Augustinian thought throughout the Middle Ages and into the modern period is difficult to overestimate, it is to be expected that his legacy would bear some traces of the apparent inconsistencies in his thought. His positive assertions about the necessity for divine grace were enshrined in the canons of the Second Council of Orange (529), but a number of his more negative contentions about human nature did not receive support there.[98] The theory of divine illumination became the dominant theory of medieval cognition, embraced by the thirteenth-century Franciscans and surviving in a modified form in the early modern epistemologies of Malebranche and Berkeley.[99] But as we shall see, this theory was naturalised by Thomas Aquinas. Augustine's assertions about the depravity of the human condition and of the necessity and sufficiency of divine grace were revived and elaborated by the Protestant reformers and, to a lesser extent, by the seventeenth-century Jansenists. His

[95] Augustine, *Soliloquies* 1.12 (NPNF 1, VII, 541).   [96] *Ibid.* 1.13 (NPNF 1, VII, 541).

[97] Augustine, *Sermons* 88.6 (*Works* III/3, 423).

[98] 'The Council of Orange', in John Leith (ed.), *Creeds of the Churches* (Atlanta, 1962), 38–45. The Council stopped short of endorsing 'double predestination'.

[99] On the fortunes of the notion of illumination in the Middle Ages see Lindberg, *Theories of Vision*, pp. 87–103; Joseph Owens, 'Faith, Ideas, Illumination and Experience', in CHLMP, pp. 440–59; Steven Marrone, *The Light of Thy Countenance: Science and Knowledge of God in the Thirteenth Century* (Leiden, 2001); Robert Pasnau, 'Henry of Ghent and the Twilight of Divine Illumination', *Review of Metaphysics* 49 (1995), 49–75. For Augustine's light metaphors see R. A. Markus, 'Augustine, Reason, and Illumination', in CHMP, pp. 362–73; F.-J. Thonnard, 'La notion de lumière en philosophie augustinienne', *Recherches Augustiniennes*, 1962, pp. 124–75; Simon Oliver, *Philosophy, God and Motion* (London, 2005), ch. 3.

teachings on the authority of the Roman Church and the sacraments were embraced by early modern Catholics and deployed against the reformers. Finally, Augustine's arguments against scepticism were rehearsed by Descartes, and in the form of the *cogito* became the foundation for his epistemological enterprise.

The next major development in medieval thought came with the reintroduction of Aristotelian texts to the West. From the twelfth century onwards, newly translated works of Aristotle were to give expression to an alternative philosophical tradition that was to have a profound impact on the course of Western thought. Aristotelian thought brought with it a more positive anthropology, an assertion of the primacy of the sensory world and, in the hands of Aquinas, a theory of cognition that invoked natural rather than divine light. Inevitably, these developments led to the formulation of new answers to the questions that Augustine had answered somewhat ambiguously: what happened to human sensory and cognitive powers after the Fall? To what extent could they be relied upon for accurate knowledge of the world? Of what value is knowledge of nature?

BAPTISING ARISTOTLE

In 1285, the English Franciscan John Pecham (*c.* 1225–92) – later to become Archbishop of Canterbury – wrote to a friend of his concerns about recent trends in philosophical theology. 'I do not disapprove of philosophical studies, insofar as they serve theological mysteries', he wrote, 'but I do disapprove of irreverent innovations in language, introduced in the last twenty years into the depths of theology against the philosophical truth and to the detriment of the Fathers, whose positions are disdained and openly held in contempt.' These developments, Pecham noted, had given rise to 'wordy quarrels, weakening and destroying with all its strength what Augustine teaches concerning the eternal rules and the unchangeable light'.[100] The general trend in question was the rise of Aristotelian philosophy in the universities and its enthusiastic adoption by a number of theologians. Up until the twelfth century Aristotle's works had been unknown in the Latin West, with the exception of two treatises on logic that had fortuitously been translated by Boethius (480–524) some 600 years before. In a relatively brief period all of this was to change. As the consequence of a remarkable investment of scholarly and editorial effort, by the end of the thirteenth century

---

[100] Quoted in Etienne Gilson, *History of Christian Philosophy in the Middle Ages* (New York, 1955), p. 359.

almost the entire Aristotelian corpus had been translated into Latin, most
of it from Greek manuscripts.[101] Not only were these ancient writings now
widely available, they were enthusiastically received by many within the
universities. By 1255, Aristotle's philosophical writings had been incorporated into the curriculum of the Faculty of Arts at Paris.[102] The introduction
of Aristotle into the medieval West was a momentous event that precipitated a revolution in Christian thought epitomized by Thomas Aquinas's
(*c.* 1225–74) masterful synthesis of Aristotelian philosophy and Christian
theology.

As Pecham's epistolary concerns indicate, however, the path for the
new theological synthesis was by no means smooth. Well before Pecham's
expressed anxieties about Thomas's theological novelties, ecclesiastical
authorities had taken action to control the contagion of Aristotelian teaching. Edicts prohibiting lectures on Aristotle's works of natural philosophy
were issued in Paris in 1210 and again in 1215, and these were enforced to
varying degrees in other parts of Europe. Yet it seems that by the middle
decades of the century these had been largely forgotten, and Aristotle's
works were prescribed for prospective Masters of Arts.[103] Controversy arose
again in the 1270s, and in 1277 Stephen Tempier, the Bishop of Paris,
condemned 219 articles in theology and natural philosophy, a number of
which were related to Aristotelian doctrines.[104] Pecham's own reservations,
moreover, were fairly representative of those of his Order. Other prominent
thirteenth-century Franciscans such as Bonaventure (1221–74) and Alexander of Hales shared Pecham's perspective, championing more traditional
Augustinian doctrines against the new ideas of Aristotle that threatened
to displace them. One of the central issues in the debate, evident from
Pecham's letter, related to Augustine's contentions about the 'unchangeable
light' and the 'eternal rules'. Pecham and a number of his fellow Franciscans
continued to hold to an epistemology that invoked divine illumination.
Aquinas, by way of contrast, had learned from Aristotle that the acquisition of knowledge was a mundane process that required no supernatural
intervention. Knowledge for Aristotle and Aquinas, moreover, began with
the very senses that in the Augustinian tradition had been associated with
the fallen condition of the human race.

[101] Bernard Dod, 'Aristoteles Latinus', CHLMP, pp. 45–79.
[102] H. Denifle and A. Chatelain, *Chartularium Universitatis Parisiensis*, 4 vols. (Delalain, 1889–97), I, 277–9.
[103] *Ibid.*, I, 70, 78f.; Dod, 'Aristoteles Latinus', CHLMP, p. 71.
[104] Denifle and Chatelain, *Chartularium*, I, 543–55; Edward Grant, 'The Condemnation of 1277, God's Absolute Power, and Physical Thought in the Late Middle Ages', *Viator* 10 (1979), 211–44.

So it was that when Aquinas came to address the fundamental question of the acquisition of knowledge he was to insist that human minds possessed a 'natural light' that made knowledge possible in the absence of either 'sanctifying grace' or 'any habitual gift superadded to nature'.[105] While Aquinas implied that his view was not at odds with the long-standing Augustinian tradition, there is little doubt that it amounted to a rejection of Augustinian illumination – as his Franciscan opponents were all too ready to point out.[106] Aquinas also differed from Augustine in insisting that our inherent capacity for knowledge – our 'natural light' – had survived the Fall intact. Adam in his innocence, he explained, had been possessed of both 'natural gifts' and 'supernatural gifts'.[107] Only the latter had been lost as a consequence of the Fall. Crucially, reason was one of the natural gifts that remained. Indeed, for Aquinas, reason was the most important of the natural gifts. The 'light of natural reason', he explained, 'since it pertains to the species of the rational soul, is never forfeit from the soul'. It is 'impossible' for it to be extinguished. [108] Aquinas was thus committed to the view that reason could not be alienated from the human soul without its ceasing to be human. Expressed in more explicitly theological terms, Aquinas was to say that the natural light of reason is nothing other than the indwelling image or likeness of God: 'the light of reason . . . is imparted to us by God. It is a likeness of the uncreated truth dwelling in us'.[109]

Thomas's distinction between natural and supernatural gifts reflects his better-known dichotomy between nature and grace. This latter distinction was inherited from Augustine, but in Aquinas given a metaphysical signif-icance lacking in the thought of his illustrious predecessor. To a degree, Aquinas's notion was premised on the new conception of the natural order

---

[105] Aquinas, ST 1a2ae. 109, 1. Cf. *Expositio super librum Boethii De Trinitate* 1.1. Aquinas explained that the act of knowing did indeed depend on God, in the sense that every natural event relies on God as the first mover. ST 1a. 79, 4. Aquinas also conceded that the natural 'intellectual light' that is in us is a participation in the uncreated light contained in the eternal types. ST 1a. 84, 5. The classic article on Thomas's understanding of *lumen naturale* is J. Guillet, 'La "lumière intellectuelle" d'après S. Thomas', *Archives d'histoire doctrinale et littéraire du moyen âge* 2 (1927), 79–88.

[106] Owens, 'Faith, Ideas, Illumination and Experience'; Pasnau, 'Twilight of Divine Illumination'.

[107] Aquinas, ST 1a. 95, 1.

[108] Aquinas, ST 2a2ae. 15, 1; *Disputed Questions on Truth* vol. II, Q. 16, A. 3 Body (p. 312). Cf. SCG 1.7 (English Dominican Fathers tr., p. 14).

[109] Aquinas, *De veritate* 11.1c. Aquinas does admit that 'at times, it is prevented from exercising its proper act, through being hindered by the lower powers'. His overall position, however, was that the intellectual faculties are not 'altered', but are merely 'impeded' as a consequence of sin. ST 2a2ae. 15, 1. Moreover it is the moral operations of reason that were more severely damaged: 'Because of sin the reason, *especially with regard to moral decision*, is blunted.' Aquinas, ST 1a2ae. 85, 3 (my emphasis). For Augustine, the intellectual faculties are 'corrupted and depraved'. *On Nature and Grace* 21.xix; 77.lxiv.

that some scholars have referred to as 'the twelfth-century discovery of nature'.[110] No longer was the world of the senses regarded as a shadowy and inferior copy of a higher spiritual realm as it had been in the Platonic-Augustinian tradition. Now it was invested with an intelligibility of its own, and it became susceptible once again to empirical investigation. The existence of an autonomous sphere of nature was the presupposition of Aquinas's distinction between natural and supernatural gifts. Human reason, belonging to the sphere of nature, was insulated from the supernatural privations that had followed the Fall and, equally importantly, retained a capacity to discern intelligibility in the natural and moral orders. The 'natural light of reason', as Aquinas expressed it, remains 'the full possession' of human beings.[111] Augustine, by way of contrast, had thought that the whole of nature was more directly dependent on the divine will. Even the most regular operations of the natural world were to be thought of as a continuous miracle.[112] The human mind was similarly the subject of constant divine interventions.

While Aquinas's belief in the persistence and integrity of human reason in lapsed human beings represented a point of departure from the Augustinian position, it was congruent with an Aristotelian epistemology that was largely unencumbered by theological considerations. The Greek philosopher had famously declared in the opening sentence of the *Metaphysics* that 'All men by nature desire to know.'[113] Aquinas agreed that our thirst for knowledge was natural, further concurring with Aristotle that this desire cannot be in vain. He concluded that human cognitive faculties had been ordered in such a way as to satisfy our desire for knowledge. Our orientation towards sense objects and the knowledge that we subsequently arrive at thus contribute to our natural good.[114] Because the natural good of the intellect is nothing other than the truth, as Aristotle had pointed out, it was reasonable to assume that both our sensory and intellectual capacities were appropriately

[110] See Marie-Dominique Chenu, *Nature, Man and Society in the Twelfth Century* (Chicago, 1968), pp. 4–18; Richard Dales, 'A Twelfth-Century Concept of Natural Order', *Viator* 9 (1978), 179–92; G. B. Ladner, 'Erneuerung', in *Reallexikon für Antike und Christentum*, ed. Ernst Dassmann, 18 vols. (Stuttgart, 1950–), 6, 246–47; G. Post, 'The Naturalness of Society and State', in G. Post (ed.), *Studies in Medieval Legal Thought* (Princeton, 1964), pp. 494–561; Harrison, *Bible and the Rise of Science*, pp. 34–43.

[111] Aquinas, ST 1a2ae. 68, 2. Dimming of this natural light is possible but arises from intemperance rather than any innate flaw. ST 2a2ae. 142, 4; ST 2a2ae. 180, 2.

[112] Augustine, *City of God* x.12.

[113] Aristotle, *Metaphysics* 980a (*Works*, p. 1552). Aquinas cites Aristotle in ST 1a. 12, 1; ST 1a2ae 3, 6; ST 2a2ae. 90, 3.

[114] Aquinas, *Sententia super Metaphysicam* I.i.3–4. But cf. ST 1a2ae. 3, 6.

organised to yield true knowledge.[115] Not surprisingly, Aquinas expressed confidence in the general reliability of our knowledge, concluding that all scientific knowledge (*omnia scientia*) is good, 'because the good of anything is that which belongs to the fulness of being which all things seek after and desire; and man as man reaches fulness of being through knowledge'.[116] In short, Aquinas was led to the conclusion that our natural orientation towards the sensory world was not an indication of our fallen state as Augustine had thought, but was the natural state of affairs ordained by God. Expression of interest in the natural world resulted not from a reprehensible curiosity directed towards the lower orders of nature, but rather from a natural inclination towards material goods.[117]

So it was that in spite of Aquinas's professed reverence for the teachings of Augustine, his views on human knowledge represented a significant departure from the teachings of the Church Father. Not only did Aquinas replace Augustine's divine light with a natural light, but he was also more inclined to observe a distinction between the natural and supernatural, investing the former with an independence and integrity that was absent in Augustine. This recognition of a 'neutral' realm of philosophy that dealt with nature using the common instruments of reason was integral to Aquinas's generally positive reception of pagan philosophy and Aristotle in particular.[118] If Bonaventure had complained that so much of the water of secular philosophy had been mixed with the wine of sacred scripture that 'it had turned from wine into water', Aquinas insisted that the introduction of Aristotle's philosophy into theology was rather the transformation of water into wine.[119] And while Aquinas also conceded that 'man had fallen into sin by adhering to visible things unduly', he nevertheless resisted the Augustinian conclusion that engagement with the visible realm was on that account undesirable. He suggested instead that the remedy for sin bears an analogy to its cause, and that the good things that God has created in the visible

[115] Aristotle, *Nicomachean Ethics* vi, 1139a; Aquinas, ST 1a. 94, 4; J. Jenkins, 'Aquinas on the Veracity of the Intellect', *The Journal of Philosophy* 88 (1991), 623–32; Norman Kretzmann, 'Infallibility, Error, Ignorance', *Canadian Journal of Philosophy*, supplementary vol. 17 (1992).

[116] Aquinas, *Sententia super De Anima* 1.i.3, *Aristotle's De Anima and the Commentary of St. Thomas Aquinas*, tr. Kenelm Foster and Silvester Humphries (New Haven, 1965), p. 45.

[117] Aquinas nonetheless considers curiosity to be a vice and he devotes a complete question to it in the *Summa theologiae* (ST 2a2ae. 167).

[118] For a discussion of the differences between Augustine and Aquinas on this issue see Armand Maurer's introduction to *Faith, Reason, and Theology* (Toronto, 1987), pp. xv–xvii.

[119] Bonaventure, *Collations on the Six Days*, in *The Works of Bonaventure*, tr. J. de Vinck (Patterson, NJ, 1960–70), v, 291; Aquinas, *Super Boethii De Trinitate* 2.3. On this metaphor see J. F. Quinn, *The Historical Constitution of St. Bonaventure's Philosophy* (Toronto, 1973), pp. 814f.

realm can therefore serve to assist in the process of human redemption.[120] Knowledge is the fulfilment of a natural, and God-given, inclination. And reason, after all, was the image of God. This can be contrasted with the position according to which our inclination towards sensory objects results from the corruption of our faculties following the Fall. Accordingly, on the Thomist view, even with attenuated rational powers the human mind can discover a range of truths – about God, his creatures, the human soul, and the moral precepts of the natural law.[121] The whole enterprise of natural theology was premised upon this optimistic view of the natural powers of the human intellect. Moreover, it was on this basis that the teachings of the pagan philosophers regarding the natural world were, in principle, acceptable to Christian thinkers, there being no compelling reason to be suspicious of learning that had sprung from the exercise of natural and universal principles of reason.

While the Thomist synthesis of Christian and Aristotelian thought was a remarkable achievement that set the agenda for much of the theological discussion of the thirteenth and fourteenth centuries, it was by no means the sole solution offered to the issues raised by Aristotelian philosophy. Neither was Thomas's retreat from Augustine's uncompromising position on original sin and the Fall universally accepted. Again, a number of Franciscan thinkers, many of whom regarded themselves as custodians of the Augustinian tradition, kept the issue of the Fall on the epistemological agenda. Even before Aquinas had set out on his mission to incorporate peripatetic ideas into Christian theology, the Oxford philosopher and theologian Robert Grosseteste (1175–1253) had shown a similar enthusiasm for the works of Aristotle, albeit one tempered with a greater fidelity to Augustinian ideas. In his commentary on Aristotle's *Posterior Analytics*, Grosseteste was thus still concerned to find a place for divine illumination and to identify the specific consequences of the Fall for human intellectual endeavour. In its original perfection, he insisted, the human intellect was capable of complete knowledge without recourse to the senses. In its fallen condition, however, the higher powers of the mind have been lulled to sleep. The senses now perform the function of rousing the mind from its somatically induced slumbers, and indeed it is repeated sensory experiences that prosecute this task best of all. Hence, while Aristotle was correct to

---

[120] Aquinas, SCG IV.56 (p. 219).
[121] Aquinas, ST I₂₂e. 91. From an Augustinian perspective such talk of a 'natural law' was, to use Ralph McInerny's phrase, redolent of 'an almost Pelagian insouciance'. Ralph McInerny, 'Ethics', in Norman Kretzmann and Eleonore Stump (eds.), *The Cambridge Companion to Aquinas* (Cambridge, 1993), pp. 196–216 (p. 213).

assert that knowledge must begin with the senses, he had been unaware of the fact that this reliance was a consequence of the Fall, rather than of a natural orientation towards material things.[122] The need for repeated experience (*experimentum*) in this scheme of things was not in order to provide examples from which inductive inferences may be drawn in the manner of a modern Baconian, but was rather to jolt reason into a belated recognition of universal ideas accessible by the illumination of the intellect. Grosseteste's emphasis on *experimentum* – best understood in this context simply as 'experience' – does not therefore qualify him as a precocious pioneer of experimental method, as some have suggested. In his own words, 'It is not in sensation that we know, but it is as a result of sensation that knowledge of the universal comes to us. This knowledge comes via the senses, but not from the senses.'[123] As Robert Southern has explained in an apt analogy, for Grosseteste use of the senses is like a blind man's use of a white cane. The cane is not the cause of his capacity for walking, but is that without which walking could not take place at all.[124] This position does not necessarily constitute a criticism of Aristotelian epistemology, but it does circumscribe the realm in which *scientia* operates, and holds it to be inferior to the *sapientia* that comes with divine illumination. The blindness of a lapsed humanity prevents it from knowing anything of ultimate significance, unless it is first illuminated by the source of all truth.[125]

One of Aquinas's contemporaries, Bonaventure, also noted that the cognitive powers implanted in us by nature 'were distorted by sin'. In the most famous of his mystical writings, *Itinerarium mentis in Deum* ('The Journey of the Mind to God'), Bonaventure states that Adam's lapse consisted in a stooping down to lesser goods, and that in this one primal act he ensnared the whole of his posterity in original sin. The Seraphic Doctor also followed Augustine in asserting that the Adamic inheritance was presently manifested in two ways: 'by ignorance in the mind, and by concupiscence in the flesh'. The first step towards the rectification of this ignorance and the attainment

[122] James McEvoy, *The Philosophy of Robert Grosseteste* (Oxford, 1982), pp. 329–35; Oliver, *Philosophy, God and Motion*, p. 66.

[123] Grosseteste, *Commentarius in Posterior Analyticorum Libros*, 1.18.205–7 (p. 269), quoted by R. Southern, *Robert Grosseteste: The Growth of an English Mind in Medieval Europe* (Oxford, 1986), p. 165. For Grosseteste as a pioneer experimentalist see Alastair Crombie, *Robert Grosseteste and the Origins of Experimental Science 1100–1700* (Oxford, 1971). Cf. B. Eastwood, 'Medieval Empiricism: the Case of Robert Grosseteste's *Optics*', *Speculum* 43 (1968), 306–21; McEvoy, *Philosophy of Grossesteste*, pp. 206–11.

[124] Southern, *Robert Grosseteste*, p. 165.

[125] Grosseteste's most famous pupil Roger Bacon also stressed the role of sin in compromising human knowledge. *The Opus Majus of Roger Bacon*, tr. Robert Burke, 2 vols. (Whitefish, MT, 2002), I, 4, 14.

of wisdom involved a recognition of the presence of sin, followed by its pur-
gation through the disciplining of the natural powers. Those who wish to
follow the contemplative path, as Bonaventure put it, 'must first eliminate
nature-deforming sin, then train the . . . natural powers'.[126] While some
commentators have pointed to parallels between Descartes' *Meditations* and
medieval meditative traditions of this kind, a case can be made that this
procedure also resembles, in important respects, the strategies adopted by
Francis Bacon and the experimental philosophers.[127] For the latter, there is
often a quite explicit acknowledgement that ignorance is the result of the
corruption of human nature, and that the disciplines associated with the
experimental method are designed to purge this inherited inclination to
make erroneous judgements.

Duns Scotus (*c.* 1266–1308) was another Franciscan who like Grosseteste
taught at Oxford. He too wished to gloss the Aristotelian claim that all
knowledge began with the senses. Scotus rightly ascribed to Aristotle the
view that the human mind is naturally oriented towards sensible things
and seeks knowledge by abstracting from particular objects in the sensory
realm. The proper object of knowledge was, then, the essence of a material
object. This was true as far as it went. Again, however, Scotus pointed
out that what Aristotle had not realised – on account of his ignorance of
the truths of revelation – was that the condition he had ascribed to the
mind as 'natural' was in fact a consequence of the Fall. The orientation
towards the sensible realm that is an inescapable feature of our present
existence is evidence of its corruption, and not some natural ordering of
the mind towards its proper end. Indeed, this had been the contention of
Augustine some 900 years earlier. Scotus further reasoned that because the

---

[126] Bonaventure, *Mystical opuscula*, in *Works* i, ii, 12.

[127] See, e.g., Pierre Mesnard, 'L'Arbre de la sagesse', *Descartes, Cahiers de Royaumont, Philosophy* ii
(Paris, 1957), 366–89, and discussion, 350–9; L. J. Beck, *The Metaphysics of Descartes: A Study of
the Meditations* (Oxford, 1965), 28–38; Pierre Hadot, *What is Ancient Philosophy?* (Cambridge, MA,
2002), pp. 264f.; Matthew Jones, 'Descartes's Geometry as Spiritual Exercise', *Critical Inquiry* 28
(2001), 40–72; Amélie Rorty, 'The Structure of Descartes' *Meditations*', in Amélie Rorty (ed.),
Essays on Descartes' Meditations (Berkeley, 1986), p. 2. In the same volume see also Gary Hatfield,
'The Senses and the Fleshless Eye: The Meditations as Cognitive Exercises', pp. 45–79; Walter
Stohrer, 'Descartes and Ignatius Loyola: La Flèche and Manresa Revisited', *Journal of the History
of Philosophy* 17 (1979), 11–27; Arthur Thomson, 'Ignace de Loyola et Descartes: L'influence des
exercices spirituels sur les œuvres philosophiques de Descartes', *Archives de philosophie* 35 (1972),
61–85; L. J. Beck, *The Metaphysics of Descartes: A Study of the 'Meditations'* (Oxford, 1965), pp. 28–38;
Z. Vendler, 'Descartes' Exercises', *Canadian Journal of Philosophy* 19 (1989), 193–224; Dennis Sepper,
'The Texture of Thought: Why Descartes' *Meditationes* Is Meditational, and Why It Matters', in
Stephen Gaukroger, John Schuster and John Sutton (eds.), *Descartes' Natural Philosophy* (London,
2000), pp. 736–50. More sceptical about the link between Descartes' work and the traditional
spiritual exercises is Bradley Rubidge, 'Descartes's *Meditations* and Devotional Meditations', *JHI*
51 (1990), 27–49.

final end of human beings is the beatific vision – the direct experience of an immaterial God – the proper object of the intellect cannot be the essences of material things, for God is not to be found there.[128] Rather the intellect was originally designed for knowledge of the entire realm of being (*ens in quantum ens*), and thus for knowledge of immaterial essences without the need for sensations. In the fallen world, however, the object of the intellect is the realm of sensory objects (*objectum de facto*), and knowledge of the essences of material things is given in sensations.[129]

The upshot of these Franciscan critiques of the Thomist synthesis was that Aristotle's epistemology was not a neutral philosophical instrument that could simply be imported uncritically into Christian theology. Previous objections to Aristotle had tended to focus on substantive claims of his natural philosophy, such as the assertion of the eternity of the world, or his view of the nature of the soul. Scotus highlighted the fact that Aristotle's fundamental epistemological premise was one that took no cognisance of sacred history or theological anthropology.[130] Accordingly, in Scotus's judgement it was compromised from the outset. Aristotle, of course, might be forgiven for his lack of awareness of the tradition of the Fall, and what it might mean for his assertion of the priority of sensory knowledge. Thomas Aquinas, perhaps, should have known better.

When in the sixteenth century the Protestant reformers came to pass judgement on the theology they had inherited from the scholastics, they were highly critical of the trend towards increasingly mild views of the Fall that dated from the time of Aquinas. Confronted with a range of more positive views of the fallen human being and its capacities, they urged a return to the more severe Augustinian position. Indeed, in certain respects they surpassed Augustine in their stress on the depravity of human nature. But on one issue they were in agreement with Scotus: Aristotle's epistemology was misconceived because it was grounded in a false view of human nature. Ignorant of those events that had taken place at the dawn of history, Aristotle had not realised that the present ordering of human faculties was the result of

---

[128] Scotus thus reinstates the Anselmian argument for the existence of God, substituting it for Thomas's 'five ways' that were based on sense experience.

[129] Duns Scotus, *Opus Oxoniense* I, d. 1, q. 3; II, d. 3, q. 8, n. 13. Translation of the relevant sections in J. Katz and R. H. Weingartner (eds.), *Philosophy in the West*, tr. J. Wellmuth (New York, 1965), pp. 560–3.

[130] This accords with Scotus's claim in the first question of his *Commentary on the Sentences of Peter Lombard* that the ultimate end of human existence cannot be known without supernatural knowledge. See Allan Wolter, 'Duns Scotus on the Necessity of Revealed Knowledge', *Franciscan Studies* 11 (1951), 231–72; Nathaniel Micklem, *Reason and Revelation: A Question from Duns Scotus* (Edinburgh, 1953).

a fall from an original perfection. His epistemology was thus fundamentally at odds with a genuinely Christian anthropology. As for Aquinas and his followers, they had unwittingly capitulated to a pagan view of human nature. Accordingly, the whole Thomist synthesis was questionable and the problem of human knowledge needed urgent reconsideration in the light of truths about human nature revealed in the history of Adam's fall from grace.

One of the principles enunciated by Shapin and Schaffer in *Leviathan and the Air Pump* is that 'solutions to the problem of knowledge are solutions to the problem of social order'.[131] This is undoubtedly true, but largely because for the Middle Ages and early modern period problems of knowledge and of social order were regarded as symptomatic of the more deep-seated problem of human sin. There are, then, instructive analogies between the spheres of knowledge and politics for the period we have just considered. It should now be evident that one of the central issues in medieval discussions of knowledge concerned the 'naturalness' of particular human propensities. Was our natural inclination to ground knowledge in sense perceptions evidence that God had intended our minds to operate that way? Or was it rather an indication of our corruption? Did all men by nature desire to know, as Aristotle had written, and were our present faculties capable of generating veridical knowledge? Or was our desire to know both the occasion of the Fall and an ongoing manifestation of an illicit curiosity that was destined to lead only to perennial frustration? The parallel issue in the sphere of political philosophy concerned the question of the natural sociability of human beings. As is well known, in the *Politics* Aristotle had contended that 'the state is a creation of nature, and that man is by nature a political animal'.[132] It followed that political systems exist because of a universal human propensity for sociability. Augustine, however, had argued to the contrary that human beings, whatever their original nature may have been, are in their present condition self-seeking, egotistical, and antisocial. In the *City of God*, he observes that 'there is nothing so social by nature, so unsocial by its corruption, as this race'.[133] For Augustine, it is precisely this propensity of fallen human beings to be given over to strife and discord that

---

[131] Shapin and Schaffer, *Leviathan and the Air Pump*, ch. 8. Cf. Margaret C. Jacob, *The Newtonians and the English Revolution, 1689–1720* (Ithaca, 1976). For a related argument that links Calvinist discipline with the early modern state see Phillip Gorski, *The Disciplinary Revolution: Calvinism and the Rise of the State in Early Modern Europe* (Chicago, 2003), esp. pp. 124f.

[132] Aristotle, *Politics* 1253a (p. 1987).

[133] Augustine, *City of God* XII.27 (Dodds edn, p. 411). For this contrast I am indebted to Cary J. Nederman, 'Nature, Sin, and the Origins of Society: The Ciceronian Tradition in Medieval Political Thought', *JHI* 49 (1988), 3–26.

justifies the existence of the state. The diverse objects of love of the citizens of the earthly city make the world inherently unstable. Only a temporal authority invested with coercive power is capable of reining in the anti-social tendencies of corrupt human beings and of bringing them together in an enforced semblance of social order. The rediscovery of Aristotle's *Politics* thus brought with it a significant dilemma for medieval thinkers: did political institutions point to a natural human propensity for sociability as Aristotle had taught, or did the existence of such institutions point rather towards the Fall and the mutual alienation of human beings that followed? Aquinas, as might be expected, opted for the Aristotelian view. Others, such as Augustinus Triumphus (*d.* 1328) and John Wyclif (*c.* 1330–84), took up something approaching an Augustinian view.[134]

In the early modern period the revival of Augustinian anthropology, accompanied as it was by an interest in the reformation of learning, prompted the question of what kinds of analogues to externally imposed, coercive institutions of political power needed to be imposed on fallen human minds in order to render them fit for that which they were no longer naturally disposed to do – that is, producing reliable knowledge. Experimental science arose out of a renewed awareness that the attainment of knowledge was not a natural, easy process, but rather one that called for the imposition of external constraints: rigorous testing of knowledge claims, repeated experiments, communal witnessing, the gradual accumulation of 'histories', the use of artificial instruments to amplify the dim powers of the senses, and the corporate rather than individual production of knowledge. These were the coercive structures of the commonwealth of learning that were to play a role equivalent to that of the state in Augustinian polity. And like the Augustinian state, this knowledge was at once divinely sanctioned yet less than ideal. It was knowledge that was fitting for a fallen race that inhabited the inherently unstable interval of time – the *saeculum* – between the coming of Christ and the final culmination of all things.

---

[134] Nederman, 'Nature, Sin, and the Origins of Society', 5. Nederman points to the emergence of a compromise 'Ciceronian' position. Plato's *Republic* prompted similar questions. Most Renaissance thinkers believed that Plato's prescriptions would have worked for the unfallen or sanctified, but were manifestly unsuitable for sinners. James Hankins, *Plato in the Italian Renaissance*, 2 vols. (Leiden, 1990), I, 142f., 227–32.

CHAPTER 2

Augustine revived

But it is impossible that nature could be understood by human reason after the fall of Adam, in consequence of which it was perverted . . .

Martin Luther, *Sermons* 1, 329

The corruption of our nature was unknown to the philosophers who, in other respects were sufficiently, and more than sufficiently, acute. Surely this stupor was itself a signal proof of original sin. For all who are not utterly blind perceive that no part of us is sound; that the mind is smitten with blindness, and infected with innumerable errors . . . corruption does not reside in one part only, but pervades the whole soul, and each of its faculties.

John Calvin, *Commentary on Genesis*

Whenever I think of this darkness of the soul, this weakness and sad servitude, I am almost out of my mind with horror. But with what grief and commotion of the mind need we reckon that the first ancestors thought the same; since they had seen the earlier light and harmony of nature and were endowed with the greatest excellency of intellect, they could reckon more correctly the greatness of their disaster, and judge to what a cruel tyrant they were subject.

Philipp Melanchthon, *Commentary on the Soul*, Preface

Princeton theologian B. B. Warfield once judiciously observed that 'the Reformation, inwardly considered, was just the ultimate triumph of Augustine's doctrine of grace over Augustine's doctrine of the Church'.[1] In speaking of a 'triumph' Warfield perhaps betrayed his own Calvinist commitments, for it is not altogether clear that the Augustinian doctrine of grace championed by the Protestants did in fact prevail. It remains true, however, that the sixteenth and seventeenth centuries witnessed a remarkable revival

---

[1] Benjamin B. Warfield, *Calvin and Augustine* (Philadelphia, 1956), pp. 321–2. For a similar sentiment see Williams, *Ideas of the Fall*, p. 425. On Augustine and the reformers, see H.-U. Delius, *Augustin als Quelle Luthers. Eine Materialsammlung* (Berlin, 1984); J. M. Lange van Ravenswaay, *Augustinus totus noster: das Augustinverständnis bei Johannes Calvin* (Göttingen, 1990); Diarmaid MacCulloch, *The Reformation* (New York, 2003), pp. 103–11.

of diverse strands of Augustinian thought.[2] Writing on the influence of the North African bishop on early modern Catholic thought, Jean Dagens has suggested that we regard the seventeenth century as the age of Augustine. Zbigniew Janowski, making a more specific argument about Augustine's influence on epistemological developments during this period, agrees that 'the role and influence of St Augustine's thought in the seventeenth century are without precedent'.[3] José Neto stresses the importance of Augustine in the theological sphere, referring to a 'revival of Augustinianism' that is 'epitomized in the Jansenist movement'.[4] Numerous writers have commented on Descartes' unacknowledged debts to Augustine. Malebranche was a self-confessed Augustinian. Leibniz's theodicy, in its basic structure, is identical to Augustine's.[5] Pascal and Arnauld, on account of their Jansenist sympathies, have an even greater claim to the label 'Augustinian'.

Neither were these developments restricted to the Continent. The impact of the Church Father's theological anthropology on the development of Protestant theology is difficult to overstate. The Augustinian understanding of Adam's Fall and of original sin had a palpable influence in Protestant circles, and amongst English Calvinists in particular. 'Is it possible to put one's finger on certain distinctive doctrines of Christianity expounded to professing English Christians of the seventeenth and eighteenth centuries?' inquires Donald Grene. 'I think that it is, and I think that these doctrines can be conveniently summed up by the word "Augustinianism".' And what, in this context, is Augustinianism? 'Augustinianism affirms strongly the fact of original sin – that is, the state in which man finds himself because of the Fall of Adam.'[6] W. M. Spellman agrees that the influence of Augustine was

---

[2] Periods of the Middle Ages have similarly been characterised as evidencing different and competing versions of Augustinianism. See Gilson, *History of Christian Philosophy*, pp. 446–71; Damasius Trapp, 'Adnotationes', *Augustinianum* 5 (1965), 147–51 (150); M. W. E. Stone, 'Augustine and Medieval Philosophy', in Eleonore Stump and Norman Kretzmann (eds.), *The Cambridge Companion to Augustine* (Cambridge, 2001), pp. 253–66.

[3] Jean Dagens, *Bérulle et les origines de la restauration catholique* (Paris, 1952); Janowski, *Cartesian Theodicy*, p. 20. Cf. A. D. Wright, *The Counter-Reformation, Catholic Europe and the Non-Christian World* (London, 1982), p. 6.

[4] José R. Maia Neto, *The Christianization of Pyrrhonism: Scepticism and Faith in Pascal, Kierkegaard, and Shestov* (Dordrecht, 1995), p. 1.

[5] See, e.g., Etienne Gilson, *La Liberté chez Descartes et la théologie* (Paris, 1913); Jean Laporte, *Le Rationalisme de Descartes* (Paris, 1950); Henri Gouhier, *La pensée métaphysique de Descartes* (Paris, 1962); G. B. Matthews, *Thought's Ego in Augustine and Descartes* (Ithaca, 1992); 'Post-medieval Augustinianism', in *Cambridge Companion to Augustine*, pp. 267–79; Menn, *Descartes and Augustine*; Janowski, *Cartesian Theodicy* and *Augustinian-Cartesian Index: Texts and Commentary* (South Bend, 2004). Less convinced about Descartes' Augustinianism is Louis-Paul Du Vaucel, 'Observations sur la philosophie de Descartes', in E. J. Dijksterhuis (ed.), *Descartes et le Cartésianisme Hollandais* (Paris, 1950).

[6] Donald Grene, 'Augustinianism and Empiricism: A Note on Eighteenth-Century Intellectual History', *Eighteenth Century Studies* 1 (1967), 33–68 (42).

deeply felt in seventeenth-century England where the doctrine of original sin 'occupied a pivotal and living position within the spiritual life of the Church and within the intellectual community as a whole'. The status of human beings, in the light of this doctrine, he adds, was one that 'engaged the serious attention of all thoughtful individuals in Tudor and Stuart England, perhaps more than any other single issue'.[7]

The Augustinian conception of the corruption of human nature and its epistemological corollaries inevitably collided with the more optimistic scholastic and Aristotelian views of the transparency of the human intellect and the sufficiency of natural light. The main fracture lines of early modern debates over the sources and reliability of human knowledge can be understood in terms of these competing anthropological commitments. However, because it is possible to see Augustine virtually wherever we look in the seventeenth century, it is important to embrace the spirit of Warfield's observation that some major controversies in the early modern period can also be understood in terms of conflicts between rival versions of Augustinianism. This was as true of the ecclesiastical sphere to which Warfield was referring as it was of the realm of knowledge which is our present concern. Perhaps the major divide here is between Descartes, whose epistemology relies on an Augustinian theodicy of free will, and Calvinists and Jansenists who adopted an Augustinian anthropology. This divide will be explored in detail in the fourth and fifth chapters. For the moment we shall focus on the Protestant Reformation and the ensuing eclipse of the epistemological optimism of medieval scholasticism.

LUTHER AND THE PUTRID PHILOSOPHER

Some indication of the change in fortunes of the fifth-century Church Father may be gleaned from the contents of a letter penned by Martin Luther on 18 May 1517. This was an auspicious year, for five months later on the Eve of All Saints (31 October) the young Augustinian monk would post his ninety-five theses on the door of the Castle-Church in Wittenberg in what is widely regarded as the event that precipitated the German Reformation. As for the earlier letter, its contents describe a neat reversal of the trend bemoaned by Pecham some two centuries earlier, and indeed a belated fulfilment of the hopes of the thirteenth-century Franciscan:

[7] Spellman, *Locke and the Problem of Depravity*, pp. 8, 9. On different meanings of 'Augustinianism', however, see M. Jordan, 'Augustinianism' in *The Routledge Encyclopedia of Philosophy*, ed. E. Craig, 10 vols. (London, 1998), I, 559–65.

Our theology and that of St. Augustine, by the grace of God, is making rapid progress in our university. Aristotle is continuing to fall from his throne, and his end is only a matter of time; and all object to hearing lectures on the text-books of the Sentences and no one need expect an audience who does not expound theology, viz. That of the Bible or St. Augustine, or some other of the honored Church teachers.[8]

Martin Luther (1483–1546) was himself an Augustinian friar and his grievances against contemporary Catholic doctrine and practice were inspired in part by his reading of the works of Augustine. On Luther's analysis much of the problem with contemporary Catholicism was owing to the Church's defection from the teachings of St Paul and St Augustine. In the universities, their position had been usurped by the pagan teachings of Aristotle, and for two centuries the works of the Greek philosopher had dominated the university curriculum. In the academy, Luther lamented, 'the blind, heathen master Aristotle rules alone', and his baleful influence had led to the corruption of Christian doctrine. The 'Church of Thomas', he wrote, is nothing other than the Church of Aristotle. Thomas, while a great man, was to be pitied, and the grand edifice of scholastic theology was dismissed as 'an unfortunate superstructure upon an unfortunate foundation'. Luther thought it 'shameless nonsense' to assert that there was no genuine conflict between Aristotle and the Catholic truth. As for Aristotle himself, he was 'a liar and a knave', 'the arch-numbskull', a 'putrid philosopher' and 'fabulator'. His writings were 'unchristian, profane, meaningless babblings'. God had sent him 'as a plague upon us for our sins'.[9] If Aristotle had been baptised by Aquinas, Luther saw it as his mission to excommunicate him.

Two related elements of Aristotle's influence were identified by Luther as particularly insidious. First was the manner in which the Greek philosopher's moral teaching had come to underscore the Catholic doctrine of merit – that one might actually attain genuine credit in God's eyes by the performance of good works. The *Nicomachean Ethics* had taught that through continued practice one acquires the virtues. As Luther himself expressed it, 'Aristotle taught that he who does much good will thereby

---

[8] Luther to John Lange, 18 May 1517, *The Letters of Martin Luther*, tr. Margaret A. Currie (London, 1908), p. 15.

[9] Luther, *Babylonian Captivity of the Church*, in *Three Treatises* (Philadelphia, 1970), p. 144; Emser, *Reply to the Answer of the Leipzig Goat*, in *Works of Martin Luther*, ed. H. E. Jacobs, 6 vols. (Philadelphia, 1915), III, 304; 'Sermon for Epiphany', I, 23 in *Sermons of Martin Luther*, ed. and tr. John N. Lenker et al., 7 vols. (Grand Rapids, 2000), I, 332; Luther, *Letter to the Christian Nobility*, *Three Treatises*, p. 93. See also G. Ebeling, *Luther: An Introduction to his Thought* (London, 1970), pp. 86–9.

become good'.[10] Such a view ran counter to the fundamental tenet of Reformation theology that human beings can never become righteous in God's sight on account of their own efforts. Rather those who are saved are 'reckoned' as righteous – virtue is imputed to them – while in fact they remain sinners.[11] This understanding of justification was opposed to the Catholic position, which the Protestants characterised as a doctrine of justification through the performance of good works. In this erroneous doctrine Luther detected the baleful influence of the Greek philosopher: 'Righteousness is not in us in a formal sense, as Aristotle maintains, but is outside us, solely in God's grace'.[12] Not surprisingly, perhaps, Luther judged Aristotle's much-lauded *Nicomachean Ethics* to be 'the worst of all books'.[13]

Aristotle's naïve assumption that human beings could acquire merit on their own account was related to a second and more basic shortcoming – a mistaken understanding of human nature. Aristotelian ethics was premised upon a view of the freedom of the will and on the basic integrity of the mental faculties. In a sense, this was the more fundamental error, for it took no cognisance of the fallen condition of humanity. Aristotle's moral philosophy was, in Luther's view, totally inconsistent with Christian anthropology, at least as it was understood within the Pauline-Augustinian tradition. It followed that scholastic theologians who had fallen under the sway of Aristotle were not only over-optimistic about the prospects for the performance of good works, but they also wrongly assumed that the mind could acquire true knowledge of the world unproblematically. Luther, by way of contrast, stressed the general incapacity of the postlapsarian mind in both its moral and intellectual operations. As a consequence of the Fall, he insisted, 'the will is impaired, the intellect depraved, and the reason entirely corrupt and altogether changed'.[14] This position was explicitly contrasted with the Thomist view that the natural powers of reason retained their efficacy even after the Fall.[15] Luther was convinced that the 'natural light' which played

[10] Luther, 'Sunday after Christmas', 6, *Sermons* III, 226.
[11] *Simul iustus et peccator* (simultaneously justified and a sinner) was Luther's famous maxim. Luther and Calvin both considered this to be the teaching of St Paul. See Luther, *Lectures on Galatians*, LW XXVI, 232 and passim.
[12] Luther, *Lectures on Galatians*, LW XXVI, 234.
[13] Luther, *Letter to the Christian Nobility*, *Three Treatises*, p. 93. Luther's attitude to Aristotle, it must be said, was not uniformly negative, and the term 'Aristotle' could itself mean quite different things. Luther seemed to have a favourable view of Aristotelian logic as an important dialectical tool. See the lengthy study of Theodor Dieter, *Der junge Luther und Aristoteles. Eine historisch-systematische Untersuchung zum Verhältnis von Theologie und Philosophie* (Berlin, 2001), esp. pp. 424f.
[14] Luther, *Lectures on Genesis 1–5*, LW I, 166. Cf. Formula of Concord, I.II.
[15] 'It is clear that the natural endowments did not remain perfect, as the scholastics rave.' LW I, 167; cf. pp. 142, 114. In *Table Talk*, Luther also complains that the school philosophers 'neither saw, nor

so central a role in Thomist epistemology had been almost completely extinguished on account of Adam's primeval transgression. That scholastic philosophers had consistently invoked the light of nature was evidence of their departure from a genuinely Christian epistemology and their uncritical reliance on pagan ideas. Our 'learned men', Luther railed, 'sink deeper into the abyss of spiritual darkness when they claim that natural light or intellect and heathen philosophy are also safe means of discovering truth'.[16]

Luther's theological anthropology, as might be expected from one whose rallying cry was *sola scriptura*, was strongly underpinned by his reading of scripture. The history of Adam provided the basic evidence for the thesis of the depravity of human nature. Accordingly, in his lectures on Genesis, Luther suggested that the consequences of the Fall were the corruption of reason, the dulling of the senses, the diminution of the powers of the body and, as a consequence of all this, the loss to posterity of much Adamic knowledge. Before the Fall, Adam's 'intellect was clearest, his memory was the best, and his will was the most straightforward'. To these mental qualities were added a range of physical perfections – 'the most beautiful and superb qualities of body and of all the limbs, qualities in which he surpassed all remaining living creatures'. Adam was also endowed with 'extraordinary perception'.[17] Remarking on the divine imperative to 'have dominion', Luther noted that Adam and Eve's command of all living things would have been impossible without 'insight into the dispositions of all the animals, into their characters and all their powers'. If we are seeking to identify outstanding philosophers, he suggested, we should look no further than 'our first parents while they were still free from sin'.[18] Eve, incidentally, 'had these mental gifts in the same degree as Adam'.[19] The vast knowledge of our first parents served to throw into high relief the relative intellectual poverty of their issue. Mired in original sin, the children of Adam are reduced to gathering scraps of knowledge in a piecemeal fashion:

There are in existence various books with descriptions of the natures of plants and animals. But how much time and how much observation were necessary until these could be collected this way through experience! There was a different light in Adam, who, as soon as he viewed an animal, came into possession of a knowledge

felt Adam's fall'. *The Table Talk or Familiar Discourse of Martin Luther*, tr. William Hazlitt (London, 1848), DXLI (pp. 235f.).

[16] Luther, 'Sermon for Epiphany', *Sermons* 1, 344. For Luther, Aristotle personified faith in the light of nature: 'Here appeared the great light of nature, who now rules in Christ's stead in all the universities viz: the great famous Aristotle.' *Sermons* 1, 331.

[17] Luther, *Lectures on Genesis*, LW 1, 62, 115. Cf. Luther, *A Commentarie vpon the Fiftene Psalmes* (London, 1577), pp. 129f.

[18] LW 1, 66. [19] *Ibid.*

of its entire nature and abilities, and, moreover, a far better one than we can acquire even when we devote an entire life to research into these things.[20]

On Luther's view, the way of acquiring knowledge by experience is the penalty for Adam's sin, and this slow accumulation of facts never really takes us to the true natures of things.[21]

Given that Adam's abilities did not arise out of 'any new enlightenment' but solely from 'the excellency of his nature', it followed that no *supernatural* gifts had been required for the acquisition of his vast knowledge. On the one hand, this view multiplied Adam's misfortunes – he had fallen not from the supernatural place to the natural, but from the natural to something even less. On the other hand, it also meant that the accomplishments of Adam were, in principle at least, within the grasp of a perfected human nature. To put it another way, the vocation of Adam in paradise is still the true calling for the Christian.[22] The rejection of this scholastic position thus undergirds the distinctively Protestant view that the original divine conception of human nature had been for the human race to seek perfection in the active worldly roles of citizen, husband, father, wife, mother and indeed, as would become increasingly common in justifications of experimental natural philosophy, in discovering the uses of the creatures and extending human dominion over nature. All of this stands in stark contrast to a medieval supernaturalism that identifies the perfection of human nature with the contemplative life of the monastery.[23] 'Man was created not for leisure, but for work, even in the state of innocence', Luther insisted. It followed that 'the idle sort of life, such as that of monks and nuns, deserves to be condemned'.[24] This new Lutheran notion of a 'vocation' to which all Christians were called was to replace the older hierarchical medieval notion of 'estates' – Clergy, Aristocracy, Laity.[25]

[20] *Ibid.*, 120.

[21] Luther also reprised the Augustinian condemnation of curiosity, regarding it as symptomatic of the unquenchable lust that is the consequence of original sin. *The Heidelberg Disputation* (1518), Proofs of the Thesis, LW xxxi, 53f.; *Sermons* I, 333.

[22] Luther, *Lectures on Genesis*, LW I, 103.

[23] See A. Ritschl, *Die christliche Lehre von der Rechtfertigung und Versöhnung*, 3 vols. (Bonn, 1870–4), III, 308.

[24] Luther, *Lectures on Genesis*, LW I, 103. Cf. Luther, *Letter to the Christian Nobility*, *Three Treatises*, p. 12.

[25] The classic account of Luther's concept of vocation is Gustaf Wingren, *Luther on Vocation*, tr. Carl C. Rasmussen (Philadelphia, 1957). See also Weber, *The Protestant Ethic and the Spirit of Capitalism*, tr. Talcott Parsons (New York, 1958), pp. 79–92; John S. Feinberg, 'Luther's Doctrine of Vocation: Some Problems of Interpretation and Application', *Fides et Historia* 12 (1979), 50–67; Karlfried Froelich, 'Luther on Vocation', *Lutheran Quarterly* 13 (1999), 195–207; Kenneth Hagen, 'A Critique of Wingren on Luther on Vocation', *Lutheran Quarterly* NS 3 (2002), 249–73. On the significance of

DEPRAVITY AND DOUBT

While Luther's position on the Fall and its catastrophic consequences is clear and uncompromising, the name most closely associated with the doctrine of human depravity is John Calvin (1509–64). Calvin was Luther's junior by twenty-five years and, as the beneficiary of the early reformer's pioneering efforts, was in a better position to develop a more systematic and rigorous theology. A jurist by training, he was adequately equipped for this task and his *Institutes of the Christian Religion* is generally recognised as the high water mark of Reformation thought. Whatever his other achievements, posterity remembers him chiefly for his championing of the distasteful doctrine of predestination and for the 'Protestant work ethic' that is generally associated with it. While notions of divine predestination may be found in St Paul, Augustine, and Luther, Calvin's clear and uncompromising statement of the doctrine has meant that this gloomy dogma is associated, often almost exclusively, with his name. For Calvin the logic of predestination was relatively simple. So depraved is human nature that individuals lack the freedom to choose the good. The initiative for salvation, then, must belong to God who in his mercy chooses to save some individuals otherwise destined, like the rest of humanity, for damnation. Such a position on human nature was relevant to Luther's insistence that justification was by divine grace and not human works.

The significance of all this in the present context is that as a consequence of the Fall, human nature was *totally* depraved. Total depravation, in this context, means that no faculty of the human mind – will, imagination, or intellect – retained its prelapsarian perfection. Calvin thus echoed Luther's sentiments about the corruption of the human intellect following the Fall, agreeing that the ancients had typically overestimated the powers of the human mind: 'The corruption of our nature was unknown to the philosophers who, in other respects, were sufficiently, and more than sufficiently, acute'. This blindness to our innate infirmity was itself 'a signal proof of original sin'.[26] But an error that was at least understandable for Aristotle and his fellow philosophers was harder to fathom when encountered in the writings of Christian authors. Calvin was dismayed to discover that while most of the Church Fathers had recognised that 'the soundness of reason in man is gravely wounded through sin', many of them, Augustine being

this for early modern natural philosophy see Peter Harrison, '"Priests of the Most High God, with respect to the Book of Nature": The Vocational Identity of the Early Modern Naturalist', in Angus Menuge (ed.), *Reading God's World* (St Louis, 2004), pp. 55–80.

[26] Calvin, *Commentary on Genesis* 3:6, *Calvin's Commentaries* I, 154.

the notable exception, had veered 'far too close to the philosophers' on this question.[27]

These considerations led Calvin to pose what was to become a fundamental question in early modern epistemological projects: 'how far the power both of the intellect and will now extends'.[28] Calvin believed that the clearest response to this question was to be found in the Augustinian formula 'that the natural gifts were corrupted in man through sin, but that his supernatural gifts were stripped from him'. Prior to sin, Adam 'was endued with a right judgment, had affections in harmony with reason, had all his senses sound and well-regulated'.[29] This harmony of the mental faculties meant that Adam named the creatures based on reason and 'certain knowledge'.[30] With the Fall, however, his mind lost the capacity to acquire true knowledge: 'Man's mind, because of its dullness, cannot hold to the right path, but wanders through various errors and stumbles repeatedly, as if it were groping in darkness, until it strays away and finally disappears. Thus it betrays how incapable it is of seeking and finding truth.'[31] To be sure, some vestiges of reason remain, significant enough to distinguish humans from brute beasts. Yet even this remaining light is 'choked with dense ignorance, so that it cannot come forth effectively'.[32] The same sentiments could be expressed in terms of a loss of the divine image. God's image was 'the perfect excellence of human nature which shone in Adam before his defection', but after the Fall it was 'so vitiated and almost blotted out that nothing remains after the ruin except what is confused, mutilated, and disease-ridden'.[33] Adam's lapse also wrought collateral damage in the physical world which, 'before the Fall, was a most fair and delightful mirror'.[34] Now its primitive

---

[27] Calvin, *Institutes* II.ii.4 (McNeill 1, 258f.).   [28] Calvin, *Institutes* II, Sections (Beveridge 1, 221).

[29] Calvin, *Commentary on Genesis*, 1:26, *Calvin's Commentaries* 1, 95. Cf. *Institutes* I.xv.3.

[30] Calvin, *Commentary on Genesis* 2:19, *Calvin's Commentaries* 1, 131. Calvin, however, was less generous than Luther in his estimates of Adam's knowledge. *Commentary on Luke* 2:40, *Calvin's Commentaries* XVI, 168.

[31] Calvin, *Institutes* II.ii.12 (McNeill 1, 271). Cf. *Commentary on Romans* 1:21, *Calvin's Commentaries* XIX, 71f.

[32] Calvin, *Institutes* II.ii.12 (McNeill 1, 270). Cf. Augustine, *On Nature and Grace* 3.iii; 21.xix; 22.xx (NPNF 1, v, 122, 127f.). Cf. 'But lest anyone think a man truly blessed when he is credited with possessing great power to comprehend truth under the elements of this world [cf. Col. 2:8], we should at once add that all this capacity to understand, with the understanding that follows upon it, is an unstable and transitory thing in God's sight, when a solid foundation of truth does not underlie it. For with the greatest truth Augustine teaches that as the free gifts were withdrawn from man after the Fall, so the natural ones remaining were corrupted.' Calvin, *Institutes* II.ii.16 (McNeill 1, 275).

[33] Calvin, *Institutes* I.xv.4 (McNeill 1, 190). Calvin suggests at one point that the divine image is now impressed on scripture which replaces human reason as the source of reliable knowledge. *Institutes* I.vii.5 (Beveridge 1, 72).

[34] Calvin, *Commentary on Genesis* 3:17, *Calvin's Commentaries* 1, 173.

transparency had been dulled, and it resisted human efforts to know it.[35] As for the creatures that had once meekly served their human master, they no longer recognised Adam's authority and became wild and unmanageable.[36] As a consequence of his sin, Adam lost both knowledge and dominion.

Like his co-reformer, Calvin was concerned to stress the difference between this understanding of the consequences of sin and the milder versions of the doctrine promulgated by Aquinas and the later scholastics. This called for a rejection of the Thomist idea that the Fall entailed only a loss of supernatural gifts.[37] Calvin also wished to refute the interpretation of the Fall promoted by Duns Scotus and other medieval Franciscans who, as Calvin saw it, wished to restrict the damage wrought by the Fall to the sensual appetites alone, while maintaining that reason had been immune:

the mind is smitten with blindness, and infected with innumerable errors . . . Corruption does not reside in one part only, but pervades the whole soul, and each of its faculties. Whence it follows, that they childishly err who regard original sin as consisting only in lust, and in the inordinate motion of the appetites, whereas it seizes upon the very seat of reason, and upon the whole heart.[38]

As for the much-vaunted 'natural light', Calvin considered it now to be 'blind' or 'extinguished'.[39]

Calvin also used the example of Adam's industry to challenge the long-standing assumption of the superiority of the contemplative over the active life.[40] Noting that God had placed Adam in the Garden of Eden to 'tend it

[35] Calvin, *Commentary on Hebrews* 11:3, *Calvin's Commentaries* XXII, 265f.

[36] Calvin, *Commentary on Genesis* 2:19, 7:8, 9:2, *Calvin's Commentaries* I, 131, 269, 290; *Commentary on Hosea* 2:18, *Calvin's Commentaries* XIII, 110.

[37] Luther, 'Lectures on Genesis: 1–5', LW I, 167, cf. 187. Calvin, *Institutes* II.i.8; II.ii.16; Calvin, *Commentary on Ezekiel* 11:9, *Calvin's Commentaries* XI, 374f. Also see the Augsburg Confession, art. 2 (Schaff, *Creeds of Christendom* III, pp. 8f.); Martin Bucer, *Common Places of Martin Bucer*, tr. and ed. D. F. Wright (Appleford, 1972), p. 122.

[38] Calvin, *Commentary on Genesis* 3:6, *Calvin's Commentaries* I, 154. Cf. Duns Scotus, *In sententias* II. xxix. 1, *Opera omnia* XIII, 267f.

[39] Calvin, *Institutes*, Prefatory Address (McNeill I, 13), I.iv.2 (McNeill I, 48), I.ii.20 (McNeill I, 280), I.ii.24 (McNeill I, 284), but cf. *Institutes* I.ii.14 (McNeill I, 273). Calvin concedes that 'some sparks of reason continue in men, however blinded they are become through the fall of Adam and the corruption of nature'. *Commentary on Malachi* 4:2. *Calvin's Commentaries* XV, 618. Moreover, there also remains what he calls 'common grace' (*generalem Dei gratiam*), *Institutes* II.ii.17 (McNeill I, 276), but it is not entirely clear what this amounts to. For differing views see H. Kuiper, *Calvin on Common Grace* (Grand Rapids, 1930); C. van Til, *Common Grace* (Philadelphia, 1947).

[40] Aquinas, ST 2a2ae. 182, 2. Calvin also challenged the attribution of this view to Augustine. *Institutes* IV.xiii.10 (McNeill II, 1264). Cf. Augustine, *City of God* VIII.4, XIX.19; *The Trinity* I.iii.20–1; VIII.i.2, VIII.vi.20, 25; Sermon 104, *Sermons* IV.81–3. Humanist Francesco Piccolomini (1523–1607) also called into question the priority of the contemplative life, initiating a debate with Jacopo Zabarella. See Heiki Mikkeli, *An Aristotelian Response to Renaissance Humanism: Jacopo Zabarella on the Nature of the Arts and Sciences* (Helsinki, 1992), ch. 2; Nicholas Jardine, 'Keeping Order in the School of

and keep it' (Gen. 2:15), Calvin observed that 'men were created to employ themselves in some work, and not to lie down in inactivity and idleness'. All men were thus to exercise 'economy, and this diligence, with respect to those good things which God has given us to enjoy'.[41] By way of contrast, 'our present-day monks find in idleness the chief part of their sanctity'.[42] The theme of the sanctity of mundane work reappears in Calvin's exegesis of the parable of the talents (Mt. 25:14–39, Lk. 19:11–27). Calvin argues that God bestows his gifts upon those whom he chooses – not, as the papists believed, according to individual merit. Those to whom God has given abilities are to employ them in the service of the common good:

Those who employ usefully whatever God has committed to them are said to be engaged in *trading*. The life of the godly, is justly compared to *trading*, for they ought naturally to exchange and barter with each other, in order to maintain intercourse; and the industry with which every man discharges the office assigned him, the calling itself, the power of acting properly, and other gifts, are reckoned to be so many kinds of *merchandise*; because the use or object which they have in view is, to promote mutual intercourse among men. Now the *gain* which Christ mentions is general usefulness, which illustrates the glory of God.[43]

Calvin continually emphasises the point that one's earthly vocation is to be for 'utility', 'profit', and 'advantage', and these accrue not to the individual, but to society.[44] Active participation in society is a necessary duty because it helps restore in part the original prelapsarian social order.[45] The Fall had wrought havoc in the original hierarchical order that had pervaded the first creation. In its original integrity, nature had been subservient to its human masters and human society had been peacefully organised. It was incumbent on Christians, out of their gratitude and obedience to God, to work towards the partial restoration of God's original order.

Luther had also insisted on the importance of exercising an earthly vocation within the sinful realities of the present world. The Christian is warned

---

Padua', in Eckhard Kessler, Daniel Di Liscia and Charlotte Methuen (eds.), *Method and Order in the Renaissance Philosophy of Nature* (Aldershot, 1997), pp. 183–209.

[41] Calvin, *Commentary on Genesis* 2:15, *Calvin's Commentaries* I, 125. Cf. *Commentary on the Psalms* 127:1–2, *Calvin's Commentaries* VI, 104f.

[42] Calvin, *Institutes* IV. xiii.10 (McNeill II, 1264).

[43] Calvin, *Harmony of the Gospels* Matthew 25:15, *Calvin's Commentaries* XVI, 443. This is a common refrain in Calvin's writings. See *Commentary on I Timothy* 4:14, *Calvin's Commentaries* XXI, 115; *Commentary on the Psalms* 127:1, *Calvin's Commentaries* VI, 104.

[44] On this notion and its influence in early modern England see David Little, *Religion, Order, and Law: A Study in Pre-Revolutionary England* (Oxford, 1970), esp. pp. 57–62. See also Weber, *Protestant Ethic*, p. 265, n. 33; E. Harris Harbison, 'The Idea of Utility in John Calvin', in E. Harris Harbison (ed.), *Christianity and History* (Princeton, 1964), pp. 249–70.

[45] Calvin, *Commentary on II Thessalonians* 3:4, *Calvin's Commentaries* XXI, 350f.

against attempting to escape the evils of the world 'by donning caps and creeping into a corner, or going into the wilderness' as the papists do. The true Christian is to 'use' the world: 'to build, to buy, to have dealings and hold intercourse with his fellows, to join them in all temporal affairs'.[46] But Calvin was even more strongly oriented towards the present world, differing from Luther not only in his approval of trade and the charging of interest, but in his emphasis on the need for Christians to be actively engaged in useful worldly affairs so that society could be transformed and restored.[47] This Calvinist conception of the sanctity of work was subsequently to become prominent in Francis Bacon's new conception of the task of philosophy and in his 'utilitarian' justifications for a new scientific programme.

The transformation of society that Calvin envisaged could not take place without considerable human effort, but consistent with his view of human nature and of the vanity of works, Calvin stressed in the *Institutes* that the human contribution to this task is made possible only by divine gifts, which include the arts and sciences.[48] Calvin also concedes that the ancients made significant contributions. He admires the 'artful descriptions of nature' provided by the philosophers, along with their endeavours in the spheres of rhetoric, polity, medicine, and mathematics. Secular authors were allowed to have been 'sharp and penetrating in their investigation of inferior things'.[49] In some of his exegetical writings he is rather more cautious, claiming that 'all the sciences which men teach us are nothing but smoke: it is a transitory thing which is soon vanished'.[50] He also invokes the Augustinian category 'curiosity', suggesting that even what remains of our mental powers is habitually diverted away from profitable subjects of investigation.[51] This ambivalence carries over into his assessment of the merits of Aristotle – 'a man of genius and learning', who was at the same time 'a heathen whose heart was perverse and depraved' and who 'employed his naturally acute powers of mind to extinguish all light'.[52] While these positions may appear to be inconsistent, Calvin's point was simply that on the one hand the abilities God gives us are to be put to use and fully

[46] Luther, 'Sermon for the Third Sunday After Easter', *Sermons* VII, 281.
[47] Ian Hart, 'The Teaching of Luther and Calvin About Ordinary Work', *Evangelical Quarterly* 67 (1995), 35–52, 121–35.
[48] Calvin, *Institutes* II.xiv.12 (McNeill I, 275).   [49] *Ibid.*, II.ii.15 (McNeill I, 274).
[50] Calvin, *Sermons on Psalm 119*, tr. Thomas Stocker (London, 1580), Sermon 13. Cf. *Commentary on Romans* 1:22, *Calvin's Commentaries* XIX, 73; *Commentary on First Corinthians*, 1:20, *Calvin's Commentaries* XX, 81–3.
[51] Calvin, *Institutes* II.ii.12 (McNeill I, 271).
[52] Calvin, *Commentary on the Psalms* 107:43, *Calvin's Commentaries* VI, 266.

exploited, but on the other, all human productions, in the larger scheme of things, are partial and transitory.

Luther and Calvin, it must be said, were far more interested in knowledge of theological truths than they were in knowledge of nature. While their respective positions are relatively unambiguous in terms of their implications for theological knowledge, it is far less clear what consequences their assertions about the limitations of fallen human minds might have for natural philosophy or, for that matter, for such domains as mathematics or morality. Neither is it possible simply to deduce from the writings of the major reformers some standard early modern 'Protestant' position on these issues. A second generation of Lutherans and Calvinists had to deal not only with each other, but with a reforming Catholicism on the one hand and the potentially destabilising radicalism of the so-called 'left wing' of the Reformation on the other. Not surprisingly, some Protestant thinkers retreated to the relative certainties of the Aristotelian paradigm, or at least to some aspects of it. Equally, while it could be asserted that human moral capacities had been irremediably wounded by the Fall, there remained the practical question of how sinful individuals were to live together in ordered societies. In light of the devastating wars of religion that came in the wake of the Reformation, the question of the rational foundations of morality and law became particularly acute. Again, some Protestant thinkers were to argue for the persistence of some aspects of moral acuity even in fallen human beings. Amongst the early modern Protestant confessions, then, there developed a diversity of views about the human mind and what befell it as a consequence of the Fall. English Calvinists remained most faithful to the positions of the original reformers, and they formulated their methods for the production of knowledge accordingly. A significant modification of the positions of Luther and Calvin, however, came with the development of Protestant scholasticism, which, as the name suggests, combined elements of Protestant thought with particular scholastic positions. In Europe, leading Protestant educationalists such as Philipp Melanchthon (1497–1560), while acknowledging the importance of the Fall, would nonetheless reintroduce the scholastic notion of 'natural light' into Protestant thinking and find a place for a legitimate *a priori* knowledge of certain features of nature.

It should also be understood that the challenge of the Protestant Reformation lay not merely in the specific content of its doctrines, but in the very fact that it presented a successful challenge to a number of long-standing authorities. Even without its Augustinian elements, it can thus be said to have precipitated what Richard Popkin has called a sceptical crisis. As for Catholicism, it underwent a reformation of its own in the sixteenth century.

Catholic thinkers were also influenced by the Renaissance revival of classical scepticism, and in movements such as Jansenism we see Catholicism's own resurgence of Augustine's views on grace and original sin. In the seventeenth century, Blaise Pascal was heir to such developments within Catholicism, which partly accounts for his animosity towards the methods of Descartes – a champion of natural light – and for certain similarities in his approach to the experimental philosophy of the English. Nevertheless, in each of these developments the agenda had been set by the Protestant reformers who insisted that the settling of epistemological questions required recourse to theological anthropology.

In sum, the key contribution of Reformation thought is that it focused attention on the human mind and its limitations. Indeed, partly because of this emphasis, the sixteenth century witnessed the emergence of the study of human nature as a distinct domain.[53] Thereafter, no project concerned with the advancement of knowledge could uncritically assume the fitness of human mental faculties or suppose that the human inclination to acquire knowledge was in itself evidence of the mind's fitness to attain that end. The assumption of a critical stance towards knowledge, while it had the potential to diminish the importance of scientific pursuits, could equally lead to a refocusing of attention on the conditions for accumulating knowledge. This latter path held the promise of an instauration of learning that would parallel the reformation of the Church. Promoters of natural knowledge, motivated by a quest to restore prelapsarian knowledge, could attempt to identify what vestiges of the divine image or of the natural light, if any, had persisted in the postlapsarian mind. This might then help to establish the broad limits of intellectual inquiry and provide answers to a range of fundamental epistemological questions: what natural things could be known? To what degree could they be known? What were suitable methods of investigation? What were the ends of human knowledge in a fallen world? As we shall see, the framing of these questions within the context of a Calvinist view of human nature, which significantly limited the efficacy of reason and the light of nature, underpinned the project of Francis Bacon, and indeed much of the programme of natural history and experimental philosophy in seventeenth-century England. By way of contrast, Descartes' constant invocation of 'the natural light' and his essentially Thomist insistence on its integrity provided the foundation for his

---

[53] See Barbara Pitkin, 'The Protestant Zeno: Calvin and the Development of Melanchthon's Anthropology', *Journal of Religion* 84 (2004), 345–78. Prior to the Renaissance, psychology, for example, was integrated into natural philosophy. See Katherine Park and Eckhard Gessler, 'The Concept of Psychology', CHRP, pp. 455–63.

epistemological project, and accounts for its divergence from the experimental philosophy that developed across the Channel. The manner in which these two quite distinct approaches to the acquisition of knowledge were informed by equally distinct theological anthropologies will be the topic of the two chapters that follow. For the moment, it is instructive to consider the resurgence of Augustinian anthropology in Catholicism.

AUGUSTINUS

The Catholic Church eventually responded to the challenge of the reformers' ideas and to the political upheavals caused by the Protestant Reformation by convening the Council of Trent (1545–1563). It must be said that a number of the concerns that prompted Luther into action had already generated other significant reform movements within the Church that predated the Council.[54] However, the business of Catholic reform took on a particular urgency in the wake of the Protestant Reformation, although 'urgency', perhaps, is a relative term. As early as 1524 both Lutherans and Catholics at the Nuremberg Reichstag had prevailed upon the Pope to convene a council to address issues raised by the Protestants, but for various reasons more than twenty years elapsed before the desired general council was to meet. Even then, it met sporadically and was dogged by controversy. Given the passage of time, one of its chief aims – the re-establishment of the peace and unity of the Church – was no longer achievable. But the council was able to make some progress with its other two main objectives, which were to bring about necessary reform within the Church, and to clarify disputed doctrine and condemn heresy.

On the matter of disputed doctrines, most members of the Council were concerned to refute Luther's contention that divine grace was appropriated by faith alone, and that human initiative played no role in the process. Grace, they insisted, also came from the sacraments and from good works, both of which required human cooperation.[55] The Tridentine deliberations on the nature and consequences of original sin revisited the ambiguous pronouncements of the Second Council of Orange (529), in effect avoiding Pelagianism while stopping short of an Augustinian position on free will

---

[54] In the 1950s Hubert Jedin proposed a generally accepted distinction between two closely related movements, the 'Catholic Reformation' and 'Counter-Reformation'. The former preceded the latter. *A History of the Council of Trent*, tr. Ernest Graf, 2 vols. (London, 1957–61). John O'Malley has recently argued for the appropriateness of a third expression, 'Early Modern Catholicism', *Trent and All That: Renaming Catholicism in the Early Modern Era* (Cambridge, MA, 2000).

[55] 'Canons and Decrees of the Council of Trent', 'Decree concerning Justification', esp. chs. xiv, xvi, in Leith (ed.), *Creeds of the Churches*, pp. 417, 418f.

and predestination. On theological matters generally, the Council tended to look back to the glories of medieval scholasticism, with the consequence that the Thomist position on a number of disputed matters was endorsed. This emphasis meant that in effect the Augustinian elements of the reformers' ideas were regarded with some suspicion, although it was commonly asserted that the Protestants had distorted the teachings of the illustrious Church Father. The prestige of Thomas was further enhanced with his elevation to the status of Doctor of the Church in 1567, four years after the final session of the Council.

No doubt the Dominicans in attendance at Trent were gratified by this general outcome, as were the members of the newly formed Society of Jesus – a group destined to become the principal agent for the propagation of reformed Catholicism. Not all those present found these developments satisfactory, however. Michel de Bay (or Baius, 1513–89), a young Professor from the University of Louvain, attended some of the final sessions of the Council. Not unreasonably, Baius thought that the Protestant appropriation of certain Augustinian doctrines was not, of itself, sufficient grounds for rejecting those doctrines.[56] Through a close study of Augustine's anti-Pelagian writings he came to the independent conclusion that prominent scholastics had overestimated the moral and cognitive capacities of fallen human beings, and had misunderstood the natural powers of Adam in his innocence. Articulating a view that was similar in many respects to Luther's, he insisted that our first father's perfections were integral to his nature, and were not owing to the supernatural elevation of that nature. The Fall was to be understood as a loss of Adam's natural perfections, as a consequence of which there followed malice of the will, a rebellion of man's lower nature, and an intellectual depravity that resulted in ignorance.[57] This stance contrasted not only with the Thomist teaching, but also with post-Tridentine restatements of that earlier position. Robert Bellarmine (1542–1621), the brilliant Jesuit theologian who was to play a significant role in the earlier stages of the Galileo affair, produced one such restatement, insisting that human nature was essentially unchanged by the Fall: 'The state of man following the fall of Adam differs from the state of Adam in what was purely natural to him (*in puris naturalibus*) no more than a man who has been

---

[56] On Baius see M. W. F. Stone, 'Michael Baius (1513–1589) and the Debate on "Pure Nature": Grace and Moral Agency in Sixteenth-Century Scholasticism', in Jill Kraye and Risto Saarinen (eds.), *Moral Philosophy on the Threshold of Modernity* (Dordrecht, 2004), pp. 51–90. I am grateful to Prof. Stone for sending me a pre-publication version to this chapter. See also Alexander Sedgwick, *Jansenism in Seventeenth-Century France: Voices from the Wilderness* (Charlottesville, 1977), pp. 6f.; William Doyle, *Jansenism* (New York, 2000), pp. 9f.

[57] Stone, 'Michael Baius'.

stripped differs from a naked man.'[58] Minimalist views of the Fall such as this prompted heated discussions about the 'pure nature' of man and the extent to which it was altered when sin entered the world.[59]

Earlier in the century Baius's conclusions might have provided a useful basis on which to conduct a constructive dialogue with the Protestant reformers. Now that the prospects for peaceful settlement with the Protestants were virtually non-existent, however, such views seemed dangerously destabilising. The apparent similarities between Baius's position and the heretical teachings of Luther were drawn to the attention of the Theological Faculties of Alcalá and Salamanca, which promptly condemned the 'Protestant' views of the Flemish professor. The verdict of the Spanish universities – Louvain was in territory then under the jurisdiction of Philip II of Spain – was reinforced by Papal Bulls from Rome issued in the years 1567 and 1579. Baius eventually recanted.[60] The damage was done, however, and the residual influence of his Augustinianism continued to be felt at Louvain, maturing into the movement that became known in the seventeenth century as 'Jansenism'.

Of Louvain's illustrious alumni, two in particular were to become famous in the seventeenth century for their commitment to the rehabilitation of Augustine's views on grace and human nature. One was Jean Duvergier de Hauranne (1581–1643), better known as Abbé de Saint-Cyran. On graduating as Master of Arts from the Sorbonne in 1600, Saint-Cyran undertook further study at the Jesuit college at Louvain. Following his return to Paris, he made the acquaintance of another student from the Flemish university, Cornelius Jansen (1585–1638). Together they studied the scriptures and the Fathers, often in the pleasant surroundings of the estates of Saint-Cyran's well-to-do family. During these periods together the seeds of a lifelong friendship were sown and, no doubt, the two men also discussed the doctrines of St Paul and Augustine that were later to became the foundations of the Jansenist creed. They parted ways in 1614, when Jansen returned to Louvain, where the embers of the controversy over the teachings of Baius

---

[58] Robert Bellarmine, *De Gratia Primi Hominis* (Heidelberg, 1612), v.12. 'Non magis differt status hominis post lapsum Adae a statu ejusdem in puris naturalibus, quam distet *spoliatus a nudo*, neque deterior est humana natura, si culpam originalem detrahas'. See also Giovanni Perrone, *Praelectiones theologicae*, 9 vols. (Rome, 1835), I, 744. For a more or less official restatement of this view in the modern era, see J. M. Herve, *Manuale Theologiae Dogmaticae*, 4 vols. (Westminster, MD, 1943), II, §§446–7.

[59] M. Lamberigts (ed.), *L'augustinisme à l'ancienne faculté de théologie de Louvain* (Leuven, 1994). See also Stone, 'Michael Baius'.

[60] Doyle, *Jansenism*, p. 9; Stone, 'Michael Baius'.

were still smouldering. Jansen's thinking about human nature and the Fall was further stimulated by the Synod of Dort (1618–19), an assembly of the Dutch Reformed Church which had met to consider the same kinds of matters that had vexed the sessions at Trent relating to justification and original sin. While the synod had been convened primarily to resolve a controversy within the Dutch Reformed Church, its canons came to be accepted throughout the reformed confessions in Europe as a statement of Calvinist orthodoxy.[61] A Dutch speaker, Jansen took a keen interest in the proceedings, writing to Saint-Cyran that the Calvinists 'follow almost entirely the doctrine of the Catholics in the matter of predestination and reprobation'.[62] By 'the doctrine of the Catholics', Jansen really meant the pure teachings of Augustine from which some contemporary Catholics had defected. From about that time he devoted himself to writing a secret work on Augustine's theology that was unencumbered by the cumulative weight of officially sanctioned interpretation. The three-volume Latin *Augustinus* eventually appeared in 1640, two years after the death of its author.

Augustinus provoked strong reactions. The Jesuits, who had attempted unsuccessfully to prevent the work's publication, now sought to have it condemned. But a number of powerful figures sprang to its defence – the ageing and imprisoned Saint-Cyran, and a new generation of Augustinian apologists which included the distinguished names of Antoine Arnauld (1612–94), Blaise Pascal (1623–62), and Pierre Nicole (1625–95). While it was Jansen who gave his name to the largely French movement that defended Augustinian principles, strictly this group owed its origins more to the work of Saint-Cyran and Angélique Arnauld – abbess of the convent at Port-Royal des Champs – whose austere vision of the spiritual life demonstrated that there was far more to Jansenism than commitment to specific theological dogmas. The ongoing conflict between Jesuits and Jansenists in seventeenth-century France was to have an enormous impact on many levels of French society. For our present purposes, however, it is the Jansenists' attitudes to human nature and knowledge that are noteworthy. For the most part, as would be expected, they tended to be hostile to the productions of human reason, which they associated with sinful pride.[63] Saint-Cyran

---

[61] On the Synod of Dort see Jonathan Israel, *The Dutch Republic: Its Rise, Greatness, and Fall 1477–1806* (Oxford, 1995), pp. 421–77.

[62] Quoted in Doyle, *Jansenism*, p. 17.

[63] Alexander Sedgwick, *Jansenism in Seventeenth-Century France*; Thomas Lennon, 'Jansenism and the Crise Pyrrhonienne', *JHI* 38 (1977), 297–306.

thus revisited Augustine's teachings on curiosity and pride, arguing that pride in the accomplishments of reason constituted a major obstacle to humble piety.[64] Again, the figure of Adam was held up as the key to an understanding of human nature. Before his fall, Adam 'was endowed with such absolute power that no creature was able to oppose him'. Moreover he enjoyed 'dominion over the whole world'. Recognition of these losses was essential for the cultivation of piety and humility, both of which were impossible 'without knowing the miserable condition to which we have been reduced by Adam's fall'.[65]

The brilliant Antoine Arnauld (1612–94), youngest brother of the reforming Abbess Angélique, was something of an exception amongst Jansenists in his more nuanced attitude towards worldly learning. Uncharacteristically, he expressed enthusiasm for the new philosophy of Descartes, with all its presupposed faith in human nature. Arnauld made his first appearance on the philosophical stage when he produced a series of responses to Descartes' *Meditations*. It was on this occasion that Arnauld identified the infamous 'Cartesian Circle'.[66] But his comments show that he was clearly impressed with Cartesian philosophy, and Descartes, for his part, regarded Arnauld as the most astute of his critics.[67] Arnauld's enthusiasm for Descartes is to be at least partly explained by the opening remark of his response to Descartes' *Meditations*: 'the basis for his entire philosophy [is] exactly the same principle as that laid down by St Augustine'.[68] No doubt this proved to be something of a back-handed compliment to Descartes, whose stated intention it had been to establish philosophy on fresh foundations, but Arnauld would not be the last commentator to make this connection. Generally, however, it must be said that Arnauld's partiality

---

[64] Steven Nadler, *Arnauld and the Cartesian Philosophy of Ideas* (Princeton, 1989), p. 18; Geneviève Rodis Lewis, 'Augustinisme et Cartésianisme à Port-Royale', in Dijksterhuis (ed.), *Descartes et le Cartésianisme Hollandais*, pp. 131–82 (136). For similar sentiments in Jansen, see *De la reformation de l'homme interieur* (Paris, 1642), pp. 50f.

[65] Saint-Cyran, *Œuvres chrestiennes et spirituelles*, 4: 6, tr. in Sedgwick, *Jansenism*, pp. 32, 33. On Saint-Cyran's comparisons of Adam's pre- and postlapsarian states see 'De la grace de Jésus-Christ, de la liberté chrétienne, et de la justification', in Jean Orcibal, *La Spiritualité de Saint-Cyran avec ses écrits de piété inédits* (Paris, 1962), pp. 233–41.

[66] According to Descartes, our proof of the existence of God is based on our clear and distinct idea of him; but it is God's existence that guarantees the truth of clear and distinct ideas in the first place. Descartes, *Objections and Replies*, CSM II, 150.

[67] Descartes, Letter to Arnauld, 4 June 1648, CSM III, 31; Letter to Mersenne, 18 March 1641, CSM III, p. 95; *Objections and Replies*, CSM II, 154.

[68] Descartes, *Objections and Replies*, CSM II, 139. Arnauld referred to the passage in Augustine's *On Free Will* II.iii.7. See also Leibniz, *New Essays on Human Understanding* tr. and ed. Peter Remnant and Jonathan Bennett (Cambridge, 1981), IV.2 (p. 367). For Arnauld's Cartesianism see Nadler, *Arnauld and Cartesian Philosophy*.

towards Descartes is inconsistent with his commitment to the principles set out in *Augustinus*, and remains rather puzzling.[69]

If Arnauld had been the most capable theologian of the French Jansenists, by far their most eloquent spokesman was Blaise Pascal. While Pascal's prodigious mathematical and scientific talent might seem to belie his commitment to a movement generally given to disparagement of worldly learning, he was strongly committed to the principles of the Port-Royal community. In spite of considerable early achievements in the realm of the natural sciences, he became increasingly ambivalent about the powers of unaided human reason. His antagonism towards Cartesian philosophy was motivated largely by what he regarded as Descartes' overconfidence in reason and the false promise of certitude that he held out to followers of his method. Like Arnauld, Pascal had 'complimented' Descartes on the fact that his chief contributions to philosophy could be found in Augustine.[70] But while Arnauld had been genuine in his praise, Pascal's ironic commendation was a pointed attempt to expose Descartes' unoriginality. The Cartesian project, in Pascal's caustic assessment, was 'useless and uncertain'. Pascal's mature views on the corruption of human nature and the paucity of reason are set out in the unfinished masterwork, the *Pensées*:

Man is nothing but a subject full of natural error that cannot be eradicated except through grace. Nothing shows him the truth, everything deceives him. The two principles of truth, reason and the senses, are not only both not genuine, but are engaged in mutual deception. The senses deceive reason through false appearances, and, just as they trick the soul, they are tricked by it in their turn. It takes its revenge. The senses are disturbed by the passions, which produce false impressions. They both compete in lies and deception.[71]

The congenital corruption of the mind, in Pascal's view, was responsible not only for ignorance, but what was worse, for curiosity. 'The chief malady of man', he rued, 'is restless curiosity about things which he cannot understand; and it is not so bad for him to be in error as to be curious to no purpose'.[72] Pascal concluded that 'once this fine reason of ours was corrupted, it corrupted everything'.[73]

[69] Ferdinand Brunetiére thus speaks of Arnauld's 'naiveté' in not seeing the incompatibility between Descartes' *Discourse* and the principles of *Augustinus*. 'Jansenistes et Cartésiens', *Etudes critiques sur l'histoire de le littérature française*, 4 vols. (Paris, 1904), IV, III–78 (140f.), cited in Nadler, *Arnauld*, p. 14, n. 1.

[70] Pascal, *L'Esprit Géométrique*, in *Œuvres complètes*, ed. J. Chevalier (Paris, 1954), p. 600.

[71] Pascal, *Pensées*, L 45 (p. 42). For Pascal's anthropology see Vincent Carraud, 'Remarks on the Second Pascalian Anthropology: Thought as Alienation', *Journal of Religion* 85 (2004), 539–55.

[72] Pascal, *Pensées*, L 744 (p. 256). [73] *Ibid.*, L 60 (p. 46).

Similar remarks can be found in the works of Pierre Nicole (1625–95), teacher of literature and philosophy at Port-Royal de Paris. Nicole contributed to the Port-Royal *Logic* (1662) but is best known for his *Moral Essays* (1671). This work extended eventually to fourteen volumes, and appeared in translation in a number of editions in England. Indeed, John Locke encountered the *Essays* while travelling in France and being rather taken with them set himself the task of translating some of them.[74] In the *Essays* Nicole stressed the importance of self-knowledge, and the very first essay is devoted to the theme of 'the weakness of man'. An abiding theme is the consciousness of human limitations that comes with self-knowledge. What we discover through scrupulous self-examination, according to Nicole, is that 'the greatest part of humane Philosophy is only a heap of things obscure, uncertain, and even false'.[75] A direct consequence of our corruption, Nicole thought, was that our learning was reduced to the historical knowledge of particular things: 'Behold then to what a low ebb the knowledge men so much boast of, is reduced, *to wit*, to the knowing a small number of Truths one by one, and that in a weak and diffident manner.'[76]

Nicole's remarks bear an interesting similarity to aspects of Francis Bacon's thought, and indeed to the kind of pessimistic views about human knowledge expressed by Robert South at the beginning of this book. But whereas for Nicole, as for Pascal, such assertions were essentially the premise of an argument designed to show that our intellectual energies are better directed towards projects designed to secure our eternal beatitude, Bacon was to make a virtue out of necessity, and suggest that the gradual accumulation of fragments of knowledge – 'natural histories' – would eventually lead to scientific knowledge. Moreover, this protracted accumulation of facts, pieced together over long periods of time by large numbers of individuals, would contribute to a kind of earthly happiness that reflected to a degree the original state of Adam in paradise. Here lies one of the fundamental differences between Jansenist and Calvinist versions of Augustinian anthropology. Jansenism remained wedded to long-standing models of Catholic spirituality that emphasised the importance of the personal piety of the individual over their social responsibilities.[77] This stance was exemplified by the strict monastic rule of St Benedict instituted at Port-Royal by Angélique Arnauld, and by the austere spirituality of the *solitaires* who lived there. Proponents of Jansenism also differed from the Calvinists on the nature

---

[74] See Jean S. Yolton (ed.), *John Locke as Translator: Three of the 'Essais' of Pierre Nicole in French and English* (Oxford, 2000).

[75] Pierre Nicole, *Moral Essayes*, 3rd edn (London, 1696), p. 17, cf. pp. 86f.

[76] *Ibid.*, pp. 19f.   [77] Sedgwick, *Jansenism*, pp. 33–46.

of the sacraments, on the cessation of miracles, on the priesthood of all believers. In short, they retained many of the 'supernaturalist' elements of medieval Catholicism. In spite of the standard Jesuit accusation that the Jansenists were crypto-Calvinists, there were these deep-seated differences. Ironically, perhaps, it was the Jesuits who most resembled the Calvinists in their this-worldly orientation, although obviously they differed in many other respects. In sum, while Jansenists and English Puritans shared elements of a common anthropology that stressed the limitations of the human mind after the Fall, they differed markedly in their prescriptions for its cure.

Reservations about human knowledge were not the sole preserve of those engaged in movements to reform the early modern Church – be they Lutherans, Calvinists, or Jansenists. Indeed, in standard histories of philosophy the impact of Augustinian anthropology on early modern theories of knowledge rarely warrants a mention. On one influential account, it was the revival of ancient scepticism that inaugurated a crisis of confidence in human knowledge, and stimulated the foundationalist modern philosophies of such figures as Descartes. Having dealt with the theological sources of mitigated religious scepticism, it is worth paying attention to one of the standard theses about the origins of modern knowledge, according to which philosophical scepticism, rather than pessimistic theological anthropology, played the major role.

THE SCEPTICAL HYPOTHESIS

Henricus Cornelius Agrippa von Nettesheim (1486–1535) is generally considered to be the first of the modern sceptical writers, his claim to priority resting upon the influential *De Incertitudine et vanitate scientarum* (Of the Uncertainty and Vanity of the Sciences, 1526).[78] Educated at the University of Cologne, the versatile Agrippa was employed variously as a soldier, teacher of theology, physician, and astrologer. Amongst his writings are works on original sin and the Pauline epistles, but the publication for which he is best known, apart from *De Incertitudine*, is the encyclopaedic *De occulta philosophia libri tres* (Three Books of Occult Philosophy, 1531). On the strength of the reputation gained from this work Agrippa was to become the model for Christopher Marlowe's Dr Faustus and, subsequently,

---

[78] On Agrippa see G. Nauert Jr, *Agrippa and the Crisis of Renaissance Thought* (Urbana, 1965); R. H. Popkin, 'Magic and Radical Reformation in Agrippa of Nettesheim', *Journal of the Warburg and Courtauld Institutes* 39 (1976), 69–103.

for Goethe's Faust.[79] His work on the vanity of the sciences enjoyed considerable popularity in the sixteenth century, running to a number of Latin editions and appearing in English, Dutch, French, and Italian – this in spite of the fact that the Faculty of Divinity of the University of Paris had ordered it to be confiscated and burned.[80] In this sceptical work Agrippa rehearsed the tradition according to which God had created Adam with a comprehensive knowledge of the natural world: 'euen as he than hath created trees ful of fruites, so also hath he created the soules as reasonable trees ful of formes & knolwedges, but thorow the sinne of the first parent al things were reueled, & obliuion the mother of ignoraunce crept in'.[81] Our ignorance, then, results from Adam's Fall – a Fall that was itself precipitated by the rash pursuit of even more learning.[82] Accumulation of knowledge will not redress our ignorance, but rather compounds our misfortune as we repeat Adam's original sinful act. 'It is better therefore and more profitable to be Idiotes, and knowe nothinge, to beleve by Faithe and charitee, and to become next unto God', Agrippa insisted, than to become 'lofty & prowde through the subtilties of science [and] to fall into the possession of the Serpente'.[83] The only prescription for our inherited malady was faith in the revealed word of God.[84]

Agrippa's denial of the power of human reason led him to appeal to a twofold revelation. One must read what God revealed to the authors of scripture. But even the contents of scripture are only fully understood by readers to whom God gives a new enlightenment. There is little here that is inconsistent with the teachings of Luther and Calvin, who similarly taught the frailty of fallen human reason and the priority of scripture. While the reformers placed less stress on the role of personal inspiration, both nonetheless believed that the meaning of scripture was open only to those whose minds had been enlivened by the Holy Spirit.[85] Agrippa also shared the reformers' view that Christian theology had been tainted by the contributions of pagan authors.[86] These parallels give some credence to the view that Agrippa's enthusiastic reading of the works of Luther

---

[79] Gerhard Ritter, 'Ein historisches Urbild zu Goethes Faust (Agrippa von Nettesheym)', *Preussische Jahrbücher* 161 (1910), 300–5.

[80] G. Nauert Jr, 'Magic and Scepticism in Agrippa's Thought', *JHI* 18 (1957), 161–82.

[81] Agrippa von Nettesheim, *Of the Vanitie and Vncertainty of Artes and Sciences*, Englished by James Sanford (London, 1569), fol. 186r.

[82] *Ibid.*, fols. 3v–4r. The role of the Fall in human ignorance was also stressed in the early work *De triplici ratione cognoscendi Deum*, in *Opera*, 2 vols. (Lyons, n.d.), II, 480–503.

[83] Agrippa, *Vanitie*, fol. 182v.

[84] *Ibid.*, fol. 187v.   [85] Calvin, *Institutes* I.viii.5 (McNeill I, 80).

[86] Agrippa, *Dehortatio gentiles theologiae*, in *Opera* II, 502–5.

in the 1520s informed the development of his sceptical outlook.[87] It has even been suggested that it was Agrippa's intention in this work to defend Protestantism, although this is difficult to square with his apparent lifelong identification with the Catholic faith.[88]

Some commentators have puzzled over the apparent inconsistency between the overt scepticism of *De Incertitudine* and the more positive teaching contained in *Occult Philosophy* – a work that did not appear in print until 1531, but which was possibly composed even before the more mature sceptical work.[89] However, the contents of *Occult Philosophy* are not necessarily at odds with a position that denies the efficacy of human reason and sense experience. Rather Agrippa exemplifies what will become the standard pattern for early modern proposals to advance the sciences – proposing a theologically informed scepticism supported by the biblical narrative of the Fall with a view to establishing the plausibility of a new approach to inquiry.[90] In the case of Agrippa, this was a reliance on revealed truths contained in a number of ancient writings. His restricted view of the sources of human knowledge – 'All thinges are contained and taught in the onely volume of the holy Bible' – was extended in *Occult Philosophy* to include other ancient works also thought to have been divinely inspired. This idea – that there had been an 'ancient philosophy' that could be recovered in the present – proved to be an attractive option for a number of Renaissance thinkers, and will be considered in more detail in the following chapter. For the moment it must be said that while Agrippa might be identified as one of the first of the modern sceptics, his writings were not informed by classical scepticism in any strong sense. While he relied on some of the ancient sceptical writers, he did not deploy any of their formal arguments to a significant degree. As in the works of the reformers, we encounter no genuinely philosophical objections to the possibility of knowledge. That task fell to later writers, who were to marshal the arguments of the classical sceptics into a more formal scepticism, and to advocate the adoption of the sceptical philosophical persona. The most important of these was Michel de Montaigne (1533–92).

While Montaigne's sceptical views are expressed primarily in the lengthy essay 'An Apology for Raymond Sebonde', his earlier writings already show indications of a sceptical outlook. As was the case with Agrippa, whose views seem to have influenced Montaigne, these were not directly informed

[87] Nauert, 'Magic and Scepticism', p. 171. It is also significant that Agrippa does not cite Sextus Empiricus, whose works were not available during Agrippa's lifetime.

[88] Panos Morphos, *The Dialogues of Guy de Brués* (Baltimore, 1953), p. 77.

[89] Nauert, 'Magic and Scepticism', 161–6.   [90] *Ibid.*

by the arguments of the ancient sceptics.[91] In an essay entitled 'It is folly to measure the true and false by our own capacity' he observed that 'to condemn a thing . . . dogmatically, as false and impossible, is to assume the advantage of knowing the bounds and limits of God's will and of the power of our mother Nature'.[92] This assertion is redolent of the kinds of arguments deployed from the thirteenth century onwards to refute certain Aristotelian dogmas in the realm of natural philosophy.[93] Some theologians had argued that if God were able to instantiate any state of affairs short of a logical contradiction, and to do so by any means, it would be folly to claim to know with certainty why the natural world was ordered in a particular way, or how certain natural events were caused. As late as the seventeenth century Pope Urban VIII was to put a similar argument to Galileo – in the latter's own words, that 'it would be excessive boldness to limit and restrict the Divine power and wisdom to some particular fancy of his own'.[94] The currency of these kinds of arguments has been plausibly used to explain the tendency towards instrumentalism in Renaissance astronomy and to support the thesis that links divine voluntarism with the emergence of an experimental approach to nature. But whatever the source of these views, Montaigne's early sceptical impulses were certainly confirmed by his later reading of the works of ancient sceptical writers.

There were two distinct schools of scepticism in the ancient world. 'Academic' scepticism took its name from Plato's Academy, where it had flourished between the third and first centuries BC.[95] Academic sceptics challenged the metaphysical certainties of Plato, seeking to revert to a more pure Socratic position that identified wisdom with the recognition of one's own ignorance.[96] Arguing that there were ultimately no criteria for adequately distinguishing between real and illusory perceptions, they

---

[91] Charles Larmore, 'Scepticism', in Daniel Garber and Michael Ayers (eds.), *The Cambridge History of Seventeenth-Century Philosophy*, 2 vols. (Cambridge, 1998), II, 1147. For Agrippa's influence on Montaigne, see Pierre Villey, *Les Sources et l'évolution des Essais de Montaigne*, 2 vols. (Paris, 1933), II, 166–70. Villey also argues that the earliest essays generally reflect a Stoic outlook that gives way to scepticism.

[92] Montaigne, *Essays*, tr. Donald Frame (Stanford, 1965), p. 132.

[93] See E. Grant, 'The Effect of the Condemnation of 1277', CHLMP, pp. 537–9. Funkenstein, *Theology and the Scientific Imagination*, pp. 121–45.

[94] Galileo, *Dialogue concerning the Two Chief World Systems*, tr. Stillman Drake (New York, 2001), p. 538.

[95] The next two paragraphs draw on the following sources: Popkin, *History of Skepticism*, and 'Theories of Knowledge', CHRP, pp. 668–84; Charles Schmitt, 'The Rediscovery of Ancient Skepticism in Modern Times', in M. Burnyeat (ed.), *The Skeptical Tradition*, (Berkeley, 1983), pp. 225–51, and *Cicero Scepticus: A Study of the Influence of the 'Academica' in the Renaissance* (The Hague, 1972); Luciano Floridi, *Sextus Empiricus: The Transmission and Recovery of Pyrrhonism* (New York, 2002).

[96] Plato, *Apology* 21c–21d.

recommended the suspension of judgement and asserted that at best there could be only probable knowledge. While the arguments of the Academics were available in the Middle Ages in Cicero's *Academica* (45 BC) and Augustine's *Against the Academics* (AD 386), it was really only with the advent of printing that they came to be more widely known and exploited. Cicero's *Academica* was first printed in 1471, and generated significant discussion from the early 1500s onwards. The Dutch Humanist Desiderius Erasmus (*c.* 1466–1536), for example, exploited the ideas of the Academics in his *In Praise of Folly* (1511), a work that was sharply critical of the scholastics and the Catholic hierarchy. In the subsequent controversy with Luther occasioned by his defence of free will in *De libero arbitrio* (1524), Erasmus also drew the sceptical conclusion that the problem of free will was beyond the capacity of human beings to solve.

The 1560s saw the publication of the works of Sextus Empiricus (second century), which brought to a Renaissance audience the arguments of the other ancient school of scepticism, Pyrrhonism.[97] Pyrrho of Elis (*c.* 320–230 BC) was the originator of the movement, exemplifying the manner in which the sceptic ought to live. However, the formalisation of Pyrrhonic thought had to wait until the first and second centuries, with the enumeration of sets of arguments favouring suspension of judgement about all knowledge claims that went beyond immediate experience. These may be found in *Outlines of Pyrrhonism* and *Against the Dogmatists*, written by Sextus. Sextus also stressed the importance of the sceptical life. The sceptic is one who, through the suspension of judgement (*epoche*), attains peace of mind or 'imperturbability' (*ataraxia*). The Pyrrhonic sceptic, moreover, did not doubt the world of appearances and lived in accordance with the prevailing laws and customs.[98]

Montaigne's 'Apology' draws quite self-consciously on the Pyrrhonic sceptics.[99] It is impossible to know certainties that lie beyond the appearances of things, he insists, and it follows that the wise individual will suspend judgement on such matters.[100] Beyond this, however, Montaigne wants to suggest that the sceptical outlook entails more than the ability to deploy a set of clever arguments designed to deflate the pretensions of the dogmatists. Scepticism is advocated as a way of life. One of the consistent themes of the 'Apology', and indeed of the *Essays* more generally, is

---

[97] Also of importance was Diogenes Laertius, *Life of Pyrrho*. See Schmitt, 'The Rediscovery of Ancient Skepticism'.

[98] Sextus Empiricus, *Outlines of Pyrrhonism*, 1.17.

[99] For elements of Academic scepticism in Montaigne, see Neto, 'Academic Skepticism in Early Modern Philosophy'.

[100] Montaigne, *Essays*, pp. 371f.

the necessity, in the face of our uncertainties, simply to adopt the customs and mores of the society in which we live.[101] As Charles Larmore has suggested, what is original about Montaigne's position is that 'it replaces, in effect, the ancient sceptical goal of *ataraxia* with the more vigorous ideal of feeling at home in interminable controversy'.[102] Such an advocacy can hardly have been more relevant than at a time when Europe had been plunged into apparently irresolvable religious controversy. Montaigne certainly made this connection himself. The view set out in the 'Apology' is at the most far remove from religious dogmatism:

It presents man naked and empty, acknowledging his natural weakness, fit to receive from above some outside power; stripped of human knowledge, and all the more apt to lodge divine knowledge in himself, annihilating his judgment to make more room for faith; neither disbelieving, nor setting up any doctrine against the common observances; humble, obedient, teachable, zealous; a sworn enemy of heresy, and consequently free from the vain and irreligious opinion produced by false sects.[103]

The lack of such equanimity in the face of religious novelty was, in Montaigne's opinion, the cause of Europe's present woes. It had blighted the lives of the English in particular. This nation, on Montaigne's reckoning, had within the span of his own lifetime not only changed its politics four times, but also 'had dispensed with constancy . . . in the most important subject there can be, to wit, religion'.[104]

Certain elements of this position lent themselves to appropriation by the forces of the Counter-Reformation, for they favoured acceptance of the prevailing religion, and were inherently biased against dogmatic claims made by would-be religious reformers. Gentian Hervet (1499–1584), secretary to the Cardinal of Lorraine, and a regular at the protracted sessions of the Council of Trent, made this point in the introduction to his Latin translation of Sextus. The sceptical arguments of Sextus, he contended, showed the poverty of human reason, and could thus provide assistance in refuting the heretical reasonings and putative certainty of the Protestant reformers.[105] Montaigne had himself implied something similar, with veiled references to 'heresy' and 'false sects', and his insistence on following the established patterns of morality and religion. As we have already seen, Erasmus also deployed sceptical arguments in his controversy with Luther over the nature of free will. For his part, Luther had given the uncompromising response: 'Spiritus sanctus non est Scepticus' (the Holy Spirit is

[101] *Ibid.*, pp. 436f. Cf. pp. 436, 440. Cf. Hadot, *What is Ancient Philosophy?*, pp. 113, 142–5.
[102] Larmore, 'Scepticism', 1150.   [103] Montaigne, *Essays*, p. 375.   [104] *Ibid.*, p. 436.
[105] Popkin, 'Skepticism', *Encyclopedia of Philosophy*, VII, 452.

not a sceptic). The most celebrated exponent of sceptical arguments in the service of the Counter-Reformation was the Jesuit priest François Véron (c. 1575–1625), who taught philosophy at La Flèche when young Descartes had been a student there. Véron developed a remarkably successful formula for countering the claims of Calvinist controversialists – one that exploited sceptical arguments to expose the difficulties of relying solely on scriptural authority for matters of religious doctrine.[106] In essence his arguments pointed to the problem of invoking a basic criterion of knowledge, when what was at issue was the criterion itself.

It is important not to overstate these apparent affinities between scepticism and Tridentine Catholicism, however, for there were significant aspects of the sceptical position that Lutherans and Calvinists, and indeed Jansenists, could agree with. The latter shared a common belief in the inherent fallibility of the human mind, and on the need to rely upon divine revelation.[107] The modern sceptics could also make reference to the Fall and its significance. As we have already seen, Agrippa attributed ignorance to the Fall. Montaigne contended that 'Christians have a particular knowledge of the extent to which curiosity is a natural and original evil in man'. 'The urge to increase in wisdom', he adds, 'was the first downfall of the human race'.[108] Montaigne's seventeenth-century disciple, Pierre Charron (1541–1603), noted that while the schools had taken the high view that the mind was 'the image of God', an 'outflowing of divinity', the sad reality was that 'the means it employs for the discovery of truth are reason and experience, both of which are very weak, uncertain, diverse, wavering'.[109] Charron attributed the weakness of the mind to 'the disease and corruption of the will': 'the will was made to follow the understanding which is its guide, its torch; but being corrupted and seized by the force of the passions, it also corrupts the understanding, whence comes the greatest part of our false judgements'.[110] The apparent similarities between this position and that advocated by the Jansenists also draws some support from the fact that in early seventeenth-century France some sceptical writers found favour with the Jansenists. When Charron was attacked by the Jesuit theologian François Garasse, who feared that Charron's corrosive

---

[106] François Véron, *La méthode nouvelle, facile et solide de convaincre de nullité la religion prétendue réformée* (Paris, 1615). This work was reprinted many times during the seventeenth century, and was translated into English, German and Dutch. I have used the English translation of 1616, *Keepe your text* (Lancashire, 1616). For a summary of the arguments see pp. 41f. See also the translator's preface to *The Rule of the Catholic Faith* (Paris, 1660), sig. A2r–A4v.
[107] Montaigne, *Essays*, pp. 415, 457.   [108] *Ibid.*, p. 368.
[109] Charron, *De la Sagesse* (Paris, 1791), pp. 109, 115; *Of Wisdome*, (London, 1606), pp. 55, 60.
[110] Charron, *De la Sagesse*, p. 120.

scepticism would undermine Catholic doctrines supported by rational argument, Saint-Cyran sprang to Charron's defence. Human reason, he insisted, was indeed as impotent as Charron had intimated.[111] In the *Pensées* we find Pascal declaring that 'Scepticism is right'.[112]

The sceptics were adjudged to be right only to a limited extent, however. While they were correct to point to the futility of human knowledge, for those who subscribed to a Christian anthropology their analysis was not informed by any genuine insight into the human condition. Such an analysis could only be provided by sacred history, which contained the account of Adam's fall from grace. The mistake of the ancient sceptics was to have regarded human ignorance as our natural condition, rather than as evidence of our corruption. The same was also true of the modern sceptics who, while they made reference to the Fall, tended to gloss it in a manner that was essentially Pelagian – or at least so their opponents argued. Charron, for example, generally attributes the Fall to our natural ignorance, rather than our ignorance to the Fall.[113] In his prelapsarian state, Adam was thus not the intellectual giant so often described in the tradition:

> The spirit is slow and heavy. This is the reason why it cannot immediately . . .
> penetrate and see objects clearly. It must proceed instead . . . by discourse, composition, and division. There, when [Adam] was deceived, he could not see deep
> into the nature of his act . . . nor anticipate the consequences. This renders him
> more entitled to forgiveness.[114]

Such a view of Adam's original condition contrasts sharply with the kinds of images of Adam set out by English writers like Robert South, and was certainly inconsistent with Jansenist views of Adam's original perfections. Indeed, one of Charron's English translators, impatient with the French author's reluctance to attribute all our failings to the Fall, interpolated more explicit references to Adam's lapse into his English version of the text.[115] According to Charron, Adam's lapse was a relatively minor infraction that did not radically change his naturally fallible nature. As far as the

[111] Jean Orcibal, *Les origines du Jansénisme* II: *Jean Duvergier de Haruanne, Abbé de Saint-Cyran, et son temps (1581–1638)* (Paris, 1947), p. 276. On the affinity between scepticism and Jansenism see T. Lennon, 'Jansenism and the *Crise Pyrrhonienne*', *JHI* 38 (1977), 297–306; Popkin, *History of Scepticism*, p. 113. But cf. Neto, *Christianization of Pyrrhonism*, pp. 6f., 25–30; Sedgwick, *Jansenism*, pp. 155f.

[112] Pascal, *Pensées*, L 691 (p. 245).

[113] I owe this insight to Neto, *Christianization of Pyrrhonism*, pp. 24, 29.

[114] Pierre Charron, 'Discours Chrestiens de la Divinité, Création, Rédemption et Octave du Sainct-Sacrament', *Œuvres* (Geneva, 1970), p. 209, tr. in *ibid.*, p. 25.

[115] In the following passage, the words in parenthesis have been added by E. Lennard, the translator: 'the wil is made to follow the vnderstanding as a guide and lampe vnto it; but being corrupted and seased on by the force of the passions (or rather by the fall of our first father *Adam*) doth likewise

Lutherans, Calvinists, and Jansenists were concerned, because the sceptics typically underestimated our original cognitive capacities, they tended to regard human ignorance as essentially incorrigible. For the sceptics, our present miseries did not result from a cosmic catastrophe precipitated by human disobedience, and were therefore to be accepted with equanimity rather than self-recrimination. For this reason they had little interest in attempting to remedy the operations of the mind, rather accepting the inevitability of ignorance and prescribing suspension of judgement as a way of dealing with it. Such a prescription would confer peace of mind and raise the sceptic beyond the petty miseries of ordinary men.

Those who adopted a Pauline or Augustinian anthropology saw matters rather differently. Their proposed solution to our present ignorance was not the Pelagian adoption of a quiescent moral persona, but rather an emphasis on the need for divine grace. Moreover, for Jansenists and Protestant reformers alike there lay the prospect of an amelioration of human ignorance through an analysis of exactly what mental faculties had been disrupted by the Fall. This was to be followed by the devising of strategies that might help to overcome these inherited infirmities. The historical figure of Adam played an important role here, for since he had once commanded nature on account of his natural gifts, it was not unreasonable to hope for the partial restoration – possibly by artificial aids and assistances – of the abilities he had once exercised more fully. Such reasoning lay at the core of the Baconian programme, important elements of which were later adopted by the Royal Society. Bacon thus explained that 'the doctrine of those who have denied that certainty could be attained at all, has some agreement with my way of proceeding'. But, he immediately adds, 'then they go on to destroy the authority of the senses and understanding; whereas I proceed to devise and supply helps for the same'.[116] Arguably, the experimental approach of the young Pascal was informed by similar convictions.[117] From this perspective, if the flaw of Aristotelianism had been an uncritical assumption of the reliability of the human mind, scepticism was equally deficient in assuming that the natural condition of the human mind was ignorance. Both extremes arose from the fact that the ancients were unaware of the biblical relation concerning the divine creation of man in

perhaps corrupt the vnderstanding, and so from hence come the greatest part of our erroneous iudgments'. *Of Wisdom* (London, 1609), p. 64. Cf. *De la Sagesse*, p. 120.

[116] Bacon, *Novum Organum* I, §37 (*Works* IV, 53). Cf. *Great Instauration* (*Works* IV, 31); *Novum Organum* I, §67 (*Works* IV, 69).

[117] Daniel C. Fouke, 'Argument in Pascal's *Pensées*', *History of Philosophy Quarterly* 6 (1989), 57–68; Jeanne Russier, *La Foi selon Pascal*, 2 vols. (Paris, 1949), II, 428.

God's image and his subsequent fall from grace. As the Lutheran reformer Philipp Melanchthon expressed it, 'philosophy has nothing to tell us about the cause of this infirmity or its remedies'.[118] Writing from his Jansenist perspective, Pascal was later to characterise the predicament of the ancients in much the same way:

> For if they realized the excellence of man they did not know his corruption, with the result that they certainly avoided sloth, but sank into pride, and if they recognized the infirmity of nature, they did not know its dignity; with the result that they were certainly able to avoid vanity, only to fall headlong into despair. Hence the various sects of Stoics and Epicureans, Dogmatists and Academicians, etc.[119]

A reliable assessment of our prospects for knowledge, then, requires a delicate balancing act. It also calls for an answer to the theological question of the extent to which the divine image persisted after the Fall, and of what capacities remained to fallen human beings. This was a question that could not even be formulated by those unfamiliar with the facts of sacred history. Accordingly, the schools of pagan philosophy could not be expected to have made any great advances in this sphere. In Pascal's judgement, the real error of the ancient sects of philosophy lay in their 'not having known that man's present condition is different from that of his original creation'.[120] This error had now infected Christian thinking, as evidenced on the one hand by Christian sceptics, and on the other by the Aristotelian Thomists and Jesuit advocates of the Molinist doctrine of 'pure nature'.

The figure of Adam, which plays no significant role in modern scepticism, thus had dual implications for those who saw themselves as subscribing to a genuinely biblical anthropology. Because of his Fall, Adam represented human loss and limitation. By the same token, on account of his (original) natural abilities, his encyclopaedic knowledge, and his earthly vocation, he symbolised the untapped potential of human nature. Again, Pascal nicely captures this dual aspect in his assertion that 'men are at once . . . unworthy through their corruption, capable through their original nature'. It follows that we are 'incapable of certain knowledge or absolute ignorance'.[121] A more optimistic appraisal, though one imbued with the same duality, was offered by the Cambridge divine and friend of John Locke, Benjamin

---

[118] Melanchthon, *Elements of Ethical Doctrine* I, in Jill Kraye (ed.), *Cambridge Translations of Renaissance Philosophical Texts*, 2 vols. (Cambridge, 1997), I, 109.

[119] Pascal, *Pensées*, L 208 (pp. 96f.). Pascal restates this point in a sustained discussion of scepticism in *Pensée* L 131. A similar position is set out in the *Port-Royal Logic* (London, 1720), pp. 5f.

[120] Pascal, *Entretien avec M. de Saci*, in *Œuvres Complètes*, ed. Jean Mesnard, 4 vols. (Paris, 1964–92), III, 152.

[121] Pascal, *Pensées*, L 444 (p. 167); L 199 (p. 92).

Whichcote (1609–83), who announced that when we consider the 'Nature of Man', we should take our conception 'not from what it is, by Defection and Apostacy; but from what God made it: What it was, and what it should be'.[122] In the sphere of knowledge, human beings are suspended between the despair of scepticism and the hope of regaining some of their original capacity for knowledge. Calvin had expressed similar views, observing that efforts of the pagan philosophers should serve as an example to Christians of what can still be accomplished with the gifts of God even though human nature has been 'despoiled of its true good'.[123]

Some of the impetus for this more positive conception of Adam – which admittedly receives less attention in the writings of the Reformation – may have been the result of the residual influence of Calvin's humanism. Konrad Burdach has shown that among certain Renaissance thinkers the myth of Adam took on a new significance, melding with the classical myth of Prometheus. The figure of Adam could thus be emblematic not only of the lost opportunities of the human race, but also of its latent potential.[124] Ernst Cassirer agreed that in the early sixteenth century the story of Adam could be as much cause for hope as for despair: 'The first man . . . becomes an expression of spiritual man, the *homo spiritualis*, and thus, all the spiritual tendencies of the epoch that are directed towards a renewal, rebirth, and regeneration of man come to be concentrated in his form'.[125] This optimism is significantly muted in Reformation thought, yet it nonetheless provided an important stimulus for activities that were thought to counter the consequences of the Fall. There is more than a little truth in Roy Battenhouse's suggestion that 'humanism's dream of a natural perfection of man-in-himself continued to haunt Calvin in his interpretation of the primal Adam and of Adam's disaster'.[126]

Early modern scepticism has a somewhat complicated relationship with contemporary developments in theology and philosophy.[127] Certainly there were those who seemed genuinely to embrace the sceptical ethos and its moral prescriptions. More frequently, however, opportunistic use was made of sceptical arguments. For this reason these arguments are deployed in a

---

[122] Benjamin Whichcote, *Moral and Religious Aphorisms* (London, 1930), §228.

[123] Calvin, *Institutes* II.ii.15 (McNeill I, 275).

[124] Konrad Burdach, *Reformation, Renaissance, Humanismus* (Berlin, 1918), pp. 171–3.

[125] Ernst Cassirer, *The Individual and the Cosmos in Renaissance Philosophy*, tr. Mario Demandi (New York, 1963), p. 93.

[126] Roy Battenhouse, 'The Doctrine of Man in Calvin and Renaissance Platonism', *JHI* 9 (1948), 447–71 (470).

[127] See Alan Kors, 'Skepticism and the Problem of Atheism in Early Modern France', in R. Popkin and A. Vanderjagt (eds.), *Scepticism and Irreligion in the Seventeenth and Eighteenth Centuries* (Leiden, 1993), pp. 185–215.

wide range of contexts and by individuals who had little sympathy with the basic moral prescriptions of scepticism. As we have seen, some Counter-Reformation figures sought to use scepticism to refute the arguments of Protestantism. Others relied on sceptical arguments to challenge the philosophical monopoly of Aristotelianism. A good example of the latter is Pierre Gassendi, whom Richard Popkin regards as exemplifying the thesis of a sceptical crisis in early seventeenth-century France. While there is little doubt that Gassendi's writing makes reference to sceptical arguments – in particular his early *Exercitationes paradoxicae adversus Aristoteleos* (1624) – it is doubtful that Gassendi regarded these arguments as anything more than a weapon to use against Aristotelianism.[128] Certainly, he was not committed to the sceptical programme in its totality, and it is unlikely that he regarded its arguments as counting decisively against the possibility of certain kinds of knowledge. Pascal also uses scepticism for his apologetic purposes. But here again we see an uncompromising rejection of the sceptical position itself. For Pascal, scepticism offers partial truths and ultimately counts only as evidence for the corruption of human nature.[129]

As mentioned at the beginning of this book, over many years Richard Popkin has developed a persuasive and influential thesis about scepticism and the origins of modern philosophy. On this thesis, Descartes' 'clear and distinct ideas' and his insistence on the reliability of the 'light of nature' were direct responses to the kind of sceptical doubts raised by Montaigne. Accordingly Popkin regards Montaigne's scepticism as 'one of the crucial forces in the formation of modern thought'.[130] Much has been written in the years since Popkin first advanced this thesis that adds to its weight and it has become firmly entrenched as a powerful explanation for the emergence of some of the characteristic features of modern philosophy. While this is not the appropriate context for a thoroughgoing evaluation of the merits

[128] Gassendi, *Exercitationes paradoxicae aduersus Aristoteleo* ii, 6, in *Opera Omnia*, 6 vols. (Lyons, 1658), iii, 192–207. For the case that Gassendi's position is more anti-Aristotelian than sceptical see Barry Brundell, *Pierre Gassendi: From Aristotelianism to a New Philosophy* (Dordrecht, 1987), esp. pp. 137–42. See also Larmore, 'Scepticism', 1155–9; Lynn Joy, *Gassendi the Atomist* (Cambridge, 1987), pp. 32–7. Francisco Sanches (*c.* 1550–*c.* 1623) – Montaigne's cousin and another pioneer in the use of sceptical arguments – had a similar goal. His *Quod nihil scitur* ('That Nothing is Known', 1581) is primarily an attack on Aristotelian doctrines.

[129] In this context José Neto has spoken of a 'Christianization of Pyrrhonism' that 'basically involves a reconstruction of Greek skepticism in terms of the doctrine of the Fall of man'. *Christianization of Pyrrhonism*, p. xv. While Neto gives a fairly accurate picture of Pascal's relation to scepticism, I would stop short of suggesting that Pascal 'reconstructs' Greek scepticism, or that he represents a 'Christianization' of it. In my view, it is in Montaigne and Charron that we see the Christianisation of Pyrrhonism and it is this attempted Christianisation that Pascal reacts against.

[130] Popkin, *History of Scepticism*, p. 54. Cf. Ernst Cassirer, *Das Erkenntnisproblem in der Philosophie und Wissenschaft der neueren Zeit*, 2 vols. (Berlin, 1906–7), i, 162, 181.

of this important thesis, it is worth making explicit three major differences between the Popkin thesis and the view that is being elaborated here.

First, while Popkin is correct to see early modern epistemological projects as responses to a kind of scepticism, these projects are not primarily responses to Montaigne and his disciples, but to the more pervasive intellectual crisis precipitated by the Reformation and Counter-Reformation. A better candidate for the 'womb of modern thought' than the 'noveau Pyrrhonisme' of Montaigne is a neo-Augustinian anthropology, chiefly associated with the reformers, but evident also in a number of the movements associated with early modern Catholicism. Montaigne's adoption of elements of ancient scepticism did not precipitate a 'sceptical crisis'. Rather Montaigne provided philosophical resources to address a crisis that already existed, and here lies his chief significance. This crisis, it must be conceded, was caused not only by the substance of a newly revived Augustinian anthropology, but also by the simple fact that the Reformation led to a plurality of competing religious beliefs. It may well be possible to view subsequent developments in early modern natural philosophy as responses to the sceptical doubts raised by Montaigne, but it is more fruitful to regard them rather as alternative solutions to the same set of problems that Montaigne was addressing. The opposition to Montaigne is not primarily a response to the sceptical doubts he raised, but rather a rejection of the solution that he proposed. The prescriptions of the early modern systems of philosophy thus have their point of departure not in the arguments of ancient or modern sceptics, but in the theological debates about human nature and the legitimacy of various sources of knowledge. It is true that ancient schools of philosophy play important supporting roles in early modern systems of knowledge, but the extent to which scepticism, or Aristotelianism, or Stoicism, or Epicureanism is exploited is ultimately dependent on their consistency with more fundamental theological convictions about God, the world, and human nature.[131]

Second, while scepticism may appear to be in conflict with the philosophical traditions of Aristotelianism and Platonism and with their prescriptions for the acquisition of knowledge, what it shares with these schools of philosophy is a general view of the goal of philosophy as the achievement of personal happiness for the philosopher. In each case, this goal is accomplished through a special kind of philosophical labour as the philosopher seeks to withdraw from, and rise above, the illusions of the mundane world. A distinctive feature of the new systems of philosophy and natural

---

[131] Partly for this reason 'eclecticism' is highly regarded in the early modern period.

philosophy, however, is an active engagement with nature. In this respect it is completely at odds with the ethos of the philosophical schools of ancient Greece. The source of this new active conception of the philosopher, whose goal is not to retreat from the natural world but rather to order it and bring it under his dominion, is the figure of the prelapsarian Adam who once possessed an encyclopaedic knowledge of nature and was capable of commanding the creatures. This positive dimension is completely lacking in scepticism, and indeed the notion of an engagement with the natural world is absent from most of the ancient philosophical traditions. It should be added that while there is no doubt that sceptical arguments can be used in discussions of epistemology, scepticism as a philosophy was directed primarily at achieving the inner mental state of 'imperturbability' (*ataraxia*).

This leads us to the third point, which is that the Popkin thesis lends support to a common view that considers early modern philosophy to be concerned primarily with epistemology *per se*.[132] This common view has arisen because the disciplines of academic philosophy and the natural sciences are now quite distinct. This was not so in the seventeenth century, however, when views about knowledge were informed by the overlapping domains of anatomy, physiology, moral psychology and, not least, theological anthropology. While Popkin himself is not guilty of this anachronistic reading, his thesis has nonetheless contributed to a common distorted view of the history of philosophy that regards Descartes as the paradigmatic modern philosopher, and which regards the discipline thereafter to be essentially preoccupied with the rather academic task of combating epistemological scepticism.[133] Providing scepticism with a central explanatory role in the development of modern philosophy almost inevitably furthers this mistaken view. The issue is not so much that Descartes is not a seminal figure, but that he is for reasons other than an apparent preoccupation with epistemology. Increasingly, Descartes scholars have come to realise that the 'father of modern philosophy' was, to paraphrase Desmond Clarke, primarily a scientist who unfortunately wrote some minor and relatively unimportant works devoted to questions of method and epistemology.[134] In this respect he has something in common with Bacon who, while not

[132] On this point see, e.g., John Cottingham, 'Doubtful Uses of Doubt: Cartesian Philosophy and the Historiography of Scepticism', in L. Catana (ed.), *Historiographies in Early Modern Philosophy and Science* (Dordrecht, forthcoming).

[133] A prominent example of this reading is Richard Rorty's *Philosophy and the Mirror of Nature* (Princeton, 1980).

[134] Clarke, *Descartes' Philosophy of Science*, p. 2. See also Gaukroger et al. (eds.), *Descartes' Natural Philosophy*, esp. pp. 1–6; Gaukroger, *Descartes' System of Natural Philosophy*.

given to the practice of natural philosophy, wrote much on how it should be prosecuted. These views, as we shall see in chapter 4, were informed by a view of human nature that rested upon precisely the kind of balance between optimism and pessimism recommended by Pascal. It is in this light that we are to view Bacon's advocacy of a middle path between two extremes: 'the presumption of pronouncing on everything, and the despair of comprehending anything'.[135] More generally, the thesis argued for in this book acknowledges the importance of discussions of knowledge and its foundations, but regards these as essentially secondary to questions of anthropology. The answers to fundamental questions about human nature were to inform issues not only of knowledge, but of religion, morality, and political philosophy. Different views on these matters can generally be related to different assessments of human nature.

It is not particularly surprising that past interpreters of Reformation thought have judged its spirit to be essentially inimical to the new science. Andrew Dickson White's *History of the Warfare of Science with Theology* (1896) – a work that has now achieved canonical status in the history of the relations between science and religion, albeit for all the wrong reasons – argues that Luther and Calvin were implacably opposed to new developments in the natural sciences generally and to the Copernican theory in particular. White reports that the German universities were imbued with 'an anti-scientific spirit' because of the baleful influence of Protestant theology.[136] While White's errors of fact and interpretation – including his use of a completely fictitious anti-Copernican quotation from Calvin – have been enumerated in detail by various critics, it is difficult not to have some sympathy with his intuition that Reformation thought would not provide a particularly fertile matrix for the development of scientific ideas. After all, if the Fall had depraved human faculties to the extent that they were completely unreliable, the prospects for a veridical science of nature would seem to be extremely limited.

What I have suggested in this chapter is that contrary to first impressions, the anthropology of the reformers, informed as it was by the biblical account of Adam's Fall, had the potential to promote a new, more critical, appraisal of human intellectual capacities. Renewed suspicion about our cognitive capabilities, I hope to demonstrate in the chapters that follow, was the starting point for the methodological discussions of the early

[135] Bacon, *Novum Organum, Works* IV, 39.
[136] A. D. White, *History of the Warfare of Science with Theology in Christendom*, 2 vols. (London, 1897), I, 126.

modern period and was particularly important in the development of what became known as the experimental philosophy. Thus, beyond the fact that the religious upheavals of the sixteenth century indirectly contributed to the reformation of learning by issuing a challenge to the prevailing authorities, the specific content of Reformation doctrines played a direct role in shaping what was to replace the older knowledge. Protestant discussions of the corruption of human nature, the concern with the abstruse distinction between 'natural' and 'supernatural' gifts, the debate about whether human nature was deprived or depraved, may appear to be marginal in an age that was to give birth to modern philosophy and science. But these questions were in fact fundamental to many fields of human endeavour, not least the science of nature. There were a number of possible responses to the doubts that had arisen about the grounds of human knowledge. Some sought refuge in those faculties of the human mind that seemed, by their very nature, to be immune from corruption. Reason, 'the light of nature', our mathematical and logical abilities – these were the most likely faculties upon which certain knowledge could be constructed. The case for the reliability of these capacities was often reinforced by an appeal to God, who was invoked as a guarantor of their integrity. This would make possible a knowledge that still possessed the degree of certainty that for Aristotle was a criterion of genuine science. Others believed that even the light of human reason had been a casualty of the Fall, and to such a degree that it was untrustworthy. For some of these individuals a more direct appeal was made to divine revelation, and knowledge was sought either in God's revealed Word, or in personal inspiration. For still others, the unreliability of reason meant knowledge of the natural world would come only after laborious experimentation, the long accumulation of many different observations, and orchestration of the efforts of numerous investigators. In this latter case, our knowledge would have a makeshift quality about it, and would lack the certainty that had been traditionally considered to be the hallmark of true science. In all of this, the figure of Adam came to symbolise not only what abilities had been lost to the human race at the Fall, but also the power over nature that might be reinstated if only the specific causes of our cognitive depredations could be correctly identified and neutralised.

CHAPTER 3

Seeking certainty in a fallen world

However, since different hypotheses are sometimes offered for one and the same motion (for example, eccentricity and an epicycle for the sun's motion), the astronomer will take as his first choice that hypothesis which is the easiest to grasp. The philosopher will perhaps rather seek the semblance of the truth. But neither of them will understand or state anything certain, unless it has been divinely revealed to him.

Andreas Osiander, Preface to Copernicus, *De Revolutionibus* (1543)

Some, following the letter of Scripture, used what the sacred writers touched on [in passing] . . . concerning cosmology and natural things in order to build a new sacred physics . . . Others, dampening down the light of the intellect, called for some other more divine and more perfect light stemming from heavenly revelation to be the foundation of philosophy, neglecting the letter of Scripture and [relying on] the intermediary of the machine of allegory.[1]

Johann Brucker, *Historia critica philosophiae* (1743)

But there are Enthusiasts in Philosophy, as well as in Religion; Men that go by no principles, but their own conceit and fancy, and by a Light within, which shines very uncertainly, and, for the most part, leads them out of the way of truth.

Thomas Burnet, *The Theory of the Earth* (1697)

One of the ways in which the Protestant Reformation had an indirect influence on the development of new approaches to philosophy was by conferring a degree of legitimacy upon projects aimed at reforms of other kinds. Advocates of new scientific approaches, for example, often pointed to the precedent of religious reformation and regarded it as providing some sanction for their own revolutionary approaches to learning.[2] Astronomer

---

[1] Johann Jakob Brucker, *Historia critica philosophiae* (Leipzig, 1743), vol. IV, pt I, bk 3, ch. 2, pp. 610f, quoted in Blair, 'Mosaic Physics', p. 36.
[2] See Harrison, *Bible and the Rise of Science*, pp. 103–7.

Johannes Kepler boldly entitled one of his major works *Astronomia Nova* (New Astronomy, 1609), at a time when the descriptor 'new' bore quite negative connotations when applied to knowledge. Kepler drew strength from the example of Luther and saw fit to identify himself as the 'Luther of astrology'.[3] Paracelsian writers described Copernicus and Paracelsus in similar terms, designating them the 'Luther and Calvin' of natural philosophy, and characterising their work as that of restoring corrupt disciplines to their primitive purity.[4] At the beginning of the seventeenth century, Francis Bacon regarded the reformation of religion as the first occasion for 'a renovation and a new spring of all other knowledges'.[5] Many of his compatriots were subsequently to locate their philosophical and scientific innovations within the context of that more general reformation inaugurated in the previous century by Luther and Calvin.[6] At the very least, then, the Protestant Reformation provided inspiration and a degree of legitimation for these new projects.

It was also the case that the arguments of the reformers provided a rich source of ammunition for those who wished to attack tradition and the authority of pagan authors in general, and Aristotle in particular. The Lutheran critique of Aristotle and his scholastic disciples, which reinforced an existing trend amongst Renaissance Platonists, was echoed in the polemical writings of reformers of knowledge for the next hundred years.[7] The Renaissance alchemist and Neoplatonist Robert Fludd (1574–1637), whose diverse interests defy precise categorisation, thus described the philosophical heritage of the Middle Ages as 'the Philosophy of the *Ethnicks*'. This philosophy, he insisted, 'is false and erroneous . . . founded upon the wisdom of the world' and has its ultimate source in 'the Prince of darknesse'.[8]

---

[3] Webster, *From Paracelsus to Newton*, p. 4.

[4] R. B., *The Difference between the Auncient Phisicke . . . and the Latter Phisicke* (London, 1585), sigs. cviii v, Hvii v; John Hester, *The Pearle of Practice* (London, 1594), Epistle Dedicatory. Cf. Anon., *Philiatros* (London, 1615), sigs. A2r–A3v.

[5] Bacon, *Advancement of Learning*, I.vi.15 (p. 42). Cf. George Hakewill, *An Apologie or Declaration of the Power and Providence of God in the Government of the World*, 3rd edn (Oxford, 1635), sig. a4v (Epistle Dedicatory).

[6] Sprat, *History*, p. 371; Thomas Culpeper, *Morall Discourses and Essayes* (London, 1655), p. 63; Samuel Hartlib, Sheffield University Library, Hartlib Papers XLVIII 17, reproduced in Webster, *Great Instauration*, Appendix 1, pp. 524–8. Cf. Noah Biggs, *Matæotechnia Medicinae Praxeos. The Vanity of the Craft of Physick* (London, 1651), To the Parliament.

[7] On the critiques of the Renaissance Platonists see James Hankins, 'Plato's Psychogony in the Later Renaissance: Changing Attitudes to the Christianization of Pagan Philosophy', in *Ancient and Medieval Philosophy*, vol. XXXII, ed. Thomas Leinkauf and Carlos Steel (Leuven, 2005), pp. 393–412.

[8] Robert Fludd, *Mosaicall Philosophy Grounded upon the Essential Truth or Eternal Sapience* (London, 1659), pp. 13, 28. Cf. pp. 33, 123.

On account of the ascendancy of Aristotle, he lamented, true philosophy lies 'buried in darkness, through the mysty and ambiguous clouds of that cavilling, brabling, heathenish Philosophy, which they so adore and follow, with their Master *Aristotle*, as if he were another Jesus rained down from heaven, to open unto mankind the treasures of the true wisdome'. The Paracelsian controversialist known simply as 'R. B'. – probably Richard Bostocke (1530–1605) – justified his call for medical reforms with the argument that contemporary Galenic medicine had been fatally compromised by its reliance on 'heathenish' Aristotelian philosophy. The received medical tradition, he concluded, was as 'false and injurious' to God's honour as was Aristotle's pagan philosophy.[9] In his *Tryal of Spirits* (1653), a work directed towards a reformation of the English universities, educational reformer William Dell (*d.* 1669) similarly contended that the 'fleshly wisdom' of Aristotle had more credence at Oxford and Cambridge than Moses or even Christ himself.[10] Religiously motivated attacks on Aristotelianism could thus provide a warrant for more comprehensive criticisms that extended to matters of philosophy, natural philosophy, and medicine.

It was not inevitable, however, that the impulse to reform natural philosophy would issue in anti-Aristotelian sentiment. If, for some, Aristotelian philosophy was the product of a mind uninformed by revelation and unenlightened by divine grace, for others the reality of the Fall meant that human minds desperately needed some features of Aristotelianism – usually the discipline of Aristotelian logic – to control and direct their wayward impulses. For reasons such as this, the Lutheran reformer and humanist Philipp Melanchthon insisted that elements of the traditional Aristotelian curriculum be maintained.[11] Johann Alsted (1588–1638), Calvinist philosopher and theologian at the University of Herborn, valued aspects of the Aristotelian method for much the same reason. Alsted wrote in his *Panacea philosophica* (1610) that before the Fall human nature had been perfect and knowledge of the world had been acquired with ease. With Adam's

---

[9] R. B., *Auncient Phisicke*, sig. Av v, title page. 'R. B'. has been identified as Richard Bostocke (Rychard Bostok) or Robert Bostocke. There is no entry for him in the *ODNB*. On his identity see David Harley, 'Rychard Bostok of Tandridge, Surrey (*c.* 1530–1605), M. P., Paracelsian Propagandist and friend of John Dee'. Unpublished MS available at http://www.nd.edu/~dharley/medicine/bostocke-paper.html#N_1. See also A. G. Debus, *The English Paracelsians* (New York, 1965), p. 24; P. H. Kocher, 'Paracelsian Medicine in England: The First Thirty Years (ca. 1570–1600)', *Journal of the History of Medicine* 2 (1947), 451–80.

[10] William Dell, *The Tryal of Spirits Both in Teachers & Hearers* (London, 1653), pp. 43, 60. Cf. John Webster, *Academiarum Examen, or the Examination of Academies* (London, 1654), pp. 109f. On Dell and Webster see Webster, *Great Instauration*, pp. 178–90.

[11] For Melanchthon's differences with Luther on these and related issues, see Günter Frank, *Die theologische Philosophie Philipp Melanchthons (1497–1560)* (Leipzig, 1995), pp. 28f., 185f.

lapse came the destruction of the divine image in man and the loss of the capacity to know nature. This catastrophic loss, however, could be ameliorated by the artificial cultivation of learning. For Alsted, this art combined elements of Raymond Lull's mnemonics and two other systems generally regarded as incompatible – Aristotelian logic and the dialectics of the French educational reformer Peter Ramus (1515–72). With this artificial assistance Alsted embarked on an encyclopaedic enterprise aimed at both restoring the knowledge of Adam and instituting a universal reformation of learning that would usher in the millennium.[12]

Alsted's most famous student was the Moravian theologian and educationalist Jan Comenius (1592–1670), whose educational reforms had an impact both on the Continent and in England. Comenius did not express virulent opposition to Aristotelianism, but argued that knowledge be grounded in a range of authorities. In his *Naturall Philosophie Reformed by Divine Light: or, A Synopsis of Physicks* (London, 1651), Comenius insisted that 'Aristotle is not to be tolerated in Christian Schools as the onely Master of Philosophie'. Rather, he suggested, 'we should be free Philosophers, to follow that which our senses, Reason, and Scripture dictate'.[13] These alternative sources to the authority of Aristotle were themselves to be justified on theological grounds. The Protestant principle of *sola Scriptura* prompted Comenius to assert that 'the seeds of true Philosophy are conteined in the holy Book of the Bible'.[14] On this analysis, the words of God were to be preferred to the words of the pagan Aristotle. Equally, however, a case could be made that God had communicated important truths in another book – the book of nature. Here, then, the contrast was between the paper books written by men, and the book of the creatures written by God. Paracelsus wrote that nature itself was a library of books that 'God himself wrote, made, and bound', and which on this account was vastly superior to anything produced in pagan antiquity.[15] To read the book of nature, for Paracelsus, was to rely on observations of the natural world, although this same metaphor

[12] See W. Schmidt-Biggeman, 'Apokalyptische Universalwissenschaft: Johann Heinrich Alsteds "Diatribe de mille annis apocalypticis"', *Pietismus und Neuzeit* 14 (1988), 50–71; L. E. Loemker, 'Leibniz and the Herborn Encyclopaedists', *JHI* 22 (1961), 323–38; R. G. Clouse, 'Johann Heinrich Alsted and English Millenarianism', *Harvard Theological Review* 62 (1969), 189–207; Howard Hotson, *Johann Heinrich Alsted 1588–1638: Between Renaissance, Reformation, and Universal Reform* (Oxford, 2000), esp. pp. 74–81.

[13] This triad of authorities may also be found in Campanella, Alsted, and one of the other Herborn encyclopaedists, John Bisterfeld. Loemker, 'Leibniz and the Herborn Encyclopaedists'.

[14] Jan Amos Comenius, *Naturall Philosophie Reformed by Divine Light: or, A Synopsis of Physicks* (London, 1651), Preface.

[15] Paracelsus, *Seven Defensiones* (1564), in *Four Treatises of Theophrastus von Hohenheim called Paracelsus*, tr. C. Lilian Tempkin et al. (Baltimore, 1941), p. 21.

was used in a variety of ways.[16] Finally, if it were assumed that the gift of reason was God-given, reliance on human reason could not be ruled out of the equation either – again, depending on one's views about its post-lapsarian reliability. Comenius's triad of 'sense, reason, and scripture' thus provided a suitable alternative to a slavish reliance upon the authority of Aristotle. In the hundred-year period that intervened between the religious reformations of the sixteenth century and the appearance of Comenius's influential works, however, the question of which of these three authorities should be the dominant one, or in what combination they might be used, was a matter of some debate. And there was a further possibility, hinted at in the title of Comenius's *Naturall Philosophie reformed by Divine Light* – that God might directly inspire certain individuals with knowledge, in much the same way that he had inspired Adam and the human authors of sacred scripture.

It is hardly surprising then, that the latter half of the sixteenth century witnessed a remarkable diversity of attempts to establish new foundations for human learning. One way of distinguishing these projects is to consider the emphasis placed on one or other of the range of available authorities: reason, scripture, experience, personal inspiration. A comprehensive survey of these projects, and of their appeals to distinct authorities, is a rather more ambitious task than is possible within the compass of this chapter. However, consideration can be given to representative examples of attempts to ground knowledge variously in reason, scripture, and personal inspiration, and of attempts to justify these appeals in the light of a renewed sense of the inherent limitations of the human mind.

VESTIGES OF HEAVENLY LIGHT

'All the works of God', Luther had declared, 'are unsearchable and unspeakable, no human sense can find them out'.[17] In our present condition, all that could be expected was an operative knowledge of the things that God had placed in the world for human use. It was Luther's sceptical conclusion that 'Here below all is incomprehensible.'[18] This seems to be a rather unpromising foundation upon which to construct a progressive view of natural knowledge. Yet, as historians have become increasingly aware, Lutheran thinkers in the German universities of the sixteenth century made major

---

[16] See Peter Harrison, '"The Book of Nature" and Early Modern Science', in K. van Berkel and Arjo Vanderjagt (eds.), *The Book of Nature in Early Modern and Modern History* (Leuven, 2006), pp. 1–27; *Bible and the Rise of Science*, pp. 193–204.
[17] Luther, *Table Talk*, LXIII (p. 28).   [18] *Ibid.*, CXXXII (p. 58).

contributions to the sciences, most conspicuously in the sphere of astronomy.[19] In certain respects this trend is not altogether surprising, for in spite of his reservations about the value of secular learning, Luther himself was reputed to have professed a particular fondness for the science of the heavens: 'I like astronomy and mathematics, which rely upon demonstrations and sure proofs.'[20]

There were good reasons for Luther's apparently uncharacteristic affirmation of this particular field of inquiry. First, there seems to be some biblical support for the utility of astronomy. According to the Genesis text, God had placed the lights in the firmament to be 'for signs and for seasons' (Gen. 1:14), thus providing a degree of legitimacy for the study of the heavens. It was also on account of their knowledge of astronomy that the kings from the East had been led to the home of the newborn Christ.[21] And there was a long-standing exegetical tradition according to which astronomy had been practised by the biblical patriarchs and prophets. Luther was clearly influenced by this tradition when he wrote that Adam and Eve had excelled at this science, and had possessed 'the most dependable knowledge of the stars and of the whole of astronomy'. This claim was to become one of the standard Lutheran defences of astronomy. [22] It was perhaps for these reasons that Luther accorded astronomy the highest praise, declaring it to have been 'the most ancient of sciences', 'the introducer of vast knowledge', and 'a fair gift of God'.[23]

[19] Peter Barker, 'The Role of Religion in the Lutheran Response to Copernicus', in M. Osler (ed.), *Rethinking the Scientific Revolution* (Cambridge, 2000), pp. 59–88; 'Theological Foundations of Kepler's Astronomy', *Osiris* 16 (2001), 88–113; Charlotte Methuen, *Kepler's Tübingen* (Aldershot, 1998); Kenneth J. Howell, *God's Two Books: Copernical Cosmology and Biblical Interpretation in Early Modern Science* (Notre Dame, 2002), ch. 2; Sachiko Kusukawa, *The Transformation of Natural Philosophy: The Case of Philip Melanchthon* (Cambridge, 1995); John W. Montgomery, 'Cross, Constellation and Crucible: Lutheran Astrology and Alchemy in the Age of the Reformation', *Ambix* 11 (1963), 65–86.
[20] Luther, *Table Talk*, DCCCXLI (p. 341). Some Luther scholars, Peter Meinhold in particular, have suggested that Luther's apparent enthusiasm for astronomy better reflects the later views of Melanchthon and that there is cause to suspect the influence of later editors. This is particularly so with the *Lectures on Genesis*. See LW I, pp. x–xii.
[21] Luther, 'Sermon for Epiphany', *Sermons*, I, 333; *Lectures in Genesis* 1:14 (LW I, 42–8). Cf. Calvin, *Commentary on Genesis* 1:14–16, 4:20, *Calvin's Commentaries* I, 83–7, 217–19; *Commentary on Isaiah* 44:25, *Calvin's Commentaries* VIII, 386f.
[22] Luther, *Lectures on Genesis*, LW I, 66; Melanchthon, 'On the Merit of the Art of Medicine (1548)' in *Orations on Philosophy and Education*, ed. Sachiko Kusukawa, tr. Christine F. Salazar (Cambridge, 1999), p. 173. Tycho Brahe similarly asserted that the study of the heavenly bodies was a venerable discipline which extended back to the time of Eden. Seth had passed on this knowledge which found its way to Abraham, who in turn had communicated it to the Egyptians during his sojourn there. The patriarchs had also transmitted astronomical knowledge to the later prophets. Howell, *God's Two Books*, pp. 78f., 82. Tycho's main source was Josephus.
[23] Luther, *Table Talk*, DCCCXLI, DCCCXLII (p. 341).

It is also possible to reconcile these concessions to astronomy with Luther's insistence on the negative noetic consequences of the Fall. When Luther asserts, for example, that 'here below' everything is incomprehensible, this particular phrase was not necessarily intended in a merely figurative sense. It is likely that it was Luther's conscious intention to exclude the celestial regions from the scope of his general scepticism. While it was universally agreed that the terrestrial realm had suffered corruption and deterioration as a consequence of Adam's Fall, the heavens were generally exempted from this fate. This was owing in part to the residual influence of Aristotle's firm dichotomy between the corruptible, terrestrial region below and the perfect and unchangeable celestial regions above.[24] Augustine had also written of the enduring importance of the heavens. God had stretched out the firmament above like a scroll for those below to read. In his exegetical writings, Augustine noted that the heavens represented the authority of scripture. The orderly motions of the heavenly lights thus continued to convey something of God's power. The regions above, he determined, had been 'kept from earthly corruption'.[25] Finally, the Aristotelian idea that genuine scientific knowledge was possible only of things that were in essence unchangeable also implied the superiority of a science of heavenly objects. Indeed, as we shall see, it would later be argued that on account of the mutability that it introduced to the sub-lunar realm, the Fall had all but made a strict science of terrestrial objects impossible.

There is little doubt that Luther was heir to these traditions. While his suggestion that things 'here below' are incomprehensible and knowledge of them but partial and incomplete, it did not follow that the same applied to things 'above', in the incorruptible regions of the heavens. Here, the works of God stood in their original, pristine condition, undamaged by the Fall and still serving as divinely instituted signs for those perceptive enough to read them. Not only did the heavens provide a glimpse into the past perfection that had once extended to the terrestrial regions, they also provided a foretaste of the life to come. At death, the souls of the blessed would journey through the heavenly spheres and see for themselves the perfections of God's creation. Indeed, it was a commonplace amongst Renaissance astronomers that the true causes of heavenly motion were available only to those who enjoyed a celestial vantage point and who

---

[24] See, e.g., Aristotle, *On the Universe*, 392a–b. For Luther's acceptance of the Aristotelian cosmos see *Lectures on Genesis*, LW 1, 30, 42–8. The idea of celestial corruptibility gradually gained ground in the sixteenth and seventeenth centuries, however. See Edward Grant, *Planets, Stars, and Orbs: The Medieval Cosmos, 1200–1687* (Cambridge, 1994), pp. 267f.

[25] Augustine, *Confessions* XIII.xv.16–18 (Chadwick edn, pp. 282f.).

could see first hand what actually transpired in the heavens. Regrettably, as one sixteenth-century writer put it, no one has 'come down from the heavens and brought back to us from there what he has seen'.[26] It was possibly sentiments such as these that inspired Galileo to furnish his first foray into astronomy with the rather presumptuous title *Sidereus Nuncius* – 'Messenger from the Stars'.[27]

But it was one thing to identify traces of a prelapsarian perfection in the heavens: quite another to suggest that fallen human beings, corrupted in both body and soul, could discover truths there. The question remained, Galileo's implicit confidence notwithstanding, whether the heavens could still be 'read' by fallen minds, or whether such a prospect had been reserved for the innocent Adam, angelic lectors, and the souls of the departed. One relevant consideration was the curious tradition that had attributed to Adam, among his various bodily perfections, an acute visual sense. It was often claimed that our first father had been assisted in his astronomical observations by this optical acuity. Luther had speculated that Adam, before his Fall, 'could have seen objects a hundred miles off better than we can see them at half a mile, and so in proportion with all the other senses'. Adam's vision, he asserted, surpassed that of the eagle and the lynx.[28] Adam could thus have shared the heavenly prospect of the angels, and would have known the truth about the causes of celestial motion on account of his sensory superiority. There were those in the seventeenth century, in England in particular, who believed that the deployment of such artificial instruments as telescopes and microscopes would redress the physical losses of the Fall, and restore in part what Adam had once known. More common in the tradition of Lutheran astronomy, however, was the attempt to identify, within the human soul, vestiges of the divine image that corresponded in some sense to the traces of divine wisdom that were still manifested in the heavens.

---

[26] Wursteisen, *New Questions in Peurbach's New Theoricas* (1568), quoted in Peter Barker and Bernard Goldstein, 'Realism and Instrumentalism in Sixteenth Century Astronomy: A Reappraisal', *Perspectives on Science* 6 (1998), 232–58 (249). Cf. Luther, 'Sermon for Epiphany', *Sermons* I, 330. Barker and Goldstein also point out that the putative instrumentalism of medieval and Renaissance astronomy was not a disciplinary principle, but a consequence of the fact that the relevant empirical data was not available to earthbound observers.

[27] On the correct translation of the title see Drake, *Discoveries and Opinions*, p. 19. For the contemporary understanding of Galileo as a celestial or angelic messenger see Pietro Redondi, 'From Galileo to Augustine', in Peter Machamer (ed.), *The Cambridge Companion to Galileo* (Cambridge, 1998), pp. 175–210 (p. 186).

[28] Martin Luther, *Table Talk*, CXXVIII (p. 57); *Lectures on Genesis 1–5*, LW I, 62; Cf. *Lectures on the Psalms*, LW XII, 117.

Luther himself may have believed that the self-evident axioms of mathematics represented just the kind of mental operations that had been uniquely insulated from the corrupting effects of the Fall. In Luther's own words, only in the realm of mathematics (which for him included astronomy) do we encounter 'demonstration and sure proofs'.[29] It is possible, then, that in the same manner in which Descartes would later seek indubitable foundations for his epistemological project, Luther located in the mathematical capacities of the mind the one faculty that still seemed to function with something like its original integrity. As we have already seen, there was a precedent for this view in Augustine's notion of the *vestigia trinitatis*. The vestiges of the divine image in the soul – memory, will, imagination – are able to discern traces of the divine image in the world. These latter consist primarily in the mathematical structure of things, and these in turn are most evident in the movements of the heavens. As far as I know, Luther nowhere explicitly set out his position in this manner. However, we find an argument very similar to this articulated by the Lutheran teacher and educational reformer Philipp Melanchthon (1497–1560).

Professor of Greek at the University of Wittenberg, Melanchthon was one of the most erudite figures in sixteenth-century Europe. While the mutual influence between Luther and Melanchthon was strong, the younger man remained faithful to a number of the principles of Renaissance humanism and took a more positive view of the achievements of pagan philosophers than Luther. Melanchthon frequently stressed the value to theology of philosophy and other 'profane disciplines', and in a number of points of doctrine was closer to both scholasticism and humanism than his co-reformers. Indeed, Calvin once wrote accusing him of being 'too philosophical' in his assessments of human nature.[30] This more positive view of the sciences was not totally divorced from the doctrine of original sin, for Melanchthon believed that formal learning provided an important check on the wayward impulses of fallen human beings. Political developments in the wake of the early stages of the German Reformation also played a role in shaping Melanchthon's convictions. He was particularly concerned lest the Church subscribe to an 'ignorant theology' of the kind professed by some of the more radical elements of the Reformation.[31] Such a philosophically uninformed theology lent itself to a social and political radicalism which, as such

---

[29] Luther, *Table Talk*, DCCCXLI (p. 341).

[30] Pitkin, 'The Protestant Zeno: Calvin and the Development of Melanchthon's Anthropology', *Journal of Religion* 84 (2004), 345–78 (347). For differences between Calvin and Melanchthon on the effects of sin see David Steinmetz, *Calvin in Context* (Oxford, 1995), pp. 29–32.

[31] Melanchthon, 'On Philosophy', *Orations*, p. 130. Melanchthon specified the Anabaptists.

events as the Peasants' War (1524–6) sufficiently attested, could result in law-lessness, rebellion, and civil upheaval. For this reason Melanchthon insisted that 'the Church has need of the entire cycle of sciences'.[32] Melanchthon also subscribed to the common view that Adam and the patriarchs had been adept at the various sciences. The most eminent parts of philosophy – including 'the teaching of the movements of the heavens' – had been prac-tised by Adam, Noah, Shem, Abraham, and Joseph, and they had 'passed on this knowledge to coming generations'.[33] This precedent provided the pur-suit of natural philosophy with a scriptural sanction. Finally, Melanchthon noted that God 'had commanded us to contemplate His work'.[34] This latter imperative implied that we had retained at least some ability to study the works of nature – and particularly those equipped with the eyes of faith – and ought to do so.

In none of this, however, does Melanchthon downplay the significance of the Fall. It is significant that in the very first credal statement of the Protestants – the Augsburg Confession (1530), authored by Melanchthon – the article on original sin appears second, preceded only by the article on God.[35] Our souls, wrote Melanchthon in the Preface to his edition of Aristotle's *On the Soul*, 'have been torn away from, and deprived of, the heavenly light'. When I think of this darkness of the soul, he confessed, 'I am almost out of my mind with horror'.[36] No truth-seeking enterprise could proceed without first attempting to identify those aspects of the soul that retained their original competence.

If the soul had kept that light and harmony which are bestowed upon it in its creation by divine providence there would be less need for other learned men, and it would examine its nature by its own sharpness of vision. However, now that – like some outstanding picture by Apelles bespattered with mud – it lies in the body, buried in hideous darkness, there is the greatest need for knowledge that should bring it forth and put it in our view, and show how great a wound the enemy inflicted on it, who overthrew the first ancestor of human kind, and show also the traces of the divine image on it, and the remains of the heavenly gifts.[37]

---

[32] *Ibid.*, p. 129. Cf. *Elements of Ethical Doctrine* I, in *Cambridge Translations of Renaissance Philosophical Texts* I, 110.

[33] Melanchthon, 'On the Merit of the Art of Medicine', *Orations*, p. 173; 'On Johannes Regiomon-tanus', *Orations*, p. 239. Like Luther, Melanchthon also commended astronomy on the basis of Genesis 1:14. 'Melanchthon to Grynaeus', 1531, *Corpus Reformatorum Philippi Melanchthonis*, ed. C. B. Bretschneider and H. E. Bindseil, 28 vols. (Halle, 1864), II, 531f.

[34] Melanchthon, 'Preface to the *Commentary on the Soul* ', *Orations*, p. 144. Cf. 'On the Life of Avicenna', *Orations*, p. 200; 'On the Life of Galen', *Orations*, p. 213.

[35] Augsburg Confession, ii.

[36] Melanchthon, 'Preface to the *Commentary on the Soul* ', *Orations*, pp. 146f.

[37] *Ibid.*, p. 146.

Here again we encounter the standard pattern for early modern epistemological enterprises: self-examination, assessment of the extent of the wound caused by sin, determination of what traces of the divine image remain. The outcomes of this procedure – and admittedly these outcomes vary among early modern thinkers – provide the foundations for any intellectual enterprise. Melanchthon came to believe that natural philosophy itself could assist in these foundational tasks. Adam and Eve would have been acutely conscious of the magnitude of their losses: 'since they had seen the earlier light and harmony of nature and were endowed with the greatest excellency of intellect, they could reckon more correctly the greatness of their disaster'.[38] Ignorant of how far they have fallen, and to what their knowledge can legitimately extend, their posterity are forced to rely on human learning. Hence, 'physics' – that is, natural philosophy – 'investigates and reveals however much the darkness of the human mind yields, and to what extent the mind can be augmented'.[39] If the scriptures teach us that we are fallen creatures, science can assist us in assessing the extent of our losses and in setting the appropriate limits to our knowledge. This is a slightly different perspective from that which will be developed by English Calvinists, for whom the scope of natural philosophy is itself determined by theological anthropology. Nonetheless, it is consistent with the widespread early modern view that human learning can play a positive role in reversing the losses of Adam's lapse.

As for 'the traces of the divine image' and 'the remains of the heavenly gifts', these provide grounds for hope that at least some philosophical enterprises might not be entirely in vain. Indeed, Melanchthon goes so far as to suggest that human beings retain something like a 'natural light'. While our souls have been 'deprived of the heavenly light', there remains 'a light . . . given to us by divine providence'.[40] This light is variously identified as the image of God, 'common notions', 'speculative principles' or 'natural law'.[41] These abilities, which Melanchthon describes as having been 'implanted in the minds of men', encompassed a knowledge of moral

[38] *Ibid.*, pp. 146f.
[39] Melanchthon, *Initia doctrinae physicae* (1543), in *Corpus Reformatorum* VIII, 179, quoted in Daniel M. Gross, 'Melanchthon's Rhetoric and the Practical Origins of Reformation Human Science', *History of the Human Sciences* 13 (2000), 5–22 (10).
[40] 'Preface to the *Commentary on the Soul*', *Orations*, p. 146; 'On Plato', *Orations*, p. 194.
[41] *Ibid.*, pp. 146, 162; *The Elements of Ethical Doctrine* 1, in *Cambridge Translations of Renaissance Philosophical Texts*, 1, 112. See also Christoph Strohm, 'Zugänger zum Naturrecht bei Melanchthon', in Günter Frank (ed.), *Der Theologe Melanchthon* (Stuttgart, 2000), pp. 339–56; Howell, *God's Two Books*, pp. 51f. For a helpful analysis of the various meanings of 'natural law' in Melanchthon see Charlotte Methuen, '*Lex Naturae* and *Ordo Naturae* in the Thought of Philip Melanchthon', *Reformation and Renaissance Review* 3 (2000), 110–25.

laws along with the laws of mathematics, logic, and physics.[42] While our moral intuitions had been irreparably damaged by the Fall, our 'notions of number and order' remain relatively intact, as seen in our ability to assent to such eternal mathematical truths as 'two plus two equals four'.[43]

Our retention of this one vestige of our prelapsarian abilities would be in vain, however, if the world remained opaque to mathematical interpretation. However, just as traces of the image of God could still be found in the mathematical abilities of the mind, they were also evident in the one region of the cosmos that had not suffered corruption on account of Adam's lapse.[44] Like Luther, and indeed most of his contemporaries, Melanchthon believed that the heavens were perfect and unchangeable. The celestial regions beyond the sphere of the moon were made of an incorruptible substance – the quintessence – and the heavenly bodies moved along their divinely ordained courses with an inexorable and eternal mathematical precision. As a consequence, the heavens were immune from the terrestrial disorder that had resulted from the sin of Adam and which had veiled God's original designs on earth.[45] For Melanchthon, then, vestiges of the divine image were evident both in the pristine perfections of the heavens and in the mathematical and dialectical faculties of the soul. The application of our mathematical abilities to the ordered movements of the heavenly bodies thus held out the prospect of genuine knowledge, for this human intellectual faculty and this subject matter were the only features of the creation, on Melanchthon's account, that had escaped the otherwise universal corruption that had ensued after the Fall.

Mathematical astronomy, then, was the one science in which fallen human beings could express some confidence. More than this, it could provide the foundation for a more comprehensive understanding of the divine order as manifested in other spheres. Melanchthon cherished the

---

[42] These are examples of an internalised 'divine law'. Philipp Melanchthon, *Loci Communes* (1543), tr. J. Preuss (St Louis, 1992), p. 70. See also Methuen, '*Lex Naturae* and *Ordo Naturae*'.

[43] Melanchthon, 'On Anatomy', in *Orations*, pp. 160f. See also Methuen, '*Lex Naturae* and *Ordo Naturae*', p. 121; Sachiko Kusukawa, '*Vinculum concordiae*: Lutheran Method by Philip Melanchthon', in Eckhard Kessler, Daniel Di Liscia and Charlotte Methuen (eds.), *Method and Order in the Renaissance Philosophy of Nature* (Aldershot, 1997), pp. 337–54.

[44] 'It is true that this entire beautiful machine of the world is a temple of God, and that traces of the Architect are engraved in many parts of it, but even more so man is the temple of God'. 'On Anatomy', *Orations*, p. 162.

[45] Melanchthon, *Initia Doctrinae Physicae*, in *Corpus Reformatorum* XIII, 253, 392–400. Cf. Daneau, *Wonderful Woorkmanship*, fol. 82v. On the significance of this see Methuen, 'The Role of the Heavens in the Thought of Philip Melanchthon,' *JHI* 57 (1996), 385–403. Nicodemus Frischlin, who lectured in mathematics and astronomy at Tübingen in the late 1560s and early 1570s, explicitly stated that the earth was cursed after the Fall, but not the heavens. *De astronomicae artis* (Frankfurt, 1586), pp. 6f. See Methuen, *Kepler's Tübingen*, pp. 90ff., 118–20.

hope that these residual mathematical abilities and their application to the study of the heavens would assist in the restoration of our original moral instincts, for through the study of the mathematical regularity of the universe we might also come to understand that God is the lawgiver who had originally instituted a parallel moral order below: 'like the order of the motions of the heavens . . . so too the whole of this political order, the bond of marriage, empires, the distinction of states, contracts, judgements, punishments, indeed all most true statutes originate from God'.[46] From a discernment of the mathematical order of the heavens we could proceed to a knowledge of the moral order below – a moral order that before the Fall had been as conspicuous as the regularities in the motions of the celestial bodies. (In a sense, Kant's later coupling of 'the starry skies above' and 'the moral law within' had precedents in the thought of Melanchthon.) Melanchthon's position is entirely consistent with Luther's conception of vocation, understood as living in conformity to a natural law that to a limited extent can still be discerned in a fallen world.[47] Moral philosophy, for Melanchthon, could also still conform to the syllogistic logical structures that characterised Aristotelian *scientia*.[48] Melanchthon also thought that study of the heavens would provide a key to unlock secrets of other terrestrial sciences. This was because he retained a belief in the existence of causal connections between the movements and positions of the heavenly bodies and earthly affairs. The importance of astrological influences on the human body, to take a single example, made knowledge of the heavens directly relevant to medicine.[49] Melanchthon was ultimately optimistic about the prospects of a relatively complete science. 'If the inner workings of nature can be ascertained', he speculated, 'then our conception of physics will be truly vast, our knowledge will be immense and divine'.[50] This was in contrast to the circumscribed knowledge of the ancients, which was 'very thin and within narrow limits'.[51] But even for true believers, complete knowledge of certain matters was to be postponed until in 'that heavenly school, the Architect shows us the image of the entire workings'.[52]

---

[46] Melanchthon, *De legibus* (1535), *Corpus Reformatorum* XI, 912, quoted in Methuen, '*Lex Naturae* and *Ordo Naturae*', p. 121. See also Barker and Goldstein, 'Theological Foundations of Kepler's Astronomy', p. 95.

[47] Paul Althaus, *The Ethics of Martin Luther*, tr. Robert Schultz (Philadelphia, 1972), ch. 2.

[48] Melanchthon, *The Elements of Ethical Doctrine* I, in *Cambridge Translations of Renaissance Philosophical Texts*, I, 110f.

[49] Melanchthon, 'On the Merit of the Art of Medicine', *Orations*, 173.

[50] Melanchthon, *Initia*, *Corpus Reformatorum* XIII, 179.

[51] Melanchthon, 'Preface to the Book on the Soul', *Orations*, p. 153.

[52] Melanchthon, 'On Anatomy', *Orations*, p. 158.

Melanchthon's general position is that education can compensate to some degree for what has been lost to the human race as a consequence of the Fall. This is not inconsistent with Augustine's view that human social institutions derive their necessity and legitimacy from the fallen condition of the earthly city. Luther also acknowledged the importance of temporal political authorities as means to rein in the sinful impulses of fallen creatures. This is most conspicuous in his 'two kingdoms doctrine' and in his support for the German princes during the Peasants' War.[53] For Melanchthon, the remnants of natural light provided a sufficient guide to establish the laws of civil society. Those laws, however, had little to do with the Gospel and with that Kingdom of Christ to which all true Christians belong. Melanchthon was to emphasise that the study of nature, inasmuch as it bore witness to the inherent lawfulness of the whole created order, could play a subsidiary role in moral and political philosophy.[54] The relative purity of our mathematical intuitions can lead us to recover in part our rather more decayed moral intuitions. This, in turn, makes possible the creation of a stable society. As Charlotte Methuen writes, 'this underlying sense of order . . . shapes Melanchthon's understanding of law as orderly behaviour, supporting orderly hierarchical society'.[55]

If Melanchthon's primary concern was with the problem of social and moral order in a fallen world, his ideas about the purity of mathematical conceptions and the importance of astronomy were to have some influence on the most important Lutheran astronomer of the sixteenth century, Johannes Kepler. According to Melanchthon, our mathematical abilities represent the vestiges not merely of particular prelapsarian intellectual abilities, but of the divine image itself. As such, they should convey something of God's nature: specifically that God is a mathematician and geometer. The 'architectonic mind', wrote Melanchthon, 'transmitted its light and its wisdom into human beings', from which we can conclude 'that God is a comprehending mind, ordering numbers and grades of things'.[56] The notion of God as a geometer was of course by no means new. Augustine had

---

[53] See, e.g., Luther, 'Secular Authority: To What Extent it should be Obeyed', in *Works of Martin Luther* III, 223–73.

[54] Melanchthon wrote that no one could be a master of method without studying Aristotle. If the Greek philosopher were to be neglected, 'a great turmoil of doctrines would follow'. 'On Aristotle', *Orations*, p. 205. For this reason Melanchthon promoted the study of Aristotelian logic in the Lutheran universities.

[55] Methuen, '*Lex Naturae* and *Ordo Naturae*', p. 123. Cf. Peter Barker, 'Kepler's Epistemology', in Kessler, Di Liscia, and Methuen (eds.), *Method and Order in Renaissance Philosophy*, pp. 354–68, esp. p. 359.

[56] Melanchthon, *De legibus, Corpus Reformatorum* IX, 908, quoted in Methuen, '*Lex Naturae* and *Ordo Naturae*', p. 122.

made such a view authoritative with his frequent assertions that 'God has ordered everything by number, measure, and weight'.[57] The idea that the divine image consists in mathematical abilities, and the inference that God is a mathematician and geometer were fundamental premises of Kepler's astronomy.

MATHEMATICAL CERTAINTIES

Johannes Kepler (1571–1630) was educated in Tübingen where he encountered the ideas of Melanchthon through the writings of Jacob Heerbrand (1521–1600), professor of theology and later Chancellor of the university.[58] Kepler subscribed to the common view that Adam and Eve had once possessed a perfect knowledge of nature, but that this had been lost after the Fall. Hence perennial confusion about the movements of the heavens and the meanings of celestial signs were to be attributed to Adam's lapse.[59] Again, however, recognition of the existence of corresponding images of God in the world and the human soul could provide the starting point for a true knowledge of the heavens and of their creator. Kepler followed Melanchthon in asserting that mathematical and geometrical truths are known by the remnants of natural light.[60] Geometry 'is coeternal with God, and by shining forth in the divine mind supplied patterns to God . . . for the furnishing of the world, so that it should become best and most beautiful and above all most like to the Creator. Indeed all spirits, souls and minds are images of God the Creator if they have been put in command each of their own bodies, to govern, move, increase, preserve, and also particularly to propagate them'. Kepler writes:

Then since they have embraced a certain pattern of the creation in their functions, they also observe the same laws along with the Creator in their operations, having derived them from geometry. Also they rejoice in the same proportions which God used, wherever they have found them, whether by bare contemplation, whether by the interposition of the senses, in things which are subject to sensation, whether

---

[57] Augustine, *Confessions* x.xii.9; *Sermon 8.1* (*Works* iii/i, 240). On these Neoplatonic elements of Melanchthon's thought see Günter Frank, 'Melanchthon and the tradition of Neoplatonism', in Jürgen Helm and Annette Winkelmann (eds.), *Religious Confessions and the Sciences in the Sixteenth Century* (Leiden, 2001), pp. 3–18.

[58] Methuen, *Kepler's Tübingen*, pp. 136f.; Barker and Goldstein, 'Theological Foundations'.

[59] Kepler, *Gesammelte Werke*, 20 vols., ed. M. Caspar et al. (Munich, 1937), iv, pp. 159–60. I am grateful to Russell Kleckley for this reference. 'Stealing golden vessels: Johannes Kepler on worldly knowledge and Christian truth', AAR Annual Meeting, Denver, November, 2001.

[60] Kepler, *De quantitatibus*, cited in Barker, 'Kepler's Epistemology', p. 360; See also *Apologia Pro Tychone contra Ursum*, tr. in N. Jardine, *The Birth of History and Philosophy of Science* (Cambridge, 1988), p. 144.

even without reflection by the mind, by an instinct which is concealed and was created with them, or whether God Himself has expressed these proportions in bodies and in motions invariably.[61]

The correspondences between the persisting divine image in the mind, and the triune images of the creator in the cosmos thus made possible an *a priori* knowledge of the mathematical ordering of the cosmos. In a well-known passage Kepler thus announced that he had long pondered three fundamental questions relating to the number, size, and motions of the heavenly orbs, and 'why they were so, and not otherwise'. His conclusion was that the 'beautiful commensurability (*harmonia*) of static objects: the sun, the fixed stars, and the intervening medium' was mirrored in the relation of 'God the Father, the Son, and the Holy Spirit'. Kepler thus draws upon the Augustinian view that vestiges of the Trinity are apparent in the created order.[62]

Those early modern thinkers who believed in the persistence of natural light after the Fall thus typically expressed confidence in *a priori* hypothesising about the natural world, on the basis of the congruence between human and divine reason. Historians Peter Barker and Bernard Goldstein observe in relation to Kepler's astronomy that 'it is the confidence that God's geometrical plan for the world is accessible through the natural light of reason that underlines the *a priori* demonstration of the structure of the world, and the defence of Copernicus's cosmic scheme'.[63] Such 'rationalist' solutions to the problem of knowledge thus correlate to some degree with optimistic views about the persistence of natural light after the Fall. The Cartesian approach was to conform to this general pattern.

There was, however, one difficulty with the discipline of mathematical astronomy, at least as it was traditionally conceived. While it was possible to arrive at demonstrative certainty, there was some doubt about whether mathematical astronomy actually described the physical state of the heavens, or merely provided a convenient device for calculating the positions of the heavenly bodies. During the Middle Ages the study of the heavenly bodies had been conducted within the two distinct disciplines of mathematics and natural philosophy. As a mathematical discipline (typified for medieval

---

[61] Kepler, *Harmony of the World*, tr. and introduced by E. J. Aiton, A. M. Duncan, and J. V. Field (Philadelphia, 1997), p. 146.

[62] Kepler, *Mysterium Cosmographicum*, 1596, p. 6, quoted in Barker and Goldstein, 'Theological Foundations'. Calvin, as might be expected, denied the doctrine of the *vestigia trinitatis*. Calvin, *Institutes* I.xv.4 (McNeill I, 190). On survivals of this idea during the Renaissance see Dennis R. Klinck, '*Vestigia Trinitatis* in Man and his Works in the English Renaissance', *JHI* 42 (1981), 13–27.

[63] Barker and Goldstein, 'Theological Foundations', pp. 25f. See also Methuen, *Kepler's Tübingen*, pp. 209f.

thinkers by Ptolemy's *Almagest*) astronomy concerned itself with predicting the movements and positions of the celestial objects, and although ideally this would cohere with what was believed to be the true physical state of the cosmos, this was not always possible. In other words, mathematical astronomy could be understood instrumentally, and often was.[64] Aquinas could thus write that mathematical hypotheses are not necessarily true, because even though they might 'save the phenomena' – that is, give valid predictions of the positions of the heavenly bodies, there might well be other models that would also give similar predictions.[65] Aquinas's concern here was to reconcile the mathematical astronomy of Ptolemy with an Aristotelian natural philosophy that sought to provide a true and causal account of the motions of the heavenly bodies. Later, the Lutheran theologian Andreas Osiander (1498–1552) was to write a Preface to Copernicus's *De Revolutionibus*, that expressed a similar view: 'When different hypotheses are offered as explanations for the same phenomenon', he wrote, 'the astronomer will take as his first choice that hypothesis which is the easiest to grasp', while 'the philosopher' will seek 'the semblance of the truth'.[66]

So the appeal to mathematical certainties as a category of knowledge immune from the corrupting influence of the Fall was only half of the story. A further condition needed to be added to the certainty of mathematical proofs, and that was that they actually describe physical reality. In any case, the instrumentalist view of mathematical astronomy was not ideal for Melanchthon's purposes, because in order to draw analogies between the law of heavenly bodies and the natural law, it was necessary to provide actual descriptions of the motions of heavenly bodies, and not just mathematical models of those motions. For this reason, Melanchthon and his Wittenberg colleagues adopted a moderate realism.[67] In Kepler's case, the

[64] The distinction reflected Aristotle's view that mathematics did not deal with real entities, but natural philosophy did. *Metaphysics* 1025b–1026a. For Aristotle, the application of mathematics to real objects took place in the 'subordinate sciences', or in what Aquinas would later call the 'middle sciences'. *Posterior Analytics* 78b34–79a; *Physics* 194a. See also W. R. Laird, *The Scientiae Mediae in Medieval Commentaries on Aristotle's Posterior Analytics* (Toronto, 1983). Not all scholars agree on the extent to which astronomy was conceived of instrumentally, however. The classic statement of the instrumentalist position is Pierre Duhem, *To Save the Phenomena: An Essay on the Idea of Physical Theory from Plato to Galileo* [1908] (Chicago, 1969). For discussions see Lindberg, *Beginnings of Western Science*, p. 261; Barker and Goldstein, 'Realism and Instrumentalism'.

[65] See C. H. Lohr, 'The Medieval Interpretation of Aristotle', p. 94, in CHLMP, pp. 80–98.

[66] Nicholas Copernicus, *On the Revolutions*, ed. Jerzy Dobrzycki, tr. Edward Rosen (Baltimore, 1978), p. xx. See also Howell, *God's Two Books*, p. 46. Cf. Robert Westman, 'The Astronomer's Role in the Sixteenth Century: A Preliminary Study', *History of Science* 23 (1980), 105–47; Owen Gingerich, 'Truth in Science: Proof, Persuasion, and the Galileo Affair', *Science and Christian Belief* 16 (2004), 13–26.

[67] Robert Westman, 'The Melanchthon Circle, Rheticus, and the Wittenberg Interpretation of the Copernican Theory', *Isis* 66 (1975), 164–93 (167).

reality of mathematical relations was guaranteed by the fact that God had instantiated a mathematical order in the cosmos, and that mathematical ideas in the divine mind were reflected by that aspect of the human soul that bore the impress of the divine image. Our mathematical ideas are thus reflections of God's ideas, and this is what gives us confidence that they can be applied to physical reality. Kepler was not unaware that his claims for mathematics would be controversial. 'I shall have the physicists [i.e. the "natural philosophers"] against me in these chapters, because I have deduced the natural properties of the planets from immaterial things and mathematical figures', he confesses. His justification for departing from the instrumentalist understanding was the argument that God had used mathematical ideas when designing the universe: 'God the Creator, since he is a mind, and does what he wants, is not prohibited, in attributing powers and appointing circles, from having regard to things which are either immaterial or based on imagination'.[68] Our access to divine ideas, via the faculty of the light of nature, thus gives us confidence in mathematical knowledge.

Galileo presented similar arguments to support his contention that the Copernican hypothesis was not merely one of a possible number of mathematical hypotheses that saved the phenomena, but that it was a true physical account of the solar system. Mathematical relations are real, Galileo insisted, and God relied upon them in designing the cosmos. In intuiting mathematical relations, human minds thus participate in the ideas of God, and while our knowledge falls short of God's in its extent, what mathematical truths we do know, we know with a certainty that equals God's:

the human intellect does understand some of them [mathematical truths] perfectly, and thus in these it has as much absolute certainty as Nature itself has. Of such are the mathematical sciences alone; that is, geometry and arithmetic, in which the Divine intellect indeed knows infinitely more propositions, since it knows all. But with regard to those few which the human intellect does understand, I believe that its knowledge equals the Divine in objective certainty, for here it succeeds in understanding necessity, beyond which there can be no greater certainty.[69]

In making these kinds of claims both Kepler and Galileo show signs of the influence of Renaissance Platonism, possibly mediated by Marsilio Ficino.[70] Insisting on the role of the divine mind in the creation and asserting the reality of *mathematica* thus amounted to an important departure from the standard Aristotelian position. To this extent, Platonism, or at least certain

---

[68] Kepler, *Mysterium Cosmographicum*, p. 123.

[69] Galileo, *Dialogue concerning the Two Chief World Systems*, p. 118; cf. p. 11.

[70] James Hankins, 'Galileo, Ficino, and Renaissance Platonism', in Jill Kraye and M. W. F. Stone (eds.), *Humanism and Early Modern Philosophy* (London, 2000), pp. 209–37 (p. 213).

aspects of it, contributed to the finding of a solution to the problem of knowledge and its foundations.

The examples of Melanchthon and Kepler show that vestiges of the original created light could be sought in the human mind and in the physical universe, providing a justification for the application of our mathematical abilities to the heavens. It is significant that this singular emphasis on mathematics was a distinctive feature of the universities of Lutheran Germany in the middle decades of the sixteenth century. Indeed, Peter Ramus remarked on this phenomenon in 1577, observing that Melanchthon had followed in the footsteps of Plato in his revival of mathematical studies.[71] But vestiges of the perfections of our prelapsarian past could also be sought elsewhere. Ancient traditions might contain remnants of the complete encyclopaedic knowledge that Adam had once possessed. If this were so, scholarly historical research into the records of past civilisations might recover these remains. Amongst the historical records of past civilisations, none was thought to be as ancient or authoritative as the Christian scriptures. Those writers inspired by Calvinism, who were less inclined to believe in the continuing efficacy of natural light, could thus look to scripture to provide a foundation not only for their theology, but also in some instances for a modest and abridged natural philosophy. The very first sentence of the Westminster Confession (1646) sets out the limitations of 'the light of nature', before asserting the reliability of God's revelation in scripture.[72] Some were to adapt this principle to the knowledge of nature. The first books of the bible in which were related the earliest history of the world were said to contain the natural philosophy of Moses who, on many accounts, had been the chief beneficiary of Adam's philosophical legacy. Advocates of a 'Mosaic philosophy' sought in the pages of scripture an alternative 'light' that could reasonably be regarded as immune from the corruption that had tainted the rest of the fallen world.

ADAM, MOSES, HERMES, SOLOMON

In his 1578 translation of Lambert Daneau's *Physica Christiana* (Christian Physics), Englishman Thomas Twyne summarised the chief argument of the work he was rendering into his native tongue: true natural philosophy is 'founded upon the assured round of Gods word and holy Scriptures', all other putative philosophies being 'established vpon the ficle foundation of

---

[71] Westman, 'The Melanchthon Circle', 171f.
[72] Westminster Confession, I.i. It is also significant that the first anthropological statements of this confession deal with the Fall and its consequences. See section VI.

mans reason & iudgement'.[73] Twyne's concise description applies to a whole genre of natural philosophy that emerged in the wake of the Protestant Reformation, known variously as 'Mosaic Philosophy', 'Christian Philosophy', or 'Pious Philosophy'.[74] The premise of these enterprises was simple: given the dubious nature of other possible foundations of knowledge – reason and experience – certainty must be sought in the more reliable foundation of scripture. Mosaic philosophers extended the principle *sola scriptura* beyond the circumscribed realm of theology to the sphere of natural philosophy.

Daneau (1530–95), whose *Physica Christiana* typifies the genre, was one of the most important of the first generation of Calvinist theologians. Educated by Calvin himself, he became professor of theology at Geneva and briefly assumed the chair of theology at the newly established University of Leiden.[75] He is best known today for his systematisation of Calvinist ethics and for his authorship of *Les Sorciers* (1564) – a dialogue on witchcraft that provides a vivid account of the nefarious practices of witches and of the 'devil's marks' that betray their true identity. Daneau shared the earlier reformers' views on the deficiencies of pagan learning. In his moral writings he argued that since none of the ancients had taken cognisance of the Fall, the precepts of classical moral theory were completely useless for postlapsarian human beings. Morality was to be grounded not in 'natural light' or 'natural law', but in the more secure foundation of what God had revealed to Moses on Mount Sinai. The Ten Commandments set down in the book of Exodus were thus to provide the foundation for moral philosophy.[76] Daneau held a similar view about the proper foundation for natural philosophy. The scientific ambitions of Aristotle and his followers were only possible because of their ignorance of their own fallibility. Because of this they had overreached themselves: 'That minde is more to be commended which knoweth it [sic] owne infirmitie, rather than that, whiche not perceiuyng the same, searcheth after the motions of the Planets, and the walles of the worlde, the foundations of the earth, and the top of the

[73] Lambert Daneau, *Wonderfull Woorkmanship*, Epistle of the Translator.
[74] For the trend to biblically oriented natural philosophy see Harrison, *Bible and the Rise of Science*, ch. 4; Ann Blair, 'Mosaic Physics and the Search for a Pious Natural Philosophy in the Late Renaissance', *Isis* 91 (2000), 32–58. The genre was first described by Johann Brucker, *Historia Critica Philosophiae* (Leipzig, 1743), IV, I, 3, 3 (pp. 610–43).
[75] For Daneau's life and career see Oliver Fatio, *Méthode et théologie: Lambert Daneau et les débuts de la scolastique réformée* (Geneva, 1976).
[76] Daneau, *Isagoges Christianae pars quinta, quae est de homine* (Geneva, 1588), fol. 110v; *Ethices Christianae libri tres* (Geneva, 1577), lib. ii. For Daneau's Calvinistic ethics, see Fatio, *Méthode et théologie*. For a brief comparison of Melanchthon and Daneau on this issue see Jill Kraye, 'Moral Philosophy', CHRP, pp. 303–86 (pp. 323f.).

heauens.'[77] Heathen philosophers, he insisted, were 'deeply drowned in darknes, [for] they were destitute of God's woord, that is to say, the true light of knowledge'.[78] The true light, for Daneau, was to be found not in the human soul, but in the scriptures.

The notion that scripture could provide an alternative 'light' for the interpretation of nature derived directly from Daneau's old teacher. In the *Institutes*, Calvin argued that the 'brightness which is borne in upon the eyes of all men' proves incapable of discerning the truth about nature without 'another and better help'. That help is nothing other than the 'light of his [God's] Word'. Calvin also compared scripture to spectacles that augment the dim remains of natural light.[79] For Daneau, too, natural light was too insecure a foundation for a reliable natural philosophy, hence his maxim that 'general natural philosophy' is to be based on neither fallible human faculties nor the writings of the ancients but is to be learned from holy scripture.[80] Regrettably, the Fathers and scholastics had not always been so discriminating in their choice of sources, falsely assuming the integrity of reason and introducing doctrines derived from the 'rabble of blind philosophers'.[81] This had led to a corruption of Christian doctrines. What was needed was a reformation of natural philosophy – one that would give rise to a truly Christian enterprise that would complement a reformed theology. If Luther and Calvin had sought to correct the theological corruptions of Catholicism by appealing to the authority of scripture, Daneau set himself an additional goal: 'to refourme the opinions of the Philosophers by the woord of God'.[82]

One of the difficulties faced by a scriptural natural philosophy was whether it could attain the degree of certainty that, according to Aristotle, was the mark of the highest science. While the particular prescriptions of Aristotelian science came into question in the sixteenth century, the Greek philosopher's conception of what counted as science proved more tenacious. The *Posterior Analytics* had laid down an ideal of scientific knowledge as demonstrative and certain. In this way were the sciences

---

[77] Daneau, *Wonderfull Woorkmanship*, fol. 4v. Daneau alludes here to passages in Augustine, *Trinity*, Bk IV, Prologue. The reference to the 'walls of the world' etc. comes from Lucretius, *De rerum naturae* 2, 73.

[78] From Twyne's tr., *Wonderful Woorkmanship*, sig. Aiii r.

[79] Calvin, *Institutes*, I.vi.1 (Beveridge I, 69f.). Cf. I.xiv.1 (Beveridge I, 160); *Commentary on Genesis*, Introduction, *Calvin's Commentaries* I, 62. Calvin also draws on the imagery of John I, in which the Word is referred to as 'the light of men', and Psalm 119:105: 'Thy word is a lamp to my feet and a light to my path'. *Institutes* I.xv.4 (McNeill I, 190); II.vii.12 (McNeill I, 361).

[80] Daneau, *Wonderfull Woorkmanship*, fol. 4v.

[81] *Ibid.*, sig. Aiii v.   [82] *Ibid.*, fol. 13v.

distinguished from mere 'opinion'.[83] The idea that science, in its purest form, dealt with demonstrative and certain truths was still promoted by influential figures during the Renaissance and well into the seventeenth century.[84] This was the kind of certainty sought by Kepler and Galileo. The conundrum that confronted advocates of a scriptural science was that the truths of revelation, most of which were contingent historical facts, did not admit of the demonstrative certainty of logically deduced propositions. Aquinas had addressed this problem by suggesting that truths of revelation derive their certainty from their source – God or the Church – thus providing alternative grounds for holding propositions to be certain.[85] In due course, Protestant theologians were to add that scriptural propositions also counted as 'scientific' knowledge. Georg Joachim Rheticus (1514–76), who served for a time as professor of mathematics and astronomy at Wittenberg, thus insisted that all passages of scripture, without distinction, bore the force of demonstration.[86] This was also the view taken by a number of Protestant theologians who were concerned to attribute the scientific status usually reserved for universal conclusions to the singular historical facts that made up the Christian revelation.[87] They did not, however, follow Aquinas in proposing two distinct kinds of certitude – one for the truths of faith and one for natural truths – but rather attempted to deny that

---

[83] Aristotle, *Posterior Analytics* 71b–72b. On the fortunes of Aristotle's idea of *scientia* in the Middle Ages and Renaissance see Charles Burnett, 'Scientific Speculations', in Peter Dronke (ed.), *A History of Twelfth-Century Philosophy* (Cambridge, 1992), pp. 151–76; Eileen Serene, 'Demonstrative Science', CHLMP, pp. 496–518; Nicholas Jardine, 'Epistemology of the Sciences', CHRP, pp. 685–771.

[84] For an excellent discussion of such notions as certainty, probability, opinion and hypothesis in seventeenth-century England see Barabara Shapiro, *Probability and Certainty in the Seventeenth-Century England* (Princeton, 1983). Also see Jardine, *Birth of History and Philosophy of Science*. For primary sources, see *Encyclopaedia Britannica*, 3 vols. (Edinburgh, 1771), s.v. 'Science' (III, 570a). Cf. Chambers, *Cyclopaedia*, I, vii.

[85] Aquinas, SCG 1.6. Aquinas distinguished between two kinds of certitude. We are certain of truths of faith on account of their cause, i.e. God. We are certain of scientific truths on account of their subject, i.e. certain premises. Aquinas concludes that 'in so far as science, wisdom and understanding are intellectual virtues, they are based upon the natural light of reason, which falls short of the certitude of God's word, on which faith is founded'. ST 2a2ae. 4, 8. Cf. ST 1a. 1, 5. For a recent discussion of this issue see Shawn Floyd, 'Achieving a Science of Sacred Doctrine', *Heythrop Journal* 47 (2006), 1–15.

[86] 'For it is written that one shall not diverge from the words of the Lord, either to the right or to the left, and that the Word itself has the force of demonstration, since it has been given to us by God.' Georg Rheticus, *G. J. Rheticus' Treatise on the Holy Scripture and the Motion of the Earth*, ed. and tr. Reijer Hooykaas (Amsterdam, 1984), pp. 65f. The circularity of this piece of reasoning seems to have escaped Rheticus, but his view was not uncommon, particularly amongst Protestant thinkers for whom the authority of scripture was paramount.

[87] Charles Lohr, 'Metaphysics', CHRP, p. 633. The problem addressed here was later to emerge in the eighteenth century as 'Lessing's dictum', which holds that the accidental truths of history can never become the proofs of necessary truths of reason.

the human mind was capable of arriving at certain premises and arguing infallibly from them.

This was the position adopted by Daneau, who argued that 'those things which in this art and knowledge wee learne out of Gods woorde, are most sure and most true, as grounded upon a most certaine foundation'. By way of contrast, claims made by merely human authors were accorded a lesser degree of certainty: 'they are not so sure and firm, bycause they bee only established by mans sence, and reason, which two thinges, are no undoubted and assured groundes. For mans reason is many times: and his senses are most times deceiuved.'[88] Viewed in this light, Daneau's intention seems to have been to provide natural philosophy with a more secure foundation than fallible reason or sense experience by grounding it in the revealed truths of scripture.

If Daneau had thought that scriptural natural philosophy was certain, it was nevertheless admitted to be limited in its scope. According to Daneau, in his 'Treatise of Naturall Philosophie' Moses had restricted himself to a single class of objects, treating 'of visible thinges onely'. The true essential nature of creatures, moreover, was now almost impossible to discern, for like the human mind they had lost their primitive perfection. Thus, in the New Testament St Paul does not 'define a creature by its owne true nature, but only by the qualitie and accident which indeede is in it', creatures 'havinge nowe lost their full and perfect nature in part, by reason of mans transgression'.[89] The modesty of the claims of the biblical philosophers was thus contrasted with the boastful pretensions of the pagan writers, whose 'rashnes in pronouncinge certainely of uncertaine things' resulted not only from a lack of awareness of their own limitations, but also from 'a moste stronge poison of humane ambition'.[90] Such ambition had led philosophers to indulge in a corrupt curiosity, and to seek knowledge that transcended their limited human capacities. Aspirations such as these, Daneau was to write in his famous work on witchcraft, led some to form a pact with the devil: 'Others some there be, who being borne away with fonde vanitie of a proude mynde, whyle they are not able to containe themselues within the compas of mans vnderstanding & capacitie, do yeelde themselves vassals to Satan'.[91]

Daneau's efforts are significant not because they were spectacularly suc-cessful – they were not, at least if gauged by their contribution to scientific achievements of the age. However, they do provide some precedents for

[88] Daneau, *Wonderfull Woorkmanship*, fol. 13v.   [89] *Ibid.*, fols. 17v, 18r.
[90] *Ibid.*, fol. 13v.   [91] Daneau, *A Dialogue of witches* (London, 1575), sigs. E2v–E3r.

the development of the mixed discipline of physico-theology in the seventeenth century.[92] Daneau's 'Christian Physics' also exemplifies a growing tendency in this period to appeal to scriptural authority as a means of legitimating natural philosophy. While it is sometimes assumed, usually on the basis of Galileo's treatment at the hands of the Inquisition, that scriptural authority was typically ranged against the new philosophies, in fact this was by no means the standard pattern. Consonance with scripture became an important means of supporting new philosophical speculations. Indeed, it is generally true to say, with Stephen Menn, that '*all* new philosophers were necessarily Mosaic philosophers, that "Mosaic philosophy" was a condition presupposed by all of the new philosophies'.[93]

One of the implications of these new combinations of contemporary physics and biblical cosmology was that the bible alone was an insufficient foundation for a comprehensive natural philosophy. For the earliest promoters of a biblical natural philosophy, such as Daneau, the apparent paucity of scientific information in the scriptures was something of an embarrassment. But there were explanations for this apparent deficiency. As we have seen, Daneau limited the scope of the natural sciences, claiming that a science so circumscribed was more in keeping with the imperfections of both the human mind and the natural world. Such a position was also consistent with a common view about the primary intention of the scriptural writers, neatly encapsulated in Cardinal Baronius's epigram that the bible informed its readers how to go to heaven, and not how the heavens go. Some of those disappointed by the absence of natural philosophy in scripture suggested that while God had inspired certain favoured individuals with an intimate knowledge of nature, this knowledge had either been lost or had survived only in cryptic oral or written traditions. The myth of the *Sepher Raziel* and Josephus' account of the pillars of Seth lent this view a certain credence. There was also a long-standing tradition that some biblical writers had in fact composed lengthy treatises devoted to natural philosophy, but that these had been tragically lost to posterity. Solomon and Job were usually identified as the most likely authors of these lost scientific works. Daneau acknowledged, for example, that scripture does not contain in detail all the 'Histories of living thynges, and of Plants', but attributed this to the fact that 'Salomens Bookes which were written copiously of the Nature of all thynges, are, through the negligence of men, perished'.[94]

---

[92] Harrison, 'Physico-Theology and the Mixed Sciences'.
[93] Stephen Menn, 'The Intellectual Setting', p. 58.
[94] Daneau, *Wonderfull Woorkmanship*, fol. 2v.

Laments for the loss of Solomon's works of natural history and natural philosophy were commonplace in the sixteenth and seventeenth centuries.[95] More often than not, Solomon himself was said to have relied upon lost works of an even earlier provenance, associated with the comprehensive antediluvian science of Noah, Seth, Enoch, and Adam.

Not surprisingly, elaborations of the first-century story of Seth's pillars were at the forefront of discussions of ancient knowledge and lacunae in its transmission. In Jean Lemaire de Belges's *Illustrations de Gaule* (1510), Josephus' modest two columns had proliferated into fourteen, the better to store the capacious learning of the first generations of men.[96] Lemaire's compatriot Gui Le Fevre de la Boderie gave the tradition a chauvinistic twist, asserting that the ancient Gauls had been the first to decipher the ancient columns, using their newfound knowledge to re-establish the mathematical arts. The pretended inventors of ancient science – the Egyptians, Greeks, and Romans – were thus exposed as boastful frauds.[97] Philipp Melanchthon also repeated the account of the pillars, although he attributed their construction to Adam rather than Seth. Melanchthon is also said to have incorporated the pillars into a more extensive structure which might have functioned something like a museum and place of worship.[98] Later in the sixteenth century the theme of antediluvian knowledge was exposed to a wide audience in the popular *Divine Weeks and Works*, the epic poem on Genesis penned by the Huguenot poet Guillaume Du Bartas (1544–90). In a section of the work entitled 'The Columns', Du Bartas provides an account of the rediscovery of Seth's pillars by Heber, the legendary founder of the Hebrews, who explains to his son the meanings of the mysterious inscriptions on the stones. In this version of events, the mathematical sciences of the quadrivium – arithmetic, astronomy, geometry, and music – are inscribed on the inside of hollow cylindrical columns.[99] This not only suggests a more extensive structure than two needles of stone, but also hints at the capacity of mathematic symbols to express, in compressed symbolic form, the totality of ancient knowledge. The traditions of ancient

[95] See, e.g., Barrough, *Method of Phisicke*, To the Reader; Comenius, *A Reformation of Schooles* (London, 1642), p. 30; Topsell, *Historie* (1658 edn), sig. A4r; Boyle, *Some Considerations touching the Usefulness of Experimental Natural Philosophy*, Works II, 309; *Some Considerations touching the Style of the Holy Scriptures*, Works II, 247ff.; William Coles, *Adam in Eden*, To the Reader. Cf. Galileo, 'Letter to the Grand Duchess Christina', in Drake, *Discoveries and Opinions*, p. 169.

[96] For discussons of antediluvian books in early modern French literature see Stephens, 'Bibliographic Myth'. I am indebted to Stephens for much of this paragraph.

[97] Gui Le Fevre de la Boderie, *La Galliade* [1582], ed. F. Roudaut (Paris, 1993), pp. 262f.

[98] Philip Melanchthon, *Chronicon Carionis* (Wittenberg, 1580), p. 17; Gottfried Vockerodt, *Exercitationes academicae* (Gotha, 1704), p. 157.

[99] Guillaume de Salluste du Bartas, *Du Bartas his Divine Weekes and Workes* (London, 1641), pp. 135–41.

knowledge and of lost books received considerable attention during the sixteenth and seventeenth centuries, and a number of authors compiled lists of antediluvian books.[100]

Speculations about 'lost books' were related to more fundamental questions about the formation and content of the biblical canon. Insistence upon the principle *sola scriptura* raised the question not only of correct interpretation of the bible, but also of the relative importance of the various books that comprised the totality of scripture. Luther had himself broached this issue when he contended that some of the individual works that had been incorporated into the ancient canon ought perhaps to have been omitted.[101] By the same token it could also be argued that the bible was not the sole deposit of writings that bore signs of divine inspiration, and that works that had been omitted may have been unjustly overlooked. In other words, in vesting religious authority solely in a collection of ancient books, the Protestant reformers had raised more fundamental questions about the basis upon which written sources might be regarded as authoritative. The most important criterion for the admission of writings into the New Testament canon was apostolic authorship, which linked the content of specific writings to the broader criterion of Apostolic succession, upon which ecclesiastical authority was based. The derivation of both the written authority of scripture and the ecclesial authority of bishops and popes could thus in principle be traced back to the person of Christ – the 'second Adam'. For the Old Testament it might similarly be reasoned that God's revelations to the first Adam were to be traced through the lineage of the ancient philosophers who had been heirs to Adamic wisdom. During the Renaissance, many contended that the secrets of Adam's knowledge had not been restricted to the canonical authors of the Old Testament such as Moses, Solomon, and Job, but were also to be found in ancient extra-biblical writings.

While the principle of *sola scriptura*, as applied in the realm of natural philosophy, might seem to render references to other ancient writings superfluous, there was nothing in the Mosaic philosophy *per se* that rendered all other written sources irrelevant to the quest for scientific truths. After all, knowledge of the creation had passed from Adam to Moses, but

---

[100] Examples include Claude Durent, *Thrésor de l'histoire des langues de cest univers* (Yverdon, 1619), pp. 115–41; Joachim J. Mader, *De bibliothecis atque archiviis* (1666); Vockerodt, *Exercitationes academicae*, pp. 147–67; Jacob Freidrich Reimmann, *Versuch einer Einleitung in die Historiam literariam antediluvianam* (Halle, 1709), pp. 1–50. For brief discussions of these works see Stephens, 'Bibliographic Myth'.
[101] Althaus, *Theology of Martin Luther*, pp. 82–6.

it could hardly have been conveyed exclusively to Moses. Moreover, given the great antiquity of the Hebrew Bible, it was highly likely that biblical insights and traditions would be present in other ancient writings, albeit in partial or distorted variants. As we have already noted, according to the 'plagiarism thesis' espoused by many of the Church Fathers, much of what was good in pagan thought had been borrowed either from biblical patriarchs and prophets or from the Hebrew Bible. This raised the possibility that fragments of Mosaic philosophy might also be discovered in non-biblical sources. In the thirteenth century, Roger Bacon (*c.* 1220–92) articulated the conventional view that God revealed the fundamentals of philosophy to Adam and that this knowledge was almost completely lost after the Fall. Bacon also suggested, however, that some aspects of Adamic philosophy were preserved and transmitted by wise men – Zoroaster, Prometheus, Atlas, Hermes, Apollo, and Asclepius. Of the biblical cast of characters, it was Solomon who had revived the ancient philosophy delivered to Adam, and the Greek philosophers Democritus, Plato, and Aristotle were heirs to this tradition. Greek philosophy represented the original revealed truths in partial and distorted versions, and these truths were subsequently corrected with the inception of Christianity.[102] Bacon's source for much of this was the Pseudo-Aristotelian *Secretum secretorum* (Secret of Secrets), a work purporting to be a letter from Aristotle to Alexander the Great.[103] Aristotle's role had been to communicate ancient Hebrew secrets to Alexander the Great, making possible his conquest of the world. These same powerful secrets, Bacon believed, might also assist the Holy Roman Empire in its contemporary struggles against Islam.[104]

Variations on this general thesis – that of the *prisca sapientia* or 'ancient philosophy' – were common in Renaissance accounts of the history of philosophy, although the personnel differed according to the philosophical predilections of those relating the history.[105] When the sceptical thinker

---

[102] Roger Bacon, *Opus Majus* I, 52–6, 64, 196. See discussions in Stephen Gaukroger, *Francis Bacon and the Transformation of Early Modern Natural Philosophy* (Cambridge, 2001), pp. 74f.; and Paolo Rossi, *Francis Bacon: From Magic to Science* (Chicago, 1968), pp. 69f.

[103] On the text and its influence see Steven J. Williams, *The 'Secret of Secrets': The Scholarly Career of a Pseudo-Aristotelian Text in the Latin Middle Ages* (Ann Arbor, 2003). For Bacon's use of it see Steven J. Williams, 'Roger Bacon and His Edition of the Pseudo-Aristotelian *Secretum secretorum*', *Speculum* 69 (1994), 57–73.

[104] Bacon, *Opus Majus* I, 63, 112, 164, 408; II, 617.

[105] D. P. Walker, *The Ancient Theology* (London, 1972); Eugenio Garin, *Giovanni Pico della Mirandola: Vita e dottrina* (Florence, 1937), pp. 75f.; Charles Schmitt, 'Perennial Philosophy: From Agostino Steuco to Leibniz', *JHI* 27 (1966), 505–32; Gaukroger, *Francis Bacon*, p. 74, n. 21; C. Blackwell, 'Thales Philosophicus: The Beginning of Philosophy as a Discipline', in Donald R. Kelley (ed.), *History and the Disciplines: The Reclassification of Knowledge in Early Modern Europe* (Rochester, 1997), pp. 61–82.

Agrippa first wrote on occult philosophy, he was attracted to the idea of an original deposit of divine wisdom and of a succession of sages – Adam, Moses, Abraham, Solomon, Hermes Trismegistus, Pythagoras, Plato – whose esoteric writings might be interpreted in such a way as to recover what had been revealed or transmitted to them.[106] The role of the contemporary magus was, as Agrippa expressed it in a phrase that now has rather different resonances, 'to recover that ancient magick'.[107] Hermes Trismegistus (the thrice-great Hermes), then believed to be an ancient Egyptian priest, came to assume a central importance in many of these accounts, following the translation of the hermetic literature in the fifteenth century by Marsilio Ficino (1433–99).[108] Genealogies of knowledge featuring the revered Hermes Trismegistus differed from Roger Bacon's in that they attempted to vindicate a Platonic Christian philosophy that would replace the prevailing Aristotelianism. In the celebrated case of Giordano Bruno, the hermetic literature was put to the quite different purpose of illustrating the superiority of Egyptian wisdom to Christianity.[109] In 1614, however, the classicist Isaac Casaubon demolished the universal assumption of the authenticity and great antiquity of the hermetic writings. Most probably, Casaubon suggested, they were forgeries that dated from the early Christian period.[110] This dealt a telling blow to hermetic versions of the ancient philosophy, although for a number of decades some of its supporters argued that while the extant hermetic literature might have post-dated the New Testament, it nonetheless represented a more ancient tradition.

The English physician and occultist Robert Fludd (1574–1637) was one who persisted with the idea that hermeticism could be integrated with Mosaic philosophy. Fludd combined elements of the fifteenth-century Neoplatonism of Ficino with his own alchemical glosses on the book of Genesis to produce a novel natural philosophy based on complex correspondences between the physical and spiritual worlds. In his *Mosaicall Philosophie* (1659), Fludd set out the view that the books of scripture 'express

---

[106] Agrippa sets out his version of the ancient philosophy in *Three Books of Occult Philosophy* (London, 1651), bk III, ch. II, ccxi ff.; and in *Oratio in praelectione . . . Trismegisti*, in *Opera* II, 1077–8.

[107] Agrippa, *Occult Philosophy*, sig. A3v. Cf. Dedication to Book III, (p. 342).

[108] On Ficino and the ancient philosophy see James Hankins, 'The Study of the "Timaeus" in Early Renaissance Italy', in A. Grafton and N. Siraisi (eds.), *Natural Particulars: Nature and the Disciplines in Renaissance Europe* (Cambridge, MA, 1999), pp. 77–119; M. O'Rourke Boyle, 'Gracious Laughter: Marsilio Ficino's Anthropology', *Renaissance Quarterly* 52 (1999), 712–41; C. S. Celenza, 'Pythagoras in the Renaissance: The Case of Marsilio Ficino', *Renaissance Quarterly* 52 (1999), 667–711.

[109] Frances Yates, *Giordano Bruno and the Hermetic Tradition* (Chicago, 1991). On the different uses of the *prisca sapientia* see Mulsow, 'Ambiguities of the *Prisca Sapientia*'.

[110] Yates, *Bruno and the Hermetic Tradition*, pp. 398–402; Anthony Grafton, *Forgers and Critics* (Princeton, 1990), pp. 62–3, 76–98.

and delineate externally such created realities, as belong unto the true Subject of the most essentiall [natural] Philosophy'. Attacking the view that the subject matter of scripture was restricted to morals and salvation, he insisted that the bible dealt with both the physical and the metaphysical.[111] I am not ashamed, he confessed, 'to attribute justly my Philosophicall principles unto my Master *Moses*, who also received them, figured or framed out by the finger of God'.[112] Anything of philosophical value in antiquity, according to Fludd, had its origins in the bible, and thus Plato and Hermes Trismegistus (but not Aristotle) had borrowed from Moses: 'The wisest amongst these Pagan Naturalists, did steal and derive their mean grounds or principles, from the true and sacred philosopher *Moses*'.[113]

As the example of Fludd shows, the tradition of ancient philosophy was very much alive in the seventeenth century. A typical account of the kind of lineage that was widely accepted was set out by the physician Gideon Harvey in his *New Principles of Philosophy* (1663):

we cannot doubt, but that Philosophy was also a *Relict* of the Forefathers, successibly conveyed to us, who did attribute the original acquisition of it to the first man *Adam*: for he in his primitive and incorrupt state, being adorned with a full and perfect Knowledge of all Beings, it is probable that after his Fall, he retained a measure of the same Knowledge; which, although being different from the former in perfection, yet by his industry had much promoted it, and so having committed it to the further accomplishment of his antediluvian Successors, to wit, *Seth, Enos, Cainan, Malaleel, Jared, Enoch, Methusalem* and *Noe*; it did attract such increase and degree of perfection from their experience that we have no great cause to admire, whence the profound learning of the postdiluvian Fathers did arive [sic] to them; who were either sacred, as *Abraham, Moses, Solomon*, &c. or prophane as the *Magicians* among the *Persians*, the *Chaldeans* of *Babylon, Brachmins* in *India*, the Priests of *Egypt*, the *Talmudists* and *Cabbalists* among the *Jews*, the *Druids* among the ancient *Britains*, and *Gauls*, with whom many of the famous Poets, *Homer, Hesiod*, as also the seven wise men of *Greece* were coetaneous.[114]

The apparent incongruity of Harvey's title – '*New* principles of philosophy' – is indicative of the residual ambivalence of seventeenth-century thinkers to anything new. While proponents of the new natural philosophy made a point of distancing themselves from the putatively unproductive

[111] Robert Fludd, *Mosaicall Philosophy Grounded upon the Essential Truth or Eternal Sapience* (London, 1659), Preface, p. 33. Cf. *Apologia compendiaria* in *Robert Fludd: Essential Readings*, ed. William Huffman (London, 1992), p. 54.

[112] Fludd, *Mosaicall Philosophy*, p. 3. Solomon was also credited with scientific knowledge. *Mosaicall Philosophy*, Preface, and *Apologia compendiaria*, in *Robert Fludd*, ed. Hoffman, p. 52.

[113] Fludd, *Mosaicall Philosophy*, p. 40, cf. pp. 28–33, 123.

[114] Gideon Harvey, *Archelogia Philosophica Nova, or New Principles of Philosophy* (London, 1663), pt 1, p. 2.

and moribund sciences of the Middle Ages, it was also important for them
to show that doing natural philosophy the 'right way' was not entirely
without historical precedent. In this regard, the situation of apologists for
the new natural philosophies paralleled that of the Protestant reformers who
were similarly susceptible to the charge that their religious innovations were
entirely novel. The question 'Where was your church before Luther?' was
a standard weapon in the arsenal of Catholic controversialists.[115] The most
common response to this question was that Protestantism represented a pure
and uncorrupted version of Christianity that could trace its origins back
to the first century, or perhaps even beyond, to the time of Adam and the
patriarchs. On this view of history, true Christianity had been represented
in all ages, even if its more corrupt manifestations had been predominant
in particular periods of history. This assertion was paralleled in the sphere
of natural philosophy by the claim that true natural philosophy had been
practised in the world since the time of Adam. Just as the dominant forms
of religiosity were to be understood as defections away from an originally
pure Christianity, so corrupt versions of natural philosophy had held sway
for much of human history. As the Protestant reformers saw themselves
as calling a wayward Church back to its true path, so the advocates of
the 'new' natural philosophy often considered themselves to be reformers
rather than innovators. It was often argued that the sources of corruption
of true philosophy and true religion were the same. Thomas Sprat made
pointed comparisons of the decay of natural philosophy and the Catholic
corruption of Christianity.[116] Isaac Newton associated apostasy from true
religion with the loss of scientific knowledge (although his unidentified
target was Trinitarian Christianity which, in his view, was a distortion of
true Christian religion). William Whiston attributed the corruption of
knowledge to rationalist speculation on the part of the Greeks denigrating,
by implication, the speculative natural philosophy of Descartes.[117] In all of

[115] For contemporary responses to this question see Bernard Richard, *Look beyond Luther* (London, 1623); Anon., *Luthers Predecessors: or, an Answer to the question of the Papists: Where was your Church Before Luther* (London, 1624); David Pareus, *A Commentary upon the Divine Revelation of the Apostle and Evangelist John* (Amsterdam, 1644), pt 1; Robert Sanderson, *A Discourse concerning the Church* (London, 1688). See also Stephen Barnett, 'Where Was Your Church Before Luther? English Claims for the Antiquity of Protestantism Examined', *Church History* 68 (1999), 14–42.

[116] See, e.g., Sprat, *History*, pp. 62, 349f., 371.

[117] Newton, 'Two Notable Corruptions of Scripture', in *Correspondence of Sir Isaac Newton*, ed. H. W. Turnbull, 7 vols. (Cambridge, 1961), III, 183–49; Snobelin, 'Isaac Newton, Heretic', 385f.; Whiston, *Astronomical Principles*, p. 289. In contrast to Newton, John Wallis used the notion of an ancient theology to suggest that the idea of a Triune God predated the New Testament. *Three Sermons*, 99–102. Some of the Cambridge Platonists had suggested something similar. See Harrison, *'Religion' and the Religions*, pp. 130–8.

this, establishing the historical pedigree of the apparently new developments in natural philosophy often involved tracing the origins of these doctrines back to Adam and those to whom he was said to have transmitted them. The implication of Harvey's title is that the 'new' natural philosophical doctrines had once been lost, but were now being recovered.

Harvey's narrative is representative of seventeenth-century English accounts of ancient wisdom in other respects. Not only does he provide a place for England's indigenous ancient philosophers, the druids, he also minimizes the significance of the hermetic sources. On this last point, he follows Francis Bacon. Bacon's approach to natural philosophy will be considered in detail in the next chapter, but it is worth pointing out at this juncture that Bacon was generally dismissive of the Renaissance genealogies of knowledge that channelled ancient wisdom through hermetic sources. In keeping with the reformation emphasis on the learning that was independent of the main currents of pagan thought, he opted for a more purely Hebrew lineage of ancient learning – a Mosaic Adam rather than a hermetic Adam.[118] Yet he was convinced that there were veins of philosophical truth amid the dross of pagan myths, so much so that in four of his works he set out to uncover what he believed to be the philosophical meanings of these legends. *De sapientia veterum* (The Wisdom of the Ancients, 1609) is Bacon's first attempt at deciphering the meanings of these legends. Here, he advances the thesis that embedded within the narratives of Greek literature were fragmentary details about the history of the world derived from earlier, biblical traditions.[119] The myths of Cupid, Pan, Prometheus, and the Sphinx were to be understood as communicating veiled truths about, amongst other things, the Creation and the Fall. Rightly understood, they also conveniently confirmed features of Bacon's own programme – the goal of re-establishing human dominion over things, the importance of combining reason and experience, and the requirement that natural philosophy be a corporate activity.[120] The meanings of these demythologised ancient legends were revisited in *De dignitate et augmentis scientarum* (1623), a

---

[118] Barbara Garner, 'Francis Bacon, Natalis Comes and the Mythological Tradition', *Journal of the Warburg and Courtauld Institutes* 33 (1970), 264–91.

[119] Bacon, *Sapientia veterum*, *Works* VI, 625–8. For Bacon on ancient mythology see Charles W. Lemmi, *The Classical Deities in Bacon: A Study of Mythological Symbolism* (Baltimore, 1930); Garner, 'Bacon and the Mythological Tradition'; Silvia Manzo, 'Holy Writ, Mythology, and the Foundations of Bacon's Principle of the Constancy of Matter', *Early Science and Medicine* 4 (1999), 115–25; J. Klein, *Francis Bacon oder die Modernisierung Englands* (Hildesheim, 1987), pp. 42–9.

[120] Bacon, *Sapientia veterum*, *Works* VI, 647f., 673, 675f., 678f. Bacon seems to have relied on the earlier work of Natalis Comes [Natale Conti], *Mythologiae sive explicationis fabularum libri decem* (Venice, 1551). See Jean Seznec, *The Survival of the Pagan Gods* (New York, 1953), pp. 219–56; Garner, 'Francis Bacon, Natalis Comes and the Mythological Tradition'.

much-expanded Latin version of the earlier *Advancement of Learning*. Here Bacon explains that the myth of Pan, for example, was 'pregnant with the mysteries and secrets of nature'. Again, these secrets had been 'borrowed' by the Greeks from the 'Hebrew mysteries', and referred to the state of the world after its first creation when it had been 'made subject to death and corruption after the Fall'.[121]

Bacon's contentions about the biblical origins of ancient myths and legends were repeated later in the century by mathematician John Wallis (1616–1703), Savilian Professor of Geometry at Oxford.[122] Other prominent Fellows of the Royal Society also followed Bacon in asserting the antiquity of the 'new' ideas about the natural world, on occasion going so far as to allocate disciplinary specialisations to particular individuals. According to Joseph Glanvill (1636–80), the patriarchs 'were well instructed in the *Knowledge of God's Works*, and contributed to the goods of Men by their useful Discoveries and Inventions'. More specifically, Adam knew the nature of the creatures, Noah was a planter of vineyards, Abraham an astronomer, Isaac was versed in Georgics, Jacob in the 'stratagem of the speckled Rods', Moses 'knew all kinds of natural knowledge', Bezaleel and Aholiah inspired architecture. Solomon was 'a deep naturalist, and a Composer of a voluminous History of Plants'. Daniel, Hananiah, Mischael, and Azariah were 'skilled in all Learning and Wisdom'.[123]

One of the key differences between the Hebrew and Greek custodians of knowledge was held to be that while the former had openly communicated their deposit of knowledge, the latter had sought to protect knowledge from the attentions of the vulgar by wrapping it in myths and allegories.[124] So successful had they been that even the most worthy minds of posterity had struggled to pierce the veil of mystery and uncover the kernel of truth within. As a consequence, Bacon pointed out, 'the river of time has carried

---

[121] Bacon, *De augmentis*, *Works* IV, 319; Cf. *De Sapientia*, *Works* VI, 709. Bacon also deals with the myths of Cupid and Coelum in the unpublished *De Principiis atque Originibus, secundum fabulas Cupidinis et Coelum* (On Principles and Origins According to the Fables of Cupid and Coelum, 1612), *Works* V, 461–500, and with Coelum and Proteus in the earlier work, *Cogitationes de Scientia Humana* (Thoughts on Human Sciences), *Works* III, 183–98, probably written before 1605.

[122] John Wallis, *Three Sermons concerning the sacred Trinity* (London, 1691), pp. 99–102. Wallis cited Natalis Comes as one of his sources. Cf. Whiston, *Astronomical Principles of Religion*, p. 289.

[123] Glanvill, *The Usefulness of Real Philosophy to Religion*, p. 41, in *Essays*.

[124] See, e.g., Sprat, *History*, p. 5. Newton himself seemed to adopt the position of the 'two-fold philosophy', hiding his anti-trinitarian views from the vulgar. See Stephen Snobelin, 'William Whiston, Isaac Newton and the Crisis of Publicity', *Studies in History and Philosophy of Science* 35 (2004), 573–603, and 'Isaac Newton, Heretic: The Strategies of a Nicodemite', *BJHS* 32 (1999), 381–419.

down to us the light and windy and has sunk the solid and weighty'.[125] Only with the rediscovery of ancient truths in modern times had it proven possible to revisit many myths and interpret them according to their true meanings – hence the interest of Bacon and others in ancient mythology. In his *Two New Sciences*, for example, Galileo suggested that the Copernican hypothesis had been implicit in Plato's philosophy, but that its mathematical foundations, 'of which Plato had remained silent', were discovered by Galileo who had 'removed their poetic mask or semblance', showing their physical truth.[126] Increasingly, the excessive secrecy and poetic whimsy of the ancients were regarded as the causes of the corruption of philosophy. Thomas Sprat attributed 'the first *Corruption* of knowledge' to the penchant of Chaldean and Egyptian wise men for wrapping up philosophical truths in mysteries. William Whiston identified Greek natural philosophy as the most significant and influential departure from universally received traditions. The Greeks 'had followed their own Reasonings', ignoring 'those Natural and Divine Doctrines which they received by Tradition from their first Founders, and which most probably were originally deriv'd from the first Parents of Mankind'.[127]

The demise of Hermes Trismegistus as a central figure in the transmission of ancient knowledge was thus not only the result of the challenge posed to his antiquity by modern methods of textual criticism. Hermeticism, in both its ancient and Renaissance manifestations, was esoteric and somewhat elitist in character. True wisdom was the preserve of a favoured few and the secrets of nature were to be closely guarded by these gifted individuals and transmitted only to those worthy to receive them. When in the seventeenth century Francis Bacon inaugurated a new conception of how natural philosophy was to be conducted, emphasising its importance in promoting the general welfare, this understanding of the role of the philosopher was one of his chief targets.[128] The excessive secrecy of the ancient sages had hindered both the transmission of knowledge and the incremental accumulation of facts which for Bacon were foundational for the scientific enterprise. For many English natural philosophers, the place

[125] Bacon, *Temporis partus masculus*, in Farington, *Philosophy of Francis Bacon*, p. 68. Cf. Bacon, *Novum Organum* I, §63 (*Works* IV, 64).
[126] Hankins, 'Galileo, Ficino, and Renaissance Platonism', p. 210.
[127] William Whiston, *Astronomical Principles of Religion, natural and reveal'd* (London, 1717), p. 289.
[128] On Bacon's conception of the natural philosopher see Gaukroger, *Francis Bacon*, p. 5; Antonio Pérez-Ramos, 'Bacon's Legacy', in Markku Peltonen (ed.), *The Cambridge Companion to Bacon* (Cambridge, 1996), pp. 311–34; Peter Harrison, 'The Natural Philosopher and the Virtues', in C. Condren, I. Hunter, and S. Gaukroger (eds.), *The Philosopher in Early Modern Europe: The Nature of a Contested Identity* (Cambridge, 2006), pp. 202–28.

of the Egyptian priest Hermes Trismegistus was given over to the Hebrew King Solomon. This distinguished line provided not merely the history of a tradition, but a justification for a renewed interest in knowledge of the natural world. Solomon's credentials as an acute naturalist were never in doubt. Edward Topsell, clerical author of popular compilations of natural history, wrote that '*Solomon*, as it is witnessed in holy Scripture, wrote of Plants, of Birds, of Fishes, and Beasts, and even then when he stood in good favour with God, therefore it is an exercise of the highest Wisdom to travel in, and the Noblest minds to study in; for in it as I will shew you . . . there is both the knowledge of God and Man'.[129] Solomon came to assume a privileged place in the line of ancient philosophers, and was second only to Adam and Moses.[130] Significantly, Francis Bacon was to call his ideal scientific institution 'the house of Salomon'. As we shall see in the next chapter, with his ambivalent attitude towards knowledge – an admiration of the wonders of nature and a reputation for an intimate familiarity with its workings, combined with counsels concerning the ultimate vanity of human learning – the figure of Solomon almost perfectly registered the mood of early modern English experimental philosophers.

As important as the intermediate links in the chain of transmission of ancient knowledge were those contemporary figures now identified as the reformers of corrupted traditions, or as rediscoverers of Adamic science. Bacon was described by an admirer as having 'discoursed with such life and light, that he may seem to have learn'd his knowledge even in the Schoole of the First Man'.[131] Descartes was more often identified as a reviver of Adamic knowledge, however. Cambridge Platonist Henry More (1614–87), in his early enthusiasm for Cartesian philosophy, reckoned Descartes to be the seventeenth-century heir to Mosaic wisdom.[132] More believed that Adam's

---

[129] Topsell, *Historie*, Epistle Dedicatory.

[130] See, e.g., Levinus Lemnius, *An Herbal for the Bible*, tr. Thomas Newton (London, 1587), p. 3; Coles, *Adam in Eden*, To the Reader; Richard Saunders, *Saunders Physiognomie and Chiromancie, Metoposcopie*, 2nd edn (London, 1671), Preface.

[131] Pierre D'Ambois de la Magdelaine, cited in Watts's introduction to *The Advancement of Learning* (1640 edn), sig. A2r.

[132] Other Platonists held similar views. See Ralph Cudworth, *A Treatise concerning Eternal and Immutable Morality* (London, 1731), pp. 55, 301; Joseph Glanvill, *The Author's Defence of the Vanity of Dogmatizing*, p. 89, in *Scepsis Scientifica* (London, 1665); *Vanity of Dogmatizing*, pp. 183, 211. In time More and the other Cambridge Platonists were to become disenchanted with Descartes. See Alan Gabbey, 'Philosophia Cartesiana Triumphata: Henry More (1646–1671)', in T. Lennon, John Nicholas, and John Davis (eds.), *Problems of Cartesianism* (Kingston and Montreal, 1982); Marjorie Nicolson, 'The Early Stage of Cartesianism in England', *Studies in Philology* 26 (1929), 356–74; Charles Webster, 'Henry More and Descartes: Some New Sources', *BJHS* 4 (1969), 359–77; A. Rupert Hall, *Henry More: Magic, Religion, and Experiment* (Oxford, 1990), pp. 146–67; J. Saveson, 'Differing Reactions to Descartes among the Cambridge Platonists', *JHI* 21 (1960), 560–7; E. A.

knowledge of the creation had been recorded in the book of Genesis by Moses, who was accordingly described as a 'Master of the most sublime and generous speculations that are in all Natural Philosophy'.[133] According to More, Moses had taught the mobility of the earth – an idea that eventually found its way to Pythagoras. The biblical author had also taught atomic philosophy, which in turn had been plagiarised by Leucippus, Democritus, and Epicurus with whom it is more traditionally associated. The revival of the corpuscular hypothesis by Gassendi and Descartes was thus the occasion of the rediscovery not only of a true philosophy of nature, but also of the true meaning of the text of Genesis. More even believed that the Cartesian hypothesis of celestial vortices was implicit in the creation narratives of Genesis.[134] It fell to others to map out the explicit connections between the ideas of Descartes and the writings of Moses. The French Cartesian Gérauld de Cordemoy (1626–84) insisted that Descartes' system of the world could easily have 'been taken out of the First Chapter of Genesis'.[135] Johan Amerpoel, in *Cartesius Mosaizans* (1677), places sections of the Genesis text side by side with extracts from Descartes' *Principles of Philosophy*, as if the latter were nothing but a commentary on the former. Christopher Wittich and Antoine Le Grand similarly argued for the congruity of the Cartesian and Mosaic accounts of the creation.[136] Best known of all attempts to construct a Cartesian version of Mosaic philosophy was Englishman Thomas Burnet's *Telluris Theoria Sacra* (Sacred Theory of the Earth, 1681), in which the biblical accounts of the creation and deluge, along with prophecies concerning the final conflagration of the world, are harmonised with a simplified Cartesian cosmology.[137]

With the eclipse of the Cartesian cosmology and the ascendancy of the mathematical system of Newton, Descartes was replaced as the modern

Burtt, *The Metaphysical Foundations of Modern Science* (Atlantic Highlands, NJ, 1952), pp. 135–50; Amos Funkenstein, *Theology and the Scientific Imagination* (Princeton, 1986), pp. 72–80. For a general account of Descartes' influence in England see G. A. J. Rogers, 'Descartes and the English', in J. D. North and J. J. Roche (eds.), *The Light of Nature* (Dordrecht, 1985), pp. 281–301.

[133] More, *Conjectura Cabbalistica*, p. 41, Epistle Dedicatory.

[134] More, *A Collection*, pp. xviii–xix; Cf. More, *Observations upon Anthroposophia Theomagica and Anima Magica Abscondita* (London, 1650), p. 65. For other advocates of a biblical science see Diodati, *Annotations upon the Holy Bible*, sig. A3r; John Edwards, *A Demonstration of the Existence and Providence of God* (London, 1696), Preface; Le Clerc, *Twelve Dissertations*, sig. A3r, A4r. Also see Hill, *English Bible*, pp. 29, 373; R. Hooykaas, 'Science and Reformation', *Journal of World History* 3 (1956), 109–39.

[135] Cordemoy, *A Discourse written to a Learned Frier* (London, 1670).

[136] Antoine Le Grand, *An Entire Body of Philosophy According to the Principles of the Famous Renate Des Cartes* (London, 1694), pp. 56–8. On Wittich see Rienk Vermij, *The Calvinist Copernicans: The Reception of the New Astronomy in the Dutch Republic* (Amsterdam, 2004), pp. 146–8.

[137] Harrison, 'Cartesian Cosmology in England'.

heir to the philosophy of the ancients. Newton's system, it was argued by his supporters, provided a new and more powerful way to understand the implicit natural philosophy of Genesis.[138] As J. E. McGuire and P. M. Rattansi demonstrated some years ago, it is also clear that Newton provided for himself a place at the end of the line of ancient philosophers. Newton believed that his discoveries were in accord with the teachings of a number of ancient philosophers – the Egyptians had subscribed to the Copernican hypothesis, Pythagoras had known the inverse-square law, Plato had spoken of the gravitational attraction between bodies.[139] In a conversation with David Gregory in May of 1694, Newton also explained how his philosophy agreed with that of the ancients and particularly that of Thales of Miletus. Even the much-maligned philosophy of Epicurus and Lucretius was true and consistent with Newtonianism, although it had been misunderstood by their contemporaries who wrongly thought that it was conducive to atheism.[140] William Stukeley's description of his friend as 'the Great Restorer of True Philosophy' was thus entirely in keeping with Newton's own conception of his achievement.[141]

For most advocates of an ancient philosophy in the later seventeenth century, recourse to ancient texts was not advocated in the first instance as a method of research. Instead it became primarily a means of independently corroborating new philosophical discoveries, and of providing them with historical legitimation. This procedure was nonetheless still related to the idea of a philosophical Fall. Writing in the last decade of the seventeenth century, clergyman John Hartcliffe nicely captured the prevailing sentiment of the period. The first motion of Adam, he wrote, was towards knowledge. But by his foolish quest for more knowledge than was appropriate he left his posterity in the dark, 'either following wrong Scents, or much in

---

[138] See Harrison, *Bible and the Rise of Science*, pp. 143–7. Not all were convinced of the congruence of Newtonian natural philosophy and scripture, however. John Hutchinson wrote his *Moses's Principia* as 'a confirmation of the Natural History of the Bible'. It had been Moses' 'chief business', thought Hutchinson, to 'determine Natural Philosophy'. In England Hutchinson's book excited considerable interest, enjoying a readership almost as wide as Newton's *Principia*, to which it had been a response. His ideas were developed and disseminated by a group of disciples who became known as the 'Hutchinsonians'. John Hutchinson, *Moses's Principia* (London, 1724–7), pt II, ii. See Albert Kuhn, 'Glory or Gravity: Hutchinson vs. Newton', *JHI* 22 (1961), 303–22.

[139] J. E. McGuire and P. M. Rattansi, 'Newton and the "Pipes of Pan"', *Notes and Records of the Royal Society* 21 (1966), 108–43; Paolo Casini, 'Newton: The Classical Scholia', *History of Science* 23 (1984), 1–58; Lawrence Principe, 'The Alchemies of Robert Boyle and Isaac Newton: Alternate Approaches and Divergent Developments', in Osler (ed.), *Rethinking the Scientific Revolution*, pp. 201–20; D. B. Haycock, '"The long-lost truth": Sir Isaac Newton and the Newtonian Pursuit of Ancient Knowledge', *Studies in History and Philosophy of Science* 35 (2004), 605–23.

[140] Newton, *Correspondence* III, 338.   [141] Haycock, 'Long-Lost Truth', p. 605.

doubt, what paths to walk in'. In spite of this depressing account, Hartcliffe concludes on a strikingly positive note:

> However there is a Providence in the conduct of Knowledg, as well as of other Affairs on Earth, and it was not designed, that all the Mysteries of Nature and of Providence should be plainly understood through all the Ages of the World; and what was made known to the Ancients only by broken Conclusions and Traditions, will be known in the latter Ages of the World, in a more perfect Way, by Principles and Theories.[142]

For Hartcliffe, the sciences of his own era represented a clear shift from reliance on inherited remnants of Adamic wisdom to freshly discovered truths. The history of lost traditions nonetheless remained important, for it provided a general legitimation of contemporary scientific enterprises and an independent source of corroboration for new discoveries.

INSPIRATION, EXPERIENCE, AND EXPERIMENT

The *Theses Theologicae* (1675) of Robert Barclay, in which are articulated the principles of the Quaker faith, begins with a proposition entitled: 'Concerning the True Foundation of Knowledge'. Here Barclay claims that the true knowledge of God comes from 'divine inward revelations' which, for Barclay at least, bear the same epistemic weight as such logical truths as the principle that the whole is greater than any one of its parts. These truths should contradict neither the external testimony of scripture nor 'right reason', yet inner inspiration was held to be superior to these alternative sources of knowledge because, to quote Barclay, it is 'evident and clear of itself'.[143] The form of Barclay's *Theses* has parallels with other credal statements of the period. The Westminster Confession, for example, also opens with a statement about the correct source of our knowledge of God, although in this instance that source is identified as scripture. Barclay's 'foundationalist' stance also echoes the approach of Descartes, both in its quest for certain foundations and in its choice of the criteria of clarity and indubitability. But while the form is common to a range of genres, the content is quite particular. Opposing the standard Calvinist elevation of the authority of scripture, Barclay declares that the bible is 'not to be esteemed the principal ground of all truth and knowledge'. As for the 'natural light' upon which the Cartesian system of natural philosophy was grounded, this was

---

[142] John Hartcliffe, *A Treatise of the Moral and Intellectual Virtues, wherein Their Nature is Fully Explained, and their Usefulness Proved* (London, 1691), pp. 296f.
[143] Barclay, *Theses Theologicae* II (Leith, p. 325).

held to be a most untrustworthy guide given our present fallen and 'corrupted' condition. Reliance upon natural light was the cause of the errors of papists and even of many Protestants.[144] Rather, Barclay insists, we must rely primarily on direct inspiration from God.

Barclay's championing of personal inspiration had important precedents in the sixteenth century in the spheres of both religion and natural philosophy. A number of radical Protestant sects – Anabaptists, Seekers, Familists, Ranters, Camisards, and Quietists – had argued for the primacy of personal inspiration, and had been labelled with the derisory designation 'enthusiasts' for their trouble.[145] But there were enthusiasts in the realm of natural philosophy as well: Paracelsians, alchemists, Behmenists (followers of Jakob Boehme), and cabbalists. Alchemists typically sought to legitimate their knowledge by providing an account of how it came by way of divine infusion.[146] The metaphysician Richard Burthogge (*c.* 1638–1703), writing at a time when the notion of personal inspiration had become disreputable, declared:

That there are *Philosophical* Enthusiasts, is as certain as that there are *Theological*; Enthusiasts in matters of Philosophy as well as Enthusiasts in matters of Divinity. *Paracelsus, Helmont,* and many other *Chymists,* are Examples of the first sort; as *H. Nicholls* the Father of the *Familists,* and others, are of the second. *Jacob Behmen* [i.e. Boehme] and Dr. *Fludd* may pass for examples of both.[147]

These philosophical enthusiasts believed that knowledge of nature could be directly communicated to human minds by the author of nature himself.

Many 'philosophical enthusiasts' were deeply indebted to hermetic and magical traditions. The Italian polymath Girolamo Cardano (1501–76), who gained notoriety by casting Christ's horoscope, claimed to have a superior understanding, communicated to him by a 'tutelary spirit' who provided him with demonstrative knowledge of 'cause and effect by means of an infallible proof'.[148] It was typically assumed that such truths were communicated on the condition of strict secrecy. The opening lines of *De magia*

---

[144] *Ibid.,* III, IV (Leith, p. 326).

[145] Seventeenth-century English radicals, influenced by such continental mystics as Sebastian Frank, often took a more positive view of the Fall. See Poole, *Milton and the Fall.*

[146] For alchemists on divine infusion, see Pamela Smith, *The Business of Alchemy: Science and Culture in the Holy Roman Empire* (Princeton, 1994), pp. 182, 228f.; N. Smith, *Perfection Proclaimed: Language and Literature in English Radical Religion, 1640–1660* (Oxford, 1989), pp. 77, 186–8, 193–9.

[147] Richard Burthogge, *Organum Vetus & Novum: Or, A Discourse of Reason and Truth* (London, 1678), p. 21. Cf. Sprat, *History,* pp. 37–8; John Sergeant, *Solid Philosophy Asserted, Against the fancies of the Ideists . . . with Reflexions on Mr. Locke's Essay Concerning Human Understanding* (London, 1697), sig. bIV.

[148] G. Cardano, *De rerum varietate* (Avignon, 1558), *Epistola,* p. 5, quoted in Rossi, *Francis Bacon,* p. 30.

veterum (1575) promise that for those who closely guard what is revealed to them, 'the eyes of your mind shall be opened to the understanding of secret things, and you shall hear all your heart's desire revealed to you through divine power'.[149] There was, however, secret and cryptic transmission of such knowledge either in encoded writings, or through a mysterious process of 'infusion' from one soul to another.[150] Truths directly revealed to individuals could thus be supplemented by accessing the tradition of secret knowledge that originated in Adam himself.

The German theosophical writer Jakob Boehme (1575–1624), described by Burthogge as both a philosophical and a religious enthusiast, combined elements of alchemy, Paracelsianism, astrology, and mysticism into a complex amalgam that was to have a far-reaching influence in Germany and England. Born in Germany, and originally a Lutheran, Boehme experienced a number of moments of divine illumination – the first in the year 1600 – details of which he imprudently published in *Aurora* (1612). This brought him to the attention of the authorities, who attempted to dissuade him from further publishing endeavours. They were ultimately unsuccessful, however, and Boehme's ideas spread throughout Germany and into England where they attracted numerous disciples. Boehme fervently believed that human reason had been 'captivated and fast bound in a close and strong Prison'. Reliance on the light of nature, he insisted, ultimately brings only darkness: 'We have a clear Example in Lucifer, and also in Adam the first Man, of what self doeth, when it getteth the Light of Nature to be its own, and when it can walk with the Understanding in its own Dominion.'[151] In order to regain the knowledge that Adam once had in his original state, we must purify ourselves and await the enlightenment of the divine spirit. While not everyone is 'fit for, or capable of the knowledge of the Eternall and Temporall Nature in its Mysterious operation', those to whom God gives the gift of his spirit are capable of reading the book of nature, and of gaining access to what Boehme referred to as 'the outer court of Natural Phylosophy, Sence, and reason'.[152] As one of Boehme's English translators later expressed it: 'the Ground of all that was in *Adam*, or any since, or shal be, is in any one of us'. The secret key that would unlock this hidden inner knowledge was the Spirit of God.[153] In order to be given this key, the

---

[149] *Ibid.*, p. 29.   [150] *Ibid.*, p. 30.
[151] Jakob Boehme, *The Way to Christ* (1622) tr. P. Erb (New York, 1978), p. 114.
[152] Jakob Boehme, *Signatura Rerum: or the Signature of all Things*, tr. J. Ellistone (London, 1651), sigs. A3v, A4v.
[153] Jakob Boehme, *The Second Booke. concerning The Three Principles of The Divine Essence* (London, 1648), 'To the Reader', sig. A4v, p. 23.

individual must participate in the necessary rituals of self-purification. The seal placed upon Adamic knowledge, according to the Behmenists, 'can be opened by no Academick, or University, or Scholastick learning: but by earnest repentance, fasting, watching, praying, knocking, and seeking in the sufferings of Iesus Christ by the Holy Ghost'.[154] Similar themes found their way into the devotional writings of seventeenth-century 'Children of the Light', as the Quakers were originally known. George Fox (1624–91) described in his journal his experience of the immediacy of God and of the knowledge that accompanied it:

I knew nothing but pureness, and innocency, and righteousness, being renewed up into the image of God by Christ Jesus, so that I say I was come up to the state of Adam which he was in before he fell. The creation was opened to me, and it was showed me how all things had their names given them according to their nature and virtue.[155]

But the same emphasis on divine inspiration was also present in more conventional medical writings. Ambroise Paré (1510–90), the most renowned surgeon of his age, wrote that after God had created Adam, 'he taught him the nature, the proper operations, faculties and vertues of all things contained in the circuit of this Vniverse'. Those now chosen by God to exercise the healing arts, he continued, may still be inspired with that same knowledge: 'But this knowledge was not buryed in oblivion with *Adam*: but by this same gift of God was given to those whom he hath chosen and ordained for Phisicke, to put their helping hands to others that stood in need thereof'.[156] This sentiment was also common amongst the Paracelsians. 'R. B'., the first of the English Paracelsian writers, wrote that Adam had enjoyed an exact knowledge of the creatures, a knowledge that had been a singular gift from God.[157] With the Fall came a corruption of our knowledge however, epitomised by the pagan traditions of Aristotle and Galen. Those who followed these heathen writers were committed to doctrines 'not founded upon the rule of Gods worde, but upon the authoritis of men reprobate of God, & such as were Idolaters and ignorant of the trueth'.[158] Unlike the prelapsarian Adam, these heathen writers had not received 'the key to wisdom' for it was God alone 'who giveth wisdome to the wise'.[159]

---

[154] *Ibid.*, Preface. Some Mosaic philosophers held this view, too. See Robert Fludd, *Mosaicall Philosophy*, p. 10.

[155] George Fox, *The Journal of George Fox*, ed. John L. Nickalls, intro. Geoffrey F. Nuttall (Cambridge, 1952), p. 27.

[156] Ambroise Paré, *The Workes of that Famous Chirurgion Ambrose Parey*, tr. Thomas Johnson (London, 1634), Preface.

[157] R. B., *Auncient Phisicke*, sigs. Fiiii r–Gi v.

[158] *Ibid.*, Author's Obtestation, sig. Bii v.   [159] *Ibid.*, sig. Bii r.

The general principle, to which R. B. appealed in support of his reformed Paracelsian medicine, was that 'there is no truth that is not derived from Christ the trueth it self'.[160]

Another Englishman, the iatrochemist Timothy Willis (1560–*c.* 1620), opened his *Search of Causes* (1616) with the assertion that 'the knowledge of trueth revealed unto the first friends of God, and by succession from them continued unto us their children, is more perfect then the wisdom of any Philosophy'. In this alchemical work, which includes a chemical reading of the biblical creation narratives, Willis insisted that Philosophers had sought in vain for the causes of all things, oblivious to the fact that the answers they sought had been revealed to biblical authors: 'In this Chronicle of the creation, there is very excellently taught the condition of all Creatures, their composition, and the state of their naturall life.'[161] But while the scriptures had preserved some of the philosophical knowledge of Adam – now translated into a more scientific form by Willis – the transmission of ancient knowledge had been greatly hindered by Adam's Fall and the 'sloth' of his immediate heirs. At this point, then, Willis departed from the standard position of the 'pious natural philosophers', claiming that through the labours of alchemists a partial redemption of the creation is possible prior to the final consummation of all things. The discovery of 'a complete elementate Compound' was to restore the original dominion that Adam had enjoyed over natural things, thus reversing one of the most catastrophic consequences of the Fall. As Willis himself expressed it, 'Man is restored to God by the suffering of one most perfect; so natural things under the ordinance of God unto man by one most exactly purified, digested and regenerated naturall compound'.[162]

In linking personal inspiration and the authority of scripture, Willis was fairly typical of those who invoked inward divine revelations as a literally impeccable source of knowledge. One of the assumptions of those who advocated this approach was that if God had originally inspired Adam with a knowledge of natural things, then communication of such knowledge to Adam's latter day progeny was possible, at least in principle. The authority of scripture, moreover, was attributed to the fact that God had inspired its human authors with a knowledge that was beyond their natural capacities. Once again, if in the past God had infused the biblical authors with such wisdom there seemed no obvious reason why he could not similarly

---

[160] *Ibid.*, ch. 1.
[161] Timothy Willis, *The Search of Causes. Containing a Theosophicall Investigation of the Possibilitie of Transmutatorie Alchemie* (London, 1616), pp. 1, 20f.
[162] *Ibid.*, p. 41.

inspire worthy individuals in the present. However, from this logic it necessarily followed, that scripture, too, must remain an important source of our knowledge. Robert Fludd, for example, had pointed out that Moses had 'conversed with God and obtained the key to both types of understanding (natural and supernatural) by divine assistance and illumination of the most Holy Spirit'.[163] Notwithstanding his belief that Plato and Hermes Trismegistus had shared in divine secrets about the world, Fludd also declared that 'heavenly wisdom is onely mystically revealed unto mankind as being reserved in the power of God, and solely discovered or opened unto the Saints, and elect, and therefore unknown unto the Pagans; or Ethnick wise-men'.[164]

It is possible to discern important differences amongst those who appealed to scriptural authority in the realm of natural philosophy. Johann Jakob Brucker (1696–1770), one of the very first historians of philosophy, was rightly to distinguish between those who appealed to the letter of scripture and those who sought more inspired allegorical readings.[165] What separates such thinkers as Lambert Daneau from those of a more enthusiastic bent was, on Brucker's analysis, the extent to which reason was demoted and revelation elevated in the quest for true knowledge. Appeals to scripture might thus be combined with varying degrees of reliance upon reason, experience, or divine revelation. Jan Comenius is a case in point. Based on the title of his *Physicae ad lumen divinum reformatae synopsis* (A Synopsis of Physics reformed by Divine Light, 1633) he might seem to be best consigned a place among the philosophical enthusiasts.[166] In his preface, however, Comenius goes on to insist that 'The seeds of true Philosophy . . . are conteined in the holy Book of the Bible', which seems to qualify him for a place in the ranks of the Mosaic philosophers. In yet a further qualification, however, he announced that reason and the senses should also take their place alongside holy writ. 'The onely true, genuine and plain way of Philosophie', Comenius states, is 'to fetch all things from sense, reason, and Scripture'.[167]

---

[163] Robert Fludd, *Apologia compendiaria*, in *Robert Fludd*, ed. Huffman, p. 46.

[164] Fludd, *Mosaicall Philosophy*, p. 10.

[165] Johann Jakob Brucker, *Historia critica philosophiae* (Leipzig, 1743), vol. IV, pt I, bk 3, ch. 2, pp. 610f. Blair, 'Mosaic Physics', p. 36.

[166] I have used the seventeenth-century English translation, *Naturall Philosophie Reformed by Divine Light: or, A synopsis of Physics* (London, 1651). In the frontispiece Comenius commends the sentiments of Juan Luis Vives: 'Nature is not to be examined by the Lamp of the Gentiles, yielding both an obscure and maligne light: but by the Torch of the Sunne, which Christ hath brought into the darknesse of the World'.

[167] Comenius, *Naturall Philosophie*, Preface. In fact Comenius condemned those whose sole resort in natural philosophy was the bible: 'they that heed the Scripture onely, and hearken neither to sense

John Webster (1611–82), a radical critic of the English universities during the Commonwealth period, had a similarly comprehensive view. *The Saints Guide* (1654) begins with a chapter devoted to 'Humane Learning', which Webster defines as 'that Science or knowledge that is or may be acquired by Natural power, capacity and industry: To the attaining of which, the immediate concourse of Gods Spirit is necessary, and the common grace of the holy Ghost requisite'. This 'acquired knowledge' was distinguished from 'infused knowledge' – 'that evidential and experimental knowledge, which men partake of, by the sending in, inflowing, and indwelling of the Spirit of Christ'.[168] Both forms of knowledge called for divine activity, but in the case of infused knowledge this activity was immediate and direct. Acquired knowledge was subsequently identified with that worldly wisdom that is 'foolishness with God', the paradigm case of which was scholastic learning, itself derived from 'the rotten rubbish of Ethnical and Babylonish ruines'.[169] His proposed reforms of the curriculum were eclectic in the extreme, combining elements of Paracelsianism, Helmontian iatrochemistry, the theosophy of Boehme and Fludd, and the corpuscular theories of Gassendi and Digby, all motivated by a Baconian ideology. The assumption was, presumably, that these were all examples of 'infused knowledge'. Webster's stated aim in all of this was a re-establishment of the knowledge that Adam had possessed by divine grant.[170]

While this talk of divine inspiration and personal experience may seem to be the very antithesis of scientific knowledge, Webster's use of the expression 'experimental knowledge' should give us pause. During this period, it should be pointed out, 'experiment' and 'experimental' had broad connotations. Throughout the Middle Ages and for much of the early modern period 'experimental' was more or less synonymous with 'experiential'. Aquinas, for example, had written that 'perception implies a certain experimental knowledge', but by this he meant nothing more than that perception

---

nor reason are either carried away beyond the world (by the sublimity of their conceptions;) or else involve things they understand not with the Colliers faith; or following the letter, propound unto themselves things, though never so absurd and superstitious, to be believed; as the Papists do in that most absurd transubstantiation of theirs &c'. *Ibid.*

[168] John Webster, *The Saints Guide*, p. 1. Also see Webster, *The Judgement Set, and the Books Opened . . . in Several Sermons* (London, 1654), 'To the Reader' (by Thomas Somerton); Webster, *Academiarum Examen*, p. 9.

[169] Webster, *Academiarum Examen*, pp. 5, 15. Webster seems to have undergone a change of mind during the 1670s, rebuking the Quakers and other 'fanatics' for claiming to be inspired in their interpretations of scripture – this in spite of an obvious earlier sympathy with many of the views of the Quakers. See 'Webster, John (1611–1682)', *ODNB*.

[170] Webster, *Academiarum Examen*, pp. 26–9.

requires sensory experience.[171] Thus Adam was said to have gained experimental knowledge (*experimentalem cognitionem*) of the animals when they paraded before him.[172] In neither instance is there any suggestion that the conducting of experiments is involved. In the context in which Webster is using it above, 'experimental' refers to direct experience, as opposed to abstract speculation or second-hand knowledge derived from books or other authorities. In fact, while in the seventeenth century the term could be used in a general sense, or in connection with the new philosophy of experiments, it was deployed primarily in a religious context.[173] The earliest occurrence of the English term in printed sources is to 'experimental witnesses of Christ's deeds' (*c.* 1449).[174] William Bonde's *Pilgrymage of perfeccyon* (1531) refers to the 'argumentes and experyments' by which Christ appeared to his disciples and of 'Experymentall knowlege of the heuenly lyfe to come'.[175] Throughout the seventeenth century it was common, especially amongst Puritan authors, to speak of 'experimental Christians', 'experimental prayer', 'experimental divinity', and 'experimental divines', in all cases the emphasis being placed on immediate, personal experience of the divine.[176] Webster's usage was typical in opposing experimental knowledge to book learning or to theoretical speculation. His earlier contemporary

---

[171] '*perceptio enim experimentalem quandam notitiam significant*'. Aquinas, ST 1a. 43, 5; Cf. 2a2ae. 45, 2; 97, 2.

[172] Aquinas, ST 1a. 96, 1.

[173] Bacon, e.g., spoke of the 'two faculties, the experimental and the rational', *Novum Organum* 1, §95 (*Works* IV, 92). Bacon distinguishes between experience and experiment: 'There remains simple experience; which, if taken as it comes, is called accident if sought for, experiment.' *Novum Organum* 1, §1 (*Works* IV, 82). Also see Peter Dear, *Discipline and Experience: The Mathematical Way in the Scientific Revolution* (Chicago, 1995), pp. 21f. Hobbes offers slightly different definitions: 'The remembrance of the succession of one thing to another, that is, of what was antecedent, and what consequent, and what concomitant, is called an experiment; whether the same be made by us voluntarily, as when a man putteth any thing into the fire, to see what effect the fire will produce upon it; or not made by us, as when we remember a fair morning after a red evening. To have had many experiments, is that we call EXPERIENCE, which is nothing else but remembrance of what antecedents have been followed with what consequents.' *Elements of Law*, I.iv.6 (Tönnies edn, 1889), p. 14. Hobbes also regarded his political philosophy, like his physics, to be experimental. *Dialogus physicus*, tr. in Shapin and Schaffer, *Leviathan and the Air Pump*, p. 391.

[174] Pecock, *The repressor of over much blaming of the clergy* (*c.* 1449), IV.iv.448, in *OED*, 2nd edn, s.v. 'experimental'.

[175] William Bonde, *Pilgrymage of perfeccyon* (London, 1531), fols. 209b, 46b.

[176] Joseph Hall, *Epistles*, 3 vols. (London, 1608–11), I, 7 (experimental divinity); Laurence Womock, *The examination of Tilenus before the triers* (London, 1657), p. 85 (experimental divines); John Woodhouse, *A catalogue of sins highly useful to self-acquaintance, experimental prayer; and above all to a suitable preparation, for a worthy partaking of the supper of the Lord* (London, 1699); J. L., *A small mite . . . Whereunto are added two new songs: the one being some brief touches on the 12 chapter of the Revelation, more fully to be enlarged in the experimental Christian* (London, 1654). See also Ralph Venning, *Orthodox paradoxes, theological and experimental* (London, 1654); Thomas Bromley, *The way to the sabbath of rest. Or, The souls progresse in the work of regeneration. Being a brief experimental discourse of the new-birth* (London, 1655); William Dimsdale, *The Quaker converted;*

and friend of Francis Bacon, John Everard (*c.* 1584–1640/41), also spoke disparagingly of 'letter learning' and 'university knowledge', arguing that it was more desirable to 'know Jesus Christ and the scriptures experimentally rather than grammatically, literally or academically'.[177] The prolific writer of religious tracts, Richard Younge (*fl.* 1636–73), followed suit, distinguishing between '*natural* and *speculative knowledge*', which the wicked share with the godly, and '*experimental,* and *saving knowledge,* which is *supernatural,* and *descendeth from above*'.[178] There could also be 'experimental knowledge' in the sphere of moral philosophy. Puritan preacher Thomas Goodwin (1600–79), an associate of Hartlib and John Dury, spoke of the necessity for 'a real and experimental' knowledge of our moral obligations. This was gained, Goodwin suggested, 'from examples of godly men whom they have lived amongst, or the observations of God's dealings with themselves or others, and not only from the word notionally'. He concluded that in the moral context 'knowledge got by experiments of mercies or judgments is of more force and evidence'.[179]

While a full study of possible links between experimental natural philosophy and experimental religion in the seventeenth century has yet to be conducted, there are some plausible connections.[180] The emphasis in Puritanism on the first-person encounter with God bears an important analogy to the replacement, in experimental philosophy, of reliance on authorities and written traditions with individual experience. The general Protestant rejection of implicit faith is also similarly suggestive of not accepting facts on the authority of others. Thus Calvin complained that the vast majority of Christians simply 'embrace every dictate of the Church as true, or leave to the Church the province of inquiring and determining'.[181] Calvin's own position was characterised, accurately enough, by Cardinal Bellarmine, as that which allowed 'individual persons to be judges in

or the experimental knowledg of Jesus Christ crucified, in opposition to the principles of the Quakers (London, 1690).

177 Quoted in Hill, *World Turned Upside Down*, p. 264.
178 Richard Younge, *No Wicked Man a Wise Man, True Wisdom described. The Excellency of Spiritual, Experimental and Saving Knowledge, above all Humane Wisdom and Learning* (London, 1666), p. 6; cf. Younge, *An Experimental Index of the Heart* (London, 1658), passim.
179 Thomas Goodwin, *Aggravation of Sin*, in *The Works of Thomas Goodwin, D.D.*, 12 vols. (Edinburgh, 1862), IV, 183. This is not to say Goodwin was a fellow-traveller with Webster. As Master of Magdalen College, Oxford in the 1650s, Goodwin defended the university against the assaults of Webster and Dell.
180 For some interesting observations on possible connections see Karen Edwards, *Milton and the Natural World: Science and Poetry in Paradise Lost* (Cambridge, 2000), pp. 47f., 64–82. See also Webster, *Great Instauration*, p. 284.
181 Calvin, *Institutes*, Prefatory Address (McNeill I, 14); *Institutes* III.ii (Beveridge I, 470). For support of implicit faith see Aquinas, ST 2a2ae. 5–8.

matters of faith'.[182] The equivalent doctrine, embodied in the words of the motto of the Royal Society – *nullius in verba* (roughly translated 'on no man's word') – enshrined the principle of not accepting established truths about the natural world without testing them against experience.[183] The parallel contrast between the experimental and speculative in the respective spheres of religion and philosophy is also important.[184]

There is another reason why this talk of the role of divine inspiration in the acquisition of scientific knowledge should not be regarded as completely inimical to the spirit of scientific investigation, and that is because virtually everyone who made knowledge claims in the early modern period took pains to attribute at least some of their achievement to the grace of God. Osiander wrote in his Preface to the *De revolutionibus* of Copernicus that neither mathematicians nor philosophers would find the truth unless it was divinely revealed to them.[185] Galileo described his telescopic discoveries as having been made 'after first being illuminated by divine grace'.[186] Johann Alsted and his old teacher, Bartholomäus Keckermann, both believed that the great philosophers of the past had benefited from divine revelations and they exhorted students in their charge to pray that the Holy Spirit might similarly inspire them.[187] George Baker wrote in his Preface to John Gerard's *Herbal* – then the standard work – that 'it was impossible for man to finde out the nature of plants, if the great worker, which is God, had not first instructed and taught him'.[188] That such allusions to divine assistance are not merely rhetorical flourishes is evident in Robert Boyle's musings about the possible role of divine inspiration in the business of scientific discovery:

And though I dare not affirm, with some of the Helmontians and Paracelsians, that God discloses to men the great mystery of chemistry by good angels, or by nocturnal visions . . . yet persuaded I am, that the favour of God does (much more than men are aware of) vouchsafe to promote some men's proficiency in the study of nature.

---

[182] Bellarmine, *Disputations* I.iii.3, in Blackwell, *Galileo, Bellarmine, and the Bible*, appendix III, p. 193.

[183] The motto is a fragment from Horace: 'Nullius addictus jurare in verba magister' (I am not bound by allegiance to the dogmas of any master), *Epistles* I.I.14.

[184] On this distinction see Peter Anstey, 'Experimental versus speculative natural philosophy', in Peter Anstey and John Schuster (eds.), *The Science of Nature in the Seventeenth Century* (Dordrecht, 2005), pp. 215–42.

[185] Osiander, Preface to Nicholas Copernicus, *On the Revolutions*, ed. Jerzy Dobrzycki, tr. Edward Rosen (Baltimore, 1978), p. xx.

[186] Galileo, *The Starry Messenger*, in *Discoveries and Opinions*, p. 28.

[187] Hotson, *Johann Heinrich Alsted*, pp. 78f.

[188] John Gerard, *The Herbal or Generall Historie of Plantes* (London, 1636), 2nd Preface. See also Parkinson, *Paradisi in Sole*, To the Reader; Jean Gailhard, *The Compleat Gentleman: or Directions for the Education of Youth* (London, 1678), p. 25.

God exercised his subtle influence, Boyle went on to say, by means of 'happy and pregnant hints'.[189]

This providential assistance, it must be conceded, can be distinguished from miraculous and mystical communications that lack any further epistemic support. Whatever subtle divine influence may have been exerted on Galileo and Boyle, to some extent their discoveries were capable of independent verification. As Boyle himself makes abundantly clear, he understood his position on the divine inspiration to be quite different from that of the Helmontians and Paracelsians. And whatever the extent of these 'hints' provided by divine providence, Boyle and Galileo thought it appropriate to publish their discoveries for the benefit of all, unlike the Renaissance magi. What these moderate invocations of the divine inspiration do indicate, however, is the extent to which in an era that sought firm foundations for knowledge God was the ultimate guarantor. Present to some degree in Kepler and Galileo, this stance is most often – and quite correctly – associated with Descartes, who in the Meditations asserted that 'man cannot achieve correct knowledge of natural things so long as he does not know God'.[190] Descartes' disciple Malebranche was even more explicit: 'The mind becomes purer, more luminous, stronger, and of greater scope as its union with God increases, because this union constitutes its entire perfection.' In this almost quasi-mystical state, the mind can grasp the divinely implanted ideas, without creaturely distractions, and thus arrive at an unimpeachable knowledge.[191] These sentiments were echoed across the Channel in the conviction of the English physician Walter Charleton (1620–1707) 'that no one thing in Nature can be known, unless the Author of Nature be first knowne'.[192] This was not a mere intellectual assent to the existence of God, moreover. Rather, knowledge of the Deity was required for 'the *Rectification* of perverted *Judgments*'.[193] Isaac Barrow, Newton's predecessor in the Lucasian Chair of Mathematics, also affirmed Descartes' basic insight: 'it seems to floowe, that every *Demonstration*, to make it effectively such, does in some sort suppose the Existence of God; not only on the

---

[189] Boyle, *Usefulness of Experimental Natural Philosophy, Works* II, 61.

[190] Descartes, *Objections and Replies*, CSM II, 290.

[191] Malebranche, *Search After Truth*, p. xxxvii. The Cartesian Pierre Poiret was even more overtly mystical. See Thomas M. Lennon, 'The Cartesian Dialectic of Creation', in Daniel Garber and Michael Ayers (eds.), *The Cambridge History of Seventeenth-Century Philosophy*, 2 vols. (Cambridge, 1998), I, 331–62.

[192] Walter Charleton, *The Darknes of Atheism Dispelled by the Light of Nature. A Physico-theological Treatise* (London, 1652). Charleton actually identifies his position with the scholastic motto: *Nulla res, qualifcunque est, intelligi potest, nisi Deus paus intelligatur*. For Charleton's approval of the method of the *Meditations*, see sig. b3r–v.

[193] *Ibid.*, sig. a2v.

Part of the knowing power or faculty, but also on the part of the knowable Object. *Cartesius* has very well observed, that to make us absolutely certain of our having attained the Truth, it is required to be known whether our Faculties of apprehending and judging the Truth be true, which can only be had from the Power, Goodness, and Truth of our Creator'.[194]

In spite of the obvious differences between the basic approaches of these individuals, and varying extents to which they drew upon divine inspiration, it is not altogether surprising to discover that they could all be lumped together as fanciful enthusiasts. The Aristotelian metaphysician John Sergeant (1622–1707) was thus to accuse the French philosophers of enthusiasm. Descartes' philosophical musings were attributed to the 'Spice of Enthusiasm; which dispos'd his Mind, already quite spent, in such a manner, that it was fit to receive Impressions of *Dreams* and *Visions*'. Malebranche was no better, for dispensing entirely with 'all *Humane Means*' of science he had joined the ranks of the philosophical zealots who 'pretend that their Light of Knowledge comes to them immediately from God'.[195] Philosophers such as these, Sergeant thought, introduce 'Fanaticism into Philosophy; built, in the main, or in great part, on a pretended *Inward Light* by means of those Imaginary and Visionary *Ideas*'.[196] But Sergeant also extended his criticisms to those prone to empiricism, and John Locke was added to Descartes and Malebranche to make up the full complement of 'philosophical fanatics'. Meric Casaubon, whose father had so effectively deflated the claims of the hermeticists, similarly regarded the experimentalists as treading the path towards a dangerous new form of enthusiasm.[197]

It was Sergeant's deep conviction that all of these elaborate attempts to find new and certain foundations for knowledge were completely unnecessary. He retained a belief in a relatively uncritical Aristotelian epistemology in which reason played an unproblematic role. He also took pains to set out the Aristotelian/Thomist view that 'true knowledge' is the 'natural end' or 'natural perfection' of human beings, and he insisted, crucially, that original sin had not hampered the attainment of that natural end:

---

[194] Isaac Barrow, *The Usefulness of Mathematical Learning Explained and Demonstrated: being Mathematical Lectures read in the Publick Schools at the University of Cambridge*, tr. John Kirby (London, 1734), [Lecture VII], pp. 109f.

[195] John Sergeant, *Solid Philosophy Asserted*, sig. b1v; *Non Ultra: or, A letter to a Learned Cartesian* (London, 1698), p. 110.

[196] Sergeant, *Solid Philosophy Asserted*, sig. A4v.

[197] Michael Heyd, 'The New Experimental Philosophy: A Manifestation of Enthusiasm or an Antidote to it?', *Minerva* 25 (1987), 423–40; Adrian Johns, 'The Physiology of Reading', in Frasca-Spada and Jardine (eds.), *Books and the Sciences in History*, pp. 291–314 (p. 301). On Casaubon's attitude to experimental philosophy see Richard Serjeantson's introduction to Meric Casaubon, *Generall Learning: A Seventeenth-Century Treatise on the Formation of the General Scholar* (Cambridge, 1999).

I see no Reason why Original Sin, which works only by giving us Corrupt Inclinations, should hinder us from concluding right in points meerly Speculative, to which our Discourse confines us; nor why an Archimedes, an Euclid, an Aristotle, or an Hippocrates, tho' Heathens, may not arrive at Truth in Mathematics, and other Sciences to which they applied themselves; nor why a man of a Wicked Life, whose Soul is Corrupted with Actual Sin added to Original, may not cast up an Accompt right, as well as he might have done had Adam never fallen.[198]

The methodological prescriptions of both Cartesians and experimentalists were thus excessive and unwarranted as far as Sergeant was concerned, for the fallen condition of the human race was an irrelevant consideration in the sphere of natural philosophy. While he did not deny the reality of original sin, he nonetheless insisted that it called for no additional compensatory mechanisms in the sphere of natural philosophy. For this reason, the philosophical insights of Aristotle, who had known nothing of original sin, were still applicable.

The challenges that confronted the traditional forms of learning in the sixteenth and seventeenth centuries stimulated a number of quite different responses, examples of which have been considered in this chapter. Many of these were destined to play only a small part in the standard narrative of the history of modern science. Biblically grounded Mosaic philosophy hardly outlasted the seventeenth century, and in the century that followed Louis Buffon was summarily to dismiss creative combinations of biblical writ and natural philosophy as 'the dark clouds of physical theology'.[199] This is not to say that congruity between science and scripture ceased to become important, but rather that increasingly the bible ceased to be regarded as a significant repository of scientific information. Perhaps the more recent advent of scientific creationism in the twentieth century might be said to hark back to these earlier attempts to base a natural philosophy on the biblical text, but the Mosaic philosophers were typically interested in integrating biblical teaching with the latest scientific theories, such as Cartesianism or Newtonianism. Moreover, the vast majority of seventeenth-century thinkers, in spite of their commitment to the literal sense of scripture, were far more likely than the modern creationists to allow that the biblical message had been 'accommodated' to the understandings of the audience to which it was first delivered. Divine inspiration is rarely invoked in accounts of scientific discovery, and is no longer regarded as a crucial feature of the acquisition of

[198] Sergeant, *Method to Science*, sig. a2v.
[199] Georges Louis Leclerc, Comte de Buffon, *Natural History, General and Particular*, tr. W. Smellie, 20 vols. (London, 1812), I, 131.

knowledge. It might be said, however, that the basic sentiment survives in a vestigial form in the idea, so beloved of the popular science writer, of the lone scientific genius who makes the major breakthrough after a sudden burst of insight. Of the approaches surveyed in this chapter, the idea that the universe has a mathematical structure has been the most influential, and is a central feature of modern physics, even if the question of the reality of mathematical constructions remains with us.

All of these attempts, in one way or another, sought ultimately to justify knowledge claims by an appeal to God. The new consciousness of the limitations of the human mind prompted attempts to seek certainty in the mathematical ideas that were a participation in the divine mind, in the written records of divine revelation, or in direct communications from the Deity. Each of these strategies also represented an attempt to re-theologise epistemology in light of the perceived failings of sciences that bracketed out the significance of the Christian revelation. What they retained from the traditional model, however, was a view of scientific knowledge as certain and demonstrable. If they dispensed with Aristotelian methods of science, they nonetheless retained the Aristotelian ideal of science. The more radical alternative was to dispense with both. A premise of the experimental approach to natural philosophy that developed in England over the course of the seventeenth century was the idea that certainty could never be achieved in the sciences, and that investigators of nature needed to lower their sights. For the experimental philosophers, guided by the Baconian vision of science as the gradual accumulation of 'historical' or experimental reports, science was to be a long-term and probabilistic enterprise. Their more restricted vision of the prospects of science was based in turn on a more sober appraisal of postlapsarian minds and senses. Experimental philosophy – which will be the subject of the next two chapters – sought the slow recovery of Adamic knowledge, but with an acute awareness that human investigators no longer possessed the perfect faculties of their first father.

CHAPTER 4

Dethroning the idols

But then we must look for the intentions of nature in things which retain their nature, and not in things which are corrupted. And therefore we must study the man who is in the most perfect state both of body and soul, for in him we shall see the true relation of the two; although in bad or corrupted natures the body will often appear to rule over the soul, because they are in an evil and unnatural condition.   Aristotle, *Politics*, 1254B

It is impossible to make a man who was born blind conceive that he does not see; impossible to make him desire sight and regret its absence. Wherefore we should take no assurance from the fact that our soul is content and satisfied with the senses we have, seeing that it has no means of feeling its malady and imperfection therein, if any there be.[1]   Montaigne, *Apology for Raymond Sebond*

For man by the fall fell at the same time from his state of innocency and from his dominion over creation. Both of these losses however can even in this life be in some part repaired; the former by religion and faith, the latter by arts and sciences. For creation was not by the curse made altogether and for ever a rebel, but in virtue of that charter, 'In the sweat of thy face shalt thou eat bread,' it is now by various labours (not certainly by disputations or idle magical ceremonies, but by various labours) at length and in some measure subdued to the supplying of man with bread; that is, to the uses of human life.
                                    Bacon, *Novum Organum* II, §52

The importance of self-knowledge to the philosophical quest had been asserted from the very inception of philosophy. The ancient maxim 'Know thyself' had adorned the temple at Delphi, and knowledge of one's own ignorance was the foundation of Socratic teaching.[2] In the early modern

---

[1] Montaigne, *Essays*, pp. 444f.
[2] Plato, *Apology* 20e–21d. See also Xenophon, *Memorabilia* IV.ii.24–9; Aristotle, *Rhetoric* II.xxi.1395a; Cicero, *Tusculan Disputations* I.xxii.52; Plutarch, *Adversus Colotem*, 1118C.

139

period, however, the quest for self-knowledge took on a new complexion as the newly revived Augustinian anthropology led to wide-ranging discussions about the defects of the human mind and the limitations of knowledge that flowed from them. Augustine himself commended the Delphic injunction, but observed that the ancients had utterly failed in their attempts to grasp the essence of human nature. Although some of the more acute pagan authorities had understood that the mind, distracted by the senses and the material realm, had literally forgotten itself, none had known that this condition was the result of the Fall.[3] In the sixteenth century, John Calvin thought it necessary to remind his readers of Augustine's criticism. True knowledge of ourselves consists in two things: 'first in considering what we were given at creation', and second, 'our miserable condition after Adam's fall'.[4] The philosophers had been right to recommend self-knowledge, but had confused 'two very diverse states of man'. Their explorations of human nature had amounted to 'seeking in a ruin for a building, and in scattered fragments for a well-knit structure'.[5] Their endeavours demonstrated that without the revealed knowledge of sacred history, man 'is puffed up with insane confidence in his own mental powers, and can never be induced to recognize their slenderness'.[6] Luther had articulated the same view, noting that reason 'knows nothing about the wretchedness of depraved nature'.[7] The pagan philosophers, and those who uncritically adopted their methods, were regarded as having been blissfully unaware of the fact that their blithe confidence in the operations of the mind was completely unwarranted. It is hardly surprising, in light of these criticisms of classical anthropology, that the early modern period witnessed renewed attempts to establish a truly 'Christian' understanding of human nature. With the revival of interest in biblical narratives, particularly in early modern England, it was inevitable that Adam would become a central figure in all those intellectual domains in which anthropology was thought to be important – theology, moral psychology, educational and political theory and, not least, natural philosophy.

---

[3] Augustine, *The Trinity*, x.ii. Cf. Bonaventure: 'If you would know yourself perfectly . . . ponder what you were, are, should have been, and can be: what you were by nature, what you now are through sin, what you should have been through effort, and what you still can be through grace.' *Mystical opuscula, Works* I, 214.

[4] Calvin, *Institutes.*, II.i.1 (McNeill I, 242). Cf. *Commentary on Genesis* 1:26, *Calvin's Commentaries* I, 94.

[5] *Ibid.*, I.xv.7 (McNeill I, 194, 196). Cf. *Commentary on Jeremiah* 6:10, *Calvin's Commentaries* IX, 329f.

[6] *Ibid.*, II.vii.6 (I, 355).

[7] Luther, *Lectures on Genesis 1–5*, LW I, 166; Luther, *Sermons* III, 231.

SELF-KNOWLEDGE AND THE SCIENCES

The importance of arriving at a correct view of human nature and the need to pay close attention to the history of Adam were persistent themes in seventeenth-century theological writings. Anglican divine Thomas Jackson (1578–1640), in spite of his rejection of elements of Calvinism, argued that a 'true estimate or experimental evaluation' of the work of Christ required first and foremost 'a Right Understanding of the Primeval State of Adam'. For Jackson, this brought with it a right understanding of human nature, itself a prerequisite for proper knowledge of God: 'We must learn to know our selves before we can attain unto the true or perfect knowledge of God . . . And this true knowledge of our selves hath a double Aspect, the one unto the *Estate from which* the other unto the Estate into which we are fallen.'[8] Plato's reservations about empirical knowledge were right, but for the wrong reasons. Our ignorance proceeds not from our embodiment, but from Adam's sin.[9] Robert Ferguson (*d.* 1714), who is perhaps better known for his lengthy career as a Whig conspirator than as a theological author, expressed reservations about the sanguine marriage of reason and religion promoted by some Fellows of the Royal Society. Applying Calvin's distinction between 'two states of man' to his inquiry into the nature of the intellect, he pointed out that reason 'may be considered either as it ought to be, and originally was; or as it exists subjectively in us, weakned, darkned and tainted by the Fall'. The distinction was crucial because 'the rational Faculty as it exists in us since the ingress of sin, differs much from what it was in its primitive Creation'.[10] In fact most members of that august body held positions that were not too remote from Ferguson's own. Robert Boyle, in his capacity as an amateur theologian, offered this list of theological fundamentals: 'a man must know much of the nature of spirits in general, and even of the father of them God himself; of the intellect, will, &. of the soul of man; of the state of *Adam* in paradise, and after his fall; of the influence of his fall upon his posterity . . .'[11] Theological writers of various persuasions were similarly conscious of the different ways in which Adam's loss was formulated in different confessions. Jackson noted that the Catholic position, endorsed at Trent, was that original sin was 'no more than a meer *Privation* of Original Justice'. This differed from his view, according to which original sin had

---

[8] Thomas Jackson, *An Exact Collection of the Works of Doctor Jackson* (London, 1654), title page, p. 3002.
[9] 'That Oblivion then or obstupefaction wherein our soules as Plato dreames, are miserably drencht by their delapse into these bodily sinks of corruption, wee may more truly derive from that pollution which we naturally draw from our first Parents.' *Originall of Unbeliefe*, p. 90.
[10] Robert Ferguson, *The Interest of Reason in Religion* (London, 1675), p. 19.
[11] Boyle, *High Veneration*, *Works* v, 144.

made a much deeper wound in human nature.[12] The unknown author of *Anthropologie Abstracted* (1655), a work devoted to an examination of human nature, concurred with Jackson's judgement, insisting that 'the Soul in supernaturalibus est *deprivata*, in naturalibus *depravata*'.[13] Puritan Divine Richard Baxter (1615–91), in his *Two Disputations on Original Sin* (1675), also alluded to 'that opinion wherein the Papists differ from our Divines; *viz.* that Grace was supernatural to *Adam*; and original sin being nothing but the privation of that Grace or Rectitude'.[14] Some measure of the gravity of these issues can be ascertained from the scale of the controversies which they were capable of generating. When in 1655 Jeremy Taylor, author of numerous popular religious works, published *Unum Necessarium* – a work which essentially denied that original sin is inherited – he unleashed a storm of controversy. Rebuttals flowed from the pens of fellow Anglicans and Puritans alike.[15] The scale of the controversy not only showed that Taylor was outside the bounds of the broadly Augustinian views of the vast majority of his contemporaries, but also serves to underscore the contemporary importance of these questions about human nature and the state of Adam in his innocence.

Taylor, however, was far from denying the significance of the Fall and in this respect shared the broad perspective of the overwhelming majority of his contemporaries. Even those groups with a relatively strong view of the integrity of reason took the doctrine of the Fall quite seriously. The so-called Cambridge Platonists, usually taken to include Benjamin Whichcote (1609–83), Henry More (1614–87), Ralph Cudworth (1617–89), Peter Sterry (1613–72), John Smith (1618–52), and Nathaniel Culverwell (1619–51), are noted for their generally high estimate of the competence of reason.[16] Benjamin Whichcote, generally considered to be the progenitor of the group, opposed what he regarded as the exaggerated pessimism of the

---

[12] Jackson, *Works*, p. 3004. See also John Davenant, *Determinationes Quaestionum Quarundam Theologicarum* (Cambridge, 1634), p. 77; Nathaniel Culverwell, *An Elegant and Learned Discourse of the Light of Nature* (1652), ed. R. Greene and H. MacCallum (Indianapolis, 2001), p. 123.

[13] Anon., *Anthropologie Abstracted: or the Idea of Humane Nature* (London, 1655), p. 43.

[14] Richard Baxter, *Two Disputations on Original Sin* (London, 1675), p. 242; cf. pp. 67, 75; *The Judgment of Non-Conformists, of the Interest of Reason, in Matters of Religion* (London, 1676), pp. 8–10.

[15] Jeremy Taylor, *Unum Necessarium* (1655), ch. 6. Responses included John Ford, *An Essay of Original Righteousness and Conveyed Sin* (n.p., 1657); John Gaule, *Sapientia Justificata* (London, 1657); Nathaniel Stephens, *Vindiciae Fundamenti* (London, 1658); Henry Jeanes, *The Second Part of the Mixture of Scholasticall Divinity* (Oxford, 1660); Burgesse, *Doctrine of Originall Sin*. For an excellent overview of the debates see Poole, *Milton and the Fall*, pp. 40–57.

[16] Sarah Hutton, 'The Cambridge Platonists', in S. Nadler (ed.), *A Companion to Early Modern Philosophy* (Oxford, 2002), pp. 308–19; Harrison, *'Religion' and the Religions*, pp. 28–60.

Puritan party, and insisted that the human mind bore within it a number of 'truths of first inscription' which could not be erased. These universal principles, manifested primarily as intuitions of basic moral truths, represented 'the light of God's creation', and were 'immutable and indispensable'.[17] Henry More repeated the argument of Thomas Aquinas, that to deny the efficacy of fallen reason completely was to destroy human nature itself: 'To take away *Reason* therefore, under what Fanatick pretense soever, is to disrobe the Priest and despoil him of his *Breast-plate*.'[18] Nathaniel Culverwell begins his *Elegant and Learned Discourse of the Light of Nature* (1652) with the biblical verse that became the unofficial motto of the group – 'the understanding of man is the candle of the Lord' (Prov. 20:27), and much of what follows is a commentary on the powers of reason. But none of this entailed a denial that reason was significantly wounded by the Fall. Henry More devoted a considerable portion of *Conjectura Cabbalistica* (1663) to an exegesis of the Genesis account of the Fall, and although his reading of it has a distinctively Platonic cast, it nonetheless concedes the gravity of the loss that accompanied the Fall. As a cosmic event, the Fall also played a crucial role in More's theodicy.[19] Culverwell's *Discourse* can be read as an attempt to fulfil Bacon's desire to clarify the scope of reason and faith. Culverwell actually begins with a paraphrase of Bacon: ''Tis a thing very material and desirable, to give unto *Reason* the things that are *Reasons*, and unto *Faith* the things that are *Faiths*, to give *Faith* her full scope and latitude, and to give *Reason* also her just bounds and limits.'[20] Culverwell immediately proceeds to the question of the Fall. 'Far be it from me', he says, 'to extenuate that great and fatal overthrow, which the sons of men had in their first and original apostasie from their God, that under which the whole Creation sigh's and groanes.' As for reason, 'this daughter of the morning is fallen from her primitive glory' and 'from her original vigour and perfection'; it 'is weakened, and vitiated', a 'feeble and diminished light'.[21] Culverwell's point is that the sorry state in which reason now languishes is not a justification for abandoning it.

A second party whose members entertained a relatively high view of the capacities of reason was a group of moderate churchmen known as

---

[17] Benjamin Whichcote, *The Works of the Learned Benjamin Whichcote, D. D.*, 4 vols. (Aberdeen, 1751), III, 20f., 31.

[18] Henry More, *A Collection*, pp. v–vi.

[19] More, *Conjectura Cabbalistica*, pp. 46, 50f., 71. On More's theodicy see Harrison '*Religion' and the Religions*, p. 58.

[20] Culverwell, *Learned Discourse*, p. 10. Cf. Bacon, *Advancement*, *Works* III, 350.

[21] *Ibid.*, pp. 10, 12, 118.

the 'Latitudinarians'.[22] The names most closely associated with this group include those of John Tillotson (1630–94), Edward Stillingfleet (1635–99), Simon Patrick (1626–1707), and John Wilkins (1614–72). Yet in the writings of these thinkers the doctrine of the Fall is treated in a quite conventional fashion – if anything, even more so than in the Cambridge Platonists. The impact of sin on reason was also clearly acknowledged. John Wilkins, often regarded as one of the leading figures of the group, stated explicitly that Adam's sin was both imputed and naturally communicated to his posterity. Original sin consisted in a 'depravation upon our natures' that makes us 'loathsome and abominable in God's eyes'. We are now 'corrupted vessels [that] pollute all the gifts that are poured into us'. Sin has completely altered us both outwardly and inwardly, infecting our understandings and memories. Indeed one mark of our fallen state is 'our aptnesse to slight and undervalue the thought of this original corruption'.[23] Simon Patrick agreed that 'we were tainted in our first Father, who hath left a foul blot and stain upon our Nature: and we feel that weakness in our reason, that strength and violence in our passions'. He further confessed: 'I loath and abhor my self, as unworthy to live and breath on the face of the earth.'[24] These are not the sentiments that one would associate with a minimalist position in relation to the consequences of original sin.

Thus, while it would be a gross exaggeration to state that there was unanimity on the nature and consequences of the Fall during this period, there was general agreement that questions relating to human nature and knowledge could not be addressed adequately without a consideration of this primeval event. Varying estimates of the severity of the Fall gave rise to different assessments of human capacities and strategies for knowledge acquisition. Jackson wrote that on the milder Catholic view of the Fall, supernatural grace 'might have been, or rather, was lost, without any Real Wound unto our Nature; Or without any other Wound, then such as the *Free-will* or right use of Reason, or other Natural Parts . . . might instantly have cured'. For the author of *Anthropology Abstracted*, the Fall wrought 'obscurity of the understanding; even in the businesse of her own

[22] Spellman, *The Latitudinarians and the Church of England, 1660–1700* (London, 1993); John Spurr, 'Latitudinarianism and the Restoration Church', *The Historical Journal* 31 (1988), 61–82; John Marshall, 'John Locke and Latitudinarianism', in R. Kroll, R. Ashcraft, and P. Zagorin (eds.), *Philosophy, Science, and Religion in England: 1640–1700* (Cambridge, 1992), pp. 253–82.

[23] John Wilkins, *A Discourse concerning the gift of Prayer* (London, 1651), pp. 74–80.

[24] Simon Patrick, *The Devout Christian* (London, 1673), pp. 447, 449. It may be significant that both Wilkins and Patrick make these claims in the context of devotional literature. For the commitments of Stillingfleet and Tillotson to the doctrine see Marshall, 'Locke and Latitudinarianism', p. 270.

proper object *(viz.) naturals and intelligibles*'.[25] Not all who stressed the importance of understanding the full implications of the Fall were agreed on the severity of its impact. Writing towards the end of the seventeenth century, James Lowde, a critic of both Locke and Malebranche, concurred that knowledge of ourselves includes 'the *true Knowledge of our Original Perfections*, and how far they are impair'd by the Fall, both what God made us at first in the state of *Innocence*, and what we have now made our selves by our *Sins*'. However, Lowde insisted that while 'the Fall did very much weaken our Faculties; yet it did not wholly alter or invert the method of acquiring, or retaining Knowledge'.[26] It is also significant that the Cambridge Platonists who retained a relatively high estimate of the powers of reason and who understood the Fall in terms of embodiment and attachment to material things gave primary place to reason rather than the senses in the attainment of knowledge. John Smith thus recommended that reason '*retract* and *withdraw* it self from all *Bodily operation* whensoever it will nakedly *discern* truth'.[27] Small wonder that the Platonists were so strongly drawn, initially at least, to the Cartesian account of knowledge. Equally, they were opposed by Baconians such as Samuel Parker (1640–88), Fellow of the Royal Society and Bishop of Oxford, who was to dismiss the Platonic philosophy as an 'ungrounded and Fanatick Fancy'.[28]

These discussions were by no means restricted to those with solely theo-logical preoccupations. The issue of human nature in relation to the Fall played a foundational role in political and educational theory, in treatises devoted to moral psychology and, most important for our present pur-poses, in works devoted to natural philosophy and theories of knowledge. Thomas Jackson himself noted the relevance of these considerations for political theory, pointing out that Adam had been granted dominion over all others by God and that this might seem to provide a biblical warrant for monarchical government. However, for Jackson, Adam's fall – which came after the grant of divine dominion – needed to be taken into consid-eration, for in much the same way that Adam's dominion over the beasts was considerably reduced after the Fall, so too his dominion over others. In what was something of an understatement, Jackson conceded that there were 'a great variety of opinions' about 'the Prerogatives or Praeeminences

---

[25] Jackson, *Works*, p. 2004. Anon., *Anthropologie Abstracted*, p. 43.

[26] James Lowde, *A Discourse concerning the Nature of Man* (London, 1694), pp. 5, 88.

[27] John Smith, *Select Discourses* (London, 1660), p. 80. Cf. Henry More, *An Antidote against Atheisme* (London, 1653), pp. 19, 31–5; Ralph Cudworth, *The True Intellectual System of the Universe* and *A Treatise Concerning Eternal and Immutable Morality*, ed. John Harrison, 3 vols. (London, 1845), III, 578.

[28] Samuel Parker, *A Free and Impartial Censure of the Platonick Philosophie* (Oxford, 1666), pp. 46, 2.

of the First Man over and above all others, which by Natural Descent have sprung from him'.[29] Much political theorising during this period was dominated by conceptions of 'the state of nature', from which speculations about Adam's original condition would seem to be directly relevant. Admittedly, a number of these conceptions of the original condition of humanity were explicitly hypothetical – Thomas Hobbes's celebrated characterisation of life in that first state as 'solitary, poor, nasty, brutish and short' being a case in point.[30] Yet for others the issue of Adam's 'dominion' both before and after his fall was directly relevant to contemporary discussions of political leadership. In Robert Filmer's (*c.* 1588–1653) vigorous defence of royal authority, *Patriarcha* – first published in 1680 but penned some forty or fifty years earlier – Adam is the central figure. According to Filmer, God granted to Adam an absolute command over the whole of creation. This monarchical authority was renewed after the Fall, and passed from Adam to the biblical patriarchs.[31] Filmer's argument was directed against the 'speculative' view, associated primarily (although not exclusively) with such 'papists' as Francisco Suárez and Cardinal Robert Bellarmine, according to whom the original condition of mankind was one of natural freedom. These men and their Protestant counterparts seemed to have forgotten, Filmer argued, 'That the desire of Liberty was the first Cause of the Fall of *Adam*'.[32] In other works Filmer had castigated Thomas Hobbes and Hugo Grotius for espousing what he regarded as unbiblical conceptions of human dominion.[33] The notion of an original freedom and equality, Filmer believed, 'was an errour which the Heathens taught'. It was excusable in 'Ethnique Authors' who were 'wanting the guide of the history of *Moses*'. For Christians, however, 'to dreame either of a *Community of things, or an equality*

---

[29] Jackson, *Works*, p. 3003. For the background of these discussions see G. Schochet, *Patriarchalism in Political Thought: The Authoritarian Family and Political Speculation and Attitudes Especially in Seventeenth-Century England* (Oxford, 1975).

[30] Thomas Hobbes, *Leviathan*, 1.13.9/14, ed. C. B. Macpherson (London, 1982), p. 186.

[31] Robert Filmer, *Patriarcha; or the Natural Power of Kings* (London, 1680), pp. 2–4, 13–14 and passim. Also see the Preface to the 2nd edn (London, 1685), by Edmund Bohun. 'All Filmer's writing', writes Glenn Burgess, 'may be understood as attempting to apply the scriptures to contemporary problems – usury, theological dispute, politics, witchcraft'. 'Filmer, Sir Robert (1588?–1653)', *ODNB*. See also Johannes Althusius, *Politica* (1614), 1, §12, abridged edn ed. and tr. F. Carney (Indianapolis, 1995), p. 38; Samuel von Pufendorf, *The Divine Feudal Law* (1695), tr. Theophilus Dorrington (Indianapolis, 2002), §§22–6 (pp. 67–74).

[32] Filmer, *Patriarcha*, pp. 3–4. In the next century moralist and theologian Samuel Clarke would object: 'That State, which Mr. Hobbes calls the State of Nature, is not in any sense a Natural State, but a State of the greatest, most unnatural, and most intolerable Corruption, that can be imagined.' S. Clarke, *Discourse upon Natural Reason*, in L. A. Selby-Bigge (ed.), *British Moralists*, 2 vols. (Dover, 1965), II, 46.

[33] The claims of Grotius regarding natural law were thus 'repugnant . . . to the truth of Holy Scripture'. *Patriarcha*, p. 31.

of all persons, is a fault scarcely pardonable'.[34] In short, proponents of the natural freedom of the human race were promoting an anthropology that was unbiblical and ahistorical – a conjecture based on mistaken assumptions about human nature. It is in this context that we are to understand Jackson's remark about a genuinely 'experimental' knowledge of human nature, by which he meant knowledge based on scripture and experience, as opposed to speculations based on reason alone. This contrast between experimental and speculative approaches also provided the basis for the major division of approaches to natural philosophy in the seventeenth century.[35]

An important part of the background of Filmer's political philosophy, and indeed seventeenth-century political thought generally, was the development of 'Federal' or 'Covenantal Theology' which provided a new explanation of the imputation of Adam's guilt to his progeny. Augustine had originally explained this puzzling aspect of the doctrine of original sin by proposing that in some sense we were all 'in Adam', and that original sin was transmitted 'seminally'.[36] Some late sixteenth-century Calvinists found Augustine's sketchy account of the transmission of Adam's guilt not entirely satisfactory, and offered an additional explanation that proposed an original covenantal agreement between God and Adam in which Adam was the representative for the whole human race.[37] As stakeholders in this covenant, the whole human race stood to benefit if Adam could hold to his part and remain obedient to God's commands. Equally, however, they became liable for whatever penalties were to befall Adam should he renege. As Bishop Edward Reynolds (1599–1676) expressed the proposition, 'We were *all one in Adam*, and with him; In him *legally* in regard of the stipulation and covenant between God and him, we were in him parties in that covenant, had interest in the mercy, & were liable to the curse which belonged to

---

[34] Filmer, *Observations Concerning the Original of Government* (London, 1652), pp. 26f. With some justification Filmer attributed to Aquinas the idea that natural law was a biblical conception (p. 29). In *The Tenure of Kings and Magistrates* (1649) Milton strongly repudiated Filmer's claims. See Poole, *Milton and the Fall*, p. 141.

[35] Anstey, 'Experimental versus Speculative Natural Philosophy'.

[36] Augustine, *City of God* XIII.14. Calvin himself openly acknowledged the counterintuitive nature of original sin: 'nothing is farther from the usual view than for all to be made guilty by the guilt of one'. Calvin, *Institutes* II.i.5 (McNeill 1, 246). The seventeenth-century embryological theory of pre-existence provided an explanation of how all human beings had literally been in Adam. Nicholas Malebranche was one who exploited this idea. Malebranche, *Search after Truth* I.vi.i (p. 27).

[37] 'Federal' from the Latin *foedus* (covenant). See David Weir, *The Origins of Federal Theology in Sixteenth-Century Reformation Thought* (Oxford, 1990); L. D. Bierma, 'Federal Theology in the Sixteenth Century: Two Traditions?' *Westminster Theological Journal* 45 (1983), 304–21. Calvinists tended to urge both seminal *and* federal explanations.

the breach of that Covenant.'[38] This view subsequently found its way into the Westminster Catechism, which explains that God made a covenant 'with Adam as a public person, not for himself only, but for his posterity'.[39] Even the Latitudinarian John Wilkins claimed that guilt is imputed to us in the present, because 'we were legally parties in that Covenant which was at first made with him [Adam]'.[40] The idea of one person representing a whole group by virtue of a contract had obvious parallels with political structures, and a number of seventeenth-century thinkers drew precisely this connection.[41] It has been plausibly argued that these covenantal conceptions and the idea of a 'public person' played an important role in the composition of Hobbes's *Leviathan* (1651).[42] Covenantal theology has also been credited with providing Filmer with a mechanism for the transmission of Adam's monarchical authority to the patriarchs.[43] This idea was also current in Protestant circles on the Continent. Lutheran jurisprudential writer Samuel Pufendorf (1632–94), whose works were so admired by John Locke, argued for an original covenant between God and mankind that was nullified with Adam's sin, necessitating a succession of further covenants.[44]

---

[38] Edward Reynolds, *Three Treatises* (London, 1631), p. 134. In England the idea can be found as early as William Perkins (1558–1602): 'Adam was not then a priuate man, but represented all mankinde.' *A Golden Chaine, or, A Description of Theologie* (London, 1592), sig. c2v. The best-known Continental exponent of federal theology was Dutch theologian Johannes Koch (Cocceius) (1603–69). See Willem van Asselt, *The Federal Theology of Johannes Coccius (1603–1669)* (Leiden, 2001).

[39] Larger Westminster Catechism, Q. 22. Cf. The Westminster Confession, vii.2, Leith (ed.), *Creeds of the Churches*, p. 202.

[40] Wilkins, *Discourse concerning Prayer*, p. 75.

[41] Among them William Perkins, Peter Bulkeley, and John Preston. See Christopher Hill, 'Covenantal Theology and the Concept of a "Public Person"' in *Collected Essays*, iii, 300–24 (304f.). Victoria Kahn, *Wayward Contracts: The Crisis of Political Obligation in England, 1640–1674* (Princeton, 2004), pp. 51, 55f. Cf. Pufendorf, *Divine Feudal Law* §§22–6 (pp. 67–74), and passim.

[42] Hobbes, e.g., spoke of the institution of a commonwealth as taking place 'when a multitude of men do agree, and covenant, every one, with every one, that to whatsoever man, or assembly of men, shall be given by the major part, the right to present the person of them all, (that is to say, to be their representative;)'. *Leviathan*, 2.18.1/20 (p. 228). Gilbert Burnet described federalism in similar terms as the view that 'a Covenant was made with all Mankind in *Adam*, as their first Parent: That he was a Person Constituted by God to represent them all; and that the Covenant was made with all Mankind in *Adam*'. Gilbert Burnet, *An Exposition of the XXXIX Articles of the Church of England* (London, 1699), p. 113. Cf. A. P. Martinich: 'Just as Adam and Jesus are representative persons in virtue of whom humans are either punished or saved, so the sovereign is a representative person in virtue of whom citizens are saved from the dangers of the state of nature.' *The Two Gods of Leviathan: Thomas Hobbes on Religion and Politics* (Cambridge, 1992), pp. 149f. Hobbes did not subscribe to covenantal theology as such, however.

[43] Ian Harris, 'The Politics of Christianity', in Rogers (ed.), *John Locke*, pp. 197–216.

[44] Pufendorf, *Divine Feudal Law* §§1, 22–6 (pp. 11, 67–74). On Pufendorf see Ian Hunter, *Rival Enlightenments* (Cambridge, 2001), pp. 148–96.

Authors of educational works also recognized that a true understanding of human nature was a fundamental prerequisite for the formulation of any realistic programme of learning. In his treatise on the education of gentlemen, Obadiah Walker (1616–99), destined to become Master of University College, Oxford, made the conventional claim that 'The most useful knowledge is that, of a mans self: and this depends upon that more universal consideration of *Quid homo potest*; naturally and artificially: i.e., what abilities are in us originally, by the gift of God; and what attainable by our own industry.'[45] Others educationalists made more explicit reference to the Fall and its significance. Jean Gailhard (*fl.* 1659–1708), a Huguenot refugee who made England his home in the 1660s, observed in his popular treatise on education that 'this intellect hath its darkness and ignorance, it is naturally blind, because of *Adam's* fall'. Failure to take this into consideration would complicate the task of instructing Adam's distant offspring, and render much of their behaviour inexplicable:

as therefore through his [Adam's] disobedience, he not only lost his supernatural privileges, as holiness, righteousness, the image of God and innocency, so all his natural gifts and faculties were thereby corrupted, and this depravation hath reached all his successors: no wonder therefore if the intellect of every young man is still involved in that blindness which is also much increased by the suggestions of Satan, and other inward corruptions.[46]

Recognition of our inherited imperfections was an important motivation for educational enterprises and, as Gailhard pointed out, this task was more urgent for Protestants, who believed that natural gifts had been corrupted by Adam's sin.

Reforms of educational practice and their accompanying justifications were closely related to arguments about how best to restore Adamic knowledge. Gailhard argued that the 'great cloud' that had been drawn over the mind might 'in some degrees be dissipated by learning'. Yet he insisted, in true Baconian fashion, that 'in these last days knowledge is not infused, but acquired with time and pains'.[47] John Milton also had the Fall in mind when he wrote in *Of Education* (1644) that 'The end of learning is to repair the ruins of our first parents by regaining to know God aright.' For Milton, moreover, pedagogical techniques were to be shaped by our knowledge of theological anthropology: 'But because our understanding cannot in this body found itself but on sensible things, as by orderly conning over [i.e. studying] the visible and inferior creature, the same method is to be

---

[45] Obadiah Walker, *Of Education: Especially of Young Gentlemen* (Oxford, 1673), Preface.
[46] Gailhard, *The Compleat Gentleman*, pp. 24f.   [47] *Ibid.*, p. 25.

followed in all discreet teaching.'[48] The Protestant reformers' efforts to extend educational opportunities to all social strata were largely motivated by their view that education would remit some of the consequences of the Fall.[49] This also explains the great enthusiasm of the Puritans for the reform of schools and universities. As the state had its role to play in the external enforcement of civic behaviour, so state-sponsored institutions could contribute to the moral formation of individuals by inculcating disciplines similarly directed at the internal control of passions and desires that had been unleashed by Adam's sin.[50]

Those writers who took as their subject the psychological maladies that assail the mind also typically took as their point of departure the fall of Adam. The dedicatory poem in Thomas Rogers's *Anatomie of the Minde* (1576) thus refers to the fact that before Adam's fall, the mind was free from perturbations, whereas in its present condition it was afflicted with disquieting passions and affections. Rogers also reminds his readers that the study of the self was to be esteemed above the study of nature: 'then must those men of necessitie bee deemed the best, who addict themselues rather to the knowing of theyr owne nature, then naturall thinges'.[51] Thomas Wright (*c.* 1561–1623) spoke in his popular *Passions of the Minde* (1601) of 'the inordinate motions of the Passions', describing how 'their preuenting of reason, their rebellion to vertue are thornie briars sprung from the infected roote of original sinne'. Understanding the rebellious nature of fractious and fallen passions, then, was central to gaining an insight into moral deliberation and rational decision-making. The passions, as Wright explained, 'augment or diminish the deformitie of actuall sins, they blind reason, they seduce the will'.[52]

---

[48] John Milton, *Of Education*, in *John Milton: The Major Works*, ed. S. Orgel and J. Goldberg (Oxford, 1991), p. 227.

[49] They also sought to promote the reading of the bible which, of course, required literacy. It is not clear, however, apart from the case of Scotland, that Protestants were any more successful in making education more widely available. See Gerald Strauss, *Luther's House of Learning: Indoctrination of the Young in Reformation Germany* (Baltimore, 1978); Paul Grendler (ed.), 'Education in the Renaissance and Reformation', *Renaissance Quarterly* 43 (1990), 774–824. On the religious aims of education in England see Webster, *Great Instauration*, pp. 100–15.

[50] Samuel Pufendorf had a similar view of education. See C. Carr and M. Seidler, 'Pufendorf, Sociality and the Modern State', *History of Political Thought* 17 (1996), 354–78 (esp. 363).

[51] Thomas Rogers, *A Philosophicall Discourse, Entituled, The Anatomie of the Minde* (London, 1576), sig AV v, Preface.

[52] Thomas Wright, *The Passions of the Minde* (London, 1601), pp. 2–3. See also Timothie Bright, *A Discourse of Melancholie* (London, 1585), p. 119; Thomas Adams, *Diseases of the Sovle: A Discovrse Divine, Moral, and Physical* (London, 1616), p. 1; *The Divells banket described in sixe sermons* (London, 1613), pp. 2–4; Thomas Goodwin, *The Vanity of Thovghts Discovered: Together with Their Danger and Cvre* (London, 1637), pp. 57f.

Many of the ideas of Wright and Rogers were incorporated in the classic medical work of the age, *The Anatomy of Melancholy* (1621). Robert Burton (1577–1640) begins his *magnum opus* with a description of the fall of Adam – 'Man's Excellency, Fall, Miseries, Infirmities; the Causes of Them'. The human being, 'this most noble creature', Burton wrote, 'is fallen from what he was, and forfeited his estate, become ... one of the most miserable creatures of the World, if he be considered in his owne nature, an unregenerate man, and so much obscured by his fall that (some few reliques excepted) he is inferiour to a beast'. All human inconveniences, including the condition of melancholy, flow from this one primeval event:

The impulsive cause of these miseries in man, this privation or destruction of God's image, the cause of death and diseases, of all temporall and eternall punishments, was the sinne of our first parent *Adam*, in eating the forbidden fruit, by the Divells instigation and allurment. His disobedience, pride, ambition, intemperance, incredulity, curiosity, from whence proceeded originall sin, and that general corruption of mankinde, as from a fountain flowed all bad inclinations, and actuall transgressions, which cause all our severall calamities, inflicted upon us for our sinnes.[53]

In the re-establishment of control over the passions, such as that which Adam had enjoyed in his innocent condition, lay the prospect of an amelioration of our present infirmities. This, in essence, was Dr Burton's primary prescription.

Even those interested in anatomy and physiology were to relate these activities to self-knowledge. An important precedent had been established by Philipp Melanchthon, whose support for the teaching of anatomy at the University of Wittenberg had been motivated partly by his conviction that the study of the body could shed light on the human condition after the Fall. For this reason, education in anatomy was not restricted to medical students, and was taught in the Arts Faculty.[54] A similar perspective was adopted by the Puritan physician and anatomist Helkiah Crooke (1576–1648), who insisted that the primary reason for studying anatomy was that it conferred self-knowledge. In the first illustrated anatomy to be published in English, *Microcosmographia* (1615), Crooke observed that 'It is no doubt an excellent thing for a man to attaine to the knowledge of

[53] Robert Burton, *The Anatomy of Melancholy*, ed. Thomas Faulker, Nicolas Kiessling and Rhonda Blair, 3 vols. (Oxford, 1989) I, 121–2.
[54] See Jürgen Helm, 'Religion and Medicine: Anatomical Education at Wittenberg and Ingolstadt', in Jürgen Helm and Annette Winkelmann (eds.), *Religious Confessions and the Sciences in the Sixteenth Century* (Leiden, 2001), pp. 51–68; Vivian Nutton, 'Wittenberg Anatomy', in Ole Grell and Andrew Cunningham (eds.), *Medicine and the Reformation* (Cambridge, 1995), pp. 11–32.

himselfe, which thing Anatomy and dissection of bodies doth teach us.' However, it was the moral applications of the discipline that Crooke had in mind. Anatomy was 'very profitable for a morall Philosopher', for in teaching 'the mutuall offices and duties of every part', this discipline would also communicate 'how to temper and order the manners and conditions of the minde'.[55] Many of his more conservative colleagues in the College of Physicians, it must be said, did not share his view that every part of the human body was morally edifying and were appropriately scandalised by the inclusion in *Microcosmographia* of plates depicting the organs of generation. On the Continent, Pierre Gassendi (1592–1655) challenged, on similar grounds, the apparent assumption of Descartes' *Meditations* that a purely introspective, psychological knowledge would provide a sufficiently robust self-knowledge. He proposed instead a 'chemical investigation' of the self, speculating that this would provide an equally compelling account of the 'internal substance' of the mind. It might be, he surmised, that we can better know the human being 'through anatomy, chemistry, so many other sciences, so many senses and so many experiments'.[56] These physical examinations of the self could ultimately serve a moral purpose. Gassendi believed that natural philosophy was useful 'in freeing us from certain Errors and Mistakes in our Understanding', for it is these that disturb the repose and tranquillity of the true philosophical life.[57] In reality, Descartes was himself not far from this position. The opening sentence of the unfinished treatise *Description du corps humain* (Description of the Human Body, 1664) makes reference to the Delphic maxim and the importance of self-knowledge. Descartes goes on to lament the fact that too little effort had been spent 'on getting to know the nature of our body', given that many of the functions of the soul 'depend solely on the body and on the disposition of its organs'.[58]

Finally, the issues of self-knowledge and the Fall were directly relevant to questions of epistemology and the methods of natural philosophy. Apparently negative assessments of human cognitive capacities could be harnessed in the service of constructive projects to advance knowledge. It is difficult to find a clearer statement of the positive ethos that accompanied these accounts of Adam's losses than the opening of Sir Thomas Browne's compendium of vulgar errors, *Pseudodoxia Epidemica* (1646). Here Browne

---

[55] Helkiah Crooke, *MIKROKOSMOGRAFIA: A Description of the Body of Man* (London, 1615), pp. 14, 15. Cf. Thomas Walkington, *The Optick Glasse of Humors* (London, 1664), pp. 1–17.

[56] Decartes, *Objections and Replies*, CSM II, 193.

[57] Pierre Gassendi, *Three Discourses of Happiness, Virtue, and Liberty* (London, 1699), p. 2.

[58] Descartes, *Description of the Human Body*, CSM I, 314.

announces what was then universally acknowledged: 'The first and father cause of common Error, is the common infirmity of humane nature.'[59] Browne continues, however, with a positive admonition: 'now our understandings being eclipsed, as well as our tempers infirmed, we must betake ourselves to reparation, and depend upon the illumination of our endeavours. For, thus we may repair our primary ruins.'[60]

Critical assessments of human capacities also provided a platform from which to mount attacks on Aristotle and the traditional science of the Schools. The strong view of the mind's debilitation provided a useful theological justification for abandoning the vain and worldly learning of the Schools which had too readily assumed the ease with which knowledge of nature could be gathered. Aristotelian philosophy, as has already been noted, was based on a relatively uncritical epistemology which assumed that the senses represent the world to us much as it really is.[61] Accordingly, the knowledge that it produced, as Francis Bacon put it, 'lay near to the senses, and immediately beneath common notions'.[62] Bacon also explained in *De sapientia veterum* (1609) that philosophers who took such an uncritical view of human nature were destined to remain in ignorance. Those who clearly understood its limitations were more likely to be spurred to industry and productive knowledge:

Among mankind, accusations against both human nature and human art proceed from a most laudable temper of mind, and tend towards a good purpose ... Those given to effusive praise of human nature and the fashionable arts rest content in admiring what they already possess, and regard the sciences cultivated among them as perfect and complete ... By way of contrast, those who accuse nature and arts, and are full of complaints against them, not only exhibit a more just and modest sense of mind, but are perpetually driven to new industry and novel discoveries.[63]

In case readers were unsure of his primary target here, Bacon went on to identify the self-satisfied flatterers of human nature as those belonging to 'the confident, assuming and dogmatic school of Aristotle'.[64]

Subsequent Baconians endorsed this verdict. Clergyman Gilbert Watts (*d.* 1657), who produced the popular 1640 English translation of Bacon's *De*

---

[59] Browne, *Pseudodoxia Epidemica*, I.i, ed. Robin Robbins, 2 vols. (Oxford, 1981), I, 5.
[60] *Ibid.*, I.v (I, 30). On Browne and the Fall see Claire Preston, *Thomas Browne and the Writing of Early Modern Science* (Cambridge, 2005), pp. 36–9.
[61] On Aristotle's reliance on commonsense observations see A. Crombie, *Robert Grosseteste*, p. 7.
[62] Bacon, *Great Instauration*, *Works* IV, 18.   [63] Bacon, *Sapientia veterum*, *Works* IV, 672.
[64] *Ibid.*

augmentis, pointed out in his introduction that human learning must be founded on a proper understanding of the human mind and its limitations:

But in the businesse in hand, the *mind of man,* the principall subject to be wrought upon, and *her speculations,* both which we so admire, are so immur'd and blockt up with corrupt notions, either from the placits of Philosophers, the depraved laws of Demonstration; or from inherent qualities in the generall nature of man, or individuate temperature of particulars.

'Nothing can be done', Watts concluded, until the deficiencies of the mind are 'subjected to examination'.[65] Watts also pointed out that the Baconian division of the sciences, based as it was on the faculties of sense, memory, and reason, was the most natural: 'the truest Partition of humane learning, is that, which hath reference to the humane faculties'.[66] The Aristotelian division of the sciences, by way of contrast, had been based on assumptions about the natures of things themselves, which presumed that they could be known in advance. Watts contended that without an appropriate understanding of the faculties of the mind, not even the fundamental task of mapping the domains of intellectual endeavour could be accomplished. Watts's criticisms were later repeated by the physician and natural philosopher Henry Power (1626–68), who also chastised the scholastics for their uncritical and superficial approach. The 'old Dogmatists and Notional Speculators', he wrote, 'onely gazed at the visible effects and last Resultances of things'. Because of this, they 'understood no more of Nature, than a rude Countrey fellow does of the Internal Fabrick of a Watch'.[67] And while Aristotle had allowed that the acquisition of knowledge was not always straightforward, it was still he who had observed that truth was 'like the proverbial door, which no one can fail to hit'.[68] The most obvious deficiency of the learning of the peripatetic Schools, it was pointed out by these critics, lay in their failure to take seriously the history of those first events in Eden, and of the mind's inherent infirmities that resulted from them. Indeed, it was argued that human sin had itself blinded philosophers to the realities of their condition.

---

[65] Bacon, *Advancement of Learning* (1640 edn), sig. ¶¶ r.

[66] *Ibid.,* sig. ¶¶ 2r. Cf. Bacon, *A Description of the Intellectual Globe, Works* IV, 501–44.

[67] Henry Power, *Experimental Philosophy in Three Books* (London, 1664), pp. 192f.

[68] Aristotle, *Metaphysics* 993b (p. 1569). In fact, Aristotle acknowledged limits to the powers of the intellect in the next sentence: 'the cause of the present difficulty is not in the facts but in us. For as the eyes of bats are to the blaze of day, so is the reason in our soul to the things which are by nature most evident of all.' This passage was cited on numerous occasions by Aquinas (who spoke of the eye of the owl rather than the bat) to illustrate the fact that the unaided intellect needed the light of revelation in order to access the most sublime truths. For scholastic authors, intellectual limitations were felt most in the supernatural rather than the natural realm.

THE DOMINION OF MIND

The advocacy of self-knowledge prompted detailed analyses of what Adam had known, how he had known it, what he had lost, and how he had lost it. Restoration divine Robert South, whose estimates of Adam's abilities we encountered in the opening lines of this book, thought that Adam had known the essences of things, could see effects dormant in their causes, and could almost predict future events. In his innocence the first man was ignorant only of sin and its consequences.[69] South's assessment was a typical one. His late contemporary John Hartcliffe (1651–1712) produced an almost identical summary of Adam's prelapsarian abilities. Adam's understanding was a direct reflection of the image of God. It 'led and controlled' the passions. It made determinations on the information provided by the senses and the imagination and gave its verdicts, not in the manner of a 'sleepy judge', but with authority. The truths which we now hold are, by comparison, 'obscure'. The acquisition of knowledge, moreover, was the basic business of paradise: 'the first motion of *Adam*, after he was furnished with a sound understanding and an obedient Will, was after Knowledg'.[70]

Adam's knowledge was most often regarded, in Protestant England at least, to have arisen out of a natural, albeit God-given, capacity. Adam was usually thought to have been created with instinctive knowledge, or at least with a natural capacity for acquiring it. This was consistent with the Protestant view that Adam had been created with many natural gifts that were forfeited by his sin. In his commentary on Psalm 127, Martin Luther had written: 'Here it appeareth that at the beginning there was planted in man by God himself, a knowledge of husbandry, of physicke, and of other artes & sciences; Afterward men of excellent wit by experience & great diligence did encrease those gifts which they had by nature. And this is but the strength of humane wisedome created in man at the beginning in Paradise.'[71] In keeping with this view, schoolmaster Alexander Gill (1565–1635) stressed that Adam's knowledge was the result of his 'naturall gifts', gifts that were subsequently 'lost and corrupted'.[72] In his *History of the Creation* (1641), George Walker concurred, arguing that Adam had a perfect knowledge of all natural things, 'arising and springing immediately from his naturall soule'.[73] Clergyman and botanist Nehemiah Grew (1641–1712), who for a time was secretary of the Royal Society, thought Adam's knowledge

[69] South, *Sermons*, p. 127.   [70] Hartcliffe, *Moral and Intellectual Virtues*, pp. 291, 296.
[71] Luther, *Commentarie vpon Fiftene Psalmes*, pp. 129f.
[72] Alexander Gill, *The Sacred Philosophy* (London, 1635), p. 116.
[73] Walker, *History of the Creation*, p. 193. Cf. Thomas Morton, *A Treatise of the Threefold State of Man* (London, 1596), p. 238.

to be natural or 'instinctual': 'he had the Faculties of his mind given him in some Equality of Perfection with the parts of his Body. And therefore, that he knew many things, by some sort of Intellectual Instinct; as Birds, and other animals do now, by that which is Phantastick.' Grew thought that 'he had this Knowledge, without Experience of studying for it'.[74] Bishop Edward Stillingfleet (1635–99) also thought that Adam had been invested with a natural knowledge of things from the time of his creation. The creatures 'were so fully known to him on his first creation, that he needed not to go to School to the wide World to gather up his conceptions of them'. This knowledge of 'the Nature, Being and Properties of those things' was required, Stillingfleet pointed out, if Adam was to exercise 'a proper dominion and use of the creatures'.[75]

This instinctual knowledge was thought to have been immediately known to Adam, or brought to consciousness by introspection, or possibly even stimulated or supplemented by sensory experience. Robert South explained that because Adam was a microcosm of the whole creation, self-knowledge would confer upon him knowledge of the cosmos. Hence, his body 'did not only contain, but also represent the soul . . . where it might see the World without travel; it being a lesser Scheme of the Creation, nature contracted, a little Cosmography or map of the universe'.[76] Stillingfleet also alluded to the ancient idea of Adam as a microcosm but added a Platonic gloss. In a sense, all of our present knowledge was recollection from a previous existence – 'the Recovery of those notions and perceptions of things which the Mind of Man once had in its pure and primitive State, wherein the Understanding was the truest Microcosm in which all the Beings of the inferior World were faithfully represented according to their true, native, and genuine Perfections'.[77] Others, however, were concerned to provide some supporting role for observation. Thomas Morton thus proposed that although Adam had been created with a deposit of knowledge, he had later added to it with 'sense, experience, observation, and by his owne industry'.[78]

In keeping with their concern to specify in some detail the cognitive capacities of the first man, seventeenth-century authors also made much of the epistemological consequences of the Fall. George Walker wrote that the Fall caused '*ignorance and errour* in mind and understanding'. Edward

---

[74] Grew, *Cosmologia Sacra*, p. 184. According to Henry Vane, Adam had an 'intuitive' insight into the natures of all material things, without need to rely on 'the report given by his senses'. *Retired Mans Observations*, p. 53.

[75] Stillingfleet, *Origines Sacrae*, p. 3.   [76] South, *Sermons*, p. 149.

[77] Stillingfleet, *Origines Sacrae*, p. 1.

[78] Morton, *Threefold State of Man*, pp. 222f. Cf. Ross, *An Exposition*, p. 50.

Reynolds, the Bishop of Norwich, declared in his *Treatise of the Passions*
that 'the fall of man working in him a generall corruption, did amongst
the rest infatuate the Mind, and as it were smother the soul with ignorance'.[79] Perhaps the most frequent metaphor deployed in these descriptions was that of the extinguishing of light. According to Thomas Morton,
'Before the fall of man his minde was enlightened with the perfect knowledge of God and of al things in the world.' Now, however, 'the natural
knowledge of man is meer darknesse and ignorance'.[80] Another author
wrote that Adam's transgressions 'contracted a black cloud over his reason,
and obnubilated its primitive clarity'.[81] According to Robert South, 'the
light within us is become darkness; and the Understanding, that should
be eyes to the blind faculty of the Will, is blind it self.'[82] Others spoke
about the diminution of specific faculties. Poet Robert Farley explained
that following the Fall Adam suffered the contraction of his once capacious memory: 'Our fraile and britle memory before / Did safely keep the
whole conceptions store.' The failure of memory necessitated the invention
of writing and an over-reliance on 'dumbe bookes'.[83] Shortness of memory also threatened the transmission of ancient wisdom. George Dalgarno
(*c.* 1616–87), author of one of the century's most important works on artificial language, pointed out that when Adam's memory deteriorated he would
have lost command over the extensive vocabulary he had originally invented
to name the creatures. This would have led to a gradual degeneration of
the primitive language, and to a loss of the knowledge embedded within
it.[84] The physician Gideon Harvey (1636/7–1702) attributed Adam's intellectual weakness to the destruction of the divine image. The Fall resulted
in 'a partial unlikenesse to God: for before he knew all things distinctly
by one operation of mind, now by many, then without error, now subject
to mistakes and errours'. As a consequence, Adam's 'distinct knowledge
of things failed him'.[85] Adam's misfortunes were, of course, his enduring
legacy. As John Hartcliffe put it, when Adam fell, he 'left his Posterity in
the dark, either following wrong Scents, or much in doubt, what paths to
walk in'.[86] Many works of the period, from a range of different disciplines,

[79] Edward Reynolds, *A Treatise of the Passions and Faculties of the Soul of Man* (London, 1647), p. 5.
[80] Morton, *Threefold State of Man*, p. 238.   [81] Anon., *Anthropologie Abstracted*, p. 43.
[82] South, *Sermons*, p. 149.
[83] Robert Farley, 'June, or Mans Young Age', from *The Kalendar of Mans Life* (London, 1638), lines
    47–66. Cf. Stillingfleet, *Origines Sacrae*, p. 1.
[84] Dalgarno, 'Of Interpretation', in *George Dalgarno on Universal Language: The Art of Signs (1661),
    the Deaf and Dumb Mans Tutor (1680), and the Unpublished Papers*, ed. David Cram and Jaap Maat
    (Oxford, 2001), p. 403.
[85] Harvey, *Archelogia Philosophica Nova*, pt 1, pp. 91f.
[86] Hartcliffe, *Moral and Intellectual Virtues*, pp. 291, 296.

offer similar accounts of Adam's original knowledge and its forfeiture after sin, and such views persisted well into the eighteenth century.[87]

As we have seen, an important element in all of these speculations was the issue of whether Adam's knowledge was a supernatural gift, and whether the Fall consisted only in a loss of supernatural gifts, as was the standard scholastic position. The contemporary significance of this recondite theological issue should not be underestimated. Had Adam's abilities resulted from a supernatural gift, the prospects for recovery of that knowledge by natural means in the present life were limited. If, on the other hand, Adam's knowledge was either innate or acquired through experience, his losses could be understood in terms of a disordering of his natural faculties. Ignorance would thus be the result of the corruption of human nature (the view of Luther and Calvin) rather than the withdrawal of any supernatural abilities (the scholastic and Tridentine position). In this latter case, the chances of regaining knowledge by natural means were somewhat better, for it would not be unreasonable to seek to ameliorate readily identifiable natural flaws in the functioning of body and mind. All of this is to say that on this common Protestant reading of the nature of the Fall, there would be strategies, outside the supernatural means of grace afforded by the Christian religion, for negotiating the natural defects of the mind that had resulted from Adam's sin. In essence, this is how we are to understand Bacon's account of the two distinct ways in which there might be a restoration of what was lost at the Fall. While the loss of *innocence* could be restored only by grace, human *dominion*, made possible by Adamic knowledge, was not a supernatural gift but a natural capacity. Though corrupted by sin, it could 'in some measure' be repaired by natural means – as Bacon put it – 'by various labours'.[88] This struggle to recover, through effort and industry in the present life, capacities that were once part of the natural endowment of human beings was integral to the Protestant vision of the earthly vocation. This vision informed seventeenth-century English projects to recover the dominion over nature that had been lost as a consequence of Adam's sin.

[87] See, e.g., Ross, *An Exposition*, p. 50; Gill, *Sacred Philosophy*, p. 116; Webster, *Academiarum Examen*, pp. 26f.; Jackson, *Originall of Unbeliefe*, p. 90; Salmon, *Clavis Alchymiae*, p. 180; Culpeper, *Complete Herbal*, p. vii; Henry More, *Conjectura Cabbalistica*, p. 41; Culverwell, *Learned Discourse*, pp. 120f.; Ferguson, *Interest of Reason in Religion*, pp. 19f., 27f.; Witty, *An Essay*, pp. 178–80; Goodwin, *Vanity of Thoughts Discovered*, p. 49; Andrewes, *Apospasmatia Sacra*, pp. 208–12; Salkeld, *Treatise of Paradise*, pp. 185–91; More, *Conjectura Cabbalistica*, pp. 41–51; Wilkins, *Discourse concerning Prayer*, pp. 77f.; Clarke, *A Discourse concerning the Unchangeable Obligations of Natural Religion*, pp. 239f.; Jonathan Edwards, 'East of Eden', *The Works of Jonathan Edwards*, vol. XVII, ed. Mark Valeri (New Haven, 1999). See also Spellman, *The Latitudinarians*, pp. 1–10, 54–71.

[88] Bacon, *Novum Organum* II §52, 334 (*Works* IV, 247).

The attribution of Adam's losses to a corruption of his nature made possible speculation about the physical and psychological causes of inherited ignorance. These individual maladies, moreover, were understood as contributing to various social evils – customs, mores, educational practices – that could also frustrate the acquisition and transmission of knowledge.[89] The individual and social elements were linked together by a standard understanding of the Fall as the partial loss of a divine image that reflected elements of God's omniscience and omnipotence. Hence with the effacing of the image of God, the human race forfeited both knowledge and power. Adam's rebellion against God was also understood as having disordered psychological, physical, social, and cosmic hierarchies.[90] In the microcosm, the passions, the senses, and the imagination usurped the authority of reason, while in the macrocosm, creatures once subject to human dominion revolted against their erstwhile masters. In the social realm, too, natural social relationships were disordered, giving rise to mutual hostility among peoples and necessitating the institution of civil authority. Finally, the physical environment itself was destabilised and became far less hospitable to its human tenants. These inter-related sets of inversions were linked together by the key metaphor of 'the rebellion of the beasts'. As we have seen, in patristic and medieval commentaries the passions were allegorically represented as the 'beasts within'. Hence, the insubordination of the lower faculties of the mind was reflected in the wildness of beasts and in the earth's resistance to cultivation. The loss of the capacity for knowledge and the loss of human dominion over nature were thus directly linked.[91] In the political sphere, 'the beasts' represented 'the mob' or 'the vulgar', who were understood as perennially prone to rebellion against their rightfully appointed rulers.

The idea that the state reflected the hierarchy of the mental faculties had been set out in Plato's *Republic* and, glossed with the Judaeo-Christian notion of the Fall, had become a powerful explanatory model in the Renaissance and early modern period. Erasmus wrote: 'As the mind is to the body, so is the prince to the state; the mind knows, the body obeys.' Because of these parallels, it was requisite for princes to learn to control their own passions, because this was directly analogous to controlling their subjects.

---

[89] According to the Larger Westminster Catechism the punishments of sin include not only 'blindness of mind, a reprobate sense, strong delusions, hardness of heart, horror of conscience, and vile affections' but such 'outward' things as 'the curse of God upon the creatures for our sakes, and all other evils that befall us in our bodies, names, estates, relations, and employments'. Q. 28.

[90] As Calvin expressed it, Adam 'perverted the whole order of nature in heaven and earth by his revolt'. Calvin, *Institutes* II.i.5. Cf. Augustine, *City of God* XIV.15.

[91] On this theme see Harrison, 'Reading the Passions'.

For Erasmus, this internal self-mastery was to be achieved through the study of philosophy, which 'frees the mind from the false opinions and ignoble passions of the masses'.[92] In his seventeenth-century treatise on the passions, Edward Reynolds drew upon these ideas, suggesting that reason was the prince of the mind, whose authority had been usurped by the passions following the Fall. It is true, he wrote, 'as well in Mans little Common-wealth, as in greater States, That there are no more pestilent and pernicious disturbers of the publicke Good, than those who are best qualified for service and imployment'.[93] In the English translation of *De Cive* (1651), Thomas Hobbes identified the state of nature with 'the dominion of the passions' – a dominion, in his view, characterised by 'war, fear, poverty, slovenliness, solitude, barbarism, ignorance, cruelty'. By contrast, the state was 'the dominion of reason' and attended with 'peace, security, riches, decency, society, elegancy, sciences, and benevolence'.[94] Like Descartes, Hobbes seems to have been reluctant to draw explicitly upon scripture to support his philosophical views. Indeed, this was a major failing in the eyes of many of his critics. Even so, it is difficult not to see in aspects of Hobbes's political philosophy a Protestant emphasis on the corruption of human nature. As Norberto Bobbio has expressed it, 'In agreement with the Augustinian-Lutheran conception of the state, Hobbes thought of the state as a remedy for the corrupt nature of man.' For Hobbes, moreover, the condition of corruption that human beings needed to abandon was 'that of the natural passions'. Philosophy was to assist in this task by classifying and describing the passions in an enterprise that was a kind of mental anatomy. Bobbio concludes that for Hobbes, 'the state was thus not a remedy for sin, but a means of disciplining the passions'.[95] All of this is in keeping with the reformers' insistence that the condition of sin cannot be expunged, but must be lived with. In the sphere of learning, too, both internal disciplines of mind and external procedural disciplines were called for in order to

---

[92] Margaret Mann Phillips, *The Adages of Erasmus* (Cambridge, 1964), pp. 217–19.

[93] Reynolds, *Treatise of the Passions*, p. 46. Bacon also considers the mind to be a microcosm of government. *Advancement of Learning* II.xxii.6 (pp. 163f.). See also Charron, *Of Wisdom*, pp. 171–3.

[94] Hobbes, *De Cive* 10.1, *The English works of Thomas Hobbes of Malmesbury*, ed. William Molesworth, 7 vols. (London, 1839–45), II, 126. Cf. *Leviathan* 2.17.1/15 (p. 223); *De Corpore Politico* II.viii.12–14 (*Works*, II, 209–11).

[95] Norberto Bobbio, *Thomas Hobbes and the Natural Law Tradition*, tr. D. Gobetti (Chicago, 1993), p. 68. See also Patricia Springborg, 'Hobbes on Religion', in Tom Sorell (ed.), *The Cambridge Companion to Hobbes* (Cambridge, 1996), pp. 346–80, esp. pp. 356f. Hobbes's incipient Augustinianism, if we may call it that, also meant that elements of his political thought could easily be appropriated by Calvinist and Jansenist authors. See Noel Malcolm, *Aspects of Hobbes*, pp. 504–7; Albert O. Hirschman, *The Passions and the Interests* (Princeton, 1997), p. 15; Franck Lessay, 'Hobbes's Protestantism', in Tom Sorell (ed.), *Leviathan after 350 Years* (Oxford, 2004), pp. 265–94.

return the mind to the dominion of reason and the natural world to the dominion of the human race.[96]

The image of the passions as 'beasts within' was also prominent in early modern accounts that linked the loss of mental powers to the loss of natural dominion. In his analysis of the generic causes of error in *Pseudodoxia Epidemica* (1646), Thomas Browne explained that because of the Fall, the 'brutall faculties' of the minds of Adam's progeny usurped the place of reason: 'The irrationall and brutall part of the soule, which lording it over the soveraigne facultie, interrupts the actions of that noble part, and choakes those tender sparkes, which Adam left them of reason.'[97] As in the earlier account of Philo, Eve's deception by the serpent was also represented as an inversion of the proper hierarchical order: Eve 'subject[ed] her reason to a beast, which God had subjected unto hers'. This reversal of the proper order of things was mirrored in Eve's temptation of Adam. Adam's fall, observes Browne, may be thought of as 'the seduction of the rationall and higher parts, by the inferior and feminine faculties'.[98] Most seventeenth-century authors who wrote on the passions also explained their insurrection in similar terms.[99]

For seventeenth-century philosophers, the passions occupied a pivotal position between mind and body. This was even the case – in fact it was especially the case – for such putatively dualist philosophers as Descartes.[100] Senault observed that 'the passions proceed from the soules marriage with the body'. Modifying the metaphor, William Ayloffe described them as 'equally Daughters of the Soul and Body'.[101] The passions could thus be

---

[96] Samuel Pufendorf, whose political philosophy develops in a different direction to Hobbes, nonetheless regards the fallen condition of man to be a vital consideration. *On the Law of Nature* II.i.6, in *The Political Writings of Samuel Pufendorf*, ed. C. Carr, tr. M. Seidler (Oxford, 1994), p. 139; Merio Scattola, 'Before and After Natural Law: Models of Natural Law in Ancient and Modern Times', in Tim Hochstrasser (ed.), *Early Modern Natural Law Theories: Context and Strategies in the Early Enlightenment* (Dordrecht, 2003), pp. 1–30.

[97] Browne, *Pseudodoxia Epidemica* I.i (pp. 5, 7). A. P. Martinich has made a case that Hobbes's doctrine of obedience to the political sovereign is indebted to a traditional understanding of the Fall as the breach of a covenant with God. *Two Gods of Leviathan*, pp. 49f., 147–50, 307f. For an alternative theological reading of Hobbes's political philosophy see Franck Lessay, 'Hobbes: une christologie politique?' *Rivista di storia della filosofia* 1 (2004), 51–72.

[98] Browne, *Pseudodoxia Epidemica* I.i (p. 5); cf. I.i (p. 8).

[99] Reynolds, *Treatise of the Passions*, pp. 435f.; Wright, *Passions of the Minde*, pp. 2f., 34f.; John Ford, *An Essay of Original Righteousness and Conveyed Sin* (n.p., 1657), pp. 46f.; William Ayloffe, *Government of the Passions according to the Rules of Reason and Religion* (London, 1700), pp. 6f., 14, 22; Gailhard, *Compleat Gentleman*, pp. 55f.; Franck, *Philosophical Treatise*, p. 161; Senault, *Man Becom Guilty*, pp. 10f.; *The Use of Passions* (London, 1671), p. 75.

[100] See esp. Susan James, *Passion and Action: The Emotions in Seventeenth Century Philosophy* (Oxford, 1997), pp. 16f.

[101] Senault, *Man Becom Guilty*, pp. 10f.; Ayloffe, *Government of the Passions*, p. 22.

described in two ways: in mental terms as promoting errors of judgement; or in physical terms as the convoluted motions of the animal spirits in the living body.[102] Study of the physical aspects of the passions thus had the potential to shed light on the material causes of error. Once again, for those who understood the insurrection of the passions as a consequence of the Fall, this called for speculation about the different physical operations of the passions in Adam before and after the Fall. Concern with the passions thus led naturally to a consideration of the fallen body, of how the Fall was to be understood in physical terms, and of the manner in which knowledge of the physiology of mental operations might contribute to a restoration of the mind's proper functioning.

THE FALLEN BODY

Most seventeenth-century Protestant writers were concerned to stress the fact that Adam's lapse was accompanied by more than just a proneness to moral and intellectual error. The Fall was held to have wrought collateral damage in the physical realm as well, and this meant that Adam's body, as well as his soul, bore the burden of his guilt. In his treatise on the Fall, clergyman George Burches described original sin as 'a pestilent infection universally dispersed over all the faculties both of Soul and body'.[103] John Wilkins wrote that the Fall had corrupted both the outward and the inward man, so that in addition to our intellectual and moral misfortunes, the body had become 'weak and vile, exposed to all manner of infirmities, diseases, sins'.[104] Richard Baxter agreed that 'When Adam sinned, each part of his body did bear its part in the guilt.'[105] The weakness and fallibility of Adam's mind were thus matched by the comparative feebleness of his body. Even Jeremy Taylor, whose relatively mild view of the effects of original sin elicited a number of sharp rejoinders, wrote that Adam 'then fell under the evills of a sickly body, and a passionate, ignorant, uninstructed soul; his sin made him sickly, his sickliness made him peevish, his sin left him ignorant, his ignorance made him foolish and unreasonable'.[106] The fallen body of Adam thus contrasted starkly with the glory of his original body.

---

[102] The passions also had social and political dimensions, and writers on the passions typically dealt with the role of the passions in social and political interactions. See James, *Passion and Action*, pp. 106f.; Harrison, 'Reading the Passions'.

[103] George Burches, *Mans Inbred Malady* (London, 1655), p. 40; Henry Ainsworth, *Annotations on the First Five Bookes of Moses* (London, 1639), fol. 15b.

[104] Wilkins, *Discourse concerning Prayer*, pp. 77, 79.

[105] Baxter, *Two Disputations*, p. 67. Cf. Burgesse, *Doctrine of Original Sin*, p. 372.

[106] Jeremy Taylor, *Deus Justificatus. Two Discourses of Original Sin* (London, 1656), p. 13.

Robert South, who so highly extolled Adam's intellectual virtues, was no less stinting in his praise of the Adamic body: 'Adam was then no less glorious in his externals; he had a beautiful body, as well as an immortal Soul. The whole compound was like a well built Temple, stately without, & sacred within.'[107] Gideon Harvey also thought that Adam had possessed a 'grandeur of body' and 'a perfection denoting strength of all the vegetative faculties, fittd for long life, and propagation'.[108]

The most tangible sign of the fallen condition of the human body was its mortality. Since death first came as a consequence of the eating of forbidden fruit (Gen. 2:17), it was widely believed that had they not fallen, Adam and Eve could have lived forever. Alexander Gill wrote that 'if *Adam* had not sinned, he might have lived a naturall life till now, and afterward; free from sicknesse, and want, abounding in all the knowledge of nature, and naturall blessings'.[109] While Aquinas had taught that the first parents had only been immortal on account of God's supernatural activity, others thought that immortality had been a natural condition – a direct consequence of the perfection of the primitive bodies. If this were the case, the curse of mortality could be explained in terms of physical changes to Adam's body. Already some medieval thinkers had speculated about those changes. Peter Alfonsi (c. 1060–c. 1140), a Spanish Jew who converted to Christianity in 1106, held that Adam had been created from the most subtle parts of the four elements, combined in exactly equal proportions. Therein lay his potential immortality. With his sin, the proportions were altered and the ensuing elemental imbalance brought mortality.[110] This explanation was consistent with the general view of the Fall as precipitating various levels of cosmic disorder. Something akin to this was suggested by Hildegard of Bingen (1098–1179), who spoke of humours rather than elements. In her *Causae et curae* she describes how Adam's humours became corrupt and bitter at the moment he fell: 'when Adam violated the divine command, in that very moment melancholy was coagulated in his blood'.[111] Her contemporary William of Conches (c. 1085–c. 1154), known for his literal readings of the Genesis narratives, provided an even more naturalistic account, arguing

---

[107] South, *Sermons*, p. 148.

[108] Harvey, *Archelogia Philosophica Nova*, pt 2, p. 75. For similar praise of the Adamic body see Jonathan Edwards, 'East of Eden', pp. 333f.; 'Sermons on Genesis', Jonathan Edwards Collection. General Collection, Beinecke Rare Book and Manuscript Library, Gen MSS 151.

[109] Gill, *Sacred Philosophy*, p. 20. See also Daneau, *Wonderfull Woorkmanship*, fol. 82v; South, *Sermons*, p. 149.

[110] Petrus Alfonsi, *Dialogi*, PL 157, 641f.

[111] Hildegard, *Causae et curae*, in Peter Dronke, *Women Writers of the Middle Ages* (Cambridge, 1984), pp. 244f.; Boas, *Essays on Primitivism*, pp. 75–7.

that it was the environmental conditions that existed beyond the bounds of Eden that brought mortality to the first family:

> For the first man was balanced between the four qualities, but when, after his expulsion from the loveliness of Paradise, he began to live on his own bread produced by the labour of his own hands in the valley of tears and misery, he began to dry up through his toil, hunger, and lack of sleep and his natural heat began to be extinguished, and the imbalance of the air and the quality of his food and drink had the same effect on him. Therefore all descended from him are corrupt, since they come from someone corrupt, and perfect health has never been found in man since that time.[112]

William's account thus provided not only a description of the fallen Adam's physical condition in humoral terms, but also an explanation of the transmission of his mortality. Physiological accounts of the Fall and the method of its transmission were thus not entirely novel.

The onset of death and mortality was only gradually felt, for according to Genesis many of the patriarchs lived remarkably long lives by modern standards: Adam reached the age of 930, his son Seth 912, and Methuselah 969.[113] After the Flood, however, the lifespan was dramatically reduced to the familiar three score years and ten (Ps. 90:10), the exception being Noah, an antediluvian by birth, who lived to the age of 950. Josephus regarded such longevity in the first ages of the world as the rule and not the exception, and this view was generally accepted.[114] Once again, naturalistic explanations were sought to account for the longevity of the antediluvians. One possibility was Adam's facility as a physician, and the corresponding capacity of the antediluvian world to provide cures. The legend of Seth postulated the existence of an 'oil of mercy' capable of relieving suffering and bringing renewed vitality. Ernaldus of Bonneval (*d. c.* 1156), whose *Hexaemeron* sets out one of the most enthusiastic accounts of the perfections of the prelapsarian age, praised Adam's knowledge of the 'essences and effects of all things', and noted that in Eden 'there was not fever but already its cure existed; there was not weakness of constitution, but already the remedy for lassitude was being produced'.[115] Some early modern thinkers

---

[112] William of Conches, *Dragmaticon* (Strasbourg, 1567), pp. 261–2, qu. in Dorothy Elford, 'William of Conches', in Peter Dronke (ed.), *A History of Twelfth-Century Philosophy*, (Cambridge, 1993), pp. 308–27 (323). See also Brian Murdoch, '*Drohtin uuerthe so!* Zur Funktionsweise der althochdeutschen Zaubersprüche', *Jahrbuch der Görres-Gesellschaft* NS 32 (1991), 11–37 (36f.).

[113] The ages of the patriarchs are given in Gen. 5, and in 9:29. On the history of this issue see Frank N. Egerton, 'The Longevity of the Patriarchs', *JHI* 27 (1966), 575–84; Almond, *Adam and Eve*, pp. 19–27.

[114] Josephus, *Antiquities* 1.104 (p. 34); Browne, *Pseudodoxia Epidemica* VII.3.

[115] Ernaldus, *Hexaemeron*, PL 1540, 1536, tr. in Boas, *Essays on Primitivism*, pp. 75, 73.

attributed the perfect health enjoyed by the first humans to Adam's ability to read the signatures of plants.[116]

Roger Bacon's thirteenth-century glosses on the pseudo-Aristotelian *Secretum* also made important references to the natural span of human life. Some of the secrets that Aristotle had apparently learned from the Hebrews dealt with the extension of human life – a topic that Bacon believed had been largely ignored in the received medical canon. The longevity of the patriarchs demonstrated that the contemporary abridgement of the life span was owing to 'accidental' factors. Aristotle's regimen involved prescriptions relating to food and drink, activity and rest, sleep and wakefulness, and control of the passions. Unfortunately, corruptions of the Latin text of the *Secretum* meant that the recipe for the crucial elixir *Gloria inestimabilis* had been lost forever. The only specific dietary recommendation to have survived the incompetence of translators and copyists was, unhappily, the ingestion of rhubarb – advice dutifully followed and subsequently recommended by Bacon himself.[117] In one of a number of anticipations of early modern positions, Bacon had also thought if we could know the composition of Adam's body, in both its upright and fallen states, our capacity for knowledge of the world would be increased.[118]

In the seventeenth century, the most general explanation for Adam's natural immortality was that he originally had a perfect body.[119] Calvinist clergyman Henry Holland (*d.* 1604) supposed that Adam's body was like the resurrected body of the saints, and thus immune to death.[120] Walter Charleton believed that the source of Adam and Eve's immortality was the Tree of Life, which had been planted in paradise for this express purpose – 'that the fruit thereof being sufficiently eaten might *instaurate* that vital *Balsam* of man as fast as it suffered *exhaustion*'.[121] Fellow physician Gideon Harvey took the alternative view that the bodies of Adam and Eve exhibited a perfect homeostatic balance: 'their primogenital temperature was by far more perfect (*comparativè*) then ours, and therefore did not consume faster then their Natures could adunite other parts in the room of the dissipated ones'. The Fall, however, altered the solubility of their 'fixed heat': 'as for

[116] Webster, *Academiarum Examen*, pp. 26–9.
[117] R. Bacon, *Fratris Rogeri Bacon De retardatione accidentium senectutis*, ed. A. Litte and E. Withington (Oxford, 1928), p. 155, cited in Williams, 'Bacon and the *Secretum secretorum*', 64f.
[118] R. Bacon, *Opus Majus* I, 617f.; *Opus minus*, in *Opera Fr. Baconis hactenus inedita*, ed. J. S. Brewer (London, 1859), pp. 370f.
[119] See, e.g., South, *Sermons*, p. 148; Gill, *Sacred Philosophy*, p. 20; Taylor, *Deus Justificatus*, p. 13.
[120] Henry Holland, *The Historie of Adam, or the foure-fold state of Man* (London, 1606), fol. 6.
[121] Charleton, *Darknes of Atheism*, p. 222. Cf. Jeremy Taylor, *Unum Necessarium*, in *The Whole Works of the Right Reverend Jeremy Taylor*, ed. R. Heber, 15 vols. (London, 1822), IX, 9.

their fixt heat, that was so arctly united and tempered, that its nexe was indissoluble, which through their Fall is become soluble'.[122] Robert South explained that it was Adam's temperance that sustained him in immortality: 'Neither was the body then subject to distempers, to die by piece meal, and languish under Coughs, Catarrs, or Consumptions. *Adam* knew no disease, so long as temperance from the forbidden fruit secured him. Nature was his Physician: and his Innocence and Abstinence would have kept him healthy to immortality.'[123]

The longevity of the patriarchs was also provided with physical explanations. The tradition that Adam had dispensed a life-giving balm was noted by Gideon Harvey, who wrote with approval of those who ascribed 'the length of life of the Patriarchs to the same mysterious Medicine, which was successively discovered to them by *Adam*'.[124] More prosaically, George Hakewill suggested that before the Flood, food was 'more *wholesome* and nutritive, and the Plants more *medicinall*'. The prevailing meteorological conditions, moreover, were thought to have been kinder to these first inhabitants of the world – 'that clymate where the *Patriarches* lived, [being] more favourable and gratious'.[125] Later in the century Nehemiah Grew similarly attributed the long lives of the patriarchs to a temperate climate and a simple diet. Contributing factors were temperance, sobriety, charity, equanimity, industry, and all the other virtues that conduce to long life. Like Hakewill, Grew believed that the Flood had brought to an end what remained of the healthy environment that had once prevailed in Eden:

But when, with the Flood, some great alteration befel the Earth: and probably, the Sun and Moon likewise, the Grand Regulators of Life and Death: When the Salubrity of the Earth, and the Air, was impaired; and herewithal, the Excellency of the Vegetable Diet, and feeding upon all sorts of Flesh, being now allowed; Men indulged themselves in all kinds of Excess: there were but too many Causes, sufficient to reduce the Life of man to a shorter measure.[126]

John Edwards agreed that the flood had altered the capacity of the earth to provide adequate sustenance for its human tenants: 'After that great Primitive Malediction', he wrote, human bodies 'stood in need of some more than ordinary Recruits, *viz.* the active and generous Spirits which are produced by feeding on Animals'.[127] Permission to eat the flesh of animals,

---

[122] Harvey, *Archelogia Philosophica Nova*, pt 2, p. 149; Pascal, *Pensées*, L 282 (p. 119). Cf. Ferguson, *Interest of Reason in Religion*, p. 20.

[123] South, *Sermons*, pp. 149f.   [124] Harvey, *Archelogia Philosophica Nova*, pt 2, p. 145.

[125] Hakewill, *Apologie*, pp. 42f.   [126] Grew, *Cosmologia Sacra*, p. 185.

[127] John Edwards, *A Demonstration*, pt 1, p. 185.

in his view, was given because of the new deficiency of the earth, and was thus not a cause of bodily infirmity but a consequence of it.

The question of the longevity of Adam and the patriarchs was important in early modern discussions of knowledge for a number of related reasons. First, the onset of mortality was generally thought to account for other physical debilitations and for alterations to Adam's mental state as well. The kinds of measures that would extend human life were likely to do so by rectifying many of the shortcomings of the body. Because the same bodily defects that led to premature death were also likely to inhibit the acquisition of knowledge, ameliorating the effects of ageing, it was argued, would also lead to gains in learning. To take a single example, in his *Discourse on the Method*, Descartes claimed that the maintenance of health is 'the chief good and the foundation of all the other goods in this life'. Descartes' emphasis on the importance of bodily health followed from his conviction that 'the mind depends so much on the temperament and disposition of the bodily organs'. The study of the body was thus an important element of the philosophical quest because, in Descartes' own words, through such studies there might be found 'some means of making men in general wiser and more skilful than they have been up till now'. For Descartes, knowledge of the functioning of the body would help optimise our mental operations. This wisdom, in turn, would assist our further investigations of the body, with the possible consequence that some of this new knowledge would liberate us from 'the infirmities of old age'.[128]

Second, long life was regarded as having been vital to the preservation and transmission of knowledge in the first ages of the world. Luther had pointed out that the longevity of the first generations of men had given rise to an unprecedented body of accumulated wisdom: 'Before Noah's flood the world was highly learned, by reason men lived a long time, and so attained great experience and wisdom.' The contracted lifespan of post-diluvian human beings, however, militated against such cumulative knowledge. 'Now', Luther complained, 'ere we begin rightly to come to the true knowledge of a thing, we lie down and die. God will not have that we should attain a higher knowledge of things.'[129] This view was reprised by a number of seventeenth-century writers. In his *Exposition of Genesis* (1626) – a work dedicated to Francis Bacon – Alexander Ross claimed that had Adam not fallen, his progeny 'should haue attained to knowledge sooner, and

---

[128] Decartes, *Discourse*, CSM I, 142. Cf. *Description of the Human Body*, CSM I, 314; Descartes to Newcastle, Oct. 1645, AT IV, 329. For Descartes on longevity see Steven Shapin, 'Descartes the Doctor: Rationalism and its Therapies', *BJHS* 33 (2000), 131–54.

[129] Luther, *Table Talk*, CLX (p. 65).

with greater ease than now, because the wit was most excellent, the senses more perfect, the life longer, the body healthier and stronger'.[130] George Hakewill agreed that in the first ages of the world 'Arts and Sciences were then to be planted, for the better effecting whereof, it was requisite, that the same men should have the experience and observation of many ages.'[131] The consequences of an abridged lifespan for contemporary projects to advance knowledge were also highlighted by Bacon in *The Advancement of Learning*. Here Bacon suggests that among the chief impediments to learning are 'shortness of life, ill conjunction of labours, [and] ill tradition of knowledge over from hand to hand'.[132] Shortness of life resulted from the Fall, and from shortness of life, barriers to the transmission of knowledge. As for the ill conjunction of labours, the unhappy cooperative enterprise to construct the tower of Babel was stymied by the imposition of a 'second curse', the confusion of tongues. In the biblical history of the world, then, the basic causes of the decay of learning were clearly set out. The connection between longevity and the transmission of knowledge was revisited in the posthumously published *New Atlantis*. In the utopian society described there, some of the inhabitants of 'Solomon's House' – Bacon's ideal scientific academy – are said to dwell in deep caves in the 'Lower Region'. These subterranean dwellings, sunk to a depth of 600 fathoms, served a number of scientific purposes including the 'conservation of bodies' and, for those prepared to live a monastic existence interred deep within the earth, for 'the prolongation of life'. From the aged cave dwellers, we are told, many things were learned.[133] Descartes also regarded 'brevity of life' as an obstacle to the acquisition and transmission of knowledge.[134]

Third, the recovery of the secret of old age was to be part of the general restoration of Adamic qualities lost as a consequence of the Fall. Paracelsian and alchemical writers who believed the processes of alchemy to be analogous to those of creation, regarded disease as that corruption of the body which had followed the Fall, rendering the human race prone to perpetual sickness. Associated with the quest for the philosopher's stone was thus a desire to reinstate the Adamic body with all its perfections, including its

[130] Ross, *An Exposition*, p. 50.
[131] Hakewill, *Apologie*, p. 42. See also Beaumont, *Considerations*, p. 95; Stillingfleet, *Origines Sacrae*, p. 11; George Dalgarno, 'On Interpretation', in Cram and Maat (eds.), *George Dalgarno*, p. 403; Josephus, *Antiquities* 1.104–6 (*Works*, p. 34).
[132] Bacon, *Advancement of Learning*, (Johnston edn), p. 7.
[133] Bacon, *New Atlantis*, *Works* III, 156f. Other utopian writers of the sixteenth and seventeenth centuries – including Campanella, Andreae, and Comenius – had also given priority to extending human life. See Webster, *Great Instauration*, p. 249.
[134] Descartes, *Discourse*, CSM I, 142.

resistance to the undesirable physical accompaniments of bodily mortality. As Lauren Kassell describes it, the alchemist's quest was 'the pursuit of a substance which, through revelation, frees man from the corruption of the Fall, restoring his health, and enabling him to commune with angels'.[135] The myth of Edenic health and wellbeing thus informed the alchemical quest. More conventional physicians also made the prolongation of life a major priority for related reasons. Physician Philip Barrough, author of the popular *Methode of Phisicke* (1583), wrote in his preface that 'there is no meanes by which a man can approch neerer unto the perfection of that nature which he first enioyed, and then lost by his fall, then by the painfull indagation of the secretes of nature'. Chief amongst these, according to Barrough, were the means to lengthen life.[136] For Francis Bacon, the prolongation of life was a major preoccupation, and he often wrote as if it were the ultimate goal of knowledge. In *Valerius Terminus* (1603) he argued that knowledge should encompass all the operations and possibilities of nature 'from immortality (if it were possible) to the meanest mechanical practice'. Extending human life, he was later to say, was the 'most noble' of all of the duties of medicine.[137] Two complete works were devoted to this theme – *The History of Life and Death* (1623) and the unpublished *De vijs mortis* ('An Inquiry concerning the Ways of Death, the Postponing of Old Age, and the Restoring of Vital Powers').[138] In the former, Bacon contests that unanimous verdict of antiquity that old age and death were natural stages of life. The human body's capacity to repair itself, he speculated, is 'potentially eternal'.[139]

As we have already seen, Descartes shared Bacon's enthusiasm for finding a cure for old age. And while the French philosopher was characteristically reticent about the biblical account of the longevity of the patriarchs, he noted in the Preface to *The Passions of the Soul* (1649) that God had provided us with the necessary means 'to be preserved in perfect health to an extreme old age'.[140] On occasion Descartes seems confident that he had

[135] Lauren Kassell, 'Reading for the Philosopher's Stone', in Marina Frasca-Spada and Nick Jardine (eds.), *Books and the Sciences in History* (Cambridge, 2000), pp. 132–50.

[136] Philip Barrough, *The Method of Phisicke* (London, 1583), To the Reader.

[137] Bacon, *Valerius Terminus*, cited in D. B. Haycock, 'Living Forever in Early Modern England', *The Center and Clark Newsletter* 43 (2004), 6–7; *Advancement of Learning, Works* IV, 372–404. Also see Haycock's forthcoming 'Projectors of Immortality: Living Forever in Early Modern Europe'.

[138] Bacon, *The History of Life and Death, Works* V, 213–335; *De vijs mortis, Philosophical Studies, c. 1611– c. 1619*, ed. Graham Rees (Oxford, 1996). See also Webster, *Great Instauration*, pp. 246–323; Gaukroger, *Francis Bacon*, pp. 95–9.

[139] Bacon, *History of Life and Death, Works* V, 218.

[140] Descartes, *The Passions of the Soul*, ed. and tr. S. Voss (Indianapolis, 1989). There is some discussion about the authorship of this preface, but it is most probably by Descartes. See *Passions*, p. 1.

knowledge of those means. He was reputed to have claimed, in response to a question from English philosopher Kenelm Digby about how to live longer, that while he might not be able to 'render a man immortal' he could extend his life span to 'equal that of the Patriarchs'.[141] In light of Descartes' relatively premature death at the age of fifty-four, this turns out to have been a rather hollow boast. But it is significant, perhaps, that many found his claims plausible enough to speculate that he must have met with an unnatural death. What remains clear is that throughout his philosophical career Descartes regarded the extension of human life as a major priority.

Finally, the quest to identify the natural causes of mortality, paralleling as it does the quest for the natural causes of human ignorance, again highlights the difference between the 'supernaturalism' of medieval Catholicism and the more naturalist orientation of post-Reformation Christendom. The Thomist position was that Adam's immortality had been a supernatural gift that was withdrawn after the Fall: 'before sin the human body was immortal not by nature, but by a gift of Divine grace; otherwise its immortality would not be forfeited through sin'.[142] For Protestant thinkers, however, it was possible that mortality was a consequence not of the withdrawal of a divine gift, but of the natural corruption of the body that followed the Fall. Moreover, if immortality (or extreme longevity) had been a natural gift, it followed that it might be restored to some degree by natural means. The historical precedent of the patriarchs' longevity supported the idea that such a partial restoration was achievable under the conditions of the earthly existence, and it was this possibility that Bacon and others sought to explore. Related to this is the fact that as modern philosophers, Bacon and Descartes tend to locate the ends of the philosophical quest within the confines of the earthly existence. Hence, philosophical wisdom was associated with the goal of prolonging the present life – even, perhaps, to the point of immortality. Aquinas had also linked the philosophical quest to immortality, but his was an immortality that was delayed until the world to come: 'by wisdom itself man is brought to the kingdom of immortality for the desire of wisdom bringeth to the everlasting kingdom (Wis. vi. 21)'.[143] This immortality was thus postponed until the general resurrection. This

---

[141] Descartes, AT xi, 671, cited in Shapin, 'Descartes the Doctor', p. 141. See also Gerald Gruman, *A History of Ideas about the Prolongation of Life* (Philadelphia, 1966), p. 79.

[142] Aquinas, ST 1a. 76, 5. Cf. ST 1a. 97, 1. Atypically for Protestant authors Alexander Ross repeats this view. *An Exposition*, p. 53.

[143] Aquinas, SCG 1.2 (p. 3).

supernaturalist understanding of the basis of immortality and longevity contrasts with Bacon's insistence that the longevity enjoyed by the first men was not to be 'imputed to grace'.[144] This stance provided the basis of his subsequent judgement that the ancients were mistaken in believing death to be natural and inevitable. Here again, the importance of distinguishing which losses were to be recovered by 'religion and faith' and which by 'arts and sciences'.

It is also significant that in medieval Catholicism the supernatural gifts lost by Adam could be restored in part through divine grace, channelled through a sacramental system presided over by the priesthood. Ultimately, of course, the final restoration of human nature took place with the beatific vision in the next world. It is in this context that we are to understand the tradition that regarded the elements of the mass as 'the medicine of immortality'. Second-century Church Father Ignatius of Antioch, with whom the expression originates, thus described how Christians 'break one Bread which is the medicine of immortality and the antidote against death, enabling us to live forever in Jesus Christ'.[145] Thomas also used the medical analogy, describing the sacraments as 'spiritual remedies for the healing of wounds inflicted by sin'.[146] Accordingly, the protocols that Bacon sought to inaugurate in the realm of the sciences may be regarded as a parallel sacramental system aimed at the restoration of corrupted Adamic abilities that were salvageable in the present life. For this reason Bacon could see his role in sacerdotal terms, establishing the scientific rituals that would minister to and restore fallen human intellectual capacities: 'I perform the office of a true priest of the sense.'[147] The custodians of Solomon's House, incidentally, similarly combined the priestly and scientific offices. On the traditional Catholic view, such ministrations to human nature were superfluous, Adam not having lost any of his natural capacities in the first place. To recall Bellarmine's words, after the Fall, human nature was no worse off in terms of its 'ignorance and infirmity' than it was before.[148]

The general principles related to the question of mortality apply also to human ignorance. Proneness to error, also a consequence of the Fall, might similarly be ameliorated by natural means. The project to repair

---

[144] Bacon, *Historia vitae*, *Works* v, 243.

[145] Ignatius of Antioch, *Letter to the Ephesians* 20.

[146] Aquinas, ST 3. 61, 2; cf. ST 3. 60, 1. As a recipient of the supernatural gifts, Adam in his innocence had not needed the sacraments.

[147] Bacon, *Great Instauration*, *Works* IV, 26.

[148] Bellarmine, *De Gratia Primi Hominis* (Heidelberg, 1612), cap. v, sec. 12.

human knowledge from its fallen state directly parallels inquiries into the possibility of redeeming the body from death. In both cases what is called for is a careful forensic investigation of the natural causes of the relevant malady followed by specific prescriptions for its cure. It is this task that Francis Bacon undertakes in his various writings on the instauration of learning.

INTELLECTUAL IDOLATRY

Bacon's first biographer, William Rawley, reports that it was as a precocious thirteen-year-old at Trinity College, Cambridge that Bacon first developed his inveterate dislike for the doctrines of Aristotle.[149] This claim is not implausible, for at home the young Bacon had been exposed to an altogether different kind of education by his mother. Anne Bacon cherished deep Puritan convictions and saw to it that her sons were taught by tutors who shared her religious orientation. From an early age, Francis and his brother Anthony were schooled in the tenets of the reformed creed and taught in the less formal style that reflected the influence of Continental Calvinism. It is hardly surprising that throughout his life Bacon exhibited some typically Calvinist preoccupations: the Fall and its consequences, the importance of the earthly vocation, the sanctity of work, and the duty to transform society. Bacon's most explicit statement of his personal religious convictions – his *Confession of Faith* (*c.* 1602) – closely mirrors the teachings of Calvin's *Institutes of the Christian Religion*. This is not to say that Bacon was a Puritan, and indeed some of his writings contain criticisms of both the Protestant reformers and their Puritan successors.[150] What remains clear is that Calvinist ideas exerted a major influence on the way in which he framed his project for the instauration of learning. With this early educational background, Bacon's first encounter with the Cambridge curriculum – dominated as it then was by Aristotelianism – would have come

---

[149] Rawley, *Life of Bacon*, *Works* I, 4. For Bacon's early education see Lisa Jardine and Alan Stewart, *Hostage to Fortune: The Troubled Life of Francis Bacon* (New York, 1999), pp. 31–8. Jardine and Stewart are somewhat sceptical of Rawley's claim.

[150] Bacon, *Confession of Faith*, *Works* VII, 215–26. For Bacon's Calvinism see Brian Vickers's remarks in *Francis Bacon: The Major Works*, ed. Brian Vickers (Oxford, 2002), pp. vi, xxvif., 560–72. See also James Spedding's observations in Bacon, *Works* VII, 21; Steven Matthews, 'Apocalypse and Experiment: The Theological Assumptions and Motivations of Francis Bacon's Instauration', Ph.D. thesis, University of Florida, 2004; John Henry, *Knowledge is Power* (London, 2002), pp. 82–92; Benjamin Milner, 'Francis Bacon: The Theological Foundations of *Valerius Terminus*', *JHI* 58 (1997), 245–64; Webster, *Great Instauration*, p. 514.

as something of a shock. One of the first texts that Bacon would have had to contend with was the 'Organon', a collection of Aristotle's writings on logic. All undergraduates were expected to become familiar with its contents, and until well into the seventeenth century university statutes prescribed monetary penalties for those guilty of transgressions against Aristotle's logic.[151] In fact, when Isaac Newton attended Trinity as an undergraduate in 1661 – almost ninety years later – he too discovered that Aristotle's 'Organon' was still an important component of the curriculum.[152] Bacon's early resistance to the Aristotelianism he encountered at university and his later ambition to establish new foundations for learning are both evident in the title of what is probably his best known philosophical work: *Novum organum* – (The New Organon, 1620).

At this point it should be unnecessary to labour the fact that Bacon has a conception of natural philosophy as an enterprise devoted to a recovery of Adamic knowledge of nature and dominion over it. Each of the two sections of the *Novum Organum* concludes with an injunction to recover the dominion over nature that was lost as a consequence of the Fall.[153] As for the impediments to this recovery, Bacon saw in the long-standing tradition of Aristotelian logic an implicit recognition of the fact that 'the human intellect left to its own course is not to be trusted'. But Bacon was convinced that the purveyors of logic had systematically misidentified the nature of mental errors and the means by which they were to be corrected. The champions of the old Organon 'have given the first place to Logic, supposing that the surest helps to the sciences were to be found in that'. In Bacon's judgement, 'the remedy is altogether too weak for the disease'. The impotence of logic in the face of the human propensity for error could be attributed to two factors. First, the logicians had simply underestimated the extent of the problem they were seeking to rectify.[154] 'The root cause of nearly all evils in the sciences', Bacon wrote, is that 'we falsely admire and extol the powers of the human mind.' As a consequence, 'we neglect to seek for its true

---

[151] The *Organon* comprised *Categories, De Interpretatione, Prior Analytics, Posterior Analytics, Topics, On Sophistical Refutations.* For its role in the curriculum see William T. Costello, *The Scholastic Curriculum at Early Seventeenth-Century Cambridge* (Cambridge, MA, 1958); Kearney, *Scholars and Gentlemen: Universities and Society in Pre-Industrial Britain* (London, 1970), pp. 81f. On the system of fines, see Merton, *Science, Technology, and Society*, p. 299.

[152] Cambridge University Library, MS. Add. 3996.

[153] Bacon, *Novum Organum* I, §129, II, §52 (*Works* IV, 115, 247); cf. *Great Instauration, Works* IV, 7; *Valerius Terminus, Works* III, 222.

[154] Bacon, *Great Instauration, Works* IV, 17. For other comments on logic see *Great Instauration*, Works IV, 7, 23f., *Novum Organum, Works* iv, 40, 48.

helps'.[155] Second, not realising that error stems from multiple failures of the human mind, they had prescribed a single generic remedy.[156]

In order to arrive at a true interpretation of nature, Bacon insists, we need to begin with an understanding of human faculties and their limitations. In the *Novum Organum*, then, Bacon identifies the senses, memory, and reason as the faculties involved in knowledge, and seeks specific 'ministrations' or 'helps' to heal their inherent infirmities.[157] These infirmities, which for Bacon 'have their foundation in human nature itself', are referred to as 'the idols of the tribe', the first category of four 'idols of the mind' to which Bacon attributes the errors of human knowledge.[158] For Bacon, the deficiencies of the senses provide the first occasion for error: 'By far the greatest hindrance and aberration of the human understanding proceeds from the dullness, incompetency, and deceptions of the senses.'[159] The senses, which are 'infirm and erring', fail us in two ways. Sometimes they provide no information; sometimes they provide false information.[160] In the first case, of things that lie beyond the threshold of visibility, nothing can be known. This applies to heavenly bodies that are too distant to see or, to cite the specific example that Bacon uses, 'the workings of spirits inclosed in tangible bodies' that 'lie hid and unobserved by men'.[161]

It is worth reminding ourselves at this point that according to a long-standing exegetical tradition, it was precisely this kind of sensory information that Adam had access to. Hildegard of Bingen had expressed the view that when Adam sinned, 'the splendor of innocence was darkened in him and his eyes, which previously saw celestial things, were extinguished'.[162] Luther described Adam's visual and auditory acuity in similar terms:

---

[155] Bacon, *Novum Organum, Works* IV, 48. The necessity for devising appropriate 'helps' and 'ministrations' is a constant theme in *The Great Instauration* and *Novum organum*. See, e.g., *Great Instauration, Works* IV, 13, 21, 23, 37, 31; *Novum Organum* I, §2 (*Works* IV, 47). Johann Alsted similarly proposed remedies for memory, judgement, and speech, each of which had become defective as a consequence of the Fall. Hotson, *Johann Heinrich Alsted*, p. 69.

[156] As Stephen Gaukroger has pointed out, Descartes is similar to the scholastics in this respect: 'All sources of error are homogenised in Descartes, and there is no need to distinguish different sources of error any more than there is for the textbook authors.' *Francis Bacon*, p. 122.

[157] Bacon, *Novum Organum* II, §10 (*Works* IV, 126).

[158] Bacon, *Novum Organum* I, §41 (*Works* IV, 54). For a discussion of the four 'idols of the mind' see §§38–68 (*Works* IV, 53–69). The other three 'idols' are: the idols of the cave, which refer to individual biases that distort knowledge; the idols of the marketplace, which arise out of the misuse of language; and the idols of the theatre, which relate to the uncritical reception of traditions. There are some similarities to Roger Bacon's earlier account of the causes of error. *Opus Majus* I, 4.

[159] Bacon, *Novum Organum* I, §50 (*Works* IV, 58).   [160] *Ibid.*; *Great Instauration, Works* IV, 26.

[161] *Ibid.*

[162] Hildegard, *Causae et Curae* II, ed. Kaiser (Leipzig, 1903), in Boas, *Essays on Primitivism*, p. 77.

After Adam had lost the righteousness in which God had created him, he was, without doubt, much decayed in bodily strength, by reason of his anguish and sorrow of heart. I believe that before the fall he could have seen objects a hundred miles off better than we can see them at half a mile, and so in proportion with all the other senses. No doubt, after the fall, he said: 'Ah, God! what has befallen me? I am both blind and deaf.'[163]

These traditions were commonplace in seventeenth-century England. According to Bishop Thomas Morton (1564–1659), in his original estate 'man had greater subtiltie of outwarde senses, arising of [sic] the exact temperament of his bodie, and being able to receave aright without errour the impression of any object'.[164] Joseph Hall asserted that Adam had a direct sensory knowledge of the internal operations of spirits, the lack of which Bacon had lamented. By means of a kind of X-ray vision, he 'saw the inside of all the creatures', while 'his Posteritie sees but their skins ever since'.[165]

Bacon thus saw his task as that of providing artificial assistance to senses that in a postlapsarian world were now inadequate for their primary task: 'I have sought on all sides diligently and faithfully to provide helps for the sense – substitutes to supply its failures, rectifications to correct its errors.' An obvious means of augmenting weakened senses was to rely on the magnifying powers of such instruments as the telescope and microscope. However, use of these glasses was then still in its infancy, and was not uncontroversial. Owing to what he called the 'incompetency' of the new magnifying devices, Bacon believed that a better 'help' for the senses was experimentation: 'For the subtlety of experiments is far greater than that of the sense itself, even when assisted by exquisite instruments.'[166] Having said this, in the optical laboratories of Solomon's House, we encounter 'helps for the sight, far above spectacles and glasses in use'. These make it possible to view distant heavenly bodies as if they are near, and 'to see small and minute bodies perfectly and distinctly'.[167] The use of improved instruments to magnify the powers of the senses thus seems to have been one of Bacon's desiderata. Later in the seventeenth century, when the utility of such instruments was better established, fellows of the Royal Society would more willingly recommend them as devices capable of overcoming the limitations of fallen senses.

[163] Luther, *Table Talk*, cxxviii (p. 57).
[164] Morton, *Threefold State of Man*, p. 223; cf. Ross, *An Exposition*, p. 50.
[165] Joseph Hall, *The Works of Joseph Hall* (London, 1634), i, 776.
[166] Bacon, *Great Instauration*, *Works* iv, 26. Cf. *Novum Organum* ii, §39 (*Works* iv, 192), where Bacon concludes that owing to the 'incompetency' of the new glasses, little new knowledge of any use had been discovered.
[167] Bacon, *New Atlantis*, *Works* iii, 163.

In *Novum Organum* Bacon has little to say about ministrations for the memory.[168] However, this was a topic that he had broached in the *Advancement of Learning*. In the earlier work he noted that knowledge is retained either in writing or in the memory.[169] Bacon was unimpressed with existing systems designed to magnify the powers of the memory – schools of the so-called 'art of memory' such as those of Raymond Lull (*c.* 1235–1316) and Peter Ramus (1515–72).[170] He also notes that it is the failures and limitations of memory that necessitate the recording of knowledge in written form. Hence, writing was already a 'help' for the memory, as for example in the case of note-taking. Bacon thus praised the formal methods of 'commonplacing' in which readers would record, under various headings in their personal commonplace books, quotations they encountered in their reading.[171] Even so, language was itself a flawed medium for both the recording and the transmission of knowledge: words being only 'tokens' of concepts, they imperfectly represented both things in the world and concepts in the memory. This imperfection was evident in the multiplicity of languages, which Bacon attributed to 'the second general curse' – the confusion of tongues at Babel (Gen. 11). Bacon regarded the science of grammar, then still an important part of university study, as an attempt to recapture the simplicity and transparency of the primitive language. Grammar was thus the means, he observed, by which 'man still striveth to reintegrate himself into those benedictions, from which by his fault he hath been deprived'. But like so many features of the scholastic educational programme, grammar was deemed 'deficient'.[172] An ideal philosophical language would recapture at least some of the elements of the original Adamic tongue. As Bacon expressed it, we must learn the language of 'the book of creation'. This, he says, 'is that speech and language which has gone out to all the ends of the earth, and has not suffered the confusion of Babel; this men must learn again, and, resuming their youth, they must become again as little children and deign to take its alphabet into their hands'.[173]

---

[168] But cf. *Novum Organum* II, §26 (*Works* IV, 162).   [169] Bacon, *Advancement, Works* III, 397.

[170] On the art of memory see Frances Yates, *The Art of Memory* (Chicago, 1966); Paolo Rossi, *Logic and the Art of Memory*, tr. Stephen Clucas (London, 2000); Mary Carruthers, *The Book of Memory* (Cambridge, 1992).

[171] Bacon, *Advancement, Works* III, 398. On commonplace books see Ann Blair, 'Note Taking as an Art of Transmission', *Critical Inquiry* 31 (2003); 'Humanist Methods in Natural Philosophy: The Commonplace Book', *JHI* 53 (1992), 541–51; Earle Havens, *Commonplace Books* (New Haven, 2001); Richard Yeo, 'Ephraim Chambers's Cyclopaedia (1728) and the Tradition of Commonplaces', *JHI* 57 (1996), 157–75.

[172] Bacon, *Advancement, Works* III, 400f.

[173] Bacon, *Historia ventorum, Works* II, 14f. This is a mixed allusion to Babel and to Ps. 19 which speaks of the language of the heavens 'going through all the earth'.

An alternative way of overcoming the curse of confused language lay in the use of 'real characters' which, as Bacon explained, 'express neither letters nor words in gross, but Things or Notions'.[174] 'Real', in this context, means that the characters were to do with things or thoughts, rather than spoken words, just as 'real, experimental philosophy' was also promoted as a philosophy that was not about wordy disputations, but about things.[175] These symbols, or 'Notes of Cogitations', were conceived of as written characters that directly represented things without the intervening medium of the spoken word, thus differing from most written languages in which spoken words represent objects or thoughts, and written words represent the spoken words. Bacon gives the example of Chinese ideographs, stating his belief that peoples in China and the 'high Levant' who do not understand each other's spoken dialects could nonetheless communicate through this common form of writing. Bacon also speculated about other kinds of symbols that had the feature of resembling the things they signified. These include the physical gestures used by the deaf and dumb, and hieroglyphics of the ancient Egyptians. There were, then, two quite distinct kinds of symbols or 'notes' being discussed, both of which directly represented thoughts – 'the one when the note hath some similitude or congruity with the notion' (e.g., hieroglyphics), the other 'having force only by contract or acceptation' (e.g. Chinese ideographs).[176] Later in the century these speculations were to inspire a number of different universal or natural language projects, some of which focused on real characters, others of which attempted to discover characters or symbols that resembled the things they stood for. While memory is not a major topic in *Novum Organum*, Bacon does make reference to the deficiencies of language and the way in which these deficiencies inhibit the business of learning. It is in this context that he speaks of the 'idols of the marketplace', which were essentially to do with the misleading 'alliances of words and names' and the incapacity of words to represent 'the true divisions of nature'. Because of these idols, Bacon pointed out, much scholarly disagreement was really to

---

[174] Bacon, *Advancement, Works* III, 399. The term 'real' was often used in conjunction with 'experimental' to describe a kind of philosophy or religion that was regarded as genuinely to do with things, rather than mere words.

[175] Thus Wilkins: 'A *Real universal Character* . . . should not signifie *words*, but *things* and *notions*' (*Essay toward a Real Character and a Philosophical Language* (London, 1684), p. 13); Hooke: 'the real, the mechanical, the experimental Philosophy' (*Micrographia*, Preface); John Ray, 'the advancement of real philosophy' (*Correspondence* (1848), p. 130).

[176] Bacon, *Advancement, Works* III, 399f. In fact, hieroglyphics turned out to be alphabetical, rather than pictorial.

do with the meanings of words.[177] Again, these observations gave impetus for the artificial language projects of the second half of the century.

If the senses are prone to providing false information, and if memory and writing are imperfect media for the storage of information, the intellect itself was deemed incapable of processing information. In his account of the idols of the tribe, Bacon was thus to speak of 'the perpetual error of the intellect', and of the fact that the intellect is 'unfit' to perform its primary duties.[178] The immediate cause of the errors of the intellect was the undesirable influence of the passions and affections: 'The human understanding is no dry light, but receives an infusion from the will and affections.' In *The Advancement of Learning*, Bacon had made a similar reference to the fact that the 'dry' soul is 'steeped and infused in the humours of the affections'.[179] Bacon's allusion to 'dry light' is a somewhat obscure reference to a corrupted maxim of the presocratic philosopher Heraclitus (*fl.* 500 BC), who was reported as having said that 'the dry soul is the wisest and best'.[180] Owing to confusions about the meaning of the original Greek, over time this fragment was rendered as 'the dry light is the wisest soul'. For Heraclitus the soul was constituted by two elements, fire (the noble element) and water (the ignoble). The wise soul is 'dry' because fire predominates. More importantly, the Baconian references to the 'drenching' of the mind by the humours also drew upon Christian traditions about what had taken place in Adam's mind as a consequence of the Fall. As we have seen, the burgeoning sixteenth- and seventeenth-century literature on the passions provided physiological accounts of the manner in which the mind is flooded by the motions of the passions, disabling it from its proper functioning.[181] When Adam fell, he lost his dominion over nature at the same time that his reason lost its dominion over the passions.

While Bacon's diagnosis of the difficulties of the intellect may have something in common with contemporary works of moral psychology, his

[177] Bacon, *Novum Organum* I, §58 (*Works* IV, 60f.). Establishing clear definitions (as Aristotle had suggested) might seem to offer a solution, but because definitions are themselves composed of words and because each language has its own names for things, the potential for confusion and disputation remained. Bacon, *Novum Organum* I, §43 (*Works* IV, 54, 192).
[178] Bacon, *Novum Organum* I, §§46, 47 (*Works* IV, 56, 58).
[179] *Ibid.*, I, §49 (*Works* IV, 57); *Advancement of Learning* I.3 (Johnston, p. 9).
[180] Heraclitus, Frg. 118, Stobaeus, *Anthology* III, 5, 8. For a discussion of the saying and its history see Charles H. Kahn, *The Art and Thought of Heraclitus* (Cambridge, 1979), pp. 245–54.
[181] See, e.g., Reynolds, *Treatise of the Passions*, pp. 6, 265; Goodwin, *Vanity of Thoughts*, pp. 49, 54, 57f.; South, *Sermons*, pp. 124f., 132f., 146; Glanvill, *Vanity of Dogmatizing*, p. 4; Ayloffe, *Government of the Passions*, p. 22. For secondary accounts see Harrison, 'Reading the Passions'; John Sutton, 'The Body and the Brain', in Gaukroger, Schuster, and Sutton (eds.), *Descartes' Natural Philosophy*, pp. 697–722.

prescription is relatively novel. In place of the usual counsels of inner self-discipline, we find in Bacon an emphasis on a new philosophical regimen that consists of externally imposed methodological constraints. It is these, rather than internally directed moral efforts, that are to overcome the inherent weakness of the mind. The intellect, he writes, 'is altogether slow and unfit, unless it be forced thereto by severe laws and overruling authority'.[182] The laws for the governing of natural philosophy set out in the *Great Instauration* involve such principles: reliance upon experimentation, the accumulation of organised sets of observations ('natural and experimental histories', as Bacon calls them), and guided communal endeavour. These new methodological prescriptions are consistent with Bacon's new vision of philosophy as less of a solitary, contemplative practice concerned with the moral formation and happiness of the individual philosopher, than a communal activity, aimed at the mastery and manipulation of nature, for the benefit of the public. As Stephen Gaukroger has expressed it, in Bacon we encounter 'the first systematic comprehensive attempt to transform the early modern philosopher from someone whose primary concern is with how to live morally into someone whose primary concern is with the understanding of and reshaping of natural processes'.[183] This new vision, in turn, was grounded in an essentially Augustinian conviction that given the irrevocable corruption of human nature, formal systems of external coercion are necessary to order the present life. In the realm of politics, this provides the justification for the coercive powers of the state. Bacon extends this to the sphere of philosophy, now understood as the re-establishment of an Adamic dominion over nature, advocating a parallel social organisation capable of stipulating the rules of the natural philosophical enterprise and overseeing their implementation. In the utopian *New Atlantis*, Bacon presages a new kind of community that presides over and regulates the acquisition of scientific knowledge. While Adam's original capacities had made possible his comprehension of the whole body of scientific knowledge, in a fallen world this was to be accomplished over time by communal labour. 'Salomon's House' was thus Bacon's model of a new kind of organisation that exercised political control over the mechanisms of knowledge generation.

In addition to the disciplines imposed on the investigator, nature itself was to be subjected to the rigours of experimentation – hence Bacon's

---

[182] Bacon, *Novum Organum* I, §47 (*Works* IV, 57). Bacon does not wholly divorce moral considerations from the practice of natural philosophy however. See, e.g., *Historia ventorum*, *Works* II, 14f.

[183] Gaukroger, *Francis Bacon*, p. 5. See also Antonio Pérez-Ramos, 'Bacon's Legacy', *Cambridge Companion to Bacon*, pp. 311–34; Harrison, 'The Natural Philosopher and the Virtues'.

notorious and oft misunderstood advocacy of extracting knowledge from nature by force. 'The secrets of nature', as he put it, 'reveal themselves more readily under the vexations of art, than when they go their own way.'[184] Part of the necessity for the manipulation of nature arose out of the conviction that as a consequence of the Fall nature itself had become unruly, insubordinate, mysterious in its operations, and opaque to the inquiring mind.[185] A number of the Church Fathers had argued that from the moment of Adam's sin the once prefect world had entered a new phase of mutability and irrevocable decline. 'The world has grown old', lamented St Cyprian, 'and does not abide in that strength in which it formerly stood; nor has it the vigour and force which it once possessed.'[186] The thesis of the world's perpetual decline was revived during the Renaissance and reached its zenith during the seventeenth century.[187] George Hakewill, who sought to refute this view, observed that 'the opinion of the Worlds decay is so generally received, not onely among the Vulgar, but of the Learned, both Divines and others, that the very commonnesse of it make it currant [sic] with many without further examination'.[188] Robert Burton was one such learned individual, who declared that 'For from the fall of our first parent *Adam*, they [God's creatures] have beene changed, the earth accursed, the influence of the starres altered, the four Elements, Beastes, Birds, Plants, are now

---

[184] Bacon, *Novum Organum* i, §98 (*Works* iv, 94f.). Cf. *Advancement of Learning* (*Works* iv, 298). For some standard misreadings of Bacon on this issue, see Susan Harding, *Whose Science? Whose Knowledge? Thinking from Women's Lives* (Ithaca, 1991), pp. 116, 43; Caroline Merchant, *The Death of Nature* (San Francisco, 1980), p. 168; Evelyn Fox Keller, *Reflections on Gender and Science* (New Haven, 1985), p. 35. For critiques of these readings see Iddo Landau, 'Feminist Criticisms of Metaphors in Bacon's Philosophy of Science', *Philosophy* 73 (1998), 47–61; Peter Pesic, 'Wrestling with Proteus: Francis Bacon and the "Torture" of Nature', *Isis* 90 (1999), 81–94.

[185] For contemporary descriptions of what befell nature after the Fall see Franck, *Philosophical Treatise*, pp. 120–60 and passim; Thomas Malvenda, *De Paradiso* (Rome, 1605), p. 202; Daneau, *Wonderfull Woorkmanship*, fol. 82r–v; Goodman, *Fall of Man*, pp. 17f., 25; Ross, *An Exposition*, p. 72; Senault, *Man becom Guilty*, pp. 319–90; Robinson, *Anatomy of the Earth*, pp. 4f. For sixteenth-century German writers on this theme, see Kathleen Crowther-Heyck, 'Wonderful Secrets of Nature: Natural Knowledge and Religious Piety in Reformation Germany', *Isis* 94 (2003), 253–73 (esp. 269f.).

[186] Cyprian, *Treatise* v, 'An Address to Demetrianus', 3 (ANF v, 458). See also David Brookes, 'The Idea of the Decay of the World in the Old Testament, the Apocrypha, and the Pseudopigrapha', in J. D. North and John Roche (eds.), *The Light of Nature* (Dordrecht, 1985), pp. 383–404. Some support was provided for the notion from such classical writers as Ovid and Lucretius. See D. C. Allen, 'The Degeneration of Man and Renaissance Pessimism', *Studies in Philology* 35 (1938), 202–27. The biblical sources for the fall of the natural world were Gen. 3:17–18 and Rom. 8:20–2.

[187] Victor Harris, *All Coherence Gone* (London, 1966); Clarence Glacken, *Traces on the Rhodian Shore: Nature and Culture in Western Thought from Ancient Times to the End of the Eighteenth Century* (Berkeley, 1973), pp. 162f., 379–92; Margaret Hodgen, *Early Anthropology in the Sixteenth and Seventeenth Centuries* (Philadelphia, 1964), pp. 254–94; George Williamson, 'Mutability, Decay, and Seventeenth-Century Melancholy', *Journal of English Literary History* 2 (1935), 121–51.

[188] Hakewill, *Apologie*, p. 13.

ready to offend us.'[189] The corrupt condition of the cosmos had important epistemological implications, and the natural world was generally regarded as having become less intelligible than it had once been. As Augustine wrote, the earth 'does not make good on its promises, it is a liar and deceives'.[190] Such ideas remained current among Bacon's contemporaries. According to the astrologer and magus John Dee (1527–1609), the earth had been severely disordered by the Fall, and the earthly chapters of the book of nature had been rendered virtually unintelligible. The terrestrial realm was 'composed of unstable elements', which resisted interpretation. (Like Melanchthon, Dee thought that the heavens still manifested a conspicuous order, and one that was susceptible to mathematical description.)[191] Gideon Harvey reasoned that before the Fall 'there was no resistence or obscurity in any of the objects; because they, being all created for the service of man, had their natures (as it were) writ upon their breast, so that herein they were at the command of the understanding'.[192] Bacon seems to have taken this tradition for granted. In *On Principles and Origins*, he explains that before the Fall, matter had been organised in the best possible configuration, thereafter suffering a deterioration.[193] Elsewhere he suggested that the original laws of nature had suffered an alteration at the Fall which would be rectified only at the end of the world.[194] For Bacon as for Harvey, moreover, nature itself seemed to have become almost wilfully impenetrable: 'But the universe to the eye of human understanding is framed like a labyrinth; such deceitful resemblances of objects and signs, natures so irregular in their lines, and so knotted and entangled.'[195] The obscurity of fallen nature thus warranted the use of the more active and intrusive methods of investigation that characterised the experimental approach.

---

[189] Burton, *Anatomy*, I, 125. See also Milton, *Paradise Lost* IX, 782–4, 942; Poole, *Milton and the Fall*, p. 181.

[190] Augustine, *Sermons* CXXCV, II (PL 38, 698). Cf. Luther, *Table Talk*, CXXXII (p. 58).

[191] Deborah Harkness, *John Dee's Conversations with Angels: Cabala, Alchemy, and the End of Nature* (Cambridge, 1999), p. 72. It was also often suggested that after the Fall the signatures of natural objects were effaced. See Bono, *Word of God*, pp. 26–84.

[192] Harvey, *Archelogia Philosophica Nova*, pt I, p. 89. Cf. Thomas Traherne: 'if nature were divested of its Corruption, the Natural Man . . . might by the Light of Nature, be fitted to understand [it]'. *Christian Ethics: Or Divine Morality* (London, 1675), p. 101.

[193] Bacon, *De principiis atque originibus*, *Works* IV, 491. Cf. *Works* VI, 250.

[194] Bacon, *A Confession of Faith*, *Works* VII, 221. This view of different sets of laws of nature for different epochs was also adopted by Newton and William Whiston. See Harrison, 'Newtonian Science, Miracles, and the Laws of Nature', 545.

[195] Bacon, *Great Instauration*, *Works* IV, 18. Cf. Descartes, for whom nature is to be observed in its normal course, rather than in circumstances that are 'more unusual and highly contrived'. *Discourse*, CSM I, 143.

Bacon's novel advocacy of an examination of nature 'out of its normal course' contravened a standard Aristotelian assumption that a distinction was to be maintained between 'natural' and 'violent' motion.[196] On this view, observations made under the conditions imposed by experimental protocols would not assist in the understanding of how nature operates when free of such human involvement. Interfering in the ordinary operations of nature would render the motions studied 'violent' rather than 'natural'. A related Aristotelian distinction was that between the natural and artificial, or nature and arts. For critics of the experimental approach, the human intrusion into nature which experimentation represented gave rise to odd hybrids that, strictly speaking, were neither one nor the other. In *Observations on Experimental Philosophy* (1666), Margaret Cavendish – probably the only woman of her era to have directly witnessed experiments being performed by fellows of the Royal Society – was to argue that experimentation produced 'Hermaphroditical Effects, that is, such as are partly Natural, and partly Artificial'.[197] In her view, experimentalists were not studying nature at all, but a monstrous creation that was partly their own fabrication. Advocacy of the experimental intrusion into nature's ordinary operations thus challenged the anthropocentric assumption of Aristotelianism, according to which there was a natural affinity between the mind and nature. For Aristotle, human desire for knowledge was answered by the intelligibility of the world. The myth of the Fall, however, suggested a disordering both of mental operations and of nature itself. Viewed through the lens of sacred history, neither nature nor the mind could be said to be operating 'naturally', both having deteriorated from the original divine plan on account of human sin. For this reason, Bacon frames the nature of his inquiry in the opening sentence of *The Great Instauration* in terms of this question: 'whether that commerce between the mind of man and the nature of things . . . might by any means be restored to its perfect and original condition, or if that may not be, yet reduced to a better condition than that in which it now is'.[198] Restoration of that 'commerce' between the mind and the natural world, on Bacon's view, called for disciplines to be applied to both.

---

[196] Aristotle, *Physics* 255. For a discussion of the distinction see Anstey, *Philosophy of Robert Boyle*, pp. 121–3. For Galileo's rejection of it see Alexander Koyré, *Galileo Studies* (Hassocks, 1978), pp. 59, 181.

[197] Margaret Cavendish, *Further Observations upon Experimental Philosophy* (London, 1666), p. 4. Cf. pp. 12f. Cf. Descartes, *Principles of Philosophy* §325, CSM I, 288; Henry Power, *Experimental Philosophy*, pp. 192f. Bacon's position is given in Paolo Rossi, *Philosophy, Technology and the Arts in the Early Modern Era* (New York, 1970), pp. 138f.

[198] Bacon, *Great Instauration*, *Works* IV, 7.

This assumption of the fallenness of the world thus gave sanction to a more active and aggressive style of experimental interrogation than that provided by Aristotelianism. It also motivated large-scale modifications of the natural environment. While the mind of man clearly stood in need of restoration, the earth itself, which in St Paul's evocative words had been 'subjected to vanity' (Rom. 8:20), was to be redeemed also. The seventeenth-century quest to re-establish human dominion over the natural world – often associated with that exploitative stance thought to typify the modern West's attitude towards nature – was thus originally conceived as a restorative project designed to return the world to its prelapsarian perfection.[199] In much the same way that the mind needed to be restored by a re-establishment of the proper hierarchical relations amongst its various faculties, so the earth's restoration was to be accomplished through the re-imposition of lost human dominion. Metaphysical poet Thomas Traherne could thus write that whereas the earth 'had been a Wilderness overgrown with Thorns, and Wild Beasts, and Serpents', now by the labour of many hands, it is 'reduced to the Beauty and Order of *Eden*'.[200] Timothy Nourse agreed that the earth needed to be liberated from 'the Original Curse of Thorns and Bryers'. Human activity could thus effect 'the *Restauration of Nature*, which may be looked upon as a *New Creation* of things'. In short, the intention of the manipulation of the natural world was, in John Donne's words, 'To rectifie nature to what she was'.[201]

Since the nineteenth century the issue of Bacon's legacy has been a matter of some debate. What is not in any doubt, however, is spectacular success of his ideas in the seventeenth century.[202] The French Académie Royale des Sciences, founded in 1666, was explicitly modelled on Baconian principles, as was the Italian Accademia della Tracia, founded in the same decade following the closure of the Accademia del Cimento. If influence can be gauged by weight of editions, then Bacon also had an enormous impact in the Netherlands, which saw forty-five printings of his works over the course of the seventeenth century. While Bacon had imitators and admirers elsewhere in Europe, his influence was most strongly felt in England, where his ideas gave a distinctive shape to English natural philosophy.

[199] Peter Harrison, 'Subduing the Earth: Genesis 1, Early Modern Science, and the Exploitation of Nature', *The Journal of Religion* 79 (1999), 86–109.
[200] Thomas Traherne, *Christian Ethicks* (London, 1675), p. 103.
[201] John Donne, 'To Sr Edward Herbert. At Julyers', lines 33f.
[202] See Gaukroger, *Francis Bacon*, pp. 2–4; Theodore Brown, 'The Rise of Baconianism in Seventeenth-Century England', in E. Hilfstein et al. (eds.), *Science and History: Studies in Honor of Edward Rosen* (Wrocław, 1978), pp. 501–22.

The Royal Society, also founded in the 1660s, regarded itself as the concrete realisation of Bacon's ideal of a scientific brotherhood, and its fellows
considered themselves the foremost exponents of his methods. Thomas
Sprat thought that the founding of the Society with its Baconian ethos
warranted the description of England as the 'Land of Experimental Knowledge' and confirmed its status as 'the Head of a Philosophical league, above
all other Countries in Europe'.[203] Sprat's judgements about the primacy of
the English in the sphere of experimental philosophy, though exaggerated
and chauvinistic, were not entirely without substance, and some historians
have cautiously repeated them. Joseph Ben-David thus observes that Baconianism conferred upon English science of the mid-seventeenth century 'a
valid strategy for conduct and a sense of coherence which were lacking in
most scientific groups elsewhere'.[204]

Bacon's most immediate appropriators were not the Fellows of the Royal
Society, however, but the Puritan 'projectors' of the 1640s and 1650s. These
individuals sought to promote reforms of learning in order to secure the
millennial restoration of all things. As we have seen, the Baconian programme itself derives much of its character from the ubiquitous narrative
of the Fall, and from the anthropological considerations that arise out of it.
The key feature of this approach is that it strikes a balance between scepticism on the one hand and, on the other, the optimistic assumption that the
acquisition of knowledge is simple and unproblematic. This middle path we
may designate 'Solomonic scepticism', that at once asserts the vanity of the
present earthly existence, and at the same time attempts to realise the latent
potentialities that reside within the human soul. Human beings are fallen,
and this brings with it significant disabilities. By the same token, the legend
of Adamic wisdom, and the realistic possibility of its present recovery, serve
to motivate the quest to repair knowledge and begin the re-establishment
of the dominion over nature that human beings were originally destined
to enjoy. Something of this admittedly precarious balancing act can be
seen in Bacon's rejection both of the over-optimistic epistemology of Aristotle and the Schools, and of the confident presumption of the magicians,

[203] Sprat, *History*, pp. 113f.
[204] J. Ben-David, *The Scientist's Role in Society: A Comparative Study* (Englewood Cliffs, NJ, 1971),
pp. 72–4, cited in Webster, *Great Instauration*, p. 515. See also Marie Boas Hall, *Promoting Experimental Learning: Experiment and the Royal Society, 1660–1727* (Cambridge, 1991), pp. 9f. There
remained a degree of diversity amongst English Baconians, however. See M. Hunter and P. Wood,
'Towards Solomon's House: Rival Strategies for Reforming the Early Royal Society', in M. Hunter
(ed.), *Establishing the New Science: The Experience of the Early Royal Society* (Woodbridge, 1989),
pp. 185–244; M. Feingold, 'Mathematicians and Naturalists: Sir Isaac Newton and the Royal Society', in J. Z. Buchwald and I. B. Cohen (eds.), *Isaac Newton's Natural Philosophy* (Cambridge, MA,
2001), pp. 77–102.

alchemists, and hermeticists who sought to replace decades of labour with isolated moments of inspiration or with a few perfunctory experiments.[205] Yet he insists that knowledge is possible and that we have a duty to pursue it. Others were less successful in following this judicious middle path. The projects of the Commonwealth period thus erred on the side of optimism, partly because of their tendency to invoke divine revelation, partly because of their focus on the capacities of the prelapsarian Adam rather than on the disabilities wrought by his Fall. Arguably, with the Restoration, this expectant optimism was significantly muted and natural philosophy became a more sober long-term enterprise. These developments are the subject of the next chapter.

[205] Bacon, *Advancement, Works* III, 362; *Temporis partus masculus, Works* III, 534; *Novum Organum* I, §54 (*Works* III, 59); *Redargutio philosophiarum, Works* III, 575.

CHAPTER 5

The instauration of learning

And as at first, mankind fell by tasting of the forbidden Tree of Knowledge, so we, their Posterity, may be in part restor'd by the same way, not only by beholding and contemplating, but by tasting too those fruits of Natural knowledge, that were never yet forbidden.

Robert Hooke, Micrographia (London, 1665), Preface

Whence, our First Enquiry ought to be, how Man's Nature came to be so Disabled from performing its Primary Operation, or from Reasoning rightly . . . Divines will tell us that this mischief happens thro' Original Sin.

John Sergeant, The Method to Science (London, 1696), sigs. a1v–a2r.

. . . we create tragedy after tragedy for ourselves by a lazy unexamined doctrine of man which is current amongst us and which the study of history does not support . . . It is essential not to have faith in human nature.

Herbert Butterfield, Christianity and History

The striking frontispiece of the 1620 edition of Bacon's *Great Instauration* bears a text from the apocalyptic book of Daniel that reads: 'Multi pertransibunt et augebitur scientia' – Many shall go to and fro, and knowledge shall be increased.[1] As Charles Webster has ably demonstrated, the turbulent decades between Bacon's death in 1626 and the Restoration of the monarchy in 1660 witnessed a remarkable marriage of Puritan millenarianism and a Baconian promotion of knowledge and learning. While it is true that the scientific writings of this period were remarkably eclectic and drew upon a variety of ancient and modern natural philosophies, it was the millenarian aspects of the Baconian programme that provided inspiration for a whole variety of scientific and technological projects. Whatever Bacon's own religious predilections, his philosophy could have been specifically

---

[1] Dan. 12:4. The Vulgate actually reads 'plurimi pertransibunt et multiplex erit scientia', which Bacon accurately cites in *Advancement, Works* III, 340. Whether the change of wording was deliberate is not clear. See Farrington's comment, *Philosophy of Francis Bacon*, p. 132.

tailored for Puritan purposes.[2] Having said this, the Puritan eschatology of
the period was characterised by a quite specific chiliastic vision. It was not
a matter of complacently awaiting the Day of Judgment, or of passively
reading the 'signs' that signalled the imminence of the millennium. Godly
individuals were to be active participants in history, directing their efforts
towards the establishment of those conditions that would usher in the final
age of the world. For the Puritans, and indeed many Protestants, the reformation of religion in the sixteenth century was the historical event that had
triggered the apocalyptic countdown. Since then, revolutions in learning
and advances in such diverse spheres as navigation and printing confirmed
them in their belief that the end time was quickly approaching. The voyages
of discovery not only expanded existing knowledge of the world, but also
raised the prospect of the gospel being preached to the whole world for
the first time – a signal occurrence that had traditionally been considered
a prerequisite for the culmination of human history. On the negative side
of the ledger, the 1620s was not a happy decade for Europe, and for Protestants in particular. The combined effects of economic depression and war
brought untold misery to millions, and Catholic forces had begun to make
significant gains in the Protestant heartlands of the Palatinate, Bohemia,
and Poland. For a time the very existence of Continental Protestantism
seemed under threat, and England seemed either unwilling or unable to
lend military support to its co-religionists. The spirit of Antichrist seemed
to loom larger than at any previous time in history. These events fuelled
an upswing of apocalyptic sentiment in Protestant Europe, and refugees
fleeing persecution and religious violence brought it with them to the
shores of England, where it melded with domestic millenarianism. On
those shores, the publication in 1627 of Joseph Mede's enormously influential *Clavis Apocalyptica* showed how biblical prophecy could be directly
applied to the interpretation of contemporary historical events, and many
were to appropriate its interpretative principles to demonstrate the imminence of the end times.[3] Along with the book of Revelation, which provided
the main subject matter for Mede's *Clavis*, the apocalyptic prophecies of
Daniel came to assume great importance for Puritan millenarians in the
revolutionary period of seventeenth-century England. The verse cited by

---

[2] Webster, *Great Instauration*, pp. 486, 514f.

[3] MacCulloch, *Reformation*, pp. 469–84; Hugh Trevor-Roper, 'Three Foreigners: The Philosophers of
the Puritan Revolution', in *The Crisis of the Seventeenth Century* (Indianapolis, 2001), pp. 219–71.
For the rise of apocalypticism, prophecy and astrology during this period see Patrick Curry, *Prophecy
and Power: Astrology in Early Modern England* (Cambridge, 1989); Christopher Hill, *Antichrist in
Seventeenth Century England* (London, 1971); Kinch Hoekstra, 'Disarming the Prophets: Thomas
Hobbes and Predictive Power', *Rivista di storia della filosofia* 1 (2004), 97–153.

Bacon took on a particular importance and often appeared in the sermons of Puritan preachers, reinforcing the message that the last days would be heralded by an unprecedented increase in knowledge.[4] The immediate context of the Daniel passage refers to the end times when 'those who are wise will shine like the brightness of the heavens, and those who lead many to righteousness, like the stars for ever and ever' (12:3). Passages such as these served to inspire Puritan activists in their efforts to reform society, to rebuild the institutions of learning, to promote arts and sciences, and to usher in a new era of peace and prosperity.

'KNOWLEDGE SHALL BE INCREASED'

One of the many immigrants to settle in England during these turbulent times was Samuel Hartlib (c. 1600–62) who, along with fellow émigré Amos Comenius, was to play a vital role in the development of an eschatologically oriented reformation of learning. A native of the Baltic port of Elbing, Hartlib had studied at Emmanuel College, Cambridge in the 1620s. He settled in London in 1628, and soon established himself at the hub of one of the most important networks of correspondence in the seventeenth century. Some sense of his commitment to the task of rebuilding the world in its final days can be gauged from the short utopian work *Macaria* which he published (but did not author) in 1641. The book describes an Edenic world subdued by agriculture and colonisation so that the whole land is once again 'like to a fruitfull Garden', thus linking an Edenic past to the coming Kingdom.[5] *Macaria* provides us with a clear sense of the specifically Puritan proactive vision of the future: 'a Reformation shall come before the day of judgment . . . therefore with alacrity let us pursue our good intentions and bee good instruments in this worke of Reformation'.[6] We encounter the same combination of the indicative and the imperative in Comenius who shared many of Hartlib's ideals, as well as his Continental Calvinist background. Comenius announced that there will be 'a multiplication of knowledge and light at the very evening of the world

---

[4] Webster, *Great Instauration*, pp. 9–12.

[5] [Gabriel Plattes], *Macaria* (London, 1641), p. 4. Hartlib himself has usually been credited with authorship of *Macaria* but it is probably the work of his colleague Gabriel Plattes. See Charles Webster, 'The Authorship and Significance of Macaria', *Past and Present* 56 (1972), 34–48. Similar Edenic images may also be found in Walter Blith, *The English Improver Improved* (London, 1652), sig. d3v; Ralph Austen, *A Treatise of Fruit Trees* (London, 1657), sig. 1r; Pettus, *History of Adam and Eve*, p. 43. See also Scott Mandelbrote, 'Représentations bibliques et édéniques du jardin à l'âge classique', *XVIIe siècle* 52 (2000), 645–54.

[6] Plattes, *Macaria*, p. 13.

Dan. 12.4 Zach. 14.7.' 'Therefore', he concluded, 'let us endeavour that this be promoted.'[7]

Puritan promoters of learning thus appropriated Bacon's incipient apocalypticism. They also took to heart his conception of science as a corporate and cumulative activity as the means to increase knowledge, and thus to hasten the millennium. Communal endeavour, moreover, was thought to secure knowledge against the errors of corrupt individual minds. 'It's in vaine to hope that humane things, prolapsed and falne to decay by the common errours of all can be restored and made entire', Comenius observed, 'without the common help and joynt assistance of all.'[8] In keeping with this principle, Hartlib took it upon himself to coordinate the disparate endeavours of those striving to improve knowledge and human welfare. Soon after his arrival in London he began to cultivate a wide circle of correspondents, drawing heavily upon his contacts in Continental communities of Protestant refugees. One of his key contacts was John Dury (1596–1680), a Calvinist minister originally from Edinburgh, but at that time in Hartlib's Polish hometown Elbing. Dury shared Hartlib's heady utopian vision of a universal republic of learning that embraced a common Protestant religion. From his London residence, and with the assistance of a secretary and a small group of copyists, Hartlib received manuscripts, reports of experiments and inventions, requests for information, and all manner of proposals for the improvement of agriculture, medicine, commerce, and chemistry. These would be copied, summarised if need be, and sent out again to his numerous correspondents. In the late 1640s, in the wake of the victory of the Parliamentary party, Hartlib sought to make his role a more formal one, designated 'the Office of Address' with official government support.[9] While his proposal was viewed favourably, it was never formally implemented. Undaunted, Hartlib continued in the role through the 1650s and garnered himself a reputation as one of Europe's key co-ordinators of scientific information. He was variously dubbed the 'hub and axeltree of knowledge', 'the great intelligencer of Europe', the 'conduit pipe' through which the learning of Europe was channelled.[10]

[7] Comenius, *A Patterne of Universall Knowledge* (London, 1651), tr. Jeremy Collier, p. 65; Cf. *Reformation of Schooles*, pp. 4, 26.

[8] Comenius, *Universal Knowledge*, p. 20.

[9] Details of the scheme are provided in *Considerations Tending to the Happy Accomplishment of Englands Reformation in Church and State* (London, 1647).

[10] Mark Greengrass, Leslie Taylor and Timothy Raylor (eds.), *Samuel Hartlib and the Universal Reformation: Studies in Intellectual Communication* (Cambridge, 1994), Introduction, p. 16; Trevor-Roper, 'Three Foreigners'.

Hartlib and Comenius had also sought to reform institutions of learning and to establish new foundations that would embody the principles and practices of Solomon's House. During Comenius's visit in 1641, the two settled upon Chelsea College – an institution founded in 1610 by James I, but now standing derelict – as the best venue for the realisation of their ambitious strategy. Comenius was to become the Dean of the college, which would reflect the Baconian ideal of a recapture of Edenic wisdom (a goal that was restated in Comenius's own *Via lucis* (The Way of Light, 1642). The ultimate plan was for Protestant England to become a beacon of learning whose light would illuminate the whole of a benighted Europe. Unfortunately, England was on the brink of its own military crisis, and the onset of civil war in 1642 meant that the Parliament had turned its attention to the more pressing matter of the war in Ireland. But there was still considerable support for educational reform amongst the Puritans. John Milton offered a somewhat belated contribution to Hartlib's efforts with his tract *Of Education* (1644). While these two may have differed on issues relating to the content of the curriculum, they shared the view that improvement of the institutions of learning was long overdue. 'To write now of the reforming of education', Milton observed, is 'one of the greatest and noblest designs that can be thought on, and for the want whereof this nation perishes'. Milton, as we have already noted, regarded education as a way of 'repairing the ruins of our first parents'.[11] His brief proposal included recommendations relating not only to the content of the curriculum, but to the kinds of practical matters that Hartlib and Comenius had also given thought to: housing, maximum enrolment, age range of pupils, along with ruminations on diet and exercise. Milton's was one of fifty works written between 1640 and 1660 devoted to the topic of educational reform. The vast majority of these were associated with the Hartlib group.[12]

If hopes for a new bricks and mortar institution that would embody the ideals of Solomon's house were dashed, the 1640s nonetheless witnessed the emergence of a number of important informal groups devoted to the promotion of knowledge, and more specifically to experimental philosophy. One of these was the 'Invisible College', about which very little is known, apart from the fact that Robert Boyle was a participant and that it convened in the two years 1646–7. Another group had begun to coalesce around the mathematician John Wallis (1616–1703) at about the same time. This latter group was devoted to the 'new philosophy' of Galileo and Bacon,

[11] Milton, *Of Education*, in *Works*, pp. 225, 226.
[12] Webster, *Samuel Hartlib and the Advancement of Learning* (Cambridge, 1971), pp. 208–11.

and included in its membership John Wilkins, Francis Glisson, George Ent, Seth Ward, and Thomas Willis.[13] Both were important precursors of the Royal Society. In spite of widespread criticism of the hidebound conservatism of the universities, the new philosophy also made inroads at these venues. And while the disruption caused by the onset of civil war may have distracted the Parliament from formal plans to establish a new foundation of godly learning, that body nonetheless resolved to reform the existing universities, seeking specifically to bring an end to the domination of the curriculum by scholasticism. Whatever the intention of the parliamentary party, it cannot be doubted that the middle decades of the century witnessed the introduction of significant aspects of the new learning of Galileo, Descartes, and Harvey at the ancient universities. At Cambridge, Henry More introduced students to Descartes' *Principles of Philosophy*, while Isaac Barrow and John Ray promoted experimental philosophy and mathematics.[14] Wallis's 'experimental philosophy club' also began meeting in Oxford in about 1648–9, hosted successively by William Petty, John Wilkins and, following Wilkins's move to Cambridge, Robert Boyle.

REVERSING BABEL

While the millenarian motivations of these groups suggest a future-oriented ethos, the history of Adam remained a central preoccupation. John Webster (1611–82), who was introduced in the third chapter, was typical in this regard. A schoolmaster and an active participant in discussions about the restructuring of social and educational institutions during the Commonwealth, Webster had diverse philosophical inspirations. Apart from a deep commitment to Baconian ideals, he approved of the theosophy of Boehme and Fludd, subscribed to the atomism of Digby, and supported elements of van Helmont's iatrochemistry (the use of chemical rather than herbal preparations in medicine). In all of this he was sharply critical of Aristotelian learning, which in his view suffered from a misplaced trust in the powers of human reason. The 'much magnified natural reason' of the peripatetic schools, he claimed, was in reality 'the fruit and effect of the forbidden tree . . . a spurious and adventitious faculty which man wanted in his innocency, and was instilled in him by *Satan* in the fall'. Confidence in human reason alone, he insisted, gave rise to knowledge that was 'fleshly, earthly, deadly and destructive'.[15] Aristotle's philosophy, in brief, was the

---

[13] C. J. Scriba, 'The Autobiography of John Wallis', *Notes and Records of the Royal Society* 25 (1970), 17–46.
[14] Webster, *Great Instauration*, pp. 134f., 150–3.   [15] Webster, *The Saints Guide*, pp. 6, 4.

corrupted knowledge of the fallen creature. It did not follow that all forms of natural philosophy were to be shunned, however, for if prosecuted properly the study of nature had two vital uses: first, it enabled the philosopher to discern 'characters' or 'hieroglyphics' of the divine power in the things of nature; second, knowledge of the operations of causes and effects would enable the investigator 'to make use of them for the general good and benefit of mankind, especially for the conservation and restauration of the health of man, and of those creatures that are usefull for him'.[16] Adamic science provided the model of this godly natural philosophy.

In speaking of the 'characters' of the natural world, Webster was not merely alluding to the ubiquitous trope of the 'book of nature', for in his conception, nature was literally written in a language that Adam had once been able to read. There was a 'Paradisical language' that Adam had spoken in Eden, and which he had used to bestow names upon the beasts. Unlike the labels of conventional language, these names were not imposed arbitrarily on things. Rather, they uniquely identified them and perfectly expressed their true natures. In Eden, Webster informs us, 'the imposition of names was adequately agreeing with their natures; otherwise it could not be univocally and truly be said to be their names, whereby he distinguished them'.[17] It followed that Adam knew 'the internal natures, virtues, effects, operations, and qualities of the creatures'; indeed Adam's encyclopaedic knowledge was nothing other than facility in the very language of nature. After the entry of sin into the world, this language of things was 'defaced and forgotten'.[18] However, Webster was encouraged by the possibility that this primitive language might be recovered, and with it Adamic learning. Indeed it was the common belief that the knowledge of the primitive tongue, if reacquired, would confer knowledge of the natures of things. Bacon himself had asserted that 'the imposition of names' was one of the summary parts of knowledge and, moreover, that 'whensoever he shall be able to call the creatures by their true names he shall again command them'.[19]

Some, like Webster, associated the Adamic language with the Renaissance doctrine of signatures, according to which natural objects (and plants particularly) bore some sign that indicated their use. The shape of the kidney bean, to take a simple example, indicates that it is to be prescribed for

---

[16] Webster, *Academiarum Examen*, p. 19.   [17] *Ibid.*, pp. 27, 29.   [18] *Ibid.*, pp. 30, 27.
[19] Bacon, *Advancement* I.vi.6 (p. 38); *Of the Interpretation of Nature, Works* III, 222. See also Walker, *History of the Creation*, pp. 193, 229; Boehme, *The Second Booke*, sig. A3r; John Pettus, *History of Adam and Eve*, p. 60; Francis Bamfield, *Miqra qadosh, The Holy Scripture* (London, 1684), title page. Also see discussions in Håkan Håkansson, *Seeing the Word: John Dee and Renaissance Occultism* (Lund, 2001), pp. 100–8; Bono, *Word of God*, ch. 8.

ailments of that organ.[20] God, it was thought, had impressed these signatures on objects to show their interior properties and their uses. The science of signatures was linked to the discipline of physiognomy, which also conveyed the inner workings of things by external signs. Webster described physiognomy as 'that laudable, excellent, and profitable science . . . from which and by certain external signs, signatures and lineaments, doth explicate the internal nature and quality of natural bodies'.[21] For Webster, knowledge of these signs had provided the basis of the natural science of Adam although, of course, this had been lost – either because of the corruption of human nature, or because the Fall had erased these once conspicuous ciphers from the surfaces of natural objects.[22] In its present state, then, the science of signatures was fragmented and imperfect, and likely to remain so unless further efforts were devoted to extending and improving it.[23]

There was also considerable speculation about the possibility that the original Adamic tongue had survived the catastrophes of the Fall and Babel, and was still spoken (or written) somewhere on the globe. Hebrew was the traditional candidate for this role, partly because of some remarks in Augustine's *City of God* suggesting that the language of the ancient Israelites had been spared the confusion of tongues.[24] The priority of Hebrew was the fundamental assumption of Cabbalism, a mystical Jewish tradition that sought hidden meanings in the Hebrew characters of scripture. Christianised versions of Cabbalism flourished during the Renaissance, finding powerful exponents amongst humanist scholars.[25] In his *Occult Philosophy*

[20] For representative adherents see Boehme, *Signatura Rerum* (London, 1651); Oswald Croll, *Of Signatures* (London, 1669); Paracelsus, *Die 9 Bücher der Natura Rerum*, in *Sämtliche Werke*, ed. Sudhoff, xi, 393. Della Porta, *Natural Magick* (London, 1658), p. 17 and passim; Richard Saunders, *Saunders Physiognomie and Chiromancie, Metoposcopie*, 2nd edn (London, 1671); Coles, *Adam in Eden*, To the Reader.

[21] Webster, *Academiarum Examen*, p. 76.

[22] *Ibid.*, pp. 27, 29. Cf. Coles, *Adam in Eden*, To the Reader; Saunders, *Saunders Physiognomie*, Preface.

[23] See also the suggestions of More, *An Antidote*, pp. 56f., and Coles, *Adam in Eden*, Preface.

[24] Augustine, *City of God* XVI.11. Supporters of this view included Browne, *Pseudodoxia Epidemica* v.xxiii; VI.i (I, 434f., 442); Gulielmus Postellus, *De originibus seu Hebraicae linguae* (Paris, 1538), sigs. Aiiir–Aivr; Agrippa von Nettesheim, *Three Books of Occult Philosophy*, pp. 162f.; J. H. Heidegger, *De historia sacra patriarchum*, 2 vols. (Amsterdam, 1667–71), I, 462f.; Richard Simon, *A Critical History of the Old Testament* (London, 1682), I.xiv (pp. 97–101); John Selden, *De Synedriis . . . veterum Ebraeorum*, Prolegomenon, cap. iii; Lightfoot, *The Works of the Learned & Reverend John Lightfoot D. D.*, 2 vols. (London, 1684), I, 1012; Thomas Brett, *A Chronological Essay on the Sacred History* (London, 1629), pp. 56–93; Simon Patrick, *A Commentary upon the first book of Moses, called Genesis* (London, 1695), pp. 218f. Also see discussion in H. Pinard de la Boullaye, *L'Etude Comparée des Religions* (Paris, 1922), pp. 158–63. Most of the language projectors of the mid-seventeenth century also believed in the priority of Hebrew. See, e.g., George Dalgarno, 'On Double and Triple Consonants' in Cram and Maat (eds.), *George Dalgarno*, p. 335; Wilkins, *Essay*, p. 5.

[25] Alison Coudert, *The Impact of the Kabbalah in the Seventeenth Century* (Leiden, 1999); Håkansson, *Seeing the Word*, pp. 170–84.

Agrippa von Nettesheim suggested that Adam's original Hebrew names 'contain in them wonderful powers of the things signified'. Because God had used speech to create the world – 'And God said . . .' (Gen. 1) – letters and words could be said to form the very structure of the cosmos. As Agrippa expressed it, 'there are therefore two and twenty Letters, which are the foundation of the world, and of creatures that are, and are named in it, and every saying, and every creature are of them, and by their revolutions receive their Name, being, and Virtue'.[26] Johannes Reuchlin (1455–1522), great-uncle to Philipp Melanchthon and pioneer of the teaching of Hebrew in the German universities, attributed Solomon's great wisdom to his ability to discern hidden scientific knowledge 'in the minutiae of grammar [and] in the letters' of the Hebrew Bible.[27] Recovery of the power of these words was often understood as the means by which Adamic knowledge and dominion were to be re-established. Reuchlin believed the whole purpose of cabbalistic interpretation was to effect a 'universal restoration, after the primordial Fall of the human race'. In an interesting variation on the *topos* of the regaining of Adamic knowledge, Reuchlin held the view that Cabbala was delivered to Adam *after* his expulsion from Eden. In a version of events that shares elements of the *Sepher Raziel* legend, Reuchlin suggested that God, in his compassion, had sent an angel to teach Adam how the divine words might be interpreted so as to repair the ruins of Edenic wisdom.[28]

Despite its obvious antiquity and its centrality in cabbalistic practices, as a candidate for the original, natural language, Hebrew suffered from the disadvantage that its written form was alphabetical, and it was thus incapable of representing things pictorially. For some, this ruled it out of contention. It was also thought that contemporary Hebrew would in any case have been a much-corrupted form of the original tongue, if for no other reason than that the modern Jews seemed to have no better knowledge of nature than anyone else. As we have seen, Bacon pointed to the fact that Chinese was written 'in characters real, which express neither letter nor words in gross'. Thomas Browne was similarly intrigued by the fact that the 'Chinoys' spoke an ancient language and used a 'common

[26] Agrippa, *Occult Philosophy*, p. 162. Pythagorean and Platonic glosses on this position were to regard the divine creative act as a numbering of things rather than a naming and hence numbers might be regarded as the basic units of the language of nature. See S. Heniger, Jr, *Touches of Sweet Harmony: Pythagorean Cosmology and Renaissance Poetics* (San Marino, 1974).

[27] Johannes Reuchlin, *On the Art of the Kabbalah*, tr. Martin and Sarah Goodman (Lincoln, NE, 1993), p. 249.

[28] Reuchlin, *Art of Kabbalah*, pp. 65, 69, 73; Håkansson, *Seeing the Word*, pp. 179f.; Wilhelm Schmidt-Biggemann, 'Christian Kabbala', in Alison Coudert (ed.), *The Language of Adam / Die Sprache Adams* (Wiesbaden, 1999), pp. 81–121.

character'. Further evidence for the priority of Chinese lay in the fact that their chronologies were said to trace their ancestry back to a founding father known as 'Poncuus', a figure often identified with the biblical Noah.[29] This combination of facts raised the enticing possibility that Noah and his family had preserved the original tongue, that the Ark had landed in China, and that in the form of writing still extant were remnants of the very first forms of writing and speech. Browne was himself doubtful about this chain of events – he had a greater interest in Egyptian hieroglyphics – but the priority of Chinese was strongly championed later in the century by John Webb, in *An Historical Essay, Endeavoring a Probability that the Language of the Empire of China is the Primitive Language* (1669).[30] While this thesis attracted some enthusiastic adherents, it was eventually acknowledged that Chinese idiograms suffered from the major shortcoming that they were difficult to draw and even more difficult to learn – not characteristics of a supposedly natural and transparent means of representation.[31] The other major contender – Egyptian hieroglyphics, which had attracted the attention of Bacon, Browne, and the Jesuit polymath Athanasius Kircher – had the advantage of obvious antiquity but were in other respects inferior to Chinese characters, not least because they were impervious to all efforts to translate them. They remained so until 1822 when, after much concerted effort, Jean-François Champollion finally deciphered them after the discovery of the Rosetta Stone.[32]

Both of these options for the recovery of the Adamic language, in the middle decades of the seventeenth century at least, gave a central place to direct divine inspiration. Webster followed Boehme in his conviction that the key to the secret language of nature would be given through the inspiration of the Spirit. Just as the key to the meaning of scripture was given only by the Spirit of God, so the knowledge of true signatures of

---

[29] Thomas Browne, 'Of Languages, and Particularly of the Saxon Tongue', *Works*, ed. Geoffrey Keynes (London, 1928), III, 71.

[30] London, 1669. Webb relied on Jesuit accounts of Chinese chronology and argued that it was also likely that the Chinese had preserved something of the primitive religion. See Harrison, *'Religion' and the Religions*, pp. 151–7.

[31] John Wilkins, *Mercury, or, the Secret and Swift Messenger*, in *Mathematical and Philosophical Works*, 2 vols. (London, 1802), II, 106f.; *Essay*, pp. 10, 451; Cave Beck, *The Universal Character* (London, 1657), Preface; Hale, *Primitive Origination*, p. 163; Robert Hooke, 'Some Observations, and Conjectures concerning Chinese Characters', *Philosophical Transactions of the Royal Society*, XVI (1696), 63–78 (65, 73); Wotton, *Reflections upon Ancient and Modern Learning* (London, 1694), p. 154.

[32] Bacon, *Advancement of Learning*, I.vi.9 (p. 39); cf. II.xvi.2 (p. 131); Browne, 'Of Languages'. Kircher thought that the Chinese language had been derived from the Egyptian. *Of the Various Voyages and Travels undertaken into China*, in Peter de Goyer and Jacob de Keyzer, *An Embassy from the east India Company of the United Provinces to the grand Tartar Cham Emperour of China* (London, 1669), pp. 75f. Cf. Kircher, *Oedipus Aegyptiacus*, pt II.

nature relied on divine inspiration.[33] According to Robert Fludd, Moses and Solomon came into their knowledge only by the assistance of the spirit. The patriarch had 'conversed with God and obtained the key to both types of understanding (natural and supernatural) by divine assistance and illumination of the most Holy Spirit'.[34] The new revelation of the true language of nature was considered to be a reversal of the curse of Babel, calling to mind the words of the Prophet Joel that were repeated by the Apostle Peter on the occasion of the linguistic miracle of Pentecost: 'I will pour out my Spirit in those days, and they will prophesy, I will show wonders in the heaven above and signs on the earth below' (Acts 2:18–19, Joel 2:29–30). Jacob Boehme's English disciple J. Ellistone thus described signatures as 'the language of Nature, which telleth for what every thing is good and profitable'. But this language was to be understood only through 'the manifestation of that Spirit, which on the Day of Pentecost gave forth the true sence and meaning of all Languages in one'.[35]

There remained a third, and less exciting, prospect for the recovery of Adamic or pre-Babel language, and that was the construction of an artificial language that possessed some of the amenity of the original language of nature. To varying degrees the universal language projects of the second half of the seventeenth century, the best known of which are those of John Wilkins and George Dalgarno, represent attempts to explore this third option. As we shall see, however, there was a sharp divergence between the apocalyptically inspired aspirations of John Webster, and the more prosaic and painstaking efforts of John Wilkins. The former sought an inspired, magical language that would provide immediate access to the secrets of nature. The later projects, however, relied upon human ingenuity and labour, and for the most part were essays attempting to lay foundations for a future enterprise. Samuel Hartlib provided an important connection between these two types of projects, because of his involvement with both.[36]

The sense of urgency that attended all of these endeavours of the interregnum enthusiasts inevitably led to a certain lack of discrimination. Virtually any form of learning, provided that it was not scholastic, could find a place in the proposed reforms. The chief commitment during this period was to eclecticism, and for this reason the disparate ideas of Paracelsus, van Helmont, Jacob Boehme, Fludd, along with the Cabbalists and Rosicrucians

---

[33] Webster, *Academiarum Examen*, pp. 7–9.
[34] Fludd, *Apologia compendiaria* in *Robert Fludd*, ed. Huffman, pp. 46, 52. Cf. *Mosaicall Philosophy*, pp. 3, 10.
[35] J. Ellistone in Boehme, *Signatura Rerum*, sig. a4r.
[36] See Gerhard Strasser, 'Closed and Open Languages: Samuel Hartlib's Involvement with Cryptology and Universal Languages', in Greengrass et al. (eds.), *Samuel Hartlib*, pp. 151–61.

all found a place at the table.[37] The chief criterion was that of potential utility. This meant that while Bacon's ideas about the organisation of scientific knowledge and his vision of a state-sponsored scientific organisation were always in the foreground, the content of his natural philosophy and his emphasis on the importance of an evaluation of the competence of the mind and the senses receded. Indeed Comenius himself had expressed dissatisfaction with the ponderous nature of scientific advance under the Baconian regime. Thus Bacon was praised for having established the method of an 'artificial induction', which Comenius conceded was 'the onely way to pierce through into the most abstruse secrets of Nature'. But the specific method of Bacon took too long, required onerous organisation, and delivered results that were uncertain: 'But because this requireth the continuall industry of many men, and ages, and is not merely laborious, but seemeth also to be uncertaine in the event and successe thereof, hence it comes to passe, that though it be a most excellent invention, yet the most part of men neglect it as unprofitable.' Accordingly, Comenius looked elsewhere, trusting that God might lend his direct assistance: 'It will be therefore requisite for us to search out some other more universall Rule, which perhaps God of his great mercy will upon our diligent endeavour vouchsafe to reveal unto us.'[38] The many years of labour demanded by the Baconian programme could not be accommodated within the contracted timetable of the Puritan millenarians. Voracious consumers of any kind of knowledge that seemed capable of improving the human lot, figures such as Comenius, Hartlib, and Webster were strongly influenced by the utilitarian and millenarian aspects of Bacon's philosophy. But while they sought to realise the kinds of practical arrangements and social organisations that Bacon had argued for, in their impatience to regain an Edenic state they were less interested in the issue of human nature itself, and in how its defects might have had a bearing on the acquisition of knowledge.

With the Restoration of the monarchy in 1660, other features of the proposed Baconian reforms came to the fore. In the middle decades of the century, the emphasis had been utopian and forward-looking, with high expectations of an almost complete recovery of Adamic knowledge. Following the Restoration, Adamic knowledge remained the focus, but the prospects for its full recovery, and the time frame that this was thought to involve were more conservative. To a degree, this development paralleled what had taken place in Continental Europe in the previous century. In the

---

[37] Stephen Clucas, 'In search of "The True Logick": Methodological Eclecticism among the "Baconian Reformers"' in Greengrass et al. (eds.), *Samuel Hartlib*, pp. 51–74; Webster, *Great Instauration*, p. 513.

[38] Comenius, *Reformation of Schooles*, p. 35. Cf. *Naturall Philosophie Reformed*, Preface.

first years of Luther's initial successes in Germany there had been high hopes that the reformation of religion would usher in a new era with reformed political and educational structures. In their more radical manifestations, these hopes culminated in the Peasants' War (1524–5), which ended in tragedy and disappointment. In the political sphere, as is well known, Luther threw in his lot with the established political authorities rather than the leaders of the rebellion. In the education realm, the Aristotelian method that had been reviled in the first heady days of the Reformation, came to be firmly established in the Lutheran universities as a means of imposing order on a curriculum that was in danger of disintegrating under the weight of competing forms of knowledge and the kinds of enthusiastic excesses that were associated with civil disorder.

The Restoration also brought in its wake a renewed sense of the vanity of human aspirations. The events of the civil war, now viewed through a Royalist lens, seemed to confirm the Puritans' own views about the inherent limitations of human nature. Now, however, there was no moderating eschatological optimism. Thus while it may seem natural that the Restoration would see some diminution in the emphasis on the depravity of the human condition, if anything, the reverse was the case. The Restoration, writes W. M. Spellman, 'witnessed a resurgence of a view of man which placed sin at the forefront of all theological discussions'. The major theological development of the period witnessed an attempt 'to restore the primitive simplicity of the Christian Fall story'.[39] By the same token, there was a significant degree of continuity between the scientific impulses of the Commonwealth period and those of the Restoration. For understandable tactical reasons, Restoration proponents of experimental philosophy tended to distance themselves from the excesses of the Commonwealth period, typically claiming Bacon as their intellectual progenitor, and silently passing over the various applications of his programme that intervened between Bacon's death and the Restoration.[40] In fact, many of the goals of the 'projectors' of the Commonwealth period would be realised, albeit in a somewhat different form, by the Royal Society.

SOLOMON'S HOUSE

The Royal Society of London was officially incorporated on 15 July 1662. From its earliest days, many of its fellows regarded the Society as an

[39] Spellman, *The Latitudinarians*, p. 55. See also Christopher Hill, 'Sin and Society', in *Essays*, II, 117–40.
[40] Webster, *Great Instauration*, pp. 492f., 499. Cf. Gaukroger, *Francis Bacon*, pp. 1f.

embodiment of the scientific ideals of Bacon's 'House of Salomon'. In his apologetic *History of the Royal Society* (1667), Thomas Sprat declared that Bacon was 'the one great Man, who had the Imagination of the whole extent of the enterprise', and while the early Society was by no means uniform in its philosophical commitments, the figure most frequently invoked as its ideological patron was Francis Bacon.[41] In November of the year of the Royal Society's incorporation, Robert Hooke (1635–1703) was appointed curator of experiments for the group, and was charged with the task of preparing several experiments to be performed on each occasion of the Society's meeting. Eventually Hooke's position attracted a salary of £80 per year, making him, in effect, the first professional research scientist.[42] While Hooke's status within the Society may not have been as elevated as that of such luminaries as Robert Boyle, his role placed him at the centre of its activities. In his experimental labours, moreover, he clearly sought to put into practice the principles articulated in Bacon's writings, while in his written works he re-enunciated those same principles. His posthumously published essay, bearing the lengthy but informative title – *A General Scheme, or Idea of the Present State of Natural Philosophy, and how its defects may be remedied by a methodical proceeding in the making experiments and collecting observations, whereby to compile a natural history, as the solid basis for the superstructure of true philosophy,* has been aptly described by Patri Pugliese as 'the most compelling rendition of Baconian principles into a solid programme of scientific investigation'.[43] Sadly, Hooke's difficult personality and his propensity to alienate influential individuals – most notable amongst them Isaac Newton – have meant that only now is Hooke taking his rightful place as one of the founding fathers of experimental science.[44]

In the *Micrographia*, one of the two first publications of the Royal Society, we encounter what is perhaps the most clear and concise account of the Baconian understanding of the relation between experimental natural philosophy and the fallen condition of human beings. Every man, Hooke wrote, 'both from a deriv'd corruption, innate and born with him, and from his breeding and converse with men, is very subject to slip into all sorts

---

[41] Sprat, *History*, p. 44. On the Baconianism of the Royal Society see Webster, *Great Instauration*, pp. 88–99, 161, 491–6.

[42] Lisa Jardine, *The Curious Life of Robert Hooke: The Man who Measured London* (San Francisco, 2004), pp. 97, 236f. Most fellows of the Royal Society were amateurs, in contrast to the Académie Royale des Sciences which was funded by the crown, and whose members were professional researchers.

[43] Patri Pugliese, 'Robert Hooke (1635–1703)', *ODNB*.

[44] Among recent attempts to provide Hooke with a more fittingly prominent place in the history of experimental science, see Jardine, *The Curious Life of Robert Hooke*; Jim Bennett et al., *London's Leonardo: The Life and Works of Robert Hooke* (Oxford, 2003); Stephen Inwood, *The Forgotten Genius* (London, 2004).

of errors'. The path to avoiding these errors lay in identifying the faculties responsible for knowledge and in rectifying their operations: 'The only way which now remains for us to recover some degree of those former perfections, seems to be by rectifying the operations of the Sense, the Memory, and Reason.' These, of course, were the three faculties identified by Bacon. Armed with this proper understanding of the workings of the mind, the inquirer must seek their specific deficiencies. Our preliminary task, Hooke wrote, is to 'recollect their several defects, so that we may better understand how to supply them, and by what assistances we may enlarge their power'. Taken together, these 'assistances' amount to the programme of experimental philosophy: 'These being the dangers in the process of humane reason, the remedies of them all can only proceed from the real, the mechanical, the experimental philosophy.'[45] The argument is reiterated in *The Present State of Natural Philosophy*, where Hooke observes that 'the Intellect is not to be suffer'd to act without its Helps, but is continually to be assisted by some Method or Engine'. Again, the first step in developing such a method involves 'an examination of the Constitution and Powers of the Soul, or an Attempt of Disclosing the Soul to itself being an Endeavour of Discovering the Perfections and Imperfections of Humane Nature'.[46]

Having surveyed the relevant 'powers of the soul', Hooke found himself agreeing with Bacon that the immediate representations made by a fallen nature to human senses are deceptive. Nature seemed 'to use some kind of art in indeavouring to avoid our discovery'. For this reason nature was to be investigated when 'she seems to be put to her shifts, to make many doublings and turnings'.[47] Nature, in short, was to be put to the test under the more stringent conditions of experiment. In addressing the need to reform the senses, Hooke stressed far more than Bacon the importance of instruments. By means of the use of 'artificial instruments', Hooke thought, there may be 'a reparation made for mischiefs, and imperfections which mankind has drawn upon itself'. Hooke referred specifically to the telescope and the microscope, the successes of the former being better established than in Bacon's era. As for the latter, Hooke helped secure the place of microscopic observation in the sphere of the natural sciences. Encouraged by pioneering efforts in the application of these artificial instruments to the

---

[45] Hooke, *Micrographia*, Preface (unpaginated). The Fall was considered to be responsible for both 'innate' corruption and that owing to 'converse with men'. The corrupting influences of 'converse with men' (which relate to Bacon's idols of the marketplace and of the theatre) were usually regarded as indirect consequences of the Fall. See, e.g., Ferguson, *Interest of Reason in Religion*.

[46] Hooke, *The Present State of Natural Philosophy*, p. 7, in *The Posthumous Works of Robert Hooke*, ed. R. Waller (London, 1705).

[47] Hooke, *Micrographia*, Preface. Cf. Glanvill, *Scepsis Scientifica*, sigs. b2v–b3r.

visual realm, Hooke expressed a firm hope 'that there may be found many mechanical inventions to improve our other Senses, of hearing, smelling, tasting, touching'.[48]

Hooke also attended closely to the corporate elements of the Baconian programme, seeing in the collective and cumulative industry of the new Society the prospects of overcoming the 'slipperiness and delusion of our memory'. Certainly he viewed his own efforts in this light. The detailed descriptions provided in *Microcosmographia* he regarded as a modest contribution to 'the foundations whereon others may raise nobler Superstructures'. The long-term success of experimental natural philosophy depended on the co-ordination of many sets of such observations on a variety of topics that were to be specified in advance and compiled under particular headings. Following Bacon's terminology, Hooke spoke of the 'compiling of a Naturall and Artificial History' which involved 'ranging and registering . . . Particulars into Philosophical Tables, as may make them most useful for the raising of Axioms and Theories'.[49] The unofficial journal of the Society – the *Philosophical Transactions*, launched in 1665 by Henry Oldenburg – also helped fulfil this function, bringing together reports of experiments and observations from fellows and numerous distinguished foreign correspondents. The very first issue contained a contribution by Hooke, and over the next few years virtually every major scientific figure of the period was represented in its pages. It remains the oldest continually published scientific journal in Europe and played a pioneering role in establishing natural science as the communal product of an international community.[50] The idea that an improved natural philosophy necessitated a proper 'ranking and registering' of particulars also found concrete realisation in the taxonomic tables of the language projects of Dalgarno, Wilkins, and others.[51]

Another early fellow of the Royal Society and one of its most vocal champions, the Anglican divine Joseph Glanvill (1636–80), also wrote at length on the link between the prescriptions of experimental natural philosophy and the Fall of the human race. His first book, *The Vanity of Dogmatizing* (1661) – a work that was revised and published under various titles throughout his life – was an attack on the Aristotelian scholasticism that he had encountered as a student at Oxford in the 1650s. Certain

[48] Hooke, *Micrographia*, Preface. Cf. Power, *Experimental Philosophy*, sig. c3v.
[49] *Ibid*. Cf. Hooke, *Present State of Natural Philosophy*, p. 7.
[50] The *Journal des sçavans* (Journal of savants) can lay claim to being the first scientific journal in the world, appearing in January 1665, two months before the *Philosophical Transactions*.
[51] In keeping with the views of the language projectors, Hooke points out that 'Words being ill set Marks on very confused Notions; the Reason of a Man is very easily impos'd on by Discourse.' *Present State of Natural Philosophy*, p. 11.

knowledge of nature, Glanvill insisted, had been possible only in Eden, hence the dogmatism of scholastically inclined natural philosophers was completely unwarranted. While Glanvill is typically associated with the Cambridge Platonists and the Latitudinarians, both of whom are generally characterised as having a more positive view of human nature than the Puritans, he nonetheless took very seriously the ramifications of sin in the realm of natural philosophy. Thus, the Fall is singled out as the 'general reason' for our 'intellectual disabilities'. Glanvill also takes it to be virtually self-evident that something is fundamentally wrong with the human mind, the 'disease of our intellectuals', as he put it, being 'too great not to be its own diagnostick'.[52] In keeping with the common verdict of the moral philosophers, he asserted that the mind of Adam, in its innocent state, was a model of proper hierarchical relations: 'Passions kept their place, as servants of the higher powers, and durst not arrogate the Throne, as now.' With Adam's revolt against God, the insurrection of the passions destroyed forever the inner harmony that made perfect knowledge possible. 'Man was never at odds with himself', Glanvill observed, 'till he was at odds with the commands of his Maker.' Thereupon, the mind fell out of tune – 'There was no jarring or disharmony in the faculties, till sin untun'd them.'[53] The rule of the passions could be represented, as it had been by Philo, by Eve's persuasion of Adam on their first day in Eden. 'The *Woman* in us', Glanvill explained, 'still prosecutes a deceit, like that begun in the *Garden*.' While we continue to judge things according to the false witness of the 'fond Feminine' we are destined to remain in ignorance.[54]

Much of Glanvill's attention focused upon Adam's sensory abilities, and how they had come to be vastly diminished. In Eden, he wrote, 'the senses, the Soul's windows, were without any spot or opacity'. As a consequence, Adam probably knew of the motion of the earth and the true relative dimensions of the heavenly bodies. 'The acuteness of his natural Opticks', Glanvill speculated, 'shew'd him much of the Coelestial magnificence and bravery without a *Galileo's* tube.'[55] In his terrestrial environment, Adam was no less capable, and could see 'the motion of the bloud and spirits

---

[52] Glanvill, *Vanity of Dogmatizing*, pp. 62f. Cf. *Scepsis Scientifica*, p. 48.

[53] *Vanity of Dogmatizing*, p. 4. Cf. pp. 13, 87, 91, 118; 'Against Confidence in Philosophy', p. 30, in *Essays on Several Important Subjects in Philosophy and Religion* (London, 1676).

[54] *Vanity of Dogmatizing*, p. 118. Cf. pp. 125, 135, *Scepsis Scientifica*, pp. 99f.; 'Against Confidence in Philosophy', p. 23, in *Essays*. Henry More has a similar view: 'Now the feminine part in Adam was so tickled with the Doctrine of the old Deceiver, that the Concupiscible began to be so immoderate, as to resolve to do any thing that may promote pleasure and experience in things.' *Conjectura Cabbalistica*, p. 46; cf. p. 71.

[55] Glanvill, *Vanity of Dogmatizing*, pp. 1, 5.

through the transparent skin' and could by sensible perception know the causes of such obscure phenomena as magnetic attraction and the fluxes of the tides.[56] Glanvill concluded that the first man's sensory apparatus 'must needs infinitely more transcend ours'.[57] From this analysis there followed the now familiar explanation of the need for 'helps' to be applied to minimise the limitations of fallen minds and bodies: 'now our *senses* being scant and limited, and Natures operations subtil and various; they must needs transcend and out-run our faculties'. Our 'deceitful and fallacious' senses 'must be assisted with *Instruments*, that may *strengthen* and *rectifie* their Operations'.[58] Five instruments in particular were thought by Glanvill to have partially compensated for the loss of Adamic abilities – the telescope, microscope, thermometer, barometer, and air pump.[59] Thus were the discoveries of Galileo, Hooke, Pascal, and Boyle attributed to their realisation of the need to supply the wants of weakened senses.

The frailty of the memory and the problem of gaps in the chain of transmission of knowledge were also taken up by Glanvill in a characteristically Baconian way. These failings were to be redressed by the establishment of organisations capable of co-ordinating the labours of successive generations of investigators. Not surprisingly, Glanvill believed that the Royal Society would play a leading role in this process. But Glanvill also believed that other modern inventions could make significant contributions on this score. The printing press, for example, had made the recording and distribution of knowledge a far more efficient process, while the compass had improved navigation and hence the geographical range of natural knowledge.[60] Still, the advancement of learning was to be a slow and incremental process, and for Glanvill all that could be expected of the present generation of philosophers was an instituting of the basic structures and methods that would establish the pattern for future centuries. Glanvill's assessment of the likely achievements of the Royal Society was accordingly modest: 'and what *one* Age can do in so *immense* an Undertaking as *That*, wherein all the generations of men are concerned, can be little *more* than to remove the *rubbish*, lay in *Materials*, and *put* things in *Order* for the *Building*'.[61]

Part of the apparent modesty of Glanvill's ambitions is to be attributed to the fact that he was sensitive to growing criticisms of the record of the

---

[56] *Ibid.*, pp. 6–8.   [57] *Ibid.*, p. 5. Cf. Philo, *Quaestiones in Genesin*, I. 32.
[58] Glanvill, *Vanity of Dogmatizing*, p. 67; 'Modern Improvements of Useful Knowledge', p. 23, in *Essays*. Cf. *Plus Ultra*, pp. 52f.
[59] Glanvill, 'Modern Improvements in Useful Knowledge', p. 23.   [60] *Ibid.*, p. 31.
[61] Glanvill, *Plus Ultra*, p. 91. Locke would later use a similar image to describe his efforts. *Essay*, Epistle to the Reader (1, 14).

Royal Society in the decades immediately following its incorporation. The standard complaint, voiced from the late 1660s, was that this august body had actually produced very little knowledge that was of any use.[62] But equally important was the fact that Glanvill was deliberately distinguishing between an 'experimental' philosophy, which in his view was grounded in a realistic estimate of human capabilities, and a 'dogmatic' philosophy, identified with the Aristotelian tradition which was presumed to have vastly overestimated the powers of the human mind. Glanvill asserted that 'the *Free* and *Real* philosophy makes men deeply sensible of the infirmities of the humane intellect, and our manifold hazards of *mistaking*, and so renders them *wary* and *modest, diffident* of the *certainty* of their *Conceptions*, and averse to the *boldness* of *peremptory asserting*.'[63] By way of contrast, the 'voluminous Schoolmen, and Peripatetical Dictators' seemed oblivious to 'the shortness of our intellectual sight, the deceptibility and imposition of our senses, the tumultuary disorders of our passions'. And with their 'shallow, unimprov'd intellects', it was these figures who were 'confident pretenders to certainty'.[64] In fact, Aristotle's philosophy was 'founded on vulgarities', dealing only with 'the unexamin'd prejudices of *Sense*' – all the less reason for modern philosophers to admire him as if he were '*Seths Pillars*, on which all knowledge is engraven'.[65] The failings of the peripatetic philosophy, moreover, were moral as well as epistemological. The same pride that had prompted Adam's Fall had blinded philosophers to their own limitations. Pride had also motivated their dogmatic confidence in their own edicts. "Tis *Pride*, and *Presumption* of ones self that causeth such fowardness and assurance', Glanvill cautioned, 'and where those *reign*, there is neither *Vertue* nor *Reason*; No *regular Government*, but a miserable *Tyranny* of *Passion* and *Self-Will*.'[66] In light of these disabilities, known through revelation and confirmed through careful self-examination, what was called for was a philosophy that threaded the narrow path between

---

[62] Prominent critics were Meric Casaubon, *A Letter of Meric Casaubon, D. D. &c. to Peter du Moulin D. D., concerning Natural Experimental Philosophie* (Cambridge, 1669), and Henry Stubbe, *Legends no Histories: or a Specimen of some Animadversions upon the History of the Royal Society . . . together with the Plus Ultra reduced to a Non-Plus* (London, 1670). For a discussion of these critiques see Harrison, '"The Fashioned Image or Poetry or the Regular Instruction of Philosophy?": Truth, Utility, and the Natural Sciences in Early Modern England', in D. Burchill and J. Cummins (eds.), *Science, Literature, and Rhetoric in Early Modern England* (Aldershot, 2007); Michael Hunter, *Science and Society in Restoration England* (Cambridge, 1981), ch. 4.

[63] Glanvill, *Plus Ultra*, pp. 146f. Cf. 'The Usefulness of Real Philosophy to Religion', p. 26, in *Essays*.

[64] Glanvill, *Vanity of Dogmatizing*, pp. 13, 14f.   [65] *Ibid.*, pp. 73, 177, 138.

[66] Glanvill, 'Against Confidence in Philosophy', p. 30, in *Essays*.

scepticism and dogmatism. Experimental philosophy had this virtue and was thus fitly described as a philosophy 'that becomes the sons of *Adam*'.[67]

John Wilkins (1614–72) was a founding fellow of the Royal Society. Indeed, he chaired its first official meeting. Wilkins had been a leading figure in 'the Invisible College', a precursor to the Royal Society that met in London and Oxford in the 1640s and 1650s. Included in its membership were Robert Boyle, John Wallis, John Evelyn, Christopher Wren, and William Petty – individuals who, like Wilkins, were also destined to play major roles in the early Royal Society.[68] Much of Wilkins's renown rests upon his *Essay Towards a Real Character and a Philosophical Language* (London, 1668) which was devoted to the development of an artificial language, but his contributions extend well beyond this. He had been an early and influential populariser of the Copernican system and when in 1649 he assumed the position of Warden of Wadham College he succeeded in transforming the Oxford college into an important centre for the new philosophy. Hooke generously observed in this connection that 'whereever he had lived, there had been the chief Seat of generous Knowledge and true Philosophy'.[69] Wilkins also played a significant role in the composition of Sprat's *History*, a work that was less a history than an articulation of the basic philosophy of the group, and a defence against the kinds of accusations that Glanvill had been concerned to address.[70]

If Hooke and Glanvill had stressed the importance of supplying 'helps' for fallen senses, Wilkins sought to alleviate the effects of the Fall on our ability to retain and communicate knowledge. 'After the fall of Adam', he pointed out, 'there were two general curses inflicted on mankind: the one upon their labours, the other upon their language.'[71] Wilkins focused his efforts on the 'second curse'. Bacon, as we have seen, spoke of two losses associated with the Fall: the loss of 'innocency' and the loss of 'dominion'. The first was to be repaired by religion, the second by arts and sciences. Wilkins agreed with Bacon that 'arts and professions' were the way to address the loss of human dominion. 'Artificial experiments', he wrote, are 'so many Essays, whereby men doe naturally attempt to restore

---

[67] Glanvill, *Vanity of Dogmatizing*, p. 223.

[68] On the early history of the society see Michael Hunter, *The Royal Society and its Fellows 1660–1700* (London, 1982), and R. Lomas, *The Invisible College* (London, 2002).

[69] Hooke, *Micrographia*, Preface.

[70] Paul Wood, 'Methodology and Apologetics: Thomas Sprat's *History of the Royal Society*', *BJHS* 13 (1980), 1–26.

[71] Wilkins, *Mercury*, p. 53. For a summary of Wilkins's views see his *Discourse concerning the Gift of Prayer* (London, 1651), pp. 74–80. Here Wilkins notes that the Fall brought about depravity of understandings, consciences, affections, wills, and memories (p. 77).

themselves from the first general curse inflicted upon their labours.'[72] Bacon, however, had also spoken of a 'second general curse', for which the best available remedy was the cultivation of the art of grammar.[73] This was a piecemeal solution, however, and the inherent ambiguities of language were primarily responsible for Bacon's 'idols of the marketplace'. Wilkins took it upon himself to find a specific 'help' that would moderate the unfortunate consequences of this second curse. Traditionally, the fractured state of human discourse was attributed to the confusion of tongues at Babel. This event provided the historical explanation for the diversity of languages and to a degree also explained their arbitrary nature. Babel was also significant because the loss of the primitive language necessarily brought with it the loss of whatever fragments of Adamic knowledge were not part of the collective memory. The 'ill conjunction of labours', which Bacon had identified as a major impediment to learning (along with 'ill tradition of knowledge'), could also be linked to the Babel event, for the confusion of tongues brought to a premature end the first cooperative technological undertaking in human history. In practice, the curse on human language was often regarded as a later manifestation of the curse placed on Adam and Eve immediately after the Fall. The fourth-century Christian poet Prudentius had long before made the fall of language contemporary with Adam's sin, rather than postponing it until Babel. The chasm which separates language and truth resulted from original sin, and the polyvalence of language thereafter is symbolised by the forked tongue of the serpent.[74] In *Paradise Lost*, Milton was thus to suggest that the Fall had infected Adam's thoughts, looks, actions, and, crucially, his words.[75] In any event, if the Adamic names and the form of writing that preserved them had persisted after the Fall, these were presumed to have been lost at Babel.[76] And even if these vestiges of the Adamic language had survived the calamity at Babel – preserved in

---

[72] Wilkins, *Mathematicall Magick. or, The Wonders That may be performed by Mechanical Geometry* (London, 1648), p. 2.

[73] Bacon, *Advancement*, II.xvi.4 (p. 132).

[74] Martha Malamud, 'Writing Original Sin', *Journal of Early Christian Studies* 10 (2002), 329–60; Michael Roberts, *Poetry and the Cult of the Martyrs: The* Liber Peristephanon *of Prudentius* (Ann Arbor, 1993).

[75] Milton, *Paradise Lost* x.608. See also John Leonard, 'Language and Knowledge in Paradise Lost', in Dennis Danielson (ed.), *The Cambridge Companion to Milton* (Cambridge, 1989), pp. 97–111; William Poole, 'The Divine and the Grammarian: Theological Disputes in the 17th-Century Universal Language Movement', *Historiographia Linguistica* 30 (2003), 273–300; Cram and Maat (eds.), *George Dalgarno*, pp. 3f.

[76] Thus Wilkins: 'The difference of characters, whereby several languages are expressed, is part of the second general curse in the confusion of tongues; for as before there was but one way of speaking, so also but one way of writing.' *Mercury*, p. 43.

Hebrew letters, Egyptian hieroglyphs or Chinese idiograms – the forms of these latter-day languages were widely acknowledged to have been significantly corrupted. To simplify matters somewhat, if language can be said to have both representational and communicative capacities, the former were thought to have been damaged by the Fall, the latter by what transpired at Babel.

Some compensation for the confusion of tongues, and hence for the loss of communicative facility of the original tongue, was already provided by Latin, the universal language of the scholarly community of the West. But the prestige of Latin had been under threat for some time. The interest of the humanist scholars in the original languages of the classics and the new Protestant focus on the biblical text had significantly raised the profiles of Greek and Hebrew. Increasingly, moreover, vernacular languages were becoming important media for the exchange of ideas. The Protestant reformers had energetically promoted new translations of the bible as alternatives to the official authoritative text, the Latin Vulgate. Latin was in any case tainted on account of its association with the rituals and administrative apparatus of the Roman Church.[77] In the sphere of the sciences, Galileo, Bacon, and Descartes had all written in the vernacular, again, to broaden the appeal of their revolutionary ideas. And of course it served the commercial interests of presses and the apologetic agendas of reformers of both religion and science to reach as wide an audience as possible. These pressures led to a considerable erosion of the dominance of Latin in the realm of print. In any case, Latin had proven itself to be in many respects a most imperfect medium for the expression of ideas, both religious and scientific. In the sixteenth century, humanist philologists and Protestant reformers had discovered that there were major discrepancies between the assumed meanings of central theological terms and the original Greek expressions of which they were supposed to be translations. Some of the most contentious doctrinal debates of the Reformation were to do with the meanings of the words of the Greek New Testament, and such fundamental terms as 'justification', 'repentance', and 'ordination' became linguistic battlefields.[78] Considerations such as these account for Wilkins's deep conviction, shared with many of those who invested time in similar projects, that a new philosophical language which emulated the original Adamic tongue would 'contribute much to the clearing of some of our

---

[77] Introduction, Vivian Salmon (ed.), *The Works of Francis Lodwick: A Study of His Writings in the Intellectual Context of the Seventeenth Century* (London, 1972), pp. 46–8.
[78] See Harrison, *Bible and the Rise of Science*, pp. 95–9.

modern differences in *Religion*'.[79] The sciences were also confronted with issues of translation, particularly in the discipline of natural history. Compilers of herbals found themselves having to identify plant species from Latin names that were translations of Greek terms taken from the classical references, often with a third language such as Arabic intervening between the Greek original and Latin name.[80] Thus for both theologians and natural historians Latin could be the problem, rather than the solution.

As we have already seen, some of the radical Baconians of the Commonwealth period had taken up the challenge provided by the 'second curse', pursuing the recovery of the primitive language and the wisdom embedded within it through the doctrine of signatures and their investigations of the Cabbala. Wilkins, however, had little time for this project:

And if you will believe the Jews, the holy spirit hath purposely involved in the words of scripture, every secret that belongs to any art or science, under such cabalisms as these. And if a man were but expert in unfolding of them, [sic] it were easy for him to get as much knowledge as Adam had in his innocency, or human nature is capable of.[81]

On balance, Wilkins seemed not to believe this. He was not so much sceptical of the tradition of Adam's encyclopaedic knowledge, however, as he was of the cabbalists' claims to be able to recover that knowledge from the words of the Hebrew Bible. There were indeed some particular instances where words of scripture may conceal genuine truths about nature, he conceded, but the general assumption that all scripture could be used for this purpose had given licence to 'men's roving and corrupt fansies' and occasioned 'many wild and strange absurdities'.[82] Wilkins's rejection of the kinds of linguistic reforms recommended by Webster were consistent with his general position that while there was room for modernisation of the curriculum, it was not to be along the lines set out by its more radical critics.

Wilkins's partner in the defence of the universities was astronomer Seth Ward (1617–89). Indeed, Ward had much in common with Wilkins: they shared an enthusiasm for the new science and Copernican astronomy; they were both founding fellows of the Royal Society, and subsequently Fellows of Wadham College; both, in time, were elevated to the episcopate. In *Vindiciae Academiarum* (1654), written in close collaboration with

[79] Wilkins, *Essay*, Epistle Dedicatory. Cf. Comenius, for whom religious differences often consist 'not in fundamentals, only in the manner of expressing them'. *The Way of Light of Comenius*, tr. E. Campagnac (London, 1938), p. 198. Consider, too, Dalgarno's lexicon of religious terms in *Ars Signorum*. See also Benjamin DeMott, 'Comenius and the Real Character', *PMLA* 70 (1955), 1068–81.
[80] Jerry Stannard, 'Medieval Herbals and their Development', *Clio Media* 9 (1974), 23–33.
[81] John Wilkins, *Mercury*, I, 41.   [82] *Ibid.*, 41f.

Wilkins, Ward expressed similar reservations about Webster's attempts to revive an Adamic language. The schoolmaster was derided as a 'credulous fanatick Reformer' given to 'canting discourse about the language of nature'. In Ward's view, Webster's 'peevish malcontented humour had brought him into the gang of the vulgar Levellers'.[83] With the Restoration of the monarchy, interest in these more ambitious projects waned as they came to be associated with the radical millenarian politics of the revolutionary era. Ironically, however, both Ward and Wilkins had an abiding interest in natural language schemes and if they did not share the mystical enthusiasms of Webster, Boehme, and Fludd, they nonetheless saw in natural or philosophical languages prospects for the furthering of knowledge.

Another associate of Wilkins who was a central figure in the natural language movements of the second half of the century was George Dalgarno (c. 1616–87).[84] A teacher at a private grammar school in Oxford, Dalgarno was proficient in shorthand and had trialled various ways of improving it. These efforts brought him to the attention of Samuel Hartlib, who suggested that with further modifications Dalgarno's version of brachygraphy could be developed into a real character that might provide the basis of a new form of scientific notation. The young schoolmaster was soon drawn into the orbit of John Wilkins, and with the encouragement of Seth Ward and the mathematician John Wallis they began work on a collaborative endeavour to develop a philosophical language and a real character. Eventually, Wilkins and Dalgarno fell out over details of the proposed scheme. Concerned to establish a claim for priority, Dalgarno hurried into print with *Ars signorum* (The Art of Signs, 1661), which lays out his model for a philosophical language. As it turned out, his haste proved to be wasted effort. Whatever the merits of Dalgarno's work, and they were not inconsiderable, it was destined to be almost completely eclipsed by Wilkins's *Essay*, which appeared seven years later in a handsome folio edition and with much fanfare. From that time until very recently Dalgarno's work has been overshadowed by that of Wilkins. In a sad irony, the only recorded use of Dalgarno's language was by Roger Daniel, who ungenerously described its inventor as *nhkpim sufa* – 'the greatest ass'.[85]

---

[83] Ward, *Vindiciae Academiarum* (Oxford, 1654), pp. 5–6.
[84] For biographical details see Cram and Maat, *George Dalgarno*, pp. 8–31; Rhodri Lewis, *Language, Mind, and Nature: Artificial Languages in England from Bacon to Locke* (Cambridge, 2007), pp. 85–117.
[85] Jaap Maat, *Philosophical Languages in the Seventeenth Century: Dalgarno, Wilkins, Leibniz* (Dordrecht, 2004), p. 133. Much of the reason that Dalgarno has been ignored lies in the mistaken view that Wilkins's *Essay* is the more perfect realisation of what was essentially the same project. See Maat, *Philosophical Languages*, pp. 31–7.

Wilkins's own scheme was presented as a realisation of particular aspects of the Baconian project, the *Essay* being intended to provide 'helps and assistances' to the memory and understanding: 'besides the best way of helping the *Memory* by natural Method, the *Understanding* likewise would be highly improved; and we should, by learning the *Character* and the *Names* of things, be instructed likewise in their *Natures*, the knowledge of both which ought to be conjoined'.[86] The assistance to the understanding was to be provided by the rational manner in which the various things to be remembered were ordered, for the problem of memory was not simply one of recording information, but of ordering it in such a way that it was accessible. Wilkins ambitiously attempted 'a regular *enumeration* and *description* of all those things and notions, to which marks or names ought to be assigned according to their respective natures', his ultimate goal being 'to reduce all things and notions into such a frame as may express their natural order, dependence, and relations'.[87] To help him complete the biological classifications of this part of the project, he drew upon the taxonomic expertise of John Ray and Francis Willoughby.

It is important to understand the ways in which Wilkins's language project differs from the earlier cabbalistic, Paracelsian, and Behmenist endeavours. While, broadly speaking, their goals are expressed in terms of the need to recover the features of a pristine ideal language, the earlier efforts sought to emulate Adam himself by seeking out the primitive language and the secrets that supposedly were embedded within it. Wilkins, Dalgarno, Lodwick, and other fellows of the Royal Society with an interest in language schemes had more modest ambitions. As the telescope and the microscope provided assistance to fallen senses, their proposed language sought to provide a 'help' for the memory and a means of bringing order to the linguistic confusion that inhibited communication of scientific ideas and promoted religious discord. While the earlier schemes such as Webster's drew upon Baconian aspirations, ultimately they relied upon supernatural inspiration for their success. Some commentators have suggested that the best way to characterise the difference between the earlier and later language projects of the seventeenth century is in terms of a shift of focus from the Fall to Babel. The more optimistic enterprises of the Commonwealth period are regarded as having focused on recapturing the past glories of a perfect Adamic language; the later projects are concerned with the more modest task of overcoming the practical difficulties caused by the

---

[86] Wilkins, *Essay*, p. 21.   [87] *Ibid.*, p. 1.

multiplicity of languages.[88] However, considerations relating to the Fall featured in the later projects too, and in significant ways.

Dalgarno, for example, thought that it was important to have a proper understanding of the Fall and its implications for the creation of a philosophical language. The connections between the design of *Ars signorum* and sacred history are not explicitly addressed in that work, but in a manuscript tract entitled 'On Interpretation', Dalgarno helpfully provides them. Here he explores the common ground 'wherein the Divine and Grammarian seem equally concerned' – the Fall of Adam.[89] In what is now a predictable pattern, Dalgarno is interested in whether Adam's mastery of language 'was a supernaturally inspired gift or a faculty proper to humane nature in its first perfection'. Dalgarno's preference is equally predictable: 'Adam by the strength and excellency of his *natural* faculties did himself invent the Language which he and Eve did then speak *without any supernatural assistance.*'[90] What is interesting about Dalgarno's position is that while he subscribes to the traditional view of Adamic wisdom – Adam was a 'great and perfect Philosopher' and a 'Master of Language' – the language used, or rather invented, by Adam was in an important sense arbitrary: 'tho I judge the first Language was rational yet in some sense it might be called arbitrary, that is he had more ways than one of expressing the same thing'.[91] In this respect then, we are in a similar position to that in which Adam found himself, inasmuch as the tokens we attach to objects are also arbitrary. But there are still ways in which Adam's language could be regarded as perfect and that the names he used could be said to be expressive of the natures of things. Both Wilkins and Dalgarno (and, later, Leibniz) proposed for their language a set of basic terms or 'radicals', arbitrarily assigned, to express various simple properties. Things would then be named by compounds of these radicals, the composition of the compound term reflecting the nature of the thing. (Think here of how the term 'philosophy' captures the nature of

---

[88] See, e.g., Benjamin DeMott, 'The Sources and Development of John Wilkins' Philosophical Language', *Journal of English and Germanic Philology* 57 (1958), 1–13 (2); David Katz, *Philo-Semitism and the Readmission of the Jews to England 1603–1655* (Oxford, 1982), pp. 43–88. Cf. Poole, 'The Divine and the Grammarian', pp. 276f.; Rhodri Lewis, 'John Wilkins's *Essay* (1668) and the context of seventeenth-century artificial languages in England', D.Phil. dissertation, Oxford, 2003, pp. 263–81.

[89] 'On Interpretation', *On Universal Language*, pp. 391–408 (p. 398). I am indebted to William Poole for drawing this MS to my attention.

[90] *Ibid.*, p. 396 (my emphasis).

[91] Dalgarno, 'The Autobiographical Treatise', 'Of Interpretation', in Cram and Maat (eds.), *George Dalgarno*, pp. 368, 396. Dalgarno reported that Adam in his innocence enjoyed 'perfection both of soule and body . . . his natural faculties were clear and distinct, not subject to error, but naturally illuminated with such a degree of knowledge that never any of his posterity can arrive at or so much comprehend what the extent of his knowledge was'. 'Of Interpretation', *ibid.*, pp. 396f.

the activity it describes – the love of wisdom – because it combines *philia* (love) and *sophia* (wisdom). The elemental terms, however cannot be further analysed in this way. Hence *philia* means 'love' and *sophia* means 'wisdom' only by convention.) Thus while the radicals were assigned to things arbitrarily, the compound terms were genuinely expressive of the nature of things.[92] In following this procedure, Dalgarno thought himself to be emulating the process by which the Adamic language was formulated, for in his view the names Adam gave to the beasts were fitting because they were compound terms that expressed an appropriate combination of properties: 'Adam as a perfect philosopher following nature and the example of his maker gave names to all living creatures, not primitive and independent words . . . but words of secondary institution inflected from other words, the primary and proper sense of which contributed to the describing of the nature of the thing . . . For unless this be granted, the commone opinion of Adams giving names to all living creatures suited to their natures will be absurd.'[93] While the process of constructing a rational language was the same then as it is now, Adam was presumably better at the business of choosing an appropriate level of generality for his radical terms, and at constructing combinations of these radicals to be expressive of the natures of things. Adam also had the advantage of a photographic memory so that he could immediately command an extensive vocabulary:

images of things that wee impress upon material objects or sounds or Characters by compact and so carry them in our memories and learn them by Art and industry, all this he did by the natural strength of his faculties without compact or study; all sounds and Characters then were indifferent to him but he was better able then wee to chuse what was in all respects most convenient. The reason of all this because all the knowledge that wee can possibly acquire by labour and paines this and much more was in him naturally without any thing of Labour or paine.[94]

The 'labours and pains' now required for the construction of such a language are considerable, as anyone who has read Dalgarno and Wilkins can attest, and it is in these labours and pains that we feel the effects of the curse. Having said this, Adam's abilities differ from ours only in degree and not kind, and hence a new formulation of an Adamic-like language is to some degree within human capabilities.

It is likely that Dalgarno's account of Adam's naming also led to one of the major differences between his scheme and that of Wilkins. In contrast

[92] Maat, *Philosophical Languages*, p. 56. It should also be said that in Dalgarno's system there were still logical links between related radicals. See *ibid.*, pp. 83–91.
[93] Dalgarno, 'Of Interpretation', in Cram and Maat (eds.), *George Dalgarno*, p. 388.
[94] *Ibid.*, p. 401.

to Wilkins, Dalgarno attempted to minimise the number of radicals or 'primitives' – a policy which would necessarily maximise the number of compound terms. The reasoning behind this strategy was that it is only the compound terms that are genuinely expressive of the natures of things and that in their naming of things both God and Adam had used compound terms.[95] Modern Hebrew was thought to have still retained these characteristics, having comparatively few simple and uncompounded roots.[96] Decisions about the number of radicals were closely related to the issue of how to determine what things or concepts were truly basic, a task that in principle rested on the division of the whole of reality into its natural categories. This issue also proved to be contentious.

One of the most basic assumptions of the language schemes of the period was that human beings agreed in their fundamental concepts of things, differing only in the linguistic labels they attached to them.[97] Because individuals share the same senses and mental facilities, when they apprehend a particular object they form a common conception of it. This was in essence the position that Aristotle had set out almost 2,000 years before in the opening lines of *De Interpretatione*: 'Now spoken sounds are symbols of affections in the soul, and written marks symbols of spoken sounds. And just as written marks are not the same for all men, neither are spoken sounds. But what these are in the first place signs of – affections of the soul – are the same for all; and what these affections are likenesses of – actual things – are also the same.'[98] In light of this understanding of the relationship between things, concepts, and language, the aim of the language projectors was to align the 'affections of the soul' that were common to all with a set of symbols that would also be common to all. Wilkins sets out the plan of the *Essay* in precisely these terms:

As men do generally agree in the same Principle of Reason, so do they likewise agree in the same *Internal Notion* or *Apprehension of things* . . . The *Names* given to these in several Languages, are such arbitrary *sounds* or *words*, as Nations of men have agreed upon, either casually or designedly, to express their Mental notions of them. The *Written word* is the figure or picture of that sound. So that if men should generally consent upon the same way or manner of *Expression* as they do agree in

---

[95] Dalgarno, 'The Art of Signs', 'Of Interpretation', in Cram and Maat (eds.), *George Dalgarno*, pp. 56, 388f.; Maat, *Philosophical Languages*, pp. 56f.

[96] Wilkins had initially agreed that Hebrew would be a good model for a philosophical language. *Mercury*, p. 57. Cf. Wilkins's critic Thomas Baker: 'The first language, the *Hebrew* was very plain and simple (a good argument of its being an Original) consisting of very few Roots, and those very simple and uncompounded.' *Reflections on Learning* (London, 1699), pp. 7f.

[97] Lewis, 'John Wilkins', ch. 4; Maat, *Philosophical Languages*, pp. 13–15, 21.

[98] Aristotle, *De Interpretatione* 16a4–16a9 (*Complete Works*, p. 25).

the same *Notion*, we should then be freed from that Curse in the Confusion of Tongues, with all the unhappy consequences of it.[99]

All this was clear enough. The next logical step, as Wilkins explained, was to arrive at 'a just *Enumeration* and description of such things or notions as are to have *Marks* or *Names* assigned to them', and it was here that the problems began.[100]

The practicality of devising classificatory tables capable of accommodating all things or concepts in a rational order presented Wilkins with difficulties that ultimately proved insuperable. This was because such a scheme seemed to presuppose both that reality could be so divided and, even more problematically, that those divisions were known in advance. Critics of the *Essay* tended to highlight this apparent weakness. In his popular *Reflections upon Learning* (1699) Thomas Baker claimed that the whole project was 'an impracticable thing'. If we are to have a language based on things rather than words, he pointed out, 'we must first be agreed about the nature of things, before we can fix Marks and Characters to represent them, and I very much despair of such an agreement'. Nature, he went on to say, 'is an inexhaustible mine, where we may always dig and yet never come at the bottom'.[101] The incompleteness of human knowledge rendered impossible the task of setting out its fundamental categories in advance. It must be said that even those involved in the scheme were sympathetic to this general point. In his private correspondence Ray declared himself to be 'ashamed' of the botanical taxonomy he had contributed. He complained that in devising the tables he been unable to follow 'nature's lead' being constrained instead by the author's method. The whole vision of constructing 'exact Philosophical tables' of anything was, in his view, highly problematic.[102]

Puzzlingly, there is evidence that Wilkins, too, was aware of at least some of these problems. At the very outset he conceded that the taxonomic scheme he was relying on – in essence a modified table of Aristotelian predicaments – was defective and could not extend to things that were as yet unknown. Indeed the perfection of such a scheme was dependent on the perfection of philosophy itself, it being the task of philosophy, in Wilkins's

---

[99] Wilkins, *Essay*, p. 20.   [100] *Ibid.*

[101] Baker, *Reflections on Learning*, pp. 18, 76; Lewis, 'John Wilkins', p. 291. Descartes had similarly thought that a true philosophical language presupposed a 'true philosophy', the existence of which presumably would obviate the need for a philosophical language. Maat, *Philosophical Languages*, pp. 27f.

[102] Ray, *Philosophical Letters*, p. 62, cited in Lewis, 'John Wilkins', pp. 303f. Cf. Benjamin DeMott, 'Science versus Mnemonics, Notes on John Ray and on John Wilkins' *Essay towards a Real Character, and a Philosophical Language*', *Isis* 48 (1957), 3–12.

view at least, 'to reduce all things into such a frame, as may express their natural order, dependence and relations'. He was also in partial agreement with Ray, that the biological taxonomies were artificial.[103] Perhaps the best construction that can be placed on Wilkins's efforts is that he sought to establish the plausibility of framing a universal language, fully cognisant of the fact that such a project could only be brought to fulfilment with the perfection of philosophy itself – a task that he thought might be left to his colleagues in the Royal Society. Wilkins's project was, after all, an 'essay': the first rather than the final word. In favour of the scheme was the witness of Aristotle (which for many, admittedly, would count against it). But it was not unreasonable to assume that God had imposed a rational order on the natural world, that it was the task of natural philosophy to discover this order, and that its disclosure would count as evidence of divine wisdom.[104] Adam's naming of the beasts was also a relevant consideration, for if the beasts had been given names according to their natures, and if this had been accomplished by natural means, it could be argued that there did in fact exist such natures in the world.

In the early eighteenth century Wilkins's attempts to frame a philosophical language were savagely satirised in Jonathan Swift's 'Academy of Lagado', where men carry around objects for use instead of words, 'since words are only names for things'. These objects, the reader is informed, 'would serve as an universal language'.[105] While Swift may be the best-known critic of Wilkins's scheme, reservations had been expressed almost from the moment of its publication. Some theologically motivated critics wondered whether repairing the ruins of Babel was such a good idea, given the fate of the original project.[106] It was not difficult to argue that in attempting to reverse the effects of the curse on language, Wilkins was simply rehearsing the proud ambition of Babel's original architects. Wilkins's latitudinarianism, a view generally associated with a marginally more generous view of human nature than prevailing versions of Calvinism, may have had something to do with these criticisms.[107] These challenges aside, there was a deep tension

---

[103] Wilkins, *Essay*, sig. 1b, pp. 1, 67. See also Lewis, 'John Wilkins', pp. 241f.; Maat, *Philosophical Languages*, pp. 156–9, 255–7.

[104] Lewis plausibly suggests this as a motivation for Hooke's 'philosophical algebra', 'John Wilkins', pp. 225f.

[105] Swift, *Gulliver's Travels*, pt III, ch. 4.

[106] Thus Baker: 'The Divisions of Tongues was [sic] inflicted by God as a Curse upon humane Ambition, and may have been continued since for the same reason; and as no Remedy has been yet found, it is most probable, it is not to be expected, nor are we to hope to unite that which God had divided.' *Reflections on Learning*, p. 19. Cf. Casaubon, *A Letter*, pp. 35f.

[107] Latitudinarians were nonetheless firmly committed to the doctrine of the Fall and can be regarded as 'largely co-extensive with the puritan movement'. Webster, *Great Instauration*, p. 497; Spellman, *The*

between Wilkins's aims and the means by which he attempted to realise them. His basic dilemma was that while his goals were directly linked to Baconian aspirations to reverse those 'curses' that had attended human sin, his proposed remedy seemed to ignore the consequences of those curses, at least as they were typically understood. In certain respects Wilkins's resort to aspects of Aristotelianism was inconsistent with the Baconian analysis of human defects. Arguably, in his invocation of Aristotelian categories he was committing the error of Aquinas in assuming that Aristotelianism was a theologically 'neutral' framework that could be deployed unproblematically in a range of different contexts. In fact, the table of Aristotelian predicaments rested on presuppositions that were compatible with neither sacred history nor the new natural philosophy. Proponents of the latter were uncomfortably aware of the impracticalities of identifying and naming the essences of things. Ray, as we have already indicated, had little confidence in his own contribution, and expressed doubts that the natures of things could be known in the kinds of ways demanded by Wilkins's project. Robert Boyle shared this scepticism, suggesting that the book of nature contained only 'Aegyptian Hieroglyphicks' and that many of its secrets would remain forever hidden from fallen human minds.[108] The corpuscular philosophy championed by Boyle, moreover, was inconsistent with the idea that natural objects could have genuine essences. The final word may be given to John Locke, who echoed Boyle's scepticism about the possibility of arriving at a true science of natural bodies. Without naming names, Locke declared in his *Essay concerning Human Understanding* (1690) that no one could attempt the perfect reformation of language 'without rendring himself ridiculous'.[109]

THE LIMITS OF REASON

Robert Boyle (1627–91) and John Locke (1632–1704) had much more in common than a shared sceptical attitude to philosophical language projects. Both have become cherished emblems of human progress in their respective fields, and they enjoy reputations as advocates of the dignity and reliability of human reason. In his 'Preliminary Discourse' to the *Encyclopédie*, Jean

---

Latitudinarians, pp. 54–71; Marshall, *John Locke: Resistance, Religion and Responsibility* (Cambridge, 1994), p. 135; Marshall, 'Locke and Latitudinarianism'.

[108] Lewis, 'John Wilkins' Essay', pp. 228 n. 62, 247f., 306f.

[109] Locke, *Essay* III.xi.2 (II, 148). There is some discussion of the extent to which Boyle and Locke shared a common view of the arbitrary nature of classification. See Jan-Erik Jones, 'Boyle, Classification, and the Workmanship of the Understanding Thesis', *Journal of the History of Philosophy* 43 (2005), 171–83.

Le Rond d'Alembert hailed Locke as the founder of 'scientific philosophy' while Voltaire referred to him as the 'Hercules of metaphysics' who had slain the serpents of scholasticism.[110] Robert Boyle is a canonical figure in the history of science, 'the father of modern chemistry' and, as every science student knows, the author of the eponymous law.[111] These reputations have important foundations in fact. Locke's insistence on the natural liberty of human beings, his advocacy of government by the consent of the governed, his defence of toleration, and his irenic and open-minded vision of Christianity, all support this characterisation. In the case of Boyle, the reasons are somewhat different, but equally compelling. He was undoubtedly the leading exponent of experimental philosophy in the seventeenth century, and while his religious commitments are well known, they are generally regarded as being of the less extreme kind. Boyle is considered to be one of the chief early modern advocates of the use of reason in the sphere of religion, largely on account of his frequently stated belief that the study of nature provides persuasive evidence of the existence of a wise and all-powerful Deity. Their rejection of Wilkins's language scheme, however, provides us with a hint that their identification as champions of the powers of unaided reason may need some modification. Indeed, in spite of their reputations, both Boyle and Locke are to be located in the tradition of theologically informed scepticism that we have been tracing in this chapter.

As Jan Wojcik has recently shown, the common reading of Boyle as an advocate of the powers of reason in the spheres of religion and natural philosophy is somewhat misleading.[112] This is not the place to rehearse her arguments in detail, but given Boyle's prominence as an advocate of experimental philosophy, some comment on his views about the Fall, human nature, and the limits of our knowledge is in order. Boyle's most direct statements on this topic are to be found in *Some Considerations about the Reconcileableness of Reason and Religion* (1675). Here he sets out the familiar claim that the human race is 'embued with Prejudices, and Errors' and that these typically 'continue undiscern'd and consequently unreform'd'.[113] Boyle enlists two modern authors to support his views. The first, surprisingly perhaps, is Descartes, who is cited to the effect that in the realm of philosophy we must always remember that we are finite and God infinite.

[110] W. M. Spellman, *John Locke* (New York, 1997), pp. 3f.
[111] Some controversy exists over the naming rights to 'Boyle's Law', there being a belated French claimant, Edmé Mariotte. Some have also thought that Hooke should have received credit for his contribution to the discovery.
[112] Jan Wojcik, *Robert Boyle and the Limits of Reason* (Cambridge, 1997), esp. pp. 212–19.
[113] Boyle, *Reason and Religion*, p. 28.

Boyle also makes reference to Descartes' suggestion that a common source of error is those prejudices acquired in infancy.[114] The other modern, as we might expect, was Bacon, whose doctrine of the 'idols' receives brief treatment. Boyle then proceeds, in language reminiscent of Bacon, to explain that the human mind 'is not sincerely dispos'd to receive the light of Truth, but receives an infusion as it were of adventitious Colours (that disguise the light) from the Will and Affections'. Human pride, moreover, prompts us to construct truth as we would want it to be, rather than as it actually is. This takes Boyle back to what transpired in Eden:

And if we consider the inbred pride of man, which is such, that if we will believe the Sacred story, ev'n *Adam* in Paradise affected to be like God knowing good and evil, we shall not so much marvel, that almost every man in particular makes the Notions he has entertain'd already, and his Senses, his Inclinations and his Interests, the Standards by which he estimates and judges of all other things, whether natural or reveal'd.

'If we admit the fall of our first Parents', Boyle continues, we will not be surprised to discover that 'our Passions and Interests, and oftentimes our Vices should pervert our Intellects'.[115]

Boyle does admit the Fall, yet he was reluctant to attribute all the limitations of human knowledge to Adam's lapse. It is significant, for example, that he was cautious about endorsing the tradition that accorded encyclopaedic knowledge to Adam. 'I will not urge the received Opinion of Divines', he wrote in *The Excellency of Theology* (1674), 'that before the Fall . . . Adam's knowledge was such, that he was able at first sight of them to give each of the Beasts a name expressive of their natures.' Boyle's reservations on this point were owing to the fact that he had closely scrutinised the Hebrew names of animals mentioned in Genesis without deriving any clearer insight into nature than that with which he had begun. He concluded that there was some doubt that Adam's knowledge in Paradise was equivalent to that 'of the Saints in Heaven'.[116] In fact, earlier in the work he had implied that recent advances in the sciences and arts had well surpassed anything that Adam could have accomplished. 'If *Adam* were now alive, and should survey that great variety of man's productions', he mused, 'he would admire to see what a new world, as it were, or set of things has been added to the primitive creatures by the industry of his posterity'.[117]

[114] *Ibid.* p. 26. According to Henri Gouhier, Descartes' account of infancy is a kind of secularised doctrine of original sin. Henri Gouhier, *La Pensée métaphysique de Descartes* (Paris, 1962).
[115] Boyle, *Reason and Religion*, p. 33.
[116] Boyle, *The Excellency of Theology compar'd with Natural Philosophy* (London, 1674), pp. 154f.
[117] Boyle, *Usefulness of Natural Philosophy*, *Works* II, 14.

Boyle thus dismissed a common view of the symmetry between the original knowledge of Adam and that of the saints in heaven. All terrestrial
knowledge, including what Adam had known in paradise, was in his view
necessarily limited by finitude. Only with the resurrection would we come
into possession of true science. At that time, just as our natures would be
completely renovated, so 'our Faculties will be Elevated and Enlarged, and
probably made capable of attaining degrees and kinds of knowledge, to
which we are here but strangers'. All the more reason, Boyle thought, that
we should value the Christian religion since it provides the only means by
which we can come to enjoy a perfect knowledge of natural philosophy.[118]

For Boyle, then, the root cause of the defects of human knowledge seemed
not to be the lapsed condition of humanity *per se*, but rather a prior set of
constraints placed on the mind and body that were present even in their first
creation. He was to speak of 'a necessary Imperfection of Humane Nature,
that whilst we remain in this mortal condition, the Soul being confin'd to
the dark prison of the Body, is capable . . . but of a dim knowledge'.[119]
For this reason, our knowledge does not extend to the essences of things,
nor even to every object, but only to those 'as God thought fit to allow
our minds in their present (and perchance lapsed) condition'.[120] Although
the Fall again receives mention here, the 'perchance' is not suggestive of a
strong endorsement of the view that the Fall is the primary cause of our
epistemic limitations. This is not to say that Boyle entertained any serious
doubts about the Fall, but rather that he was uncertain of how it affected
our capacity for knowledge. Most likely he regarded the Fall as evidence of
our tendency to make poor judgements rather than as the ultimate cause
of them. As for the necessity of these limitations, they seem to follow, as
implied above, from the kind of creatures we are – souls imprisoned in
bodies. It is our relatively modest position in the scale of being that limits
our capacity for knowledge, particularly when we compare ourselves to
the omniscient God. This comparison means that our knowledge of both
natural and supernatural things will be considerably circumscribed: 'We
purblind mortals, that are not of the highest order of God's creatures, may
justly think of ourselves incompetent judges of the extent of the power and
knowledge of God . . . whose power may justly be supposed to reach farther
than our limited intellect can apprehend.'[121] All of this means that we must
entertain only modest expectations of the reach of natural philosophy. Thus

---

[118] Boyle, *Excellency of Theology*, pp. 154f. Similar remarks may by found in *Seraphic Love*, *Works* I,
283–90; *Usefulness of Natural Philosophy*, *Works* II, 33.
[119] Boyle, *Excellency of Theology*, p. 154.   [120] Boyle, *Things above Reason*, *Works* IV, 445.
[121] Boyle, *Appendix to the First Part of The Christian Virtuoso*, *Works* VI, 676f.

Boyle frequently stresses the fact that there is no 'clearness and certainty' in physics.[122]

There has been considerable discussion in the secondary literature about the impact of Boyle's theological voluntarism on his approach to natural philosophy. According to a widely accepted thesis, 'voluntarists' (who emphasise the divine will and believe that God arbitrarily determined the order of the cosmos) tend to be empiricists, while 'intellectualists' (who stress the divine rationality and goodness, and thus the inherent rationality of the natural order) tend to be rationalists.[123] Boyle is generally taken to be representative of the former position, Descartes of the latter. There are some deficiencies in this thesis, but for our present purposes it should be sufficient to point out that what ultimately drives experimentalism and its relatively modest vision of what can be achieved in the realm of natural philosophy is not a particular conception of God and how he makes his decisions, but rather a view of human nature.[124] The experimental approach is justified primarily by appeals to the weakness of our sensory and cognitive capacities. For many seventeenth-century English thinkers these weaknesses were understood as consequences of the Fall. Boyle and Locke, for their part, also place stress on the incapacities that necessarily attend the kind of beings that we are. But in both cases, the more important issue is the nature of human capacities rather than the nature of the Deity. And if the idea of a fall away from an originally perfect knowledge begins to decline in importance towards the end of the seventeenth century, it nonetheless played a crucial role by drawing attention to the question of the capacities of human nature in the present world.

Boyle, incidentally, was by no means the only fellow of the Royal Society to harbour deep misgivings about the prospects of formulating a perfect science. The physician and botanist Henry Power (*c.* 1626–68), whose *Experimental Philosophy* (1664) was the first to acquaint the general public with the

[122] Boyle, *Excellency of Theology*, p. 153.
[123] See M. B. Foster, 'The Christian Doctrine of Creation and the Rise of Modern Natural Science', *Mind* 43 (1934), 446–68; J. E. McGuire, 'Boyle's Conception of Nature,' *JHI* 33 (1972), 523–42; Francis Oakley, 'Christian Theology and the Newtonian Science: The Rise of the Concept of Laws of Nature', *Church History* 30 (1961), 433–5; John Henry, 'Henry More versus Robert Boyle', in Sarah Hutton (ed.), *Henry More (1614–87): Tercentenary Essays* (Dordrecht, 1990), pp. 55–76; James E. Force and Richard H. Popkin, *Essays on the Context, Nature, and Influence of Isaac Newton's Theology* (Dordrecht, 1990); P. M. Heimann, 'Voluntarism and Immanence: Conceptions of Nature in Eighteenth Century Thought', *JHI* 39 (1978), 271–83; Margaret J. Osler, *Divine Will and the Mechanical Philosophy: Gassendi and Descartes on Contingency and Necessity in the Created World* (Cambridge, 1994); Wojcik, *Robert Boyle*, pp. 189–211.
[124] For difficulties with this thesis see Harrison, 'Voluntarism and Early Modern Science', and 'Was Newton a Voluntarist?'

discoveries of microscopy, wrote that human senses were framed 'as might best manage this particular engine we call the Body, and best agree with the place of our habitation (the earth and the elements we were to converse with) and not to be critical surveyors, and adequate judges of the immense Universe'.[125] John Ray, whose ambivalence about Wilkins's philosophical language we have already noted, expressed a similar sentiment in his classic *Wisdom of God Manifested in the Works of Creation* (1691), declaring that 'our Eyes and Senses, however armed or assisted, are too gross to discern the curiosity of the Workmanship of Nature . . . and our understanding too dark and infirm to discover and comprehend all Ends and uses to which the infinitely wise Creator did design them'.[126] The most systematic exposition of this view of the limitations of human knowledge, however, was provided by John Locke.

The work for which Locke is best known, the *Essay concerning Human Understanding* (1690), had its genesis in a casual discussion on the topics of religion and morality that took place among a group of friends in Locke's London house early in 1671. By any ordinary criterion the occasion was not a success. There was certainly no resolution of the issues under discussion and on parting the participants found themselves in a state of complete puzzlement. But the meeting did plant the seed of an idea in Locke's mind and, on his own account, he came away with the insight that 'before we set about enquiries of that nature it [is] necessary to examine our own abilities, and see what objects our understandings were or were not fitted to deal with'.[127] This was the idea that was to give rise to the *Essay concerning Human Understanding*. Locke's basic insight, it need hardly be pointed out, was of a piece with the general trend in seventeenth-century England, to direct attention to the question of human nature before pursuing knowledge claims. Locke's doubts about the prospects of a robust knowledge of nature are evident to the reader as soon as the book is opened. The title page of the fourth and subsequent editions of the *Essay* bears this epigraph: 'As thou knowest not what is the way of the Spirit, nor how the bones do grow in the womb of her that is with child: even so thou knowest not the works of God, who maketh all things.' These words, reputed to be those of Solomon, are taken from Ecclesiastes 11:5. While they have often escaped the attention of commentators, they set the tone for the essay and

---

[125] Power, *Experimental Philosophy*, Preface, sig. b r.
[126] Ray, *Wisdom of God*, p. 58. Although not published until 1691, this work was composed in the 1650s.
[127] Locke, *Essay*, Epistle to the Reader, 1.i.7 (1, 10).

provide an important link to the tradition of 'Solomonic' scepticism.[128] In the Epistle to the Reader, Locke informs the reader that his concern is the analysis of errors and their causes. In order to provide 'some service to human understanding', he states, it will prove necessary to 'break in upon the sanctuary of vanity and ignorance'.[129] Errors arise in our understanding, he goes on to say, because of overgenerous estimates of the capabilities of the human mind. Accordingly, the *Essay* was intended as an analysis of the powers of the mind, 'how far they reach, to what things they are in any degree proportionate; and where they fail us . . .' – all this to the end that 'we may learn to content ourselves with what is attainable in this state'.[130] The problem of preceding philosophies came from their failure to acknowledge the limits of reason, and their tendency to 'require demonstration, and demand certainty, where probability only is to be had'.[131] Thus the philosophies that had sought certain conclusions based on logical demonstration had been nothing more than evidence of human hubris. Locke's obvious debt to Bacon was acknowledged elsewhere, in the posthumously published *Of the Conduct of the Understanding* (1706). Here Locke repeats Bacon's observations about the incompetence of logic to address the manifold errors of the mind. 'There are several weaknesses and defects in the understanding', he observes, 'either from the natural temper of the mind or ill habits taken up'. Of these defects, he continues, 'there are as many possibly to be found, if the mind were thoroughly studied, as there are diseases of the body, each whereof clogs and disables the understanding to some degree, and therefore deserves to be looked after and cured'.[132]

For a figure typically regarded as a standard bearer for the Enlightenment and the philosopher (along with Bacon) most closely associated with the rise of empirical science, Locke's vision of the reach of natural philosophy is a rather sober one. Armed with Baconian 'experiments' and 'histories', Locke thought, the industrious investigator can penetrate further into the

---

[128] The original epigraph comes from Cicero, *De natura deorum* 1.30 and reads, in rough translation: 'How much more fitting it would have been, Velleius, for you to have confessed your ignorance of the things of which you were ignorant, than to have spouted the nonsense you did, and aroused your own disgust.' For a discussion of the epigraphs and their significance see Stephen Buckle, 'British Sceptical Realism: A Fresh Look at the British Tradition', *European Journal of Philosophy* 7 (1999), 1–29.

[129] Locke, *Essay*, Epistle to the Reader (1, 14). Locke acknowledges his debt to Bacon in *Of the Conduct of the Understanding*, 5th edn, ed. Thomas Fowler (Oxford, 1901), p. 4.

[130] Locke, *Essay*, Introduction, 4 (1, 28f.).   [131] *Ibid.*, Introduction, 5 (1, 30).

[132] Locke, *Conduct of the Understanding*, p. 4; cf. p 35. On the disease metaphor in Locke's *Conduct* see Nicholas Wolterstorff, *John Locke and the Ethics of Belief* (Cambridge, 1996), pp. 94f. For Locke's often unrecognised indebtedness to Bacon see Peter Anstey, 'Locke, Bacon and Natural History', *Early Science and Medicine* 7 (2002), 65–92; Neal Wood, 'The Baconian Character of Locke's "Essay"', *Studies in History and Philosophy of Science* 6 (1975), 43–84.

natures of things than the scholastic philosophers had ever managed. But this experimental knowledge falls well short of the status of science:

I deny not, but a man, accustomed to rational and regular experiments, shall be able to see farther into the nature of bodies, and guess righter at their yet unknown properties, than one that is a stranger to them: But yet, as I have said, this is but judgment and opinion, not knowledge and certainty. This way of getting and improving our knowledge in substances only by experience and history, which is all that the weakness of our faculties in this state of mediocrity, which we are in this world, can attain to; makes me suspect, that natural philosophy is not capable of being made a science.[133]

This verdict is repeated in Locke's *Thoughts concerning Education* (1693), in which he observes that we shall never be able to make a science out of natural philosophy because the 'Works of Nature are contrived by a Wisdom, and operate by ways too far surpassing our Faculties to discover, or Capacities to conceive, for us ever to be able to reduce them into a Science'.[134] Because the workmanship of God far surpasses the comprehension of the most ingenious of men, philosophical taxonomies of the kind proposed by Wilkins are sheer fantasies. Locke wrote that it is in vain that we 'pretend to range things into sorts, and dispose them into certain classes, under names, by their real essences'. 'A blind man', he concluded, 'may as soon sort things by their colours.'[135]

For Locke, as for Boyle, however, our current 'state of mediocrity' seems to be less the result of a catastrophic Fall than of the fact that our proper station is quite literally a 'mediocre' or middle state between angelic perfection and the lower orders of the beasts.[136] The capacities we do have, however, are well suited to our current state. According to Locke, God had 'fitted our senses, faculties, and organs, to the conveniences of life, and the business we have to do here' – that business not being the quest for a complete knowledge of the operations of nature, but that of learning about God through the creatures, discovering the nature of our moral

---

[133] Locke, *Essay* IV.xii.10 (1, 349). Cf.: 'But as to a perfect science of natural bodies (not to mention spiritual beings) we are, I think, so far from being capable of any such thing, that I conclude it lost labour to seek after it.' *Essay* IV.iii.29 (1, 222). See also *Essay* III.vi.9 (1, 64). In this context Locke means 'science' in the Aristotelian sense of knowledge that is certain and demonstrable. For Locke's views on the nature of natural philosophy see Peter Anstey, 'Locke on Method in Natural Philosophy', in Peter Anstey (ed.), *The Philosophy of John Locke: New Perspectives* (London, 2003), pp. 26–42.
[134] Locke, *Some Thoughts Concerning Education* §190, ed. John Yolton and Jean Yolton (Oxford, 1989), p. 244.
[135] Locke, *Essay* III.vi.9 (II, 64).
[136] For Locke's thoughts on the chain of being see the *Essay* III.6.12 (II, 68).

duties, and providing for the practical necessities of life.[137] In this respect we are no different from Adam. In contrast to Glanvill, and in keeping with Boyle's view, Locke had little time for an Adam equipped with super-sensitive organs of perception, for these he regarded as incompatible with the nature of human beings. While conceding that our present senses were indeed 'dull and weak', he pointed out that any significant improvement in their acuity would be accompanied by a host of inconveniences. Were our hearing more sensitive, we would be distracted by a perpetual noise, and would 'in the quietest retirement be less able to sleep or meditate, than in the middle of a sea fight'. Microscopic or telescopic vision would also prove to be more a burden than a boon. One possessed of an extraordinary 'quickness and tenderness of sight' could not, Locke supposed, 'endure bright sun-shine, or so much as open day-light; nor take in but a very small part of any object at once'.[138] As for Adam's supposed ability to name things according to their natures, this is also treated with scepticism. Adam was merely the first to impose names on things, but his naming would be no different to ours were we in his situation. Indeed, we still possess the same naming capacities as Adam: 'The same liberty also that Adam had of affixing any new name to any idea, the same has any one still.'[139]

The ideal conditions for acquiring knowledge to which our present state was to be compared, then, were represented not by Adam in paradise, but by the situation of angelic beings – 'spirits' that might have the ability 'to frame and shape to themselves organs of sensation or perception, as to suit them to their present design, and the circumstances they would consider'.[140] It is a measure of Locke's commitment to empiricism that in his scheme of things even spiritual beings would rely on sense perceptions for their knowledge of material bodies. Elsewhere, he was to affirm that spirits, 'of a higher rank than those immersed in flesh', have knowledge and ideas 'much more perfect than ours', and indeed 'may have as clear ideas of the radical constitution of substances, as we have of a triangle, and so perceive how all their properties and operations flow from thence: But the manner how they come by that knowledge exceeds our conceptions'.[141] It follows from Locke's adherence to the idea that God placed humans on a specific rung on the ladder of being that had Adam possessed the remarkable intellectual abilities so often attributed to him, he would in fact not have been human at all, but a creature occupying a more elevated rank in the *scala naturae*.

[137] Locke, *Essay* II.xxiii.12 (I, 402).
[138] *Ibid.* Cf. Power, *Experimental Philosophy*, Preface.
[139] Locke, *Essay* III.vi.51 (II, 470).   [140] *Ibid.*, II.xxiii.13 (I, 404).
[141] *Ibid.*, III.xi.23 (II, 160).

Nonetheless, it seems clear that Locke's assessment of human nature was shaped to a considerable degree by the Augustinian tradition. This influence is particularly conspicuous in the *Two Tracts upon Government*, written between the years of 1660 and 1662 in the wake of the failure of the Puritan experiment. For Locke, while the events of the immediate past had shown the folly of Puritan political aspirations, they had paradoxically confirmed one of that movement's most fundamental convictions, namely, the deep corruption of human nature. The Puritan project, however laudable in its original conception, had served to demonstrate how the best motives are inevitably diverted towards evil. Instead of establishing a godly commonwealth, they had succeeded only in reducing England to 'chaos' and 'a heady ferment of passions'. Their proud ambition was the consequence of neither reason nor knowledge of the divine will, but was instead a demonstration of 'predatory lust under the guise of Christian liberty and religion'.[142] Locke thus welcomed the Restoration of the monarchy. Without legitimately instituted political power, Locke urged, there would be 'no peace, no security, no enjoyments, enmity with all men and safe possession of nothing, and those stinging swarms of miseries that attend anarchy and rebellion'.[143] The Hobbesian cadences of this statement are unmistakable, as a number of commentators have pointed out.[144] It is not unreasonable to think that the common currency of fallen human nature informed the views of both Locke and Hobbes. Locke himself provides support for this reading. 'Ever since man threw himself into the pollution of sin', he wrote, 'he sullies whatever he takes into his hand, and he that at first could make the best and perfectest nature degenerate cannot fail now to make other things so.' Political anarchy is one result of our 'frail nature' and 'corruption'.[145]

This early conviction persisted well beyond the aftermath of the civil wars. If anything, it was reinforced during Locke's three-year sojourn in France in the years 1675–9. Here he encountered the writings of the Jansenist theologian Pierre Nicole. Locke was particularly taken with Nicole's *Essais de Morale* (1671–8), and set himself the task of translating three of them

---

[142] Locke, *Two Tracts*, in *Political Essays*, ed. Mark Goldie (Cambridge, 1997), p. 56.

[143] *Ibid.*, p. 37.

[144] See, e.g., J. Gough, *John Locke's Political Philosophy* (Oxford, 1950), p. 180; M. Cranston, *Locke: A Biography* (London, 1957), p. 62. See also Locke, *Political Essays*, ed. Goldie, p. 37 n. 19.

[145] Locke, *Two Tracts*, in *Political Essays*, p. 36. Thus John Dunn on the *Two Tracts*: 'The cognitive insouciance and the insubordinate disposition of fallen men necessitate an elaborate structure of human authorities.' *Political Thought of John Locke*, p. 15. John Spellman agrees that Locke's *Two Tracts* were premised on 'the irreversible corruption and inherent sinfulness of all men'. *Locke and the Problem of Depravity*, pp. 49–62. Cf. Marshall, *John Locke*, pp. 27, 32, 63; John Colman, *John Locke's Moral Philosophy* (Edinburgh, 1983), p. 12; Ian Harris, 'The Politics of Christianity', in Rogers (ed.), *John Locke*, pp. 197–216 (p. 207).

into English. In a journal entry dated 15 August 1676, probably intended as a preface to his translations, he observed:

when we a little consider what our author says and experience vouches concerning the shortness of our lives and the weakness of our understandings, what small progress men of the quickest parts make in real knowledge, and how little of useful truth we discover after a long search and infinite labour, we shall find there was reason enough to desire all needless difficulties should be removed out of the way.[146]

It is likely, John Marshall writes, that Locke 'broadly agreed with Nicole's vision of men's corrupted nature, the centrality of corrupt self-love among the passions, and the essential role of God's grace in enlivening and saving men'.[147] Indeed the affinity between Locke's philosophy and Jansenism was noted at the time by Voltaire, who on one occasion described Locke as 'the Pascal of the English'.[148]

Perhaps the chief significance of Locke's encounter with Nicole was that it provided independent corroboration, as it were, of what in England was the dominant view. Nicole's position, as restated by Locke, was entirely consistent with the theological consensus in England at the time, where all groups, including the relatively optimistic Latitudinarians, stressed the depravity of the human condition.[149] There is little in the later political writings to suggest that Locke ever abandoned these convictions. While his unpublished 'Essay on Toleration' (1667) represents a change of heart on the question of toleration (possibly the result of his experience in Europe of Catholics, Lutherans and Calvinists living together in relative peace), he was still to identify 'depraved ambitious human nature' as the reason for men's desire to have dominion over other men.[150] In the *Two Treatises on Government* (1690), Locke writes that 'Adam was created a perfect man, his body and mind in full possession of their strength and reason'. In the state of innocence he had been able to 'govern his actions according to the dictates of the law of reason which God had implanted in him'. For this reason the original grant of government was not given to Adam until after the Fall, when he was 'much distant in condition' from his first creation. In theory, the prescriptions of the law of nature would have been sufficient to ensure a 'great and general community' were it not for

---

[146] Locke, *Essay*, pp. 254–7, quoted in Marshall, *John Locke*, p. 134.

[147] Marshall, *John Locke*, p. 134. Cf. Kim Parker, *The Biblical Politics of John Locke* (Waterloo, Ontario, 2004), pp. 53f.

[148] Voltaire, *Eloge et Pensées de Pascal*, in Louis Moland (ed.), *Œuvres complètes de Voltaire*, 52 vols. (Paris, 1877–85), XXXI, 42.

[149] Spellman, *The Latitudinarians*, p. 55; Marshall, *John Locke*, p. 135.

[150] Marshall, *John Locke*, p. 64.

the 'corruption, and viciousness of degenerate Men'.[151] By implication, civil government was a prerequisite for peace in the postlapsarian world.[152] Locke's rambling and repetitive *Third Letter concerning Toleration* (1692) is peppered with references to 'depraved' and 'corrupt human nature'.[153] Even in the *Essay*, according to John Dunn, Locke only claims that human beings are potentially or intermittently rational, given that all human judgements 'are clouded by the corrupt passions released by the Fall'.[154]

Locke had two further occasions to reflect on the biblical narrative of the Fall and its contemporary significance. His famous refutation of Robert Filmer's *Patriarcha* entailed a careful exegesis of the narrative of Adam's creation and Fall. As we have already seen, Filmer's case for absolutism was grounded in the idea that Adam was the first monarch; that his authority came from a divine grant rather than the consent of those he governed; that this power was conveyed to the patriarchs and from them to all monarchs; and that there had never in all of history been a 'state of nature' in which individuals had been free. All of this was buttressed with supporting references from scripture.[155] Locke's demolition of this argument in his *Two Treatises* involved an alternative reading of Genesis and one which, arguably, was more faithful to the literal account than Filmer's. Locke upbraided Filmer for having read his personal political views into the text, declaring that 'our own ill grounded opinions, however by us called "probable", cannot authorize us to understand scripture contrary to the direct and plain meaning of the words'.[156] A consideration of that 'plain meaning' of the relevant texts led Locke to the conclusion that 'Adam had not, either by natural right of fatherhood, or by positive donation from God, any such authority over his children, or dominion over the world, as is pretended'.[157] The other puzzling feature of Filmer's account seized upon by Locke concerned the issue of succession. Even if God had granted absolute political power to Adam, Locke pointed out, it was not clear how this power would pass to his offspring.[158] On this issue, Filmer had simply invoked the commonplace principle of Adam as a representative person – 'what was given to Adam, was given in his person to his posterity'.[159] This view was common currency,

---

[151] Locke, *Two Treatises of Government*, 12th edn, ii.vi.56 (Laslett edn p. 305); i.iii.16 (p. 152); ii.ix.128 (p. 352).

[152] Cf. Marshall, *John Locke*, p. 145 n. 38.

[153] See, e.g., Locke, *A Third Letter for Toleration*, in *Works* vi, 351f., 362, 400, 446, 467, 543.

[154] Dunn, *Political Thought of John Locke*, p. 194.   [155] Filmer, *Patriarcha*, p. 13 and *passim*.

[156] Locke, *Two Treatises* i.iv.36 (p. 165).   [157] *Ibid.*, ii.i.1 (p. 267). Cf. pp. 161, 291.

[158] *Ibid.*, i.ix.95–8 (pp. 211–13).

[159] Robert Filmer, *The Anarchy of a Limited or Mixed Monarchy*, in J. P. Sommerville (ed.), *Filmer: Patriarcha and other Writings* (Cambridge, 1991), p. 138.

as we have seen, because it was presupposed in one of the standard explanations of how Adamic guilt came to fall upon succeeding generations. It was by virtue of this principle, then, that both Adam's monarchical authority and his guilt could be transmitted to his posterity (although the former, problematically, was conveyed patrilineally to particular persons).[160] Locke was to deny that Adam possessed such a representative capacity, and did so again in the rather different context of his account of Christianity.

In the first sentence of *The Reasonableness of Christianity as Delivered in the Scriptures* (1695) Locke announced: 'It is obvious to any one, who reads the New Testament, that the doctrine of redemption, and consequently of the Gospel, is founded upon the supposition of Adam's fall.' For Locke, arriving at a proper understanding of the nature of Adam's fall was as fundamental for a right conception of Christianity as it was for political philosophy. What quickly emerges in this work, however, is that while Locke still holds to the idea of the Fall, he has abandoned the Augustinian/Calvinist understanding of it. This was as a consequence of applying the two criteria cited in his title – reasonableness and the witness of scripture – to the question of what Adam had lost on his expulsion from paradise. Locke argues, plausibly enough, that on a strictly literal reading of Genesis and St Paul, Adam had lost only 'immortality and bliss' as a consequence of sin. It was these things, then, that were restored by Christ's redemptive work.[161] Mortality and the loss of bliss might have indirectly made the acquisition of knowledge more difficult, but Locke did not seem to think that the Fall had directly wrought havoc with the mind or the senses. Neither did Locke find any conclusive biblical evidence to support the Augustinian view that moral guilt is inherited by all of the descendants of Adam, 'whom millions had never heard of, and no one had authorized to transact for him, or to be his Representative'. According to the New Testament, Locke concludes, 'every one's sin is charged upon himself only'.[162] Such a view, happily, also accords with commonsense conceptions of justice and of the goodness of God

---

[160] Harris, 'The Politics of Christianity'; Parker, *Biblical Politics of John Locke*, p. 149; Spellman, *John Locke*, pp. 74f.

[161] Locke, *Reasonableness of Christianity*, *Works* VII, 10. Also see the MS '*Homo ante et post lapsum*', reproduced in Victor Nuovo (ed.), *John Locke: Writings on Religion* (Oxford, 2002), p. 231. This is very close to Thomas Hobbes's reading, *Leviathan* III.38.2/25 (p. 479). Locke returned to this issue in his *Paraphrase and Notes on the Epistles of St Paul* (1705–7). See Parker, *Biblical Politics of John Locke*, pp. 63–5.

[162] *Ibid.* pp. 7, 10. Locke's contemporary, Bishop Gilbert Burnet, had made a similar point about the Augustinian view which he equated with Federal theology: 'And since the Foundation of this is a supposed Covenant with *Adam* as the Representative Head of Mankind, it is strange that a thing of that great consequence, should not have been more plainly Reported in the History of the Creation.' Burnet, *An Exposition*, p. 115.

himself.[163] It is also very similar to a position briefly sketched out earlier by Locke in his commonplace book, in which the Fall is said to have introduced private possessions and labour, disparities in living conditions, along with 'coviteousness, pride & ambition which *by fashen & example* spread the corruption which has soe prevailed over man kind'.[164] This follows from the Genesis text in which the necessity of labour is attributed to the Fall (Gen. 3:17–19). In Locke's well-known doctrine, property only becomes private when mixed with human labour. Thus with private possessions, themselves necessitated by the Fall, came social inequalities and a host of consequent evils. Adam's lapse did introduce corruption into the world, but it was mostly engendered by social rather than inherited factors. Much of this was also consistent with the views of Locke's Arminian friend and leader of the Dutch Remonstrants, Philip van Limborch (1633–1712), whom he had met during his voluntary exile in the Netherlands during the mid-1680s.[165] Van Limborch pointed out in his *Theologia Christiana* (1686) that the expression 'original sin' was not to be found in scripture, and while he conceded that 'we are now born less pure than Adam was created', he described that loss of purity as 'only a natural Inclination of attaining that which is grateful to the Flesh, which is properly owning the Constitution of the Body, which we derive from our next immediate parents'.[166] This was inherited corruption in only a weak sense, and wholly in accordance with Locke's view, expressed in the *Essay*, that our cognitive limitations are owing to our status as embodied creatures and the corrupting influences of our upbringing.

Brief comment should be made at this juncture on Locke's *Some Thoughts concerning Education* (1693), a work that in his day rivalled the *Essay* in popularity. This book is directly relevant to the present discussion because it sets out some of the practical implications of what is the best-known contention of the *Essay*: that at birth the human mind is a blank sheet or *tabula*

---

[163] For Locke's sensitivity to this issue see 'Peccatum originale' (1661), in Nuovo (ed.), *Writings on Religion*, pp. 229f.; Locke, Journal, 1 August 1680, in *Political Essays*, ed. Goldie, p. 277. The notion of Adam as a public person was also inconsistent with Locke's conception of personal identity. See Ian Harris, *The Mind of John Locke: A Study of Political Theory in its Intellectual Setting* (Cambridge, 1994), pp. 301f.

[164] Locke, 'Homo ante et post lapsum' (1662), in Nuovo (ed.), *Writings on Religion*, p. 231 (my emphasis). See also Dunn, *Political Thought of John Locke*, p. 115; Jacob Viner, '"Possessive Individualism" as Original Sin', *Canadian Journal of Economics and Political Science* 29 (1963), 548–59.

[165] On the Locke–Limborch connection see Spellman, *Locke and the Problem of Depravity*, pp. 130–7; Israel, *Radical Enlightenment*, pp. 464–71.

[166] From the English translation of *Theologia Christiana*, Philip van Limborch, *A Complete System, or Body of Divinity . . . founded on Scripture and Reason*, tr. William Jones, 2 vols. (London, 1713), 1, 190, quoted in Spellman, *Locke and the Problem of Depravity*, p. 132.

rasa.[167] If there are, in fact, no innate principles or ideas in the mind, it follows that it is education or training that plays the most significant role in determining the nature of the person. Locke's faith in the efficacy of education and his apparent assertion of the essential innocence of the neonate have sometimes been interpreted as an uncompromising repudiation of the pessimistic Augustinian tradition and a major catalyst for the liberation of humanity from the bleak vision of human nature fostered by early modern Protestants. However, to claim that at birth the mind is a *tabula rasa* is not necessarily to claim that it is innocent or free from bias towards good or evil. Whatever his successors might have made of the doctrine, Locke himself still believed that human beings are constitutionally selfish and wilful.[168] We should also recall that Locke was by no means the first to advance the idea of the mind as a blank slate, and that it had long been regarded as quite compatible with the view of innate corruption. Prominent advocates of original sin were thus happy to affirm the view that the mind was a 'blank sheet' at birth. These included Thomas Aquinas, who had cited Aristotle to the effect that the mind is at first 'like a clean tablet on which nothing is written'. A number of Locke's contemporaries also saw nothing in this principle that counted against even stronger versions of original sin than Aquinas had been prepared to countenance.[169] It is also possible to conceive of the educational programme set out in *Thoughts concerning Education* as the development of a long-standing Puritan emphasis on the value of education as remitting some of the worst effects of the Fall. Huguenot émigré Jean Gailhard exemplifies both of those points. Although a staunch opponent of Locke on a number of issues, he was to agree that the child is 'a smooth table upon which any thing can be written'. But this was simply one of the premises establishing the importance of education. The other was original sin, thus: 'Learning doth also afford us help, and rules, how to master our passions . . . Now these passions are seated in the heart, wherein reason ought to preside . . . but this part of man is much sensible of the sad effects of *Adam's* sin.'[170] Education could be regarded, on analogy with the coercive powers of the state and the discipline of the

---

[167] 'Let us then suppose the mind to be, as we say, white paper, void of all characters, without any ideas.' Locke, *Essay* II.i.2 (I, 121).

[168] Locke, *Thoughts concerning Education* §§35, 132, 167 (pp. 104, 193, 223).

[169] Aquinas, ST Ia. 79, 2. On the history of the idea see Neal Wood, 'Tabula Rasa, Social Environmentalism, and the "English Paradigm"', *JHI* 53 (1992), 647–68; Spellman, *John Locke*, pp. 84f.

[170] Gailhard, *Compleat Gentleman*, 28. Cf. Milton, 'Of Education', in *Prose Works of John Milton*, ed. J. A. St John and Charles Sumner (London, 1848–64), III, 462f. See also Webster, *Great Instauration*, pp. 100f. On earlier Puritan attitudes to education see John Morgan, *Godly Learning: Puritan Attitudes towards Reason, Learning, and Education, 1560–1640* (Cambridge, 1988).

Baconian experimental regimen, as a therapy aimed at remedying the anarchic tendencies of wayward passions. There is clear evidence that this was how Locke's general position was interpreted into the eighteenth century. If Locke's epistemology could be appropriated by the forces of Enlightenment it could equally serve to reinforce the more sober assessments of human capacity that originally inspired it. In Isaac Watts's *Logick* (1725) – a standard logic text based on Lockian principles which appeared in more than twenty editions over the course of the eighteenth century – the author announces that the science of logic is designed 'to rescue our Reasoning Powers from their unhappy Slavery and Darkness'. This new form of logic, inspired by Locke and distinguished from the noisy and wordy wrangling of the Schools, was intended to guard us against 'the foolish and evil Dispositions that are found in fallen Man' and 'to raise us in some measure from the Ruins of our Fall'.[171]

All of this seems to confirm W. M. Spellman's considered verdict that one of the central aims of Locke's philosophical career was 'to fully illuminate the nature of the Fall'.[172] It is true that to a degree Locke's lifelong engagement with the Fall narrative was a function of the intellectual milieu of Restoration England in which so many issues were framed within the limits of a broadly shared theological conception of human nature. It would have been difficult to make a significant contribution to contemporary debates – such as those concerning the philosophical justification for particular forms of government – without coming to terms with this formative myth. But Locke was also committed to the idea of a Fall on his own account. His reading of scripture, his vision of Christianity (minimalist though it might have become), and not least his own experiences, led to an acceptance of the doctrine. There is also the intriguing possibility that he initially formulated his opposition to innatism under the influence of the prevailing understandings of original sin according to which the Fall had obliterated whatever moral notices had originally been stamped on the human soul by God.[173] Undeniably, Locke's final position on the Fall represents something of a watershed. With Locke, two of the fundamental characteristics of Calvinist and Lutheran versions of Christianity – the principle of *sola scriptura* and a strong commitment to the doctrine of original sin – become

---

[171] Isaac Watts, *Logick: Or, the Right Use of Reason in the Enquiry after Truth, with a Variety of Rules to guard against Error* (London, 1725), pp. iii, vi, 4f.

[172] Spellman, *Locke and the Problem of Depravity*, p. 103. For an alternative reading of Locke see Peter Schouls, *Reasoned Freedom: John Locke and Enlightenment* (Ithaca, 1992), pp. 193–203.

[173] Thus Marshall: 'Locke would seem to have originally believed in . . . a moderate view of the Fall, one that obliterated many but not all innate principles.' *John Locke*, p. 32. Also see Locke, *Essays on the Law of Nature*, ed. W. von Leyden (Oxford, 1954), p 137.

disengaged. The plain sense of scripture, Locke discovered, did not seem to support Augustine's bleak doctrine of inherited guilt. Neither, incidentally, did it seem to support the idea of Adam as a peerless natural philosopher. Locke's Adam is a figure whose prelapsarian capacities are not much different from ours, and thus in many respects our natural condition is similar to that of Adam in his innocence – with regard to our naming of things, in relation to the formation of our political institutions, inasmuch as we bear the burden of guilt for our own transgressions, and in the means by which we must acquire our knowledge. Where we do differ from Adam, however, is in the social matrix into which we are born. The corrupting influences of our human environment place us at a considerable disadvantage, and these influences are themselves the consequence of sin. When Bacon and Hooke had spoken of the deficiencies of human nature, they had distributed blame across innate infirmities and social conditioning.[174] Locke shifted the balance in favour of social factors. We are still inherently limited beings, but this by virtue of our rank in the cosmic hierarchy rather than original sin. We are born into conditions that further compromise our already weak abilities, and these can be regarded as a consequence of the corrupt natures of those who are around us from birth. That said, Locke's estimate of the reach of the human mind is not so different from those who attributed human weaknesses to an inherited disposition. Viewed in this light, the *Essay concerning Human Understanding* was not an epistemological manifesto for a progressive and triumphalist modern science, nor was it (for its author at least) the philosophical harbinger of an Enlightenment that would place its unqualified trust in the powers of reason. Rather it was an attempt to establish the narrow limits of our knowledge of the world, and point the way to a more certain science – the science of morals. Human beings, Locke insisted, can never possess 'a universal or perfect comprehension of whatsoever is', yet they 'have light enough to lead them to knowledge of their Maker, and the sight of their own duties'.[175] Knowledge relating to 'our conduct' and 'our eternal estate' constituted 'the proper science' and the 'greatest interest' of the human race.[176] Locke's late views on toleration and government are indeed in tune with the broad spirit of the Enlightenment and no doubt had a significant role in those movements. But these

---

[174] Bacon, *Novum Organum* §§38–68 (*Works* IV, 53–69); Hooke, *Micrographia*, Preface.

[175] Locke, *Essay*, Introduction, 5 (I, 29); Cf. Locke, *Essay* II.xxiii.13 (I, 404).

[176] *Ibid.*, Introduction, 6 (I, 31); IV.xii.11 (II, 350). For a similar reading of Locke see Spellman, *Locke and the Problem of Depravity*, pp. 5–7, 104–6, and passim. Cf. Richard Ashcroft, 'Locke wrote the *Essay* . . . in order to secure the ends of religion and morality.' 'Faith and Knowledge in Locke's Philosophy', in John Yolton (ed.), *John Locke: Problems and Perspectives* (Cambridge, 1969), p. 198.

views, like his epistemology, were grounded in a sober assessment of human nature that was entirely consistent with the anthropology of the Protestant reformers. As Victor Nuovo has recently put it, perhaps we should now think of Locke 'not merely as a progenitor of the Enlightenment, but as one of the last of the Reformers'.[177]

ANTHROPOLOGY ABANDONED

Locke met Isaac Newton in the spring of 1689. He had read the *Principia* during his exile in France and while, like most readers, he found its mathematics impenetrable, this had not prevented him from writing a favourable review of the work. In spite of Newton's notoriously difficult personality the two became close friends and they exchanged ideas on a number of topics of common interest. Much of their correspondence concerns the interpretation of scripture and the slender biblical foundations of the doctrine of the Trinity, but for their immediate posterity their names were linked as dual founders of a new form of knowledge.[178] According to one dominant eighteenth-century French reading of history, and one still remarkably influential, Newton and Locke, with some help from Bacon and Descartes, were inaugurators of the modern, enlightened age. Jean d'Alembert thus suggested that if Locke had created a scientific philosophy suited to the modern era, Newton was the originator of a scientific physics. Both were said to have shared an unwavering commitment to the empirical approach to knowledge.[179] D'Alembert (and, before him, Voltaire) allowed that Descartes had been both iconoclast and innovator. But their countryman's speculative methods were judged to have been seriously deficient when compared with a more rigorous English experimentalism, the chief representatives of which were Bacon, Locke, and Newton. As we have already seen, Locke's posthumous enlistment in the cause of Enlightenment is not without its difficulties, and there are other problems with the version of history promoted by the *philosophes*.[180] My concern in this final

[177] Nuovo (ed.), *Writings on Religion*, p. lvii. Cf. Spellman, *John Locke*, pp. 4–7.
[178] Peter Walmsley, *Locke's Essay and the Rhetoric of Science* (Lewisburg, PA, 2003), p. 20; J. R. Milton, 'Locke's Life and Times', in Vere Chappell (ed.), *The Cambridge Companion to Locke* (Cambridge, 1994), pp. 5–25.
[179] Jean Le Rond d'Alembert, 'Discours préliminaire', *Encyclopédie, ou Dictionnaire Raisonné des Sciences, des Arts et des Métiers*, vol. I, (Paris, 1751), pp. xxliv–xxlv. Cf. 'Expérimental', vol. VI (Paris, 1756), pp. 298–301; Voltaire, *Letters Concerning the English Nation*, ed. Nicholas Cronk (Oxford, 1999), letters 13–16. See also P. M. Rattansi, 'Voltaire and the Enlightenment Image of Newton', in H. Lloyd-Jones (ed.), *History and Imagination* (London, 1981), 218–31.
[180] Israel, *Radical Enlightenment*, pp. 522–6; Brian Young, 'Newtonianism and the Enthusiasm of Enlightenment', *Studies in History and Philosophy of Science* 35 (2004), 645–63.

section will be to consider one aspect of this history – the assumption present not only in the propaganda of the French Enlightenment but also in more recent histories of science, according to which Newton may be regarded as the culmination of the tradition of English experimental philosophy that began with Bacon. If this were the case, we would expect to find in Newton's works discussions of the effects of the Fall, or at the very least some systematic account of the limits of knowledge and the way in which experimental philosophy compensates for these. As it turns out, such anthropological concerns are almost completely absent from the Newtonian corpus. In spite of extensive and well-documented interests in the sphere of theology Newton showed little interest in the Fall of Adam or the doctrine of original sin. Neither does he anywhere discuss at any length the issue of the limitations of human knowledge. On the face of it, this is inconvenient for the central thesis of this book, according to which advocacy of a certain kind of experimentalism is closely linked to such considerations. The question that needs further (if necessarily brief) consideration is whether Newton's methodological prescriptions differ significantly from the pattern of Baconian 'natural and experimental histories' and, if so, whether these differences can be related in any way to his silence on the questions of theological anthropology that had so preoccupied his predecessors.

Newton's extra-curricular preoccupations – chronology, alchemy, Church history, biblical prophecy, and theology – have been the subject of much scholarly discussion over the past few decades. It has long been known that Newton was passionately opposed to the central tenet of Christian orthodoxy, the doctrine of the Trinity. From his voluminous manuscript writings – Newton wrote several million words on religious topics – we now know that he also cherished other heterodox views, rejecting infant baptism, the natural immortality of the soul, and the existence of the devil.[181] The abandonment of these beliefs was not, as it was for some deistically inclined contemporaries, the consequence of rationalism or religious scepticism. Newton remained fervently committed to what he believed was genuine Christianity, understood as the simple biblical faith practised by the early Church. According to Newton's carefully reconstructed history of the Church, the minimalist creed of the first Christians had been corrupted by the introduction of doctrines that reflected Greek philosophy rather than

---

[181] Frank Manuel, *The Religion of Isaac Newton* (Oxford, 1974); James Force and Richard Popkin (eds.), *Essays on the Context, Nature, and Influence of Isaac Newton's Theology* (Dordrecht, 1990); Stephen Snobelen, 'Isaac Newton, Heretic: The Strategies of a Nicodemite', *BJHS* 32 (1999), 381–419; 'Lust, Pride, and Amibition: Isaac Newton and the Devil', in James E. Force and Sarah Hutton (eds.), *Newton and Newtonianism: New Studies* (Dordrecht, 2004), pp. 155–82.

biblical truths. Chief amongst these was the idea of a triune God, which, according to Newton's somewhat idiosyncratic version of Church history, had been inserted into the Christian creeds at the instigation of the Church Father Athanasius (*c.* 296–373).[182]

On the subject of original sin Newton had little to say even in his private papers. This is one of the striking features of Newton's theological writings when compared with those of his contemporaries. In none of the manuscript sources listing what Newton considered to be the basic tenets of Christian belief is a significant place accorded to the Fall or original sin.[183] In his 'Theological Notebook' brief reference is made to the classic verse in Romans 5 which speaks of sin entering the world through the transgressions of one man. Newton simply observes in this context that the curse from which we are redeemed is the curse of the Law, rather than the curse of original sin.[184] While Newton's silence on this issue may seem surprising when we consider the prominent place of theological anthropology in a wide range of contemporary writings, it is nonetheless consistent with his personal religion with its credal minimalism and strict Biblicism. It is likely that Newton considered the doctrine of original sin to be a late interpolation into Christian theology and one that, like the notion of a Triune God, rested on rather flimsy biblical foundations. A denial of original sin would also cohere with Newton's rejection of infant baptism (understood within the Catholic tradition as a washing away of original sin), his scepticism about Satan (a central figure in the Fall narrative), and his occasional expression of Pelagian views.[185] But there is a more obvious connection between Newton's rejection of the deity of Christ and his silence on original sin. As Locke rightly declared in *The Reasonableness of Christianity*, the idea of the Fall was the foundation upon which the whole edifice of the doctrine of Christ's redemption was constructed. And as Athanasius himself had long ago pointed out, there was a vital connection between the nature of Christ and the atoning work that he had to perform. Such was the extent of our fallen condition that only God himself could repair it.

---

[182] Yahuda MS 15, Bodmer MS 'On the Church'.

[183] 'Seven Statements on Religion', Keynes MS 6; 'A Short Scheme of the True Religion', Keynes MS 7; 'Twelve Articles on Religion', Keynes MS 8; 'Three Paragraphs on Religion', Keynes MS 9.

[184] Keynes MS 2, pt 1, xxii *Christi Satisfactio, & Redemptio vivi*. There is a heading 'xxix *Status Naturæ et Gratiæ*', but unhelpfully nothing is written there. Insofar as he has any conception equivalent to that of original sin, it would be understood as something like the universal human propensity towards idolatry. Richard S. Westfall, *Never at Rest: A Biography of Isaac Newton* (Cambridge, 1983), p. 355; Rob Iliffe, '"The Idols of the Temple": Isaac Newton and the Private Life of Anti-Idolatry', Ph.D. dissertation, University of Cambridge, 1989.

[185] Part 2 of the 'Theological Notebook' opens with a statement to the effect that a man sins not through necessity, but through choice. Keynes MS 2, pt 2.

Necessarily, the redeemer must participate in the Godhead.[186] In orthodox theology, then, the doctrines of original sin and of the divinity of Christ were inextricably linked. Newton's vehement rejection of the Trinity was thus entirely consistent with his telling silence on the issue of original sin.

On the thesis being pursued in this volume it would be expected that Newton's agnosticism with regard to theological anthropology, unusual for his period, would have had a bearing on the way in which he formulated his ideas about scientific method. Specifically, he ought to have been less concerned with justifying his methods by appealing to particular theories of human nature and more open to the prospect of a knowledge of nature that was certain and complete. As it turns out, Newton's approach to natural philosophy was quite distinctive. Considered in the context of the seventeenth century, Newton's methodology, according to Peter Dear, makes him 'a curious and novel exception'. Rob Iliffe agrees that the basic methodological principles of Newton's masterwork, the *Principia*, 'went boldly against the grain of most contemporary approaches to natural philosophy'.[187] These judgements are borne out by the confusion and controversy that greeted Newton's first methodological pronouncements in the early 1670s.[188]

One of the chief differences between Newton's methods and those of his contemporaries in the Royal Society lies in Newton's confidence that his procedure would yield results that were virtually certain. Where his predecessors and peers had tended to settle for probabilistic conclusions, Newton boldly sought mathematical demonstrability, proceeding, in his own words, 'in imitation of the method by wch Mathematitians are wont to prove their doctrines'.[189] Such a method would, in his view, give rise to a new kind of natural science that rejected 'probabilities' and was 'supported by the greatest evidence'.[190] At the same time, Newton wished to present himself

[186] Athanasius, *De Incarnatione* §6, §10.

[187] Peter Dear, 'Method and the Study of Nature', in Daniel Garber and Michael Ayers (eds.), *The Cambridge History of Seventeenth-Century Philosophy*, 2 vols. (Cambridge, 1998), I, 147–77 (166); Rob Iliffe, 'Abstract Considerations: Disciplines and the Incoherence of Newton's Natural Philosophy', *Studies in History and Philosophy of Science* 35A (2004), 427–54 (446). Newton's investigations of light, Iliffe adds, 'represented a deliberate and ambitious attempt to transform contemporary natural philosophy, and closer to home, the nature of enquiry at the Royal Society' (437).

[188] See, e.g., Hooke's complaints, *Isaac Newton's Papers and Letters on Natural Philosophy*, ed. I. Bernard Cohen and Robert E. Schefield (Cambridge, MA, 1978), p. 111. See also Zev Bechler, 'Newton's 1672 Optical Controversies: A Study in the Grammar of Scientific Dissent', in E. Yahuda (ed.), *The Interaction between Science and Philosophy* (Atlantic Highlands, NJ, 1974), pp. 115–42; Alan Gross, 'On the Shoulders of Giants: Seventeenth-Century Optics as an Argumentative Field', in R. A. Harris (ed.), *Landmark Essays on Rhetoric of Science* (Marwah, NJ, 1997), pp. 19–38.

[189] Newton to Oldenburg, 21 September 1672, *Correspondence of Sir Isaac Newton*, ed. H. W. Turnbull, 7 vols. (Cambridge, 1961), I, 237.

[190] Newton, *The Optical Papers of Isaac Newton, Vol. 1: The Optical Lectures 1670–1672*, ed. Alan Shapiro (Cambridge, 1984), I, 89.

as an experimentalist, an identification associated with the very probabilism he wished to avoid. This tension is nowhere better expressed than in the opening sentence of the *Opticks*, where Newton announces his intention to 'propose and prove' the properties of light 'by Reason and Experiments'.[191] This stance contrasted with the more modest experimentalism of most of his compatriots. Sprat, for example, had written earlier that the results of experiment must be reported not 'as *unalterable Demonstrations*, but as *present appearances*'.[192] The proposed union of reason and experiment suggested a greater faith in our rational capacities than most seventeenth-century experimentalists had been willing to countenance. Indeed Newton's eighteenth-century legacy tended to split precisely along the lines of reason and experiment. I. Bernard Cohen and George Smith rightly observe that Newton engendered 'two related but rather different traditions of doing science'.[193] These were those of the experimentalist and the mathematical theoretician.

Much of the apparent oddness of Newton's approach arises out of his claim to be able to treat the phenomena of light and gravity from both physical and mathematical points of view. This particular combination of approaches, Newton believed, would enable him to argue 'more securely' or with 'certainty'.[194] Historians of science now routinely interpret Newton's novelty as resulting from the (then) illicit introduction of the methods of mixed mathematics into natural philosophy.[195] Related to this disciplinary

---

[191] Newton, *Opticks: or, A Treatise of the Reflections, Refractions, Inflections & Colours of Light*, based on the 4th edn, ed. I. Bernard Cohen et al. (New York, 1979), p. 1.

[192] Sprat, *History*, p. 108.

[193] I. Bernard Cohen and George E. Smith (eds.), *The Cambridge Companion to Newton* (Cambridge, 2002), Introduction, p. 31. On tensions between the methods of the *Opticks* and the *Principia* see George Smith, 'The Methodology of the *Principia*', in *Cambridge Companion to Newton*, pp. 138–73; P. Anstey, 'The Methodological Origins of Newton's Queries', *Studies in History and Philosophy of Science* 35A (2004), 247–69; P. Achinstein, 'Newton's Corpuscular Query and Experimental Philosophy', in P. Bricker and R. I. G. Hughes (eds.), *Philosophical Perspectives on Newtonian Science* (Cambridge, MA, 1990), pp. 135–73; I. Bernard Cohen, *The Newtonian Revolution* (Cambridge, 1980); J. E. McGuire, 'Newton's "Principles of Philosophy": An Intended Preface for the 1704 *Opticks* and a Related Draft Fragment', *BJHS* 5 (1970), 178–186.

[194] Newton, *The Principia: Mathematical Principles of Natural Philosophy*, tr. I. Bernard Cohen and Anne Whitman (Berkeley, 1999), bk 1, sec. 11, Scholium (p. 589); Definition 8 (p. 408). Newton to Oldenburg, 6 Feb. 1676, *Correspondence* 1, 96. On these features of Newton's method see Ernan McMullin, 'Conceptions of Science in the Scientific Revolution', in David Lindberg and Robert Westman (eds.), *Reappraisals of the Scientific Revolution* (Cambridge, 1990), pp. 27–92, esp. pp. 67–70.

[195] See, e.g., Andrew Cunningham, 'How the *Principia* got its Name: Or, Taking Natural Philosophy Seriously', *History of Science* 28 (1991), 377–92; 'Getting the Game Right: Some Plain Words on the Identity and Invention of Science', *Studies in History and Philosophy of Science* 19 (1998), 365–89; Peter Dear, 'The Mathematical Principles of Natural Philosophy: Toward a Heuristic Narrative for the Scientific Revolution', *Configurations* 6 (1998), 173–93.

transgression was Newton's apparent assumption that he could practice a demonstrative science while dispensing with the essentialism upon which such a procedure typically depended.[196] We are now in a position to see a further source of apparent inconsistency: Newton had combined two approaches – 'rationalist/mathematical' and 'experimental' – that had arisen as distinct and arguably mutually inconsistent ways of making knowledge in a fallen world. These approaches had been separated not only on account of lingering Aristotelian prejudices about the separate subject matters of mathematics and natural philosophy, but also because they were based on divergent assessments of our post-lapsarian mental capacities. Small wonder, perhaps, that Newton's natural philosophy can be characterised as 'incomprehensible' and 'incoherent'.[197]

Newton's general approach to the question of method represents a significant point of departure from what had come before. Rather than seeking foundations for knowledge, as Bacon and Descartes had done, he sought ways of rendering the world intelligible by whatever combination of approaches seemed to work. This meant (in addition to seeking scientific knowledge in ancient texts and arcane alchemical practices) exploiting both experimental and mathematical methods, even though each of these approaches had originally been inspired by quite different estimates of the capacities of fallen human minds and of the intelligibility of the fallen world. What for others would have amounted to an inconsistent combination of methods was possible for Newton because he was not constrained by any specific theological doctrine of epistemological incapacity. In other words, he had no interest in showing how his method was consistent with a particular theological anthropology. His theological concern lay elsewhere. As he famously wrote in the *Opticks*, by pursuing his method it might be possible to 'know by natural Philosophy what is the first Cause'.[198] Given that uncovering the designs of God was one of his principal objects, his approach to the natural world could be said to be hermeneutical rather than

---

[196] Dear, 'Method and the Study of Nature', pp. 166–70.

[197] Rob Iliffe, 'Butter for Parsnips: Authorship, Audience and the Incomprehensibility of the *Principia*', in M. Biagioli and P. Galison (eds.), *Scientific Authorship: Credit and Intellectual Property in Science* (London, 2003), pp. 33–65.

[198] Newton, *Opticks*, p. 405. Cf. 'General Scholium', *Principia*, p. 943; Keynes MS 7, fol. 1r. For Newton's commitment to natural theology see I. Bernard Cohen, 'Isaac Newton's *Principia*, the Scriptures and the Divine Providence', in Sidney Morgensbesser et al. (eds.), *Philosophy, Science and Method* (New York, 1969), pp. 523–48; Michael Ben-Chaim, 'The Discovery of Natural Goods: Newton's Vocation as an "Experimental Philosopher"', *BJHS* 34 (2001), 395–416; Stephen Snobelen, 'To Discourse of God: Isaac Newton's Heterodox Theology and his Natural Philosophy', in Paul Wood (ed.), *Science and Dissent in England, 1688–1945* (Aldershot, 2004), pp. 39–65. Newton, however, was a more cautious natural theologian than many Newtonians.

epistemological. For this reason he elaborated related sets of rules for the interpretation of scripture and the interpretation of nature.[199] In pursuing these interpretative strategies Newton showed himself to be interested less in re-establishing a lost dominion over nature than in uncovering some underlying uniformity and intelligibility that would in turn point to the power and wisdom of God.

The past few decades have seen a number of attempts to relate Newton's heterodox religious views to his natural philosophy.[200] Certainly, the general point can be made that Newton's natural philosophical pursuits were at least partly motivated by his religious convictions. This, however, would also be true for most of his contemporaries, and falls short of establishing a connection between specific religious convictions and the content of natural philosophy. Some commentators have proposed a connection between Newton's extreme and heterodox monotheism and his apparent theological voluntarism. Newton's God is a God of dominion, who directly controls the creation without the need for the second person of the Trinity mediating between God and his creation.[201] But as I have argued elsewhere, Newton's voluntarism is questionable and in any case voluntarism is entirely consistent with Trinitarian theology.[202] The considerations set out above hint at a possible alternative way of connecting Newton's heterodoxy to his philosophy. It was Newton's rejection of the deity of Christ that indirectly led to his agnosticism about the fallen state of human nature. This in turn enabled him to combine two methodological principles that arose out of conflicting theological anthropologies. The essentially 'optimistic' premises of mathematical natural philosophy are brought together with the 'pessimistic' programme of experimental philosophy in a way possible

---

[199] On parallels between Newton's biblical hermeneutics (his 'Rules of Interpretation') and his natural philosophical method ('rules of reasoning in philosophy' in the *Principia*), see Stephen Snobelen, '"God of gods, and lord of lords": The Theology of Isaac Newton's General Scholium to the *Principia*', *Osiris* 16 (2001), 169–208; M. Mamiani, 'The Rhetoric of Certainty: Newton's Method in Science and in the Interpretation of the Apocalypse', in M. Pera and W. R. Shea (eds.), *Persuading Science* (Canton, OH, 1991), pp. 157–72. Peter Redpath, *Masquerade of the Dream Walkers: Prophetic Theology from the Cartesians to Hegel* (Amsterdam: 1998), pp. 18f.; Scott Mandelbrote, '"A Duty of the Greatest Moment": Isaac Newton and the Writing of Biblical Criticism', *BJHS* 26 (1993), 281–302.

[200] Ayval Lesham, *Newton on Mathematics and Spiritual Purity* (Dordrecht, 2003); James E. Force, 'The Nature of Newton's "Holy Alliance" between Science and Religion: From the Scientific Revolution to Newton (and Back Again)', in Osler (ed.), *Rethinking the Scientific Revolution*, pp. 247–70; Snobelen, 'To Discourse of God'.

[201] See especially James Force, 'Newton's God of Dominion: The Unity of Newton's Theological, Scientific and Political Thought', in Force and Popkin (eds.), *Essays on Newton's Theology*, pp. 75–102.

[202] Harrison, 'Was Newton a Voluntarist?'

only for someone lacking strong commitments to any of the prevailing models of theological anthropology. This lack of interest in anthropology – exceptional for his time – enabled him to construct an equally exceptional natural philosophical method. So Newton's theological heterodoxy did inform his natural philosophy insofar as it enabled him to adopt more easily methodologies that were ultimately incompatible with the more conventional theological positions of his contemporaries.

The state of human nature in light of the Fall was important for Boyle and Locke, even though they tended to diminish its role as a significant inhibitor of learning. Ultimately it is not important that Locke diverges from the strong view of inherited incapacity. What is significant is that the prevalence of such a view within his social milieu forced him to reflect critically on the mind and its limitations. If he was eventually to demur from the common view of the original causes of the debilitation of the mind, he nonetheless affirmed the inherent weakness of the mind and the limited scope of its reach. This is to say that his anthropology was consistent with what had been expressed throughout the century. As he himself put it, what we were able to discover in 'our present condition' with 'dull and weak' faculties was rather modest: 'We are able, by our senses, to know and distinguish things; and to examine them so far, as to apply them to our uses, and several ways to accommodate the exigencies of this life . . . But it appears not, that God intended we should have a perfect, clear, and adequate knowledge.'[203] In downplaying the significance of the Fall as an account of how we came to be in this state, Locke was in essence 'naturalising' our corrupt and weak condition. Michael Losonsky rightly suggests that Locke's strategy 'was to accept the curse as an unavoidable characteristic of human beings'.[204] But however it subsequently came to be theorised, this acceptance of the limitations of knowledge was to become a crucial feature of modern experimental science, much of the success of which relies upon the modesty of its ambitions and its capacity to ask the 'small question'. Equally, without the residual influence of the eschatological orientation of the seventeenth-century Protestants, along with Calvinist notions of vocation, the usefulness of earthly works, and the need to progress gradually towards the human transformation of the natural and social realms, this account of human nature might have degenerated into a quiescent scepticism.

[203] Locke, *Essay* II.xxiii.12 (I, 402).
[204] Michael Losonsky, 'Locke on Meaning and Signification', in G. A. J. Rogers (ed.), *Locke's Philosophy: Content and Context* (Oxford, 1996), pp. 123–42.

Newton's approach signals a more significant departure from the original justifications of experimental natural philosophy. But this is not a consequence of any diminution in the significance of theological considerations in the sphere of natural philosophy. Newton's stance, along with that of Boyle, is indicative of a gradual move away from theological anthropology towards a more exclusive focus on physico-theology.[205] The capacity of both experimental and mathematical natural philosophy to provide evidence of divine providence and design became more important than whether their respective epistemological foundations were in accord with theological conceptions of human nature. This development can be partly explained by the fact that one of the original concerns of those advancing anthropological justifications of their methods had been to critique the putatively naïve and uncritical methods of Aristotelianism, and do so within a context of post-Reformation debates about the extent of the damage wrought by the Fall. With experimental and mathematical methods now more secure, and Aristotelianism less so, attention could be directed away from theological foundations towards theological outcomes. The religious legitimacy of the new forms of knowledge increasingly came to rest on their capacity to deliver a robustly theistic view of the natural world, rather than on whether their methods accorded with a quite specific conception of human nature. Regarding the latter issue, it was also the case that the consensus that had once existed amongst English Protestants on the nature and extent of original sin was slowly dissolving. This is evident in the vigorous debates of the second half of the century, in the rise of Socinianism, in Newton's studious ignoring of the whole issue, and in the fact that Boyle and Locke sought to move the problem of intellectual incapacity out of the context of discussions of the Fall and into a more broad metaphysical framework. Equally important is the fact that there is considerable tension between arguments to the effect that divine design can be discerned in the natural world, and claims that the world is fallen and that we have lost the capacity to interpret it. The strong sense of the fallenness of human beings and their world that is characteristic of Calvinism has often been accompanied by an ambivalence about natural theology or even downright hostility towards it.[206] The claim that design is evident in the world assumes both the intelligibility of nature and our minds' capacity to detect that intelligibility. Both sit uneasily with a strong view of the Fall and its noetic consequences. Already in Boyle we see that the pendulum has begun to swing away from an emphasis on original sin towards physico-theology. This continues with Newton, although,

---

[205] Israel, *Radical Enlightenment*, pp. 456–63.   [206] The locus classicus for this tension is Rom. 1:20.

like Boyle, he was content to exploit an experimental method that owed its origins to a theological position to which he no longer subscribed.

It is partly on account of Newton's unparalleled achievements in the sphere of natural philosophy that there has been a tendency for historians to view the theological interactions between science and religion in seventeenth-century England in terms of Newtonianism and subsequent eighteenth-century developments.[207] This has meant that the dominant theme in discussions of that relation has been the rise of physico-theology and the quest for evidence of design in nature. This vision has been broadened somewhat by the work of Charles Webster and others, who have added the dimension of Protestant eschatology to the picture. My contention has been that a vital third theological component has been consistently overlooked in these discussions. It is now time to accord theological anthropology a significant place in the articulation and defence of early modern experimental philosophy.

This is not to say that the difference between the two traditions brought into an uneasy partnership by Newton were immediately forgotten. The divide between English experimentalism and the more speculative approach of such Continental figures as Descartes, Spinoza, and Leibniz was deep seated and remained a central feature of the rhetoric of the respective camps. The latter thinkers, whose 'rationalism' is typically contrasted with British 'empiricism', expressed considerable impatience with the mass of observations and experiments demanded by the Baconian regimen, and were disappointed by the modesty of the conclusions drawn from them.[208] Leibniz, presuming to speak for them all, complained that the Baconian method, as exemplified by Boyle's practice, was tedious, labour intensive, and ultimately insufficient to provide the kind of certainty that genuine science required. In a lengthy but revealing passage he expresses what he sees to be the essential difference between the respective approaches:

The art of discovering the causes of phenomena, or genuine hypotheses, is like that of deciphering: an inspired guess often provides a generous short-cut. Lord Bacon started putting the art of experimenting into the form of rules, and the Honourable Robert Boyle was a gifted practitioner of it. But unless we add to that

---

[207] This is equally true for issues of method which sometimes assume the existence of a univocal Newtonian tradition. See Paul Wood, 'Science, Philosophy and the Mind', in Roy Porter (ed.), *The Cambridge History of Science, vol. vi: Eighteenth Century Science* (Cambridge, 2003), pp. 800–24, esp. p. 824.

[208] Spinoza, Letter to Oldenburg, April 1662, *The Collected Works of Spinoza*, ed. and tr. Edwin Curley (Princeton, 1985), I, 178. See also Israel, *Radical Enlightenment*, pp. 253–6; M. B. Hall, *Robert Boyle on Natural Philosophy: An Essay with Selections from his Writings* (Bloomington, 1966), p. 43.

the art of using experiments and of drawing conclusions from them, we can lay
out a king's ransom and still achieve less than an acute thinker could discover in
a moment. M. Descartes, who certainly fits that description, said something to
the same effect in one of his letters, referring to the English Chancellor's method.
And Spinoza (whom I am quite prepared to quote when he says something good)
offered a similar reflection in one of his letters to the Secretary of the Royal Society
of England, the late Mr Oldenburg; it was published among the posthumous works
of that discerning Jew. He was commenting on a work of Mr Boyle's, who, it must
be said, does spend rather too long on drawing from countless fine experiments
no conclusion except one which he could have adopted as a principle, namely that
everything in nature takes place mechanically – a principle which can be made
certain by reason alone, and never by experiments, however many of them one
conducts.[209]

A natural philosophy based on 'inspired guesses', on what 'an acute thinker
could discover in a moment', and principles 'made certain by reason alone',
as contrasted with 'countless fine experiments' amounts to a significant difference over the powers of the mind, or, at the very least, the causes of its
propensity for error. This, in turn, may be attributed to a different reading
of Adam's incapacity following his Fall – one that insists that fallen human
minds still retain something of their access to divine ideas. As we have
seen, by the end of the seventeenth century the explicit theological justifications for experimentation were already being written out of accounts of
scientific method. Nonetheless, the divide between the methods of inspired
guesswork and experimentation persisted. In the middle of the eighteenth
century David Hume, who had little time for the doctrines of the Fall
and original sin, would still defend English experimentalism against the
'other scientific method' in terms of the former being more in keeping with
the imperfections of human nature. In a passage from his *Enquiry into the
Principles of Morals* (1751) he nicely sets out the key issues:

we can only expect success, by following the experimental method, and deduc-
ing general maxims for a comparison of particular instances. The other scientific
method, where a general abstract principle is first established, and is afterwards
branched out into a variety of inferences and conclusions, may be more perfect in
itself, but suits less the imperfection of human nature and is a common source of
illusion . . .[210]

[209] Leibniz, *New Essays on Human Understanding* IV.12, ed. and tr. Peter Remnant and Jonathan Bennett
(Cambridge, 1981), p. 454. For Spinoza's letter see *Collected Works* I, 182.
[210] David Hume, *An Enquiry into the Principles of Morals*, ed. L. A. Selby-Bigge, 3rd edn revised by
P. H. Nidditch (Oxford, 1975), p. 174.

Notably absent from Hume's remarks is reference to a theological account of human imperfection. In time, even the more general theme of cognitive limitation was to disappear from such methodological reflections, and the last traces of the theological origins of this approach were erased. Henceforth, experimentation will present itself as a central and relatively unproblematic feature of modern science.

Conclusion

One of the crowning glories of the Victorian Gothic revival is London's Natural History Museum in South Kensington. When the museum first opened in 1881, a terracotta statue of Adam overlooked proceedings from a vantage point at the pinnacle of the most lofty gable. Whether this was the original conception of the designer, Alfred Waterhouse, or of the chief scientific sponsor of the museum, Richard Owen, is not known. But whatever the origins of the idea, it was a fitting symbolic gesture. Much as the protoplast had surveyed the creation, named and classified the creatures, and bent them to his ends, those who now laboured within the confines of the museum also sought to bring order to the unruly diversity of nature and to organise the whole of the living world into a kind of material encyclopaedia. As recent visitors to the museum may be aware, the original statue of Adam can no longer be seen, for some time after the end of World War II it was toppled from its commanding position – whether an accident, an act of mindless vandalism, or an ideological statement, has never been ascertained.[1] This particular fall of Adam might also be vested with symbolic significance, for the twentieth century witnessed the final stages of the secularisation of scientific knowledge, along with the development of a degree of historical amnesia about the role of religion in its early modern origins. Of course, already in the Victorian era, in spite of its symbolic recognition of our first father, there had been a major reassessment of the mythology surrounding Adam and his status as a scientist. In one of the lengthy 'dissertations' of the eighth edition of the *Encyclopaedia Britannica* (1853), Richard Whately made this observation about primitive knowledge:

The earliest history of mankind, by far, that we possess, is that contained in the book of Genesis. It is extremely brief and scanty; especially the earliest portion of

---

[1] Colin Cunningham, *The Terracotta Designs of Alfred Waterhouse* (London, 2000), p. 15; Carla Yanni, *Nature's Museums: Victorian Architecture and the Culture of Display* (Baltimore, 1999), pp. 142f. The portal sculpture of the Oxford University Museum also depicts Adam. See Yanni, *Nature's Museums*, p. 86.

it. But it plainly represents the first of the human race, when in the Garden of Eden, as receiving direct communications from God. We have no detailed account, however, of the instruction they received; and even part of what the history does record is but obscurely intimated.[2]

Whately expresses no overt scepticism regarding the biblical account of the creation, nor even of the idea that Adam was the recipient of divine communications. He does point out, however, that we have no idea what information God impressed upon Adam, implying that the issue of Adamic science is irrelevant for those currently engaged in the pursuit of learning. The knowledge of the patriarch is revisited in the article on astronomy. Here, the account of the pillars of Seth is given short shrift. Josephus, it is pointed out, ascribed the origins of astronomy to 'the antediluvian patriarchs'. But as for the pillars which preserved this ancient wisdom: 'The fables relating to the two columns of brick and marble which these sages are said to have erected, and on which they engraved the elements of their astronomy, to preserve them from the universal destruction by fire and water to which, they are said to have learned from Adam, the earth was doomed, are not worth the trouble of repetition.'[3] Although deemed not worthy of repetition, the 'fables' are nonetheless repeated, presumably because they still retained some cultural authority. The tradition about Adamic science and its subsequent fate was thus taken seriously, if only for the purposes of relegating it to the margins of intellectual life. Given the prevalence of the idea of Adamic science in the early modern period, we should not be surprised to discover its lingering presence in the nineteenth century. Indeed, faint reverberations of these early modern ideas about the debilitation of reason by original sin have persisted in the thinking of those influenced by Reformation theology even in the twentieth century.[4]

[2] Richard Whately, 'Rise, Progress, and Corruptions of Christianity', *The Encyclopaedia Britannica, or Dictionary of Arts, Sciences, and General Literature*, 8th edn (Edinburgh, 1852–60), I, 449. The 'dissertations' were meant to cover broad topics, thus providing some thematic continuity, as opposed to the individual entries which dealt with quite specific topics.

[3] *Encyclopaedia Britannica* (1853), III, 781.

[4] The Dutch Calvinist theologian Abraham Kuyper (1837–1920) suggested that had it not been for sin, controversy in the sciences would be unknown. On account of sin, disharmony has been generated with the human being, and human understanding has been 'darkened'. Abraham Kuyper, *Principles of Sacred Theology* (Grand Rapids, 1980), pp. 78, 83, 175; Del Ratzsch, 'Abraham Kuyper's Philosophy of Science', *Calvin Theological Journal* 27 (1992), 277–303. The mathematical philosophy of Kuyper's countryman, L. E. J. Brouwer (1881–1966), seems also to have been informed by the notion of a fall from grace. Brouwer attributed the imperfections of the mathematical sciences to a generic defect in the human condition. See 'Consciousness, Philosophy and Mathematics', in *Proceedings of the Tenth International Congress of Philosophy* (Amsterdam, 1949), II, 1235–49. I am grateful to Eric James for drawing my attention to Brouwer's views. See also D. H. Th. Vollenhoven, *De Noodzakelijkheid eener Christelijke Logica* [The Necessity of a Christian Logic] (Amsterdam, 1932).

That sacred history was marginalised in discussions of the basis of scientific knowledge is not particularly surprising. The uneasy relationship between the rational principle of design and the more fragile historical concept of the Fall was resolved in favour of the former. With the rise of historical criticism in the nineteenth century, the meaning of biblical narratives came to be understood in the context of the imagined social milieu in which they had originally circulated. The idea that these stories provided a unique and privileged perspective on universal history became increasingly difficult to sustain. In any case, as was apparent even in the late seventeenth century, the cognitive limitations of the human mind, once acknowledged, could be provided with alternative metaphysical explanations. The fallibility of human minds could thus be attributed to our particular station in the chain of being, or regarded as a necessary consequence of free will, and these could replace explanations that made reference to a primeval fall from perfection. Nonetheless, the significance of the Fall narrative and of theological debates about the extent of our debilitation as the result of sin had been that they focused attention on the basic question of the limits of the mind, and thus promoted critical epistemologies and the quest for solid foundations upon which to construct knowledge.

It is a curious irony that with the advent of the theory of evolution by natural selection an alternative myth became available to account for the flaws in our knowledge-making processes. According to evolutionary epistemology, our minds have evolved primarily for the purpose of promoting the survival of the species. Hence, like other minds, they are not geared towards truth, *per se*, but rather, to the preservation of the organism. Any capacity to intuit ultimate truths about the universe would, on this account, be an accidental by-product of the evolution of the brain. Intriguingly, evolutionary epistemology rehearses two themes that were prevalent in the seventeenth century: first, that the early history of human beings provides important insights into the present functioning of our mental apparatus; second, that as Descartes stressed, the survival of the body is an important consideration in any discussion of how our minds have been 'designed' – whether by God or the processes of natural selection – to operate.[5] It is also curious that the notion of a fundamental flaw in human character has been preserved in popular works of anthropology, sociobiology, and evolutionary psychology – disciplines that are not noted for their congruity with theology. Since the appearance of Konrad Lorenz's *On Aggression* (1963), a number of authors have pointed to the inherent aggression of human beings,

---

[5] Descartes, *Meditations*, CSM II, 57.

attributing it to our bestial origins.[6] This theory of innate aggression, one anthropologist has complained, is simply 'original sin revisited'.[7] Most recently Steven Pinker has joined the discussion in *The Blank Slate: The Modern Denial of Human Nature* (2002), in which he echoes some of the views of such earlier popularisers as Lorenz and suggests that the findings of sociobiology (such as they are) have something in common with traditional Christian views of human nature. Belatedly, some theologians have also noted affinities between some of the doctrines of sociobiology and the idea of original sin.[8]

To say more about the earlier period that has been the subject of this book, however, it should by now be clear that the myth of Adam and the idea of a Fall were ubiquitous features of seventeenth-century discussions of knowledge and its foundations, particularly in the English context. This is the most general thesis of the book, and I take it to be fairly well established. One possible explanation for this situation is that those proposing new foundations for knowledge sought to vest their schemes of knowledge with theological legitimacy, and thus appealed to this basic tenet of Christian doctrine. There is undoubtedly some truth in this explanation, but it fails to account for why new foundations for knowledge were sought in the first place and why they took the particular forms they did. The experimental approach to the study of nature was in many respects counter-intuitive, and the application of mathematics to the physical world was also unprecedented in important respects. The more ambitious claim of this book, then, has been that the event of the Protestant Reformation, the crisis of authority that it precipitated, and the new theological anthropology that it promoted, together challenged the Aristotelian-scholastic dominance of human learning and necessitated the establishment of new foundations for knowledge. Of particular importance were the reformers' views of human nature, which amounted to a revival of elements of Augustine's theological anthropology. Along with these, the Protestant emphasis on the historical

[6] Konrad Lorenz, *Das sogenannte Böse: zur Naturgeschichte der Aggression* (1963); Eng. trans., *On Aggression* (London, 1966). Cf. Robert Ardrey, *African Genesis* (London, 1961); Desmond Morris, *The Naked Ape* (London, 1967). Also see Bernhard Kleeberg, 'Die vitale Kraft der Aggression: Evolutionistische Theorien des bösen Affen "Mensch"', in Ulrich Bröckling et al. (eds.), *Disziplinen des Lebens. Zwischen Anthropologie, Literatur und Politik* (Tübingen, 2004), pp. 203–22.

[7] M. F. Ashley Montagu, 'The New Litany of "Innate Depravity", or Original Sin Revisited', in A. Montagu (ed.), *Man and Aggression*, 2nd edn (New York: Harper and Rowe, 1973), pp. 3–18.

[8] Steven Pinker, *The Blank Slate: The Modern Denial of Human Nature* (London, 2002). For a theologian on these issues see Patricia Williams, *Doing without Adam and Eve: Sociobiology and Original Sin* (Minneapolis, 2001).

sense of biblical narratives made Adam a central figure in a wide range of discussions relating to science, technology, politics, and religion.

Of all the new systems of knowledge of the seventeenth century, it is experimental philosophy that is most indebted to Calvinist ideas of human nature. Here we encounter a critical scrutiny of human faculties along with frank appraisals of their inherent limitations. But this apparently pessimistic assessment was combined with a remarkable optimism about what could be achieved if limited human capabilities were acknowledged, accounted for, and guided in their efforts by a carefully specified methodological regimen. The commitment to the pursuit of knowledge and technology was thus tempered by the realisation that this knowledge would be but partial and probable, that it would be attained only after much drudgery and labour, and that it would require the coordinated efforts of many individuals. These notions occupy a vitally important place in the genealogy of modern science, and they remain as features of the scientific enterprise to the present. It is thus the recognition of the radically circumscribed nature of human knowledge that has made possible the advances of modern science. Exponents of the virtues of empirical knowledge have come to a common agreement that the key to doing science, as historian Jon Roberts has expressed it, is to 'think small'.[9] This 'key', I have suggested, originates in the new and critical appraisals of human nature associated with the Reformation and the early modern resurgence of Augustinianism. This interpretation of the origins of experimental science runs contrary to a long-standing view, first articulated by French *philosophes*, that associates the origins of science with a new and unqualified faith in the powers of reason. More recently, in explaining why science emerged in Western Christendom (and not in Islamic or Chinese culture), Toby Huff has reiterated this common view: 'Insofar as science is concerned, individuals must be conceived to be endowed with reason, the world must be thought to be a rational and consistent whole, and various levels of universal representation, participation, and discourse must be available.'[10] Sociologist Rodney Stark has similarly spoken of the 'victory of reason', which supposedly accounts for the scientific superiority of the West.[11] My suggestion is that these

---

[9] Jon H. Roberts and James Turner, *The Sacred and the Secular University* (Princeton, 2000), p. 36.

[10] Toby Huff, *The Rise of Early Modern Science: Islam, China and the West*, 2nd edn (Cambridge, 2003), p. 219.

[11] Rodney Stark, *The Victory of Reason: How Christianity Led to Freedom, Capitalism and Western Success* (New York, 2005); *For the Glory of God: How Monotheism Led to Reformations, Science, Witch-Hunts and the End of Slavery* (Princeton, 2004).

interpretations are misleading in at least two respects, for experimentalism was justified by appeals to the fallibility of reason and the opacity of nature.

It is true, however, that the experimental philosophy was not the only response to the early modern problem of knowledge. There were also those who sought to identify some aspect of human nature that would be impervious to the corrupting effects of the Fall. Individuals such as Kepler and Descartes found what they believed to be an impeccable source of knowledge in the light of reason, understood as the image of God. This so-called rationalist tradition was no less a response to the crisis of knowledge than was the experimental philosophy. While in certain respects this position is closer to the uncritical epistemologies of Aristotle and Thomas Aquinas, its proponents nonetheless posed critical questions about human knowledge, and looked for a source of indubitable truths. Ultimately they were each to circumvent fallible human capacities and vest the certainty of their systems of knowledge in God. This is most obvious in Malebranche, for whom the most secure knowledge was only so because it entailed participation in the divine mind.[12] Galileo had earlier expressed a similar view about our knowledge of mathematical truths, while Kepler also believed that we could have confidence in an *a priori* demonstration of the nature of the universe because God's geometrical plan was directly accessible through the light of nature that persisted even in fallen human beings. Descartes also grounded his epistemological project in a God known through the light of nature. The quest for certitude led to mathematics. Both Kepler and Descartes were to assert the reality of mathematical relations – Kepler on account of his Platonist commitments, Descartes because he believed that God had created mathematical relations. In this respect they rejected the Aristotelian contention, reflected in the Thomist organisation of the sciences, that mathematics is a human abstraction, and thus without a role in pure natural philosophy. This, then, was an alternative solution to the sceptical crisis provoked by the Reformation, but one equally important in the lineage of modern science, for it established a place for a genuinely mathematical physics, the best-known example of which is Newton's *Philosophiae naturalis principia mathematica* (Mathematical Principles of Natural Philosophy, 1687).

As we have seen, Newton is in certain respects a poor exemplar for a thesis that stresses the importance of the Fall in the development and acceptance

---

[12] Malebranche, *Search for Truth*, Preface (p. xxxvii); III.ii.6 (p. 231); Nicholas Jolley, 'Intellect and Illumination in Malebranche', *Journal of the History of Philosophy* 32 (1994), 209–24; Tad Schmaltz, 'Malebranche on Ideas and the Vision in God', in Steven Nadler (ed.), *The Cambridge Companion to Malebranche* (Cambridge, 2000), pp. 58–86.

of experimental philosophy. In spite of his famous profession to 'fain no hypotheses' and his apparent humility when it came to postulating the causes of phenomena, there were elements of his natural philosophy that seemed to smack of the dogmatic and speculative attitudes of the Cartesians. He also seemed still to cherish the ambition of a demonstrative and certain science. However, these apparent inconsistencies can be explained partly by his indifference to the anthropological considerations that had led his contemporaries to opt for either mathematical demonstration or experimental probability but not both. Newton does share with Boyle and the other experimentalists a conviction that the realm of nature is not fully knowable – hence his refusal to speculate, in public at least, about the causes of gravity. On the other hand, he sought a degree of certainty in his mathematical physics more in keeping with the optimism of Descartes. Perhaps we may regard Newton as also emblematic of what Steven Shapin calls 'the fragmented knowledge-making legacies of the seventeenth century' and of the basic divide in which diffidence was opposed to ambition.[13] The question of whether science deals with idealised mathematical quantities, or whether it deals with facts garnered from accumulated observations or generated under experimental conditions, is a divide that remains with us to the present. In the seventeenth century, I have suggested, each of these options was proposed as a distinct solution to the difficulties generated by a renewed consciousness of human fallibility.

The fact that the second half of this book focuses almost exclusively on the development of experimental science in the English context leaves open a number of important questions about experiment and its justifications elsewhere in Europe during this period. While there is undoubtedly something quite distinctive about English experimental philosophy, and while it is also true that 'speculative' and mathematical forms of natural philosophy were more predominant in Continental Europe, it could hardly be said that experimental practices were restricted to English shores. Further investigation is needed in order to determine the extent to which, if at all, other centres of experiment framed their activities in similar theological terms. Italy, for example – a uniformly Catholic nation with an important experimental tradition – might seem to represent a major obstacle to any attempt to apply my general thesis more broadly. While a comparison of the rhetoric of experiment in these two national contexts is beyond the scope of this volume, it is worth pointing out that in at least some circumstances experiment played a rather different role in Italian natural philosophy. Galileo's

[13] Steven Shapin, *The Scientific Revolution* (Chicago, 1996), p. 117.

credentials as an experimentalist are not in doubt, yet he was critical of the 'experimental history' approach of Englishman William Gilbert's *De Magnete* (1600). He wished that Gilbert were 'more of the mathematician' and complained that his results 'are not rigorous, and lack that force which must unquestionably be present in those adduced as necessary and eternal scientific conclusions'.[14] Such criticism is consistent with an 'optimistic' reading of human nature and its capabilities, and is also suggestive of a different role for experiment. The very possibility of a natural philosophy that was both experimental and, at the same time, capable of arriving at necessary and certain truths was denied by most English experimental philosophers on the grounds of epistemic impairment. Galileo himself, it must be said, never really resolved the problem of how his lofty conception of science, which still bore the impress of traditional Aristotelian ideals, might be made consistent with the contingent results of contrived experiments.[15] In England a resolution of this problem was achieved simply by abandoning the requirement that natural philosophy be a demonstrative science. The apparently robust experimentalism of the short-lived Accademia del Cimento which flourished in Florence between 1657 and 1667 might also appear as a counter-example to a thesis linking pessimistic theological anthropology with experimental natural philosophy. However, the reported experiments of the Cimento academicians, while superficially similar to those performed by Fellows of the Royal Society, did not have a comparable epistemic status to those of their English counterparts. Crudely put, reports of experiments were designed to persuade others of natural philosophical positions held on other grounds.[16] These brief remarks are not intended as a substitute for further in-depth studies of the relationship between theology and experimental natural philosophy in other national contexts, but they do suggest that carefully attending to different meanings and uses of 'experiment' might obviate what seem to be *prima facie* objections to applications of the thesis of this book beyond the English context.

If experimental practices of various kinds were not confined within the borders of England, neither were commitments to Calvinist anthropology. While the discrete set of theological beliefs that I have associated with the rise of experimental natural philosophy in England may have been exclusive to that country, broadly similar views could be found elsewhere in Europe. Again, it would not be unreasonable to inquire whether such

[14] Galileo, *Dialogue concerning the Two Chief World Systems*, p. 471.
[15] Dear, *Discipline and Experience*, p. 127.
[16] See especially Luciano Boschiero, 'Natural Philosophical Contention in the Accademia del Cimento: The Properties and Effects of Heat and Cold', *Annals of Science* 60 (2003), 329–49.

theological views correlate with the kind of experimentalism so enthusiastically promoted in England. Did Dutch Calvinism, for example, give rise to a similar culture of experiment, defended in terms of a comparable theological understanding of human nature? Some aspects of the history of natural philosophy in the Netherlands support an affirmative answer to this question. Thus, Gisbert Voetius explicitly criticised Cartesian claims for the certainty of clear and distinct ideas on the grounds that in the postlapsarian state, no man is free from error.[17] But Voetius could not be regarded as an advocate of experimental methods. If anything, he was a rather conservative defender of Aristotelian science. In any case, there was another Calvinist faction in the Dutch republic that actually favoured Cartesian science. This suggests that there were additional cultural forces at work here that had a bearing on the way in which theological doctrines were deployed in the contexts of natural philosophy. Once again, the nexus between experimental philosophy and Dutch Calvinism seems less simple than in the case of England, but on that account no less worthy of further investigation. It is surely significant, too, that the only surviving traces of the early modern doctrine of epistemic impairment are to be found in some present-day manifestations of the Dutch Reformed tradition.[18]

If the myth of the Fall played an important role in the emergence of science, it is also worth reflecting on whether it may have been important in the development of other characteristic features of Western modernity. As was the case with natural philosophy, such an influence may be difficult to discern. This is partly because one of the standard narratives attributes many of the distinctive features of modernity to the Enlightenment, the spirit of which, however defined, seems antipathetic to notions of a Fall and human incapacity. Moreover, from the late seventeenth century onwards there was a tendency to 'naturalise' the vices – both intellectual and moral – of a fallen humanity and to integrate them into a new view of human nature. This is already present in the thought of Boyle and Locke (and indeed Leibniz), for whom our intellectual infirmities are as well explained by our station in the scale of being as by the primitive history of the human race reported in scripture. Over the course of the eighteenth century our cognitive incapacities began to lose the moral disapprobation that they had

---

[17] Voetius, *Disputationes Theologicae Selectae*, 5 vols. (Utrecht, 1659), III, 701. For the Calvinist scepticism of Voetius see Theo Verbeek, 'From "Learned Ignorance" to Scepticism: Descartes and Calvinist Orthodoxy', and Ernestine van der Wall, 'Orthodoxy and Scepticism in the Early Dutch Enlightenment', both in Richard H. Popkin and Arjo Vanderjagt (eds.), *Scepticism and Irreligion in the Seventeenth and Eighteenth Centuries* (Leiden, 1993), pp. 31–45, 121–41.

[18] See n. 4 above. Also Alvin Plantinga, *Warranted Christian Belief* (Oxford, 2000), pp. 199–240.

once attracted on account of their association with the Fall. Indeed, in some cases it might even be said that moral valence of the consequences of sin was reversed. This is evident in the sphere of moral philosophy and its troubled disciplinary offspring, economics. The insatiability of human desire, once the distinctive mark of the fallen mind, became the signal feature of human existence to which could be attributed the origin of human society and the capitalist economy. Already in the third of his *Essais*, Pierre Nicole had pointed to the role played by calculating self-interest in the formation of societies. The self-love of fallen human beings, so strong an element of Augustinian anthropology, had led to cooperation, the development of societies, and the invention of many human amenities. However these communities, to use John Marshall's apt description, were 'economically thriving but vicious'.[19] Society could thus be based on a prudential self-interest, although Nicole's view was that the stability of such societies ultimately depended on a reorientation of self-love to love of God and love of others.

In the less palatable scheme of Bernard Mandeville (*c.* 1670–1733), human vice also provides a vital foundation for public welfare. In Mandeville's unforgettable formulation, private vices give rise to public benefits.[20] While this thesis outraged contemporary moral philosophers, it was a succinct and prescient statement of the foundations of modern economics. Mandeville insisted that 'not the Good and Amiable, but the Bad and Hateful qualities of Man, his Imperfections and the want of Excellencies which other creatures are endued with, are the first causes that made Man sociable beyond other Animals the moment he lost paradise'. Had man not fallen, Mandeville argues, he would never have become 'that sociable Creature he is today'. The very possibility of progress thus arises out of the 'multiplicity of desires' that typify our fallen condition, and the forces of nature that conspire against their gratification. These physical obstacles are similarly attributed to the Fall, for the Globe we inhabit resists our desires 'since it has been curs'd'.[21] Mandeville concludes that all 'Trade, Art, Science, Dignity or Employment' are the outcomes not of our 'Amiable Virtues', such as they are, but of our imperfections and the variety of our appetites.[22] Mandeville thus presents an account of the human condition that might have been drawn directly from Augustine himself. According to the latter, fallen man

---

[19] Marshall, *John Locke*, p. 178.
[20] Bernard Mandeville, *The Fable of the Bees: or Private Vices, Publick Benefits*, ed. F. B. Kayne, 2 vols. (Oxford, 1924), title page.
[21] *Ibid.*, I, 344.   [22] *Ibid.*, I, 346.

'pursues one thing after another, and nothing remains permanently with him. So what with his corn and wine and oil, his needs are so multiplied that he cannot find the one thing needful, a single and unchangeable nature, seeking which he would not err, and attaining which he would cease from grief and pain.'[23] But that which in Augustine is the occasion for regret and self-recrimination becomes for Mandeville the matter-of-fact foundation of human civilisation.

Adam Smith's better-known deliberations on the same topic proved to be more publicly acceptable, not least because Smith gave a more prominent role to human virtues in the production of social goods. Smith also gave due deference to the Deity in his invocation of 'the invisible hand'. Nonetheless, for Smith as for Mandeville human foibles provided the basis of sociability. Thus the human propensity for self-deceit – 'the fatal weakness of mankind' – was the engine of economic development:[24]

It is well that nature imposes on us in this manner. It is this deception which rouses and keeps in continual motion the industry of mankind. It is this which first prompted them to cultivate the ground, to build houses, to found cities and commonwealths, and to invent and improve all the sciences and arts . . .[25]

Again in Smith the fundamental human incapacity is naturalised. We are not precipitated into a deceiving world on account of our own culpability, for it is *nature* that imposes on us. This imposition, moreover, is the very condition of human progress.[26] The Fall becomes, as it was for many of the Church Fathers, a *felix culpa*, a 'fortunate flaw', and Smith's economic theory, like Descartes' epistemology, may be regarded as a theodicy. Indeed, as anthropologist Marshall Sahlins has pointed out, 'the genesis of economics was the economics of Genesis'. Wide-ranging human desires, to which Augustine and Luther had attributed the bondage of the will, became in modern liberal-bourgeois ideology the very condition of human freedom.[27] Economic historians have also drawn attention to the

[23] Augustine, *De Vera Religione* XXI.41 (PL 34, 139).
[24] Adam Smith, *The Theory of Moral Sentiments* III.4, ed. D. D. Raphael and A. L. Macfie (Oxford, 1976), pp. 156–61.
[25] *Ibid.*, IV.1.10 (p. 183).
[26] Some commentators argue that for Smith, human weaknesses are not a consequence of the Fall, but are deliberately planned by God to secure human happiness. See Lisa Hill, 'The Hidden Theology of Adam Smith', *European Journal of Economic Thought* 8 (2001), 1–29. Others have suggested that in stressing the social merits of human weakness, Smith is elaborating an Augustinian theodicy. Anthony Waterman, 'Economics as Theology: Adam Smith's *Wealth of Nations*', *Southern Economic Journal* 68 (2002), 907–21.
[27] Marshall Sahlins, 'The Sadness of Sweetness: The Native Anthropology of Western Cosmology', *Current Anthropology* 37 (1996), 395–428 (397f.). I am grateful to Marina Bollinger for drawing this

postlapsarian condition of human beings as the premise of economics. Lionel Robbins observes, in his celebrated formulation of the subject matter of Economic Science, that

We have been turned out of Paradise. We have neither eternal life nor unlimited means of gratification. Everywhere we turn, if we choose one thing we must relinquish others which, in different circumstances, we would wish not to have relinquished. Scarcity of means to satisfy ends of varying importance is an almost ubiquitous condition of human behaviour. Here, then, is the unity of the subject of economic science, the forms assumed by human behaviour in disposing of scarce means.[28]

In the history of the parent discipline of economics, moral philosophy, we also find the Fall and its consequences playing an important role. In classical morality the question of what one ought to do could be answered by identifying those actions that would promote the attainment of man's true end. Knowledge of the true end or final cause of human beings thus lay at the core of moral reasoning. In medieval Christian formulations, which brought together Aristotelian assumptions and Christian ethical doctrines, while moral imperatives would conform to divine injunctions communicated through revelation, this did not count against the fact that they could be known independently through reason by reference to man's final end. However, fallen reason, as the Reformers understood it, was incapable of discerning the final cause of human existence, and thus was useless as a guide to action. Alasdair MacIntyre has argued that this new conception of the depravity of reason, promoted by Protestants and Jansenists, accounts for the abject failure of eighteenth-century moral philosophy. For while on the one hand the Enlightenment inherited a set of moral precepts for which it had to provide rational justification, on the other hand it was heir to a newly impoverished reason that was totally inadequate for the task of constructing a coherent moral philosophy.[29] This, of course, assumes the failure of eighteenth-century moral philosophy – a reasonable enough assumption perhaps. However, it must be said that the intuitionist school represented an attempt to redress this problem by grounding moral philosophy in observations of human nature – hence, the 'experimental'

---

reference to my attention. Cf. Albert O. Hirschman, *The Passions and the Interests* (Princeton, 1997), pp. 15f., and passim.

[28] Lionel Robbins, *An Essay on the Nature and Significance of Economic Science*, 2nd edn (London, 1952), p. 15, cited in Sahlins, 'Sadness of Sweetness', 397. Cf. Hill, 'Sin and Society', p. 118.

[29] Alasdair MacIntyre, *After Virtue*, 2nd edn (Notre Dame, 1984), p. 53. On this general theme see especially Mark Painter, *The Depravity of Wisdom: The Protestant Reformation and the Disengagement of Knowledge from Virtue in Modern Philosophy* (Aldershot, 1999).

approach to morals that was thought to provide an alternative to the sanguine assumptions of the rationalists about the integrity of right reason, and its capacity to specify moral duties.

Turning to the history of philosophy more generally, it has been recently suggested by Stephen Mulhall that the myth of the Fall continued to exert a significant influence on the philosophy of late modernity. The thought of Nietzsche, Heidegger, and Wittgenstein, Mulhall argues, bears the unmistakable stamp of this Christian doctrine. These figures 'share a conception of human beings as standing in need of redemption', along with the conviction that 'we are flawed in our very structure and composition'. This is not the place to embark on a detailed analysis of Mulhall's interesting arguments, but there is surely some merit in his conclusion that 'it will be far more challenging than many seem to think to construct a conception of the human condition that genuinely transcends the Christian theological horizon within which Western culture has developed'.[30] Some measure of support for this contention comes from the reappearance of original sin in the guise of the 'scientific' thesis of innate aggression.

Some of the implications of the renewed focus on the fallenness of the human condition for the sphere of political philosophy have received attention in this book. Controversies about the most appropriate form of government frequently turned upon the original condition of human beings and what was required to constrain them in their present fallen state. There is, perhaps, a general case to be made for the importance of the idea of the Fall in the development of modern political institutions – institutions which have been often regarded as the products of an 'enlightened' view of human nature, of an emancipation of individuals from repressive religious conceptions and institutions, and of a growing faith in the powers of reason. Some brief observations have already been made about Hobbes's contractualism in this regard. It is intriguing that Jansenism has recently been recognised as having played a major role in the establishment of modern political institutions on the Continent. Jansenists are now credited with the expulsion of the Jesuits from France, and for having provided intellectual resources for resistance to the Monarchy. William Doyle suggests that this group is ultimately responsible for 'the "desacralization" of the monarchy which led to regicide, both before and after the French Revolution'.[31] As a consequence, the story of the origins of the French Enlightenment is being rewritten with

---

[30] Stephen Mulhall, *Philosophical Myths of the Fall* (Princeton, 2005), pp. 118, 120f.
[31] Doyle, *Jansenism*, p. 4. Cf. D. K. van Kley, *The Religious Origins of the French Revolution: From Calvin to the Civil Constitution, 1560–1791* (New Haven, 1996); J. W. Merrick, *The Desacralization of the French Monarchy in the Eighteenth Century* (Baton Rouge, 1992).

credit being diverted from the *philosophes* to those individuals, inspired by the ideas of Augustine, who most vigorously opposed them.

All of this suggests that if the considerations set out in this book are basically correct, there is a need for a revision of common assumptions about the connections between science, the Enlightenment, and modernity. The birth of modern experimental science was not attended with a new awareness of the powers and capacities of human reason, but rather the opposite – a consciousness of the manifold deficiencies of the intellect, of the misery of the human condition, and of the limited scope of scientific achievement. Equally, a common understanding of the origins of modernity, which assumes an intimate connection between science and secularisation, can be sustained only with a recapturing of the ancient notion of *saeculum*. For Augustine, the present age – the *saeculum senescens* – is to be understood as the interval between the incarnation and the second coming of Christ. There is a certain tension in this age of spiritual awakening, for while the divine plan of salvation has been revealed, history has yet to reach its predestined culmination.[32] The human institutions that characterise this epoch are recognisably deficient, yet for all that are divinely sanctioned for their limited purposes. Theologian John Milbank thus aptly describes the *saeculum* as 'the interval between the fall and *eschaton* where coercive justice, private property and impaired natural reason must make shift to cope with the unredeemed effects of sinful humanity'.[33] Science, for many of its seventeenth-century proponents, was one such deficient institution, motivated by a vision of Adamic wisdom that had once been, and would be again. For now, however, it was devoted to the generation of a makeshift knowledge that would alleviate some of the burdens of the human condition in the hope of a better future in both the present world and that which was to come.

---

[32] Augustine, *Two Books on Genesis against the Manichees* 1.23.40, *Augustine on Genesis*, tr. Ronald Teske, FaCh 84 (Washington DC, 1991), 86f. For discussions of Augustine's views see R. A. Marcus, *Saeculum: History and Society in the Theology of Augustine* (London, 1970); Mark Vessey, Karla Pollmann, and Allan D. Fitzgerald (eds.), *History, Apocalypse, and the Secular Imagination: New Essays on Augustine's City of God* (Bowling Green, OH, 1999); Eric Voegelin, *History of Political Ideas I: Hellenism, Rome, and Early Christianity*, in *Collected Works of Eric Voegelin*, xix (Columbia, 1997), pp. 211f. Already in the New Testament, there is a tension between what Rudolf Bultmann describes as the 'no longer' and the 'not yet'.

[33] John Milbank, *Theology and Social Theory: Beyond Secular Reason* (Oxford, 1990), p. 9.

Bibliography

PRIMARY SOURCES

Adams, Thomas, *Diseases of the Soule: A Discovrse Divine, Moral, and Physical* (London, 1616).

The Divells banket described in sixe sermons (London, 1613).

Agrippa von Nettesheim, Cornelius, *Opera*, 2 vols. (Lyons, n.d.).

Of the Vanitie and Vncertainty of Artes and Sciences, tr. James Sanford (London, 1569).

Three Books of Occult Philosophy (London, 1651).

Ainsworth, Henry, *Annotations on the First Five Bookes of Moses* (London, 1639).

Althusius, Johannes, *Politica* (1614) abridged edn, ed. and tr. F. Carney (Indianapolis, 1995).

Andrewes, Lancelot, *Apospasmatia Sacra* (London, 1657).

Anon., *Anthropologie Abstracted: or the Idea of Humane Nature* (London, 1655).

Luthers Predecessors: or, an Answer to the question of the Papists: Where was your Church Before Luther (London, 1624).

Philiatros (London, 1615).

The Apocrypha and Pseudepigrapha of the Old Testament, ed. R. H. Charles, 2 vols. (Oxford, 1977).

Aristotle, *The Complete Works of Aristotle*, ed. J. Barnes, 2 vols. (Princeton, 1984).

Augustine, *Augustine on Genesis*, tr. Ronald Teske, FaCh 84 (Washington DC, 1991).

City of God, tr. Marcus Dodd (New York, 1950).

On the Trinity, tr. Stephen Mackenna, FaCh 45 (Washington DC, 1992).

The Confessions, tr. H. Chadwick (Oxford, 1991).

The Works of Augustine, ed. John E. Rottelle, 20 vols. (New York, 1997–2000).

Austen, Ralph, *A Treatise of Fruit Trees* (London, 1657).

Ayloffe, William, *The Government of the Passions According to the Rules of Reason and Religion* (London, 1700).

B., R. [R. Bostocke?], *The Difference between the Auncient Phisicke . . . and the Latter Phisicke* (London, 1585).

Bacon, Francis, *De vijs mortis, Philosophical Studies, c. 1611–c. 1619*, ed. Graham Rees (Oxford, 1996).

The Major Works, ed. Brian Vickers (Oxford, 2002).

The Works of Francis Bacon, ed. James Spedding, Robert Ellis, and Douglas Heath, 14 vols. (London, 1857–74).

Bacon, Roger, *Fratris Rogeri Bacon De retardatione accidentium senectutis*, ed. A. Little and E. Withington (Oxford, 1928).

Opus minus, in *Opera Fr. Baconis hactenus inedita*, ed. J. S. Brewer (London, 1859).

The Opus Majus of Roger Bacon, tr. Robert Burke, 2 vols. (Whitefish, MT, 2002).

Baker, Thomas, *Reflections on Learning* (London, 1699).

Bamfield, Francis, *Miqra qadosh, The Holy Scripture* (London, 1684).

Barrough, Philip, *The Method of Phisicke* (London, 1583).

Barrow, Isaac, *The Usefulness of Mathematical Learning Explained and Demonstrated: being Mathematical Lectures read in the Publick Schools at the University of Cambridge*, tr. John Kirby (London, 1734).

Baxter, Richard, *The Judgment of Non-Conformists, of the Interest of Reason, in Matters of Religion* (London, 1676).

Two Disputations on Original Sin (London, 1675).

Beck, Cave, *The Universal Character* (London, 1657).

Bellarmine, Robert, *De Gratia Primi Hominis* (Heidelberg, 1612).

Biggs, Noah, *Matæotechnia Medicinae Praxeos. The Vanity of the Craft of Physick* (London, 1651).

Blith, Walter, *The English Improver Improved* (London, 1652).

Boehme, Jakob, *The Second Booke. concerning The Three Principles of The Divine Essence* (London, 1648).

The Way to Christ [1622], ed. P. Erb, Classics of Western Spirituality (New York, 1978).

Bonaventure, St, *Collations on the Six Days*, in *The Works of Bonaventure*, tr. J. de Vinck (Patterson, NJ, 1960–70), v, 291.

The Life of St Francis, in *Bonaventure: The Soul's Journey into God, The Tree of Life and The Life of St Francis*, tr. Ewert Cousins (London, 1978).

Bonde, William, *Pilgrymage of perfeccyon* (London, 1531).

Boyle, Robert, *The Excellency of Theology compar'd with Natural Philosophy* (London, 1674).

The Works of the Honourable Robert Boyle, ed. Thomas Birch, 6 vols. [1772] (Hildesheim, 1966).

Brett, Thomas, *A Chronological Essay on the Sacred History* (London, 1629).

Bright, Timothie, *A Discourse of Melancholie* (London, 1585).

Bromley, Thomas, *The Way to the sabbath of rest. Or, The souls progresse in the work of regeneration* (London, 1655).

Browne, Thomas, *Pseudodoxia Epidemica*, ed. Robin Robbins, 2 vols. (Oxford, 1981).

Works, ed. Geoffrey Keynes (London, 1928).

Brucker, Johann Jakob, *Historia critica philosophiae* (Leipzig, 1743).

Bucer, Martin, *Common Places of Martin Bucer*, tr. and ed. D. F. Wright (Appleford, 1972).

Buffon, Georges Louis Leclerc, Comte de, *Natural History, General and Particular*, tr. W. Smellie, 20 vols. (London, 1812).

Burches, George, *Mans Inbred Malady* (London, 1655).

Burgesse, Anthony, *The Doctrine of Original Sin* (London, 1658).

Burnet, Gilbert, *An Exposition of the XXXIX Articles of the Church of England* (London, 1699).

Burthogge, Richard, *Organum Vetus & Novum: Or, A Discourse of Reason and Truth* (London, 1678).

Burton, Robert, *The Anatomy of Melancholy*, ed. Thomas Faulker, Nicolas Kiessling and Rhonda Blair, 3 vols. (Oxford, 1989).

Calvin, John, *Calvin's Commentaries*, 22 vols. (Grand Rapids, 1984).
Institutes of the Christian Religion, tr. Henry Beveridge, 2 vols. (London, 1953).
Institutes of the Christian Religion, ed. John McNeill, tr. F. Battles, 2 vols. (Philadelphia, 1960).
Sermons on Psalm 119, tr. Thomas Stocker (London, 1580).

Cardano, Girolamo, *De rerum varietate* (Avignon, 1558).

Casaubon, Meric, *A Letter of Meric Casaubon, D. D. &c. to Peter du Moulin D. D., concerning Natural Experimental Philosophie* (Cambridge, 1669).

Cavendish, Margaret, *Further Observations upon Experimental Philosophy* (London, 1666).

Charleton, Walter, *The Darknes of Atheism Dispelled by the Light of Nature. A Physico-theological Treatise* (London, 1652).

Charron, Pierre, *De la Sagesse* (Paris, 1791).
Of Wisdom (London, 1609).
Of Wisdome (London, 1606).

Clarke, Samuel, *A Discourse concerning the Unchangeable Obligations of Natural Religion* (London, 1706).
Discourse upon Natural Reason, in L. A. Selby-Bigge (ed.), *British Moralists*, 2 vols. (Dover, 1965).

Coles, William, *Adam in Eden: or, Natures Paradise* (London, 1657).

Comenius, Jan Amos, *A Patterne of Universall Knowledge*, tr. Jeremy Collier (London, 1651).
A Reformation of Schooles (London, 1642).
Naturall Philosophie Reformed by Divine Light: or, A synopsis of Physics (London, 1651).
The Way of Light of Comenius, tr. E. Campagnac (London, 1938).

Comes [Conti], Natalis, *Mythologiae sive explicationis fabularum libri decem* (Venice, 1551).

Copernicus, Nicholas, *On the Revolutions*, ed. Jerzy Dobrzycki, tr. Edward Rosen (Baltimore, 1978).

Cordemoy, Géraud de, *A Discourse written to a Learned Frier* (London, 1670).

Croll, Oswald, *Of Signatures* (London, 1669).

Crooke, Helkiah, *MIKROKOSMOGRAFIA: A Description of the Body of Man* (London, 1615).

Cudworth, Ralph, *A Treatise concerning Eternal and Immutable Morality* (London, 1731).

The True Intellectual System of the Universe and A Treatise Concerning Eternal and Immutable Morality ed. John Harrison, 3 vols. (London, 1845).

Culpeper, Nicholas, *Complete Herbal* (Ware, 1995).

Culpeper, Thomas, *Morall Discourses and Essayes* (London, 1655).

Culverwell, Nathaniel, *An Elegant and Learned Discourse of the Light of Nature* (1652), ed. R. Greene and H. MacCallum (Indianapolis, 2001).

d'Alembert, Jean Le Rond, and Denis Diderot (eds.), *Encyclopédie, ou Dictionnaire Raisonné des Sciences, des Arts et des Métiers*, 35 vols. (Paris, 1751–72).

Dalgarno, George, *George Dalgarno on Universal Language: The Art of Signs (1661), the Deaf and Dumb Mans Tutor (1680), and the Unpublished Papers*, ed. David Cram and Jaap Maat (Oxford, 2001).

Daneau, Lambert, *A Dialogue of witches* (London, 1575).

Ethices Christianae libri tres (Geneva, 1577).

Isagoges Christianae pars quinta, quae est de homine (Geneva, 1588).

The Wonderfull Woorkmanship of the World (London, 1578).

Davenant, John, *Determinationes Quaestionum Quarundam Theologicarum* (Cambridge, 1634).

Dell, William, *The Tryal of Spirits Both in Teachers & Hearers* (London, 1653).

della Porta, Giambattista, *Natural Magick* (London, 1658).

Descartes, René, *Œuvres de Descartes*, ed. Charles Adam and Paul Tannery, 13 vols. (Paris, 1897–1913).

The Passions of the Soul, ed. and tr. S. Voss (Indianapolis, 1989).

The Philosophical Writings of Descartes, tr. John Cottingham, Robert Stoothoff, Dugald Murdoch, and Anthony Kenny, 3 vols. (Cambridge, 1984–91).

Dimsdale, William, *The Quaker converted; or the experimental knowledg of Jesus Christ crucified, in opposition to the principles of the Quakers* (London, 1690).

Diodati, John, *Pious and Learned Annotations upon the Holy Bible*, 2nd edn (London, 1648).

Du Bartas, Guillaume de Salluste, *Du Bartas his Divine Weekes and Workes* (London, 1641).

Duns Scotus, John, *Opera omnia*, 12 vols. (Lyons, 1638).

Durent, Claude, *Thrésor de l'histoire des langues de cest univers* (Yverdon, 1619).

Edwards, John, *A Demonstration of the Existence and Providence of God* (London, 1696).

Edwards, Jonathan, *The Works of Jonathan Edwards* (New Haven, 1957–).

Farley, Robert, 'June, or Mans Young Age', from *The Kalendar of Mans Life* (London, 1638).

Ferguson, Robert, *The Interest of Reason in Religion* (London, 1675).

Filmer, Robert, *Observations Concerning the Original of Government* (London, 1652).

Patriarcha; or the Natural Power of Kings (London, 1680), 2nd edn (London, 1685).

The Anarchy of a Limited or Mixed Monarchy, in *Filmer: Patriarcha and Other Writings*, ed. J. P. Sommerville (Cambridge, 1991).

Fischer, Kuno, *Geschichte der neueren Philosophie*, 6 vols. (Mannheim, 1860).

Metaphysik oder Wissenschaftslehre (Stuttgart, 1852).

Fludd, Robert, *Mosaicall Philosophy Grounded upon the Essential Truth or Eternal Sapience* (London, 1659).

Robert Fludd: Essential Readings, ed. William Huffman (London, 1992).

Ford, John, *An Essay of Original Righteousness and Conveyed Sin* (n.p., 1657).

Fox, George, *The Journal of George Fox*, ed. John L. Nickalls, intro. Geoffrey F. Nuttall (Cambridge, 1957).

Gailhard, Jean, *The Compleat Gentleman: or Directions for the Education of Youth* (London, 1678).

Galilei, Galileo, *Dialogue concerning the Two Chief World Systems*, tr. Stillman Drake (New York, 2001).

Discoveries and Opinions of Galileo, tr. Stillman Drake (New York, 1957).

Gassendi, Pierre, *Opera Omnia*, 6 vols. (Lyons, 1658).

Three Discourses of Happiness, Virtue, and Liberty (London, 1699).

Gaule, John, *Sapientia Justificata* (London, 1657).

Gerard, John, *The Herbal or Generall Historie of Plantes* (London, 1636).

Gill, Alexander, *The Sacred Philosophy* (London, 1635).

Glanvill, Joseph, *Essays on Several Important Subjects in Philosophy and Religion* (London, 1676).

Plus Ultra: or the Progress and Advancement of Knowledge (London, 1668).

Scepsis Scientifica, or, Confest ignorance, the way to science (London, 1665).

The Author's Defence of the Vanity of Dogmatizing, in *Scepsis Scientifica* (London, 1665).

The Vanity of Dogmatizing. or, Confidence in opinions manifested in a discourse of the shortness and uncertainty of our knowledge, and its causes: with some reflexions on peripateticism, and an apology for philosophy (London, 1661).

Goodwin, Thomas, *The Vanity of Thovghts Discovered: Together with Their Danger and Cvre* (London, 1637).

The Works of Thomas Goodwin, D. D., 12 vols. (Edinburgh, 1862).

Grew, Nehemiah, *Cosmologia Sacra: or a Discourse of the Universe as it is the Creature and Kingdom of God* (London, 1701).

Hakewill, George, *An Apologie or Declaration of the Power and Providence of God in the Government of the World*, 3rd edn (Oxford, 1635).

Hale, Matthew, *The Primitive Origination of Mankind* (London, 1677).

Hall, Joseph, *Epistles*, 3 vols. (London, 1608–11).

The Works of Joseph Hall (London, 1634).

Hartcliffe, John, *A Treatise of the Moral and Intellectual Virtues, wherein Their Nature is Fully Explained, and their Usefulness Proved* (London, 1691).

Harvey, Gideon, *Archelogia Philosophica Nova, or New Principles of Philosophy* (London, 1663).

Heidegger, J. H., *De historia sacra patriarchum*, 2 vols. (Amsterdam, 1667–71).

Hester, John, *The Pearle of Practice* (London, 1594).

Hobbes, Thomas, *The English Works of Thomas Hobbes of Malmesbury*, ed. William Molesworth, 7 vols. (London, 1839–45).

Leviathan, ed. C. B. Macpherson (Harmondsworth, 1982).

Holland, Henry, *The Historie of Adam, or the foure-fold state of Man* (London, 1606).

Hooke, Robert, 'Some Observations, and Conjectures concerning Chinese Characters', *Philosophical Transactions of the Royal Society* XVI (1696), 63–78.

Micrographia (London, 1665).

The Present State of Natural Philosophy, in *The Posthumous Works of Robert Hooke*, ed. R. Waller (London, 1705).

Hume, David, *An Enquiry into the Principles of Morals*, ed. L. A. Selby-Bigge, 3rd edn revised by P. H. Nidditch (Oxford, 1975).

Hutchinson, John, *Moses's Principia* (London, 1724–7).

Jackson, Thomas, *A Treatise of the Originall of Unbeliefe* (London, 1625).

An Exact Collection of the Works of Doctor Jackson (London, 1654).

Jansen, Cornelius, *De la reformation de l'homme interieur* (Paris, 1642).

Jeanes, Henry, *The Second Part of the Mixture of Scholasticall Divinity* (Oxford, 1660).

Josephus, Flavius, *The Works of Josephus*, tr. William Whiston (Peabody, 1993).

Kepler, Johannes, *Harmony of the World*, tr. and introduced by E. J. Aiton, A. M. Duncan, and J. V. Field (Philadelphia, 1997).

Mysterium Cosmographicum [1621], tr. A. M. Duncan (Norwalk, CT, 1999).

Kircher, Athanasius, *Of the Various Voyages and Travels undertaken into China*, in Peter de Goyer and Jacob de Keyzer, *An Embassy from the east India Company of the United Provinces to the grand Tartar Cham Emperour of China* (London, 1669)

Oedipus aegyptiacus, 4 vols. (Rome, 1652–4).

L., J., *A small mite* (London, 1654).

Le Clerc, Jean, *Twelve Dissertations out of Monsieur Le Clerk's Genesis* (London, 1696).

Le Fevre de la Boderie, Gui, *La Galliade*, ed. F. Roudaut (Paris, 1993).

Le Grand, Antoine, *An Entire Body of Philosophy According to the Principles of the Famous Renate Des Cartes* (London, 1694).

Leibniz, G. W., *New Essays on Human Understanding*, ed. and tr. Peter Remnant and Jonathan Bennett (Cambridge, 1981).

Theodicy, tr. E. M. Huggard (La Salle, 1985).

Lemnius, Levinus, *An Herbal for the Bible*, tr. Thomas Newton (London, 1587).

Lightfoot, John, *The Works of the Learned & Reverend John Lightfoot D. D.*, 2 vols. (London, 1684).

Locke, John, *Essay concerning Human Understanding*, ed. A. C. Fraser, 2 vols. (New York, 1959).

Essays on the Law of Nature, ed. W. von Leyden (Oxford, 1954).

Of the Conduct of the Understanding, 5th edn, ed. Thomas Fowler (Oxford, 1901).

Some Thoughts Concerning Education, ed. John Yolton and Jean Yolton (Oxford, 1989).

Two Tracts, in *Political Essays*, ed. Mark Goldie (Cambridge, 1997).

Two Treatises of Government, 12th edn, ed. Peter Laslett (Cambridge, 1960).

Works, 10th edn, 10 vols. (London, 1801).

Lowde, James, *A Discourse concerning the Nature of Man* (London, 1694).

Luther, Martin, *A Commentarie vpon the Fiftene Psalmes* (London, 1577).

Luther's Works, ed. J. Pelikan and H. Lehman, 55 vols. (St Louis, 1955–75).

Sermons of Martin Luther, ed. and tr. John N. Lenker et al., 7 vols. (Grand Rapids, 2000).

Table Talk, tr. William Hazlitt (Philadelphia, 1848).

The Letters of Martin Luther, tr. Margaret A. Currie (London, 1908).

Three Treatises (Philadelphia, 1970).

Works of Martin Luther, ed. H. E. Jacobs, 6 vols. (Philadelphia, 1915).

Mader, Joachim. J., *De bibliothecis atque archiviis* (Helmstedt, 1666).

Malebranche, Nicolas, *Œuvres de Malebranche*, ed. A. Robinet, 20 vols. (Paris, 1958–68).

The Search after Truth, ed. and tr. Thomas Lennon and Paul Olscamp (Cambridge, 1997).

Malvenda, Thomas, *De Paradiso* (Rome, 1605).

Mandeville, Bernard, *The Fable of the Bees: or Private Vices, Publick Benefits*, ed. F. B. Kayne, 2 vols. (Oxford, 1924).

Melanchthon, Philipp, *Chronicon Carionis* (Wittenberg, 1580).

Corpus Reformatorum Philippi Melanchthonis, ed. C. B. Bretschneider and H. E. Bindseil, 28 vols. (Halle, 1864).

Loci Communes [1543], tr. J. Preuss (St Louis, 1992).

Orations on Philosophy and Education, ed. Sachiko Kusukawa, tr. Christine F. Salazar (Cambridge, 1999).

Milton, John, *John Milton: The Major Works*, ed. S. Orgel and J. Goldberg (Oxford, 1991).

The Prose Works of John Milton, ed. J. A. St John and Charles Sumner (London, 1848–64).

Montaigne, Michel de, *Essays*, tr. Donald Frame (Stanford, 1965).

More, Henry, *A Collection of Several philosophical Writings of D. Henry More*, 2nd edn (London, 1662).

An Antidote against Atheisme (London, 1653).

Conjectura Cabbalistica. Or, a Conjectural Essay of Interpreting the Mind of Moses (London, 1653).

Observations upon Anthroposophia Theomagica and Anima Magica Abscondita (London, 1650).

Morton, Thomas, *A Treatise of the Threefold State of Man* (London, 1596).

Newton, Isaac, *Correspondence of Sir Isaac Newton*, ed. H. W. Turnbull, 7 vols. (Cambridge, 1961).

Isaac Newton's Papers and Letters on Natural Philosophy, ed. I. Bernard Cohen and Robert E. Schefield (Cambridge, MA, 1978).

Opticks: or, A Treatise of the Reflections, Refractions, Inflections & Colours of Light, based on the 4th edn, ed. I. Bernard Cohen et al. (New York, 1979).

The Optical Papers of Isaac Newton, vol. I: The Optical Lectures 1670–1672, ed. Alan Shapiro (Cambridge, 1984).

The Principia: Mathematical Principles of Natural Philosophy, tr. I. Bernard Cohen and Anne Whitman (Berkeley, 1999).

Nicole, Pierre, *Moral Essayes*, 3rd edn (London, 1696).

Paracelsus, *Die 9 Bücher der Natura Rerum*, in *Sämtliche Werke*, ed. K. Sudhoff and W. Matthiessen, 15 vols. (Munich, 1922–33).

Four Treatises of Theophrastus von Hohenheim called Paracelsus, tr. C. Lilian Tempkin et al. (Baltimore, 1941).

Paré, Ambroise, *The Workes of that Famous Chirurgion Ambrose Parey*, tr. Thomas Johnson (London, 1634).

Pareus, David, *A Commentary upon the Divine Revelation of the Apostle and Evangelist John* (Amsterdam, 1644).

Parker, Samuel, *A Free and Impartial Censure of the Platonick Philosophie* (Oxford, 1666).

Pascal, Blaise, *L'Esprit Geometrique*, in *Œuvres complètes*, ed. J Chevalier (Paris, 1954).

Oeuvres Complètes, ed. Jean Mesnard, 4 vols. (Paris, 1964–92).

Pensées, tr. A. J. Krailsheimer (London, 1966).

Patrick, Simon, *The Devout Christian* (London, 1673).

Perkins, Wilkins, *A Golden Chaine, or, A Description of Theologie* (London, 1592).

Perrone, Giovanni, *Praelectiones theologicae*, 9 vols. (Rome, 1835).

Pettus, John, *Volatiles for the History of Adam and Eve* (London, 1674).

Philo of Alexandria, *The Works of Philo*, tr. C. D. Younge (Peabody, 1992).

Plato, *Collected Dialogues*, ed. Edith Hamilton and Huntington Cairns (New York, 1961).

Plattes, Gabriel, *Macaria* (London, 1641).

Postellus, Gulielmus, *De originibus seu Hebraicae linguae* (Paris, 1538).

Power, Henry, *Experimental Philosophy in Three Books* (London, 1664).

Pufendorf, Samuel von, *The Divine Feudal Law* [1695], tr. Theophilus Dorrington (Indianapolis, 2002).

The Political Writings of Samuel Pufendorf, ed. C. Carr, tr. M. Seidler (Oxford, 1994).

Reimann, Jacob Friedrich, *Versuch einer Einleitung in die Historiam literariam antediluvianam* (Halle, 1709).

Reynolds, Edward, *A Treatise of the Passions and Faculties of the Soul of Man* (London, 1647).

Three Treatises (London, 1631).

Rheticus, Georg, *G. J. Rheticus' Treatise on the Holy Scripture and the Motion of the Earth*, ed. and tr. Reijer Hooykaas (Amsterdam, 1984).

Richard, Bernard, *Look beyond Luther* (London, 1623).

Rogers, Thomas, *A Philosophicall Discourse, Entituled, The Anatomie of the Minde* (London, 1576).

Salkeld, John, *A Treatise of Paradise* (London, 1617).

Salmon, William, *Clavis Alchymiae* (London, 1691).

Sanderson, Robert, *A Discourse concerning the Church* (London, 1688).

Saunders, Richard, *Saunders Physiognomie and Chiromancie, Metoposcopie*, 2nd edn (London, 1671).

Selden, John, *De Synedriis et praefectiurus juridicus veterum Ebraeorum* (Amsterdam, 1679).

Senault, Jean-François, *Man Becom Guilty, Or the Corruption of Nature by Sinne, according to St. Augustin's Sense* (London, 1650).

The Use of Passions (London, 1671).

Sepher Rezial Hemelach: The Book of the Angel Rezial, tr. Steve Savedow (Weiser, 2000).

Sergeant, John, *Non Ultra: or, A letter to a Learned Cartesian* (London, 1698).

Solid Philosophy Asserted, Against the fancies of the Ideists. . . . with Reflexions on Mr. Locke's Essay Concerning Human Understanding (London, 1697).

The Method to Science (London, 1696).

Simon, Richard, *A Critical History of the Old Testament* (London, 1682).

Smith, Adam, *The Theory of Moral Sentiments*, ed. D. D. Raphael and A. L. Macfie (Oxford, 1976).

Smith, John, *Select Discourses* (London, 1660).

South, Robert, *Sermons Preached upon Several Occasions* (Oxford, 1679).

Spinoza, Benedict, *The Collected Works of Spinoza*, ed. and tr. Edwin Curley (Princeton, 1985).

Sprat, Thomas, *History of the Royal Society of London* (London, 1667).

Stephens, Nathaniel, *Vindiciae Fundamenti* (London, 1658).

Stillingfleet, Edward, *Origines Sacrae* (London, 1702).

Stubbe, Henry, *Legends no Histories: or a Specimen of some Animadversions upon the History of the Royal Society . . . together with the Plus Ultra reduced to a Non-Plus* (London, 1670).

Taylor, Jeremy, *Deus Justificatus. Two Discourses of Original Sin* (London, 1656).

The Whole Works of the Right Reverend Jeremy Taylor, ed. R. Heber, 15 vols. (London, 1822).

Thomas Aquinas, *Aristotle's De Anima and the Commentary of St. Thomas Aquinas*, tr. Kenelm Foster and Silvester Humphries (New Haven, 1965).

Summa contra gentiles, tr. English Dominican Fathers (New York, 1924).

Topsell, Edward, *The History of Four-Footed Beasts and Serpents* (London, 1658).

Traherne, Thomas, *Christian Ethics: Or Divine Morality* (London, 1675).

van Limborch, Philip, *A Complete System, or Body of Divinity . . . founded on Scripture and Reason*, tr. William Jones, 2 vols. (London, 1713).

Vane, Henry, *Retired Mans Observations* (London, 1655).

Venning, Ralph, *Orthodox paradoxes, theological and experimental* (London, 1654).

Véron, François, *Keepe your text. Or a short discourse, wherein is sett downe a method to instruct, how a Catholike (though but competently learned) may defend his fayth against the most learned protestant, that is, if so the protestant will tye himselfe to his owne principle and doctrine, in keeping himselfe to the text of the scripture* (Lancashire, 1616).

La méthode nouvelle, facile et solide de convaincre de nullité la religion prétendue reformée (Paris, 1615).

The Rule of the Catholic Faith (Paris, 1660).

Vockerodt, Gottfried, *Exercitationes academicae* (Gotha, 1704).

Voltaire [François-Marie Arouet], *Letters Concerning the English Nation*, ed. Nicholas Cronk (Oxford, 1999).

Œuvres completes de Voltaire, ed. Louis Moland, 52 vols. (Paris, 1877–85).

Walker, Obadiah, *Of Education: Especially of Young Gentlemen* (Oxford, 1673).

Walkington, Thomas, *The Optick Glasse of Humors* (London, 1664).

Wallis, John, *Three Sermons concerning the sacred Trinity* (London, 1691).

Ward, Seth, *Vindiciae Academiarum* (Oxford, 1654).

Watts, Isaac, *Logick: Or, the Right Use of Reason in the Enquiry after Truth, with a Variety of Rules to guard against Error* (London, 1725).

Webb, John, *An Historical Essay, Endeavoring a Probability that the Language of the Empire of China is the Primitive Language* (London, 1669).

Webster, John, *Academiarum Examen, or the Examination of Academies* (London, 1654).

The Judgement Set, and the Books Opened . . . in Several Sermons (London, 1654).

The Saints Guide, or, Christ the Rule, and Rule of Saints (London, 1654).

Whichcote, Benjamin, *Moral and Religious Aphorisms* (London, 1930).

The Works of the Learned Benjamin Whichcote, D.D., 4 vols. (Aberdeen, 1751).

Whiston, William, *Astronomical Principles of Religion, natural and reveal'd* (London, 1717).

Wilkins, John, *A Discourse concerning the Gift of Prayer* (London, 1651).

An Essay toward a Real Character and a Philosophical Language (London, 1684).

Mathematicall Magick. or, The Wonders That may be performed by Mechanical Geometry (London, 1648).

Mercury, or, the Secret and Swift Messenger, in *Mathematical and Philosophical Works*, 2 vols. (London, 1802).

Willis, Timothy, *The Search of Causes. Containing a Theosophicall Investigation of the Possibilitie of Transmutatorie Alchemie* (London, 1616).

Witty, John, *An Essay towards a Vindication of the Vulgar History of the World*, 2 vols. (London, 1705).

Womock, Laurence, *The examination of Tilenus before the triers* (London, 1657).

Woodhouse, John, *A catalogue of sins highly useful to self-acquaintance, experimental prayer; and above all to a suitable preparation, for a worthy partaking of the supper of the Lord* (London, 1699).

Wotton, William, *Reflections upon Ancient and Modern Learning* (London, 1694).

Wright, Thomas, *The Passions of the Minde* (London, 1601).

Wylie, J. A., *History of the Scottish Nation*, 3 vols. (Edinburgh, 1886).

Younge, Richard, *An Experimental Index of the Heart* (London, 1658).

No Wicked Man a Wise Man, True Wisdom described. The Excellency of Spiritual, Experimental and Saving Knowledge, above all Humane Wisdom and Learning (London, 1666).

SECONDARY SOURCES

Achinstein, P., 'Newton's Corpuscular Query and Experimental Philosophy', in P. Bricker and R. I. G. Hughes (eds.), *Philosophical Perspectives on Newtonian Science* (Cambridge, MA, 1990), pp. 135–73.

Aertsen, Jan, 'Aquinas's Philosophy in its Historical Setting', in Norman Kretzmann and Eleonore Stump (eds.), *The Cambridge Companion to Aquinas* (Cambridge, 1993), pp. 12–37.

Allen, D. C., 'The Degeneration of Man and Renaissance Pessimism', *Studies in Philology* 35 (1938), 202–27.

Almond, Philip, *Adam and Eve in Seventeenth-Century Thought* (Cambridge, 1999).

Althaus, Paul, *The Ethics of Martin Luther*, tr. Robert Schultz (Philadelphia, 1972). *Theology of Martin Luther*, tr. R. Schultz (Philadelphia, 1966).

Anderson, L., 'The *Imago Dei* Theme in John Calvin and Bernard of Clairvaux', in W. H. Neusner (ed.), *Calvinus Sacrae Scripturae Professor* (Grand Rapids, 1994), pp. 180–97.

Anstey, Peter, 'Experimental versus Speculative Natural Philosophy', in Peter Anstey and John Schuster (eds.), *The Science of Nature in the Seventeenth Century* (Dordrecht, 2005), pp. 215–42.

'Locke on Method in Natural Philosophy', in Peter Anstey (ed.), *The Philosophy of John Locke: New Perspectives* (London: Routledge, 2003), pp. 26–42.

'Locke, Bacon and Natural History', *Early Science and Medicine* 7 (2002), 65–92.

'The Methodological Origins of Newton's Queries', *Studies in History and Philosophy of Science* 35A (2004), 247–69.

The Philosophy of Robert Boyle (London, 2000).

Ardrey, Robert, *African Genesis* (London, 1961).

Bammel, C. P., 'Adam in Origen', in Rowan Williams (ed.), *The Making of Orthodoxy: Essays in Honour of Henry Chadwick* (Cambridge, 1989), pp. 62–93.

Banner, W. A., 'Origen and the Tradition of Natural Law Concepts', *Dumbarton Oaks Papers* 8 (1954), 51–92.

Barker, Peter, 'Kepler's Epistemology', in Eckhard Kessler, Daniel Di Liscia and Charlotte Methuen (eds.), *Method and Order in the Renaissance Philosophy of Nature* (Aldershot, 1997), pp. 354–68.

'The Role of Religion in the Lutheran Response to Copernicus', in M. Osler (ed.), *Rethinking the Scientific Revolution* (Cambridge, 2000), pp. 59–88.

'Theological Foundations of Keplar's Astronomy', *Osiris* 16 (2001), 88–113.

Barker, Peter and Bernard R. Goldstein, 'Theological Foundations of Kepler's Astronomy', in John Hedley Brooke, Margaret J. Osler, and Jitse van der Meer (eds.), *Science in Theistic Contexts*, *Osiris*, 2nd series 17 (2001), 88–113.

'Realism and Instrumentalism in Sixteenth Century Astronomy: A Reappraisal', *Perspectives on Science* 6 (1998), 232–58.

Barnett, Stephen, 'Where Was Your Church Before Luther? English Claims for the Antiquity of Protestantism Examined', *Church History* 68 (1999), 14–42.

Battenhouse, Roy, 'The Doctrine of Man in Calvin and Renaissance Platonism', *JHI* 9 (1948), 447–71.

Bechler, Zev, 'Newton's 1672 Optical Controversies: A Study in the Grammar of Scientific Dissent', in E. Yahuda (ed.), *The Interaction between Science and Philosophy* (Atlantic Highlands, NJ, 1974), pp. 115–42.

Beck, L. J., *The Metaphysics of Descartes: A Study of the 'Meditations'* (Oxford, 1965).

Bell, David, *Wholly Animals: A Book of Beastly Tales* (Kalamazoo, 1992).

Ben-Chaim, Michael, 'The Discovery of Natural Goods: Newton's Vocation as an "Experimental Philosopher"', *BJHS* 34 (2001), 395–416.

Ben-David, J., *The Scientist's Role in Society: A Comparative Study* (Englewood Cliffs, NJ, 1971).

Bennett, Jim et al., *London's Leonardo: The Life and Works of Robert Hooke* (Oxford, 2003).

Bertrand, D. A., 'Adam prophète', in P. Maraval (ed.), *Figures de l'Ancien Testament chez les Pères*, Cahiers de Biblia patristica 2 (Strasbourg, 1989), pp. 61–81.

Bierma, L. D., 'Federal Theology in the Sixteenth Century: Two Traditions?', *Westminster Theological Journal* 45 (1983), 304–21.

Bierwaltes, W., 'Augustins Interpretation von Sapientia 11,21,' *Revue des Études Augustiniennes* 15 (1969), 51–61.

Blackwell, C., 'Thales Philosophicus: The Beginning of Philosophy as a Discipline', in Donald R. Kelley (ed.), *History and the Disciplines: The Reclassification of Knowledge in Early Modern Europe* (Rochester, 1997), pp. 61–82.

Blackwell, Richard J., *Galileo, Bellarmine, and the Bible* (Notre Dame, 1991).

Blair, Ann, 'Humanist Methods in Natural Philosophy: The Commonplace Book', *JHI* 53 (1992), 541–51.

'Mosaic Physics and the Search for a Pious Natural Philosophy in the Late Renaissance', *Isis* 91 (2000), 32–58.

'Note Taking as an Art of Transmission', *Critical Inquiry* 31 (2003), 85–107.

Blumenberg, Hans, 'Augustins Anteil an der Geschichte des Begriffs der theoretischen Neugierde', *Revue des Etudes Augustiniennes* 7 (1961), 35–70.

'*Curiositas* und *veritas*: Zur Ideengeschichte von Augustin, Confessiones x 35', *Studia Patristica* 6, Texte und Untersuchungen 81 (1962), 294–302.

Boas, George, *Essays on Primitivism, and Related Ideas* (Baltimore, 1966).

Bobbio, Norberto, *Thomas Hobbes and the Natural Law Tradition*, tr. D. Gobetti (Chicago, 1993).

Bonner, G., 'Augustine and Pelagianism', *Augustinian Studies* 23 (1992), 33–52; 24 (1993), 27–47.

Bono, James, *The Word of God and the Languages of Man* (Madison, 1995).

Boullaye, H. Pinard de la, *L'Etude Comparée des Religions* (Paris, 1922).

Boyancé, P., 'Etymologie et théologie chez Varron', *Revue des Etudes Latines* 53 (1975), 99–115.

Boyle, M. O'Rourke, 'Gracious Laughter: Marsilio Ficino's Anthropology', *Renaissance Quarterly* 52 (1999), 712–41.

Bray, Gerald, 'Original Sin in Patristic Thought', *Churchman* 108 (1994), 1–37.

Brooke, John Hedley, *Science and Religion: Some Historical Perspectives* (Cambridge, 1991).

Brookes, David, 'The Idea of the Decay of the World in the Old Testament, the Apocrypha, and the Pseudepigrapha', in J. D. North and John Roche (eds.), *The Light of Nature* (Dordrecht, 1985), pp. 383–404.

Brouwer, L. E. J., 'Consciousness, Philosophy and Mathematics', in *Proceedings of the Tenth International Congress of Philosophy* (Amsterdam, 1949), II, 1235–49.

Brown, Theodore, 'The Rise of Baconianism in Seventeenth-Century England', in E. Hilfstein et al. (eds.), *Science and History: Studies in Honor of Edward Rosen* (Wrocław, 1978), pp. 510–22.

Brundell, Barry, *Pierre Gassendi: From Aristotelianism to a New Philosophy* (Dordrecht, 1987).

Brunetière, Ferdinand, 'Jansenistes et Cartésiens', *Etudes critiques sur l'histoire de le littérature française*, 4 vols. (Paris, 1904).

Buckle, Stephen, 'British Sceptical Realism: A Fresh Look at the British Tradition', *European Journal of Philosophy* 7 (1999), 1–29.

Burdach, Konrad, *Reformation, Renaissance, Humanismus* (Berlin, 1918).

Burgess, Glenn, 'Filmer, Sir Robert (1588?–1653)', in Brian Harrison and Colin Matthew (eds.), *Oxford Dictionary of National Biography* (Oxford, 2004).

Burnett, Charles, 'Scientific Speculations', in Peter Dronke (ed.), *A History of Twelfth-Century Philosophy* (Cambridge, 1992), pp. 151–76.

Burtt, E. A., *The Metaphysical Foundations of Modern Science* (Atlantic Highlands, NJ, 1952).

Butterfield, Herbert, *Christianity and History* (London, 1949).

Carr, C. and M. Seidler, 'Pufendorf, Sociality and the Modern State', *History of Political Thought* 17 (1996), 354–78.

Carraud, Vincent, 'Remarks on the Second Pascalian Anthropology: Thought as Alienation', *Journal of Religion* 85 (2004), 539–55.

Carruthers, Mary, *The Book of Memory* (Cambridge, 1992).

Casini, Paolo, 'Newton: The Classical Scholia', *History of Science* 23 (1984), 1–58.

Cassirer, Ernst, *Das Erkenntnisproblem in der Philosophie und Wissenschaft der neueren Zeit*, 2 vols. (Berlin, 1906–7).

Celenza, C. S., 'Pythagoras in the Renaissance: The Case of Marsilio Ficino', *Renaissance Quarterly* 52 (1999), 667–711.

Chadwick, Henry, *Early Christian Thought and the Classical Tradition: Studies in Justin, Clement, and Origen* (New York, 1966).

The Early Church (Harmondsworth, 1993).

Chenu, Marie-Dominique, *Nature, Man and Society in the Twelfth Century* (Chicago, 1968).

Clarke, Desmond, 'Descartes' Philosophy of Science', in John Cottingham (ed.), *The Cambridge Companion to Descartes* (Cambridge, 1992), pp. 258–85.

Descartes' Philosophy of Science (University Park, 1982).

Clouse, R. G., 'Johann Heinrich Alsted and English Millenarianism', *Harvard Theological Review* 62 (1969), 189–207.

Clucas, Stephen, 'In search of "The True Logick": Methodological Eclecticism among the "Baconian Reformers"', in Mark Greengrass, Leslie Taylor and Timothy Raylor (eds.), *Samuel Hartlib and the Universal Reformation* (Cambridge, 1994), pp. 51–74.

Cohen, I. Bernard, 'Isaac Newton's *Principia*, the Scriptures and the Divine Providence', in Sidney Morgensbesser et al. (eds.), *Philosophy, Science and Method* (New York, 1969), pp. 523–48.

   The Newtonian Revolution (Cambridge, 1980).

Cohen, I. Bernard and George E. Smith (eds.), *The Cambridge Companion to Newton* (Cambridge, 2002).

Colman, John, *John Locke's Moral Philosophy* (Edinburgh, 1983).

Colpe, C., 'Von der Logoslehre des Philon zu der des Clemens von Alexandrien', in A. M. Ritter (ed.), *Kerygma und Logos* (Göttingen, 1979), pp. 68–88.

Costello, William T., *The Scholastic Curriculum at Early Seventeenth-Century Cambridge* (Cambridge, MA, 1958).

Cottingham, John, 'Doubtful Uses of Doubt: Cartesian Philosophy and the Historiography of Scepticism', in L. Catana (ed.), *Historiographies in Early Modern Philosophy and Science* (Dordrecht, forthcoming).

Coudert, Alison, *The Impact of the Kabbalah in the Seventeenth Century* (Leiden, 1999).

Cranston, M., *Locke: A Biography* (London, 1957).

Crombie, Alastair, *Robert Grosseteste and the Origins of Experimental Science 1100–1700* (Oxford, 1971).

Crowther-Heyck, Kathleen, 'Wonderful Secrets of Nature: Natural Knowledge and Religious Piety in Reformation Germany', *Isis* 94 (2003), 253–73.

Cunningham, Andrew, 'Getting the Game Right: Some Plain Words on the Identity and Invention of Science', *Studies in History and Philosophy of Science* 19 (1998), 365–89.

   'How the *Principia* got its Name: Or, Taking Natural Philosophy Seriously', *History of Science* 28 (1991), 377–92.

Cunningham, Colin, *The Terracotta Designs of Alfred Waterhouse* (London, 2000).

Curry, Patrick, *Prophecy and Power: Astrology in Early Modern England* (Cambridge, 1989).

Dagens, Jean, *Bérulle et les origines de la restauration catholique* (Paris, 1952).

Dales, Richard, 'A Twelfth-Century Concept of Natural Order', *Viator* 9 (1978), 179–92.

Daston, Loraine, 'Curiosity in Early Modern Science', *Word & Image* 11 (1995), 391–404.

Dear, Peter, 'Method and the Study of Nature', in Daniel Garber and Michael Ayers (eds.), *The Cambridge History of Seventeenth-Century Philosophy* 2 vols. (Cambridge, 1998), I, 147–77.

   'The Mathematical Principles of Natural Philosophy: Toward a Heuristic Narrative for the Scientific Revolution', *Configurations* 6 (1998), 173–93.

Discipline and Experience: The Mathematical Way in the Scientific Revolution (Chicago, 1995).

Debus, A. G., *The English Paracelsians* (New York, 1965).

Delius, H.-U., *Augustin als Quelle Luthers. Eine Materialsammlung* (Berlin, 1984).

Delumeau, Jean, *Le Péché et la peur: La culpabilisation en Occident XIIIe–XVIIIe siècles* (Paris, 1983).

DeMott, Benjamin, 'Science versus Mnemonics: Notes on John Ray and on John Wilkins' *Essay towards a Real Character, and a Philosophical Language*', *Isis* 48 (1957), 3–12.

'Comenius and the Real Character', *PMLA* 70 (1955), 1068–81.

'The Sources and Development of John Wilkins' Philosophical Language', *Journal of English and Germanic Philology* 57 (1958), 1–13.

Denifle, H. and A. Chatelain, *Chartularium Universitatis Parisiensis*, 4 vols. (Paris, 1889–97).

Dieter, Theodor, *Der junge Luther und Aristoteles. Eine historisch-systematische Untersuchung zum Verhältnis von Theologie und Philosophie* (Berlin, 2001).

Diggins, John Patrick, 'Arthur O. Lovejoy and the Challenge of Intellectual History', *JHI* 67 (2006), 181–209.

Dillon, J., 'Philo Judaeus and the Cratylus', *Liverpool Classic Monthly* 3 (1978), 37–42.

Dilthey, Wilhelm, 'Die Funktion der Anthropologie in der Kultur des 16. und 17. Jahrhunderts', in *Weltanschauung und Analyse des Menschen seit Renaissance und Reformation. Wilhelm Diltheys Gesammelte Schriften* II (Leipzig, 1914).

Dobbs, Betty Jo Teeter, *The Janus Faces of Genius: The Role of Alchemy in Newton's Thought* (Cambridge, 1991).

Dod, Bernard, 'Aristoteles Latinus', in Norman Kretzmann et al. (eds.), *The Cambridge History of Later Medieval Philosophy* (Cambridge, 1988), pp. 45–79.

Dooley, Brendan, *The Social History of Skepticism: Experience and Doubt in Early Modern Culture* (Baltimore, 1999).

Doyle, William, *Jansenism* (New York, 2000).

Dronke, Peter, *Women Writers of the Middle Ages* (Cambridge, 1984).

Du Vaucel, Louis-Paul, 'Observations sur la philosophie de Descartes', in E. J. Dijksterhuis (ed.), *Descartes et le Cartésianisme Hollandais* (Paris, 1950), pp. 113–30.

Duhem, Pierre, *To Save the Phenomena: An Essay on the Idea of Physical Theory from Plato to Galileo* [1908] (Chicago, 1969).

Dunn, John, *Political Thought of John Locke* (Cambridge, 1969).

Eastwood, B., 'Medieval Empiricism: the Case of Robert Grosseteste's *Optics*', *Speculum* 43 (1968), 306–21.

Ebeling, G., *Luther: An Introduction to his Thought* (London, 1970).

Edwards, Karen, *Milton and the Natural World: Science and Poetry in Paradise Lost* (Cambridge, 2000).

Egerton, Frank N., 'The Longevity of the Patriarchs', *JHI* 27 (1966), 575–84.

Elford, Dorothy, 'William of Conches', in Peter Dronke (ed.), *A History of Twelfth-Century Philosophy* (Cambridge, 1993), pp. 308–27.

Encyclopaedia Britannica, 3 vols. (Edinburgh, 1771).

Farington, B., *Philosophy of Francis Bacon* (Liverpool, 1964).

Fatio, Oliver, *Méthode et théologie: Lambert Daneau et les débuts de la scolastique réformée* (Geneva, 1976).

Feinberg, John S., 'Luther's Doctrine of Vocation: Some Problems of Interpretation and Application', *Fides et Historia* 12 (1979), 50–67.

Feingold, M., 'Mathematicians and Naturalists: Sir Isaac Newton and the Royal Society', in J. Z. Buchwald and I. B. Cohen (eds.), *Isaac Newton's Natural Philosophy* (Cambridge, MA, 2001), pp. 77–102.

Floridi, L., 'The Diffusion of Sextus Empiricus's Works in the Renaissance', *JHI* 56 (1995), 63–85.

'The Rediscovery of Ancient Scepticism in Modern Times', in M. Burnyeat (ed.), *The Skeptical Tradition* (Berkeley, 1983), pp. 225–51.

Sextus Empiricus: The Transmission and Recovery of Pyrrhonism (New York, 2002).

Floyd, Shawn, 'Achieving a Science of Sacred Doctrine', *Heythrop Journal* 47 (2006), 1–15.

Force, James E., 'Newton's God of Dominion: The Unity of Newton's Theological, Scientific and Political Thought', in Force and Popkin (eds.), *Essays on Newton's Theology*, pp. 75–102.

'The Nature of Newton's "Holy Alliance" between Science and Religion: From the Scientific Revolution to Newton (and Back Again)', in M. Osler (ed.), *Rethinking the Scientific Revolution* (Cambridge, 2000), pp. 247–70.

Force, James E. and Richard H. Popkin, *Essays on the Context, Nature, and Influence of Isaac Newton's Theology* (Dordrecht, 1990).

Foster, M. B., 'The Christian Doctrine of Creation and the Rise of Modern Natural Science', *Mind* 43 (1934), 446–68.

Fouke, Daniel C., 'Argument in Pascal's *Pensées*', *History of Philosophy Quarterly* 6 (1989), 57–68.

Frank, Günter, 'Melanchthon and the Tradition of Neoplatonism', in Jürgen Helm and Annette Winkelmann (eds.), *Religious Confessions and the Sciences in the Sixteenth Century* (Leiden, 2001), pp. 3–18.

Die theologische Philosophie Philipp Melanchthons (1497–1560) (Leipzig, 1995).

Froelich, Karlfried, 'Luther on Vocation', *Lutheran Quarterly* 13 (1999), 195–207.

Funkenstein, Amos, *Theology and the Scientific Imagination* (Princeton, 1986).

Gabbey, Alan, 'Philosophia Cartesiana Triumphata: Henry More (1646–1671)' in T. Lennon, John Nicholas, and John Davis (eds.), *Problems of Cartesianism* (Kingston and Montreal, 1982).

Garin, Eugenio, *Giovanni Pico della Mirandola: Vita e dottrina* (Florence, 1937).

Garner, Barbara, 'Francis Bacon, Natalis Comes and the Mythological Tradition', *Journal of the Warburg and Courtauld Institutes* 33 (1970), 264–91.

Gaukroger, Stephen, *Descartes: An Intellectual Biography* (Oxford, 1995).

Descartes' System of Natural Philosophy (Cambridge, 2002).

Francis Bacon and the Transformation of Early Modern Natural Philosophy (Cambridge, 2001).

Gaukroger, Stephen (ed.), *The Soft Underbelly of Reason: The Passions in the Seventeenth Century* (London, 1998).

Gaukroger, Stephen, John Schuster, and John Sutton (eds.), *Descartes' Natural Philosophy* (London, 2000).

Geoffrey, David L. (ed.), *A Dictionary of Biblical Tradition in English Literature* (Grand Rapids, 1992).

Gilson, Etienne, 'The Future of Augustinian Metaphysics', in *A Monument to St. Augustine* (London, 1934).

History of Christian Philosophy in the Middle Ages (New York, 1955).

La Liberté chez Descartes et la théologie (Paris, 1913).

Gingerich, Owen, 'Truth in Science: Proof, Persuasion, and the Galileo Affair', *Science and Christian Belief* 16 (2004), 13–26.

Ginzberg, Louis, *The Legends of the Jews*, tr. Henrietta Szold, 7 vols. (Philadelphia, 1937–66).

Glacken, Clarence, *Traces on the Rhodian Shore: Nature and Culture in Western Thought from Ancient Times to the End of the Eighteenth Century* (Berkeley, 1973).

Gough, J., *John Locke's Political Philosophy* (Oxford, 1950).

Gouhier, Henri, *La pensée métaphysique de Descartes* (Paris, 1962).

La philosophie de Malebranche et son expérience religieuse (Paris, 1978).

Grafton, Anthony, *Forgers and Critics* (Princeton, 1990).

Grant, Edward, 'The Condemnation of 1277, God's Absolute Power, and Physical Thought in the Late Middle Ages', *Viator* 10 (1979), 211–44.

'The Effect of the Condemnation of 1277', in Norman Kretzmann et al. (eds.), *The Cambridge History of Later Medieval Philosophy* (Cambridge, 1988), pp. 537–9.

Planets, Stars, and Orbs: The Medieval Cosmos, 1200–1687 (Cambridge, 1994).

Greengrass, Mark, Leslie Taylor, and Timothy Raylor (eds.), *Samuel Hartlib and the Universal Reformation: Studies in Intellectual Communication* (Cambridge, 1994).

Grendler, Paul (ed.), 'Education in the Renaissance and Reformation', *Renaissance Quarterly* 43 (1990), 774–824.

Grene, Donald, 'Augustinianism and Empiricism: A Note on Eighteenth-Century Intellectual History', *Eighteenth Century Studies* 1 (1967), 33–68.

Gross, Alan, 'On the Shoulders of Giants: Seventeenth-Century Optics as an Argumentative Field', in R. A. Harris (ed.), *Landmark Essays on Rhetoric of Science* (Marwah, NJ, 1997), pp. 19–38.

Gross, Daniel M., 'Melanchthon's Rhetoric and the Practical Origins of Reformation Human Science', *History of the Human Sciences* 13 (2000), 5–22.

Gross, Julius, *Entstehungsgeschichte des Erbsündendogmas: Von der Bibel bis Augustinus* (Munich, 1960).

Gruman, Gerald, *A History of Ideas about the Prolongation of Life* (Philadelphia, 1966).

Gschwandtner, Christina, 'Threads of Fallenness according to the Fathers of the First Four Centuries', *European Explorations in Christian Holiness* 2001, 19–40.

Guerlac, Henry, 'Theological Voluntarism and Biological Analogies in Newton's Physical Thought', *JHI* 44 (1983), 219–29.

Guillet, J., 'La "lumiere intellectuelle" d'après S. Thomas', *Archives d'histoire doctrinale et littéraire du moyen âge* 2 (1927), 79–88.

Hadot, Pierre, *What is Ancient Philosophy?* (Cambridge, MA, 2002).

Hagen, Kenneth, 'A Critique of Wingren on Luther on Vocation', *Lutheran Quarterly* NS 3 (2002), 249–73.

Håkansson, Håkan, *Seeing the Word: John Dee and Renaissance Occultism* (Lund, 2001).

Hall, Marie Boas, *Promoting Experimental Learning: Experiment and the Royal Society, 1660–1727* (Cambridge, 1991).

Robert Boyle on Natural Philosophy: An Essay with Selections from His Writings (Bloomington, 1966).

Hanby, Michael, *Augustine and Modernity* (London, 2003).

Hankins, James, 'Galileo, Ficino, and Renaissance Platonism', in Jill Kraye and M. W. F. Stone (eds.), *Humanism and Early Modern Philosophy* (London, 2000), pp. 209–37.

Plato in the Italian Renaissance, 2 vols. (Leiden, 1990),

'Plato's Psychogony in the Later Renaissance: Changing Attitudes to the Christianization of Pagan Philosophy', in Thomas Leinkauf and Carlos Steel (eds.), *Ancient and Medieval Philosophy*, vol. XXXII (Leuven, 2005), pp. 393–412.

The Study of the 'Timaeus' in Early Renaissance Italy, in A. Grafton and N. Siraisi (eds.), *Natural Particulars: Nature and the Disciplines in Renaissance Europe* (Cambridge, MA, 1999), pp. 77–119.

Hannaway, O., *The Chemists and the Word: The Didactic Origins of Chemistry* (Baltimore, 1975).

Harbison, E. Harris, 'The Idea of Utility in John Calvin', in E. Harris Harbison (ed.), *Christianity and History* (Princeton, 1964).

Harding, Susan, *Whose Science? Whose Knowledge? Thinking from Women's Lives* (Ithaca, 1991).

Harkness, Deborah, *John Dee's Conversations with Angels: Cabala, Alchemy, and the End of Nature* (Cambridge, 1999).

Harris, Ian, 'The Politics of Christianity', in G. A. J. Rogers (ed.), *Locke's Philosophy: Content and Context* (Oxford, 1996), pp. 197–216.

The Mind of John Locke: A Study of Political Theory in its Intellectual Setting (Cambridge, 1994).

Harris, Victor, *All Coherence Gone* (London, 1966).

Harrison, Peter, '"Priests of the Most High God, with respect to the Book of Nature": The Vocational Identity of the Early Modern Naturalist', in Angus Menuge (ed.), *Reading God's World* (St Louis, 2004), pp. 55–80.

'"The Book of Nature" and Early Modern Science', in K. van Berkel and Arjo Vanderjagt (eds.), *The Book of Nature in Early Modern and Modern History* (Leuven, 2006), pp. 1–26.

'"The Fashioned Image or Poetry or the Regular Instruction of Philosophy?": Truth, Utility, and the Natural Sciences in Early Modern England', in D. Burchill and J. Cummins (eds.), *Science, Literature, and Rhetoric in Early Modern England* (Aldershot, 2007), pp. 15–36.

'Newtonian Science, Miracles, and the Laws of Nature', *JHI* 56 (1995), 531–53.
'Physico-theology and the Mixed Sciences: Theology and Early Modern Natural Philosophy', in Peter Anstey and John Schuster (eds.), *The Science of Nature in the Seventeenth Century* (Dordrecht, 2005), pp. 165–83.
'Reading the Passions: The Fall, the Passions, and Dominion over Nature', in S. Gaukroger (ed.), *The Soft Underbelly of Reason: The Passions in the Seventeenth Century* (London, 1998), pp. 49–78.
'Religion' and the Religions in the English Enlightenment (Cambridge, 1990).
'Subduing the Earth: Genesis 1, Early Modern Science, and the Exploitation of Nature', *The Journal of Religion* 79 (1999), 86–109.
'The Influence of Cartesian Cosmology in England', in Stephen Gaukroger, John Schuster, and John Sutton (eds.), *Descartes' Natural Philosophy* (London, 2000), pp. 168–92.
'The Natural Philosopher and the Virtues', in C. Condren, I. Hunter, and S. Gaukroger (eds.), *The Philosopher in Early Modern Europe: The Nature of a Contested Identity* (Cambridge, 2006), pp. 202–28.
'Voluntarism and Early Modern Science', *History of Science* 40 (2002), 63–89.
'Was Newton a Voluntarist?', in James E. Force and Sarah Hutton (eds.), *Newton and Newtonianism: New Studies* (Dordrecht, 2004), pp. 39–64.
The Bible, Protestantism and the Rise of Natural Science (Cambridge, 1998).
Hart, Ian, 'The Teaching of Luther and Calvin About Ordinary Work', *Evangelical Quarterly* 67 (1995), 35–52, 121–35.
Hatfield, Gary, 'The Senses and the Fleshless Eye: The Meditations as Cognitive Exercises', in Amélie Rorty (ed.), *Essays on Descartes' Meditations* (Berkeley, 1986), pp. 45–79.
Havens, Earle, *Commonplace Books* (New Haven, 2001).
Haycock, David, '"The long-lost truth": Sir Isaac Newton and the Newtonian Pursuit of Ancient Knowledge', *Studies in History and Philosophy of Science* 35 (2004), 605–23.
'Living Forever in Early Modern England', *The Center and Clark Newsletter* 43 (2004), 6–7.
'Projectors of Immortality: Living Forever in Early Modern Europe', forthcoming.
Heimann, Peter, 'Voluntarism and Immanence: Conceptions of Nature in Eighteenth-century Thought', *JHI* 39 (1978), 271–83.
Helm, Jürgen, 'Religion and Medicine: Anatomical Education at Wittenberg and Ingolstadt', in Jürgen Helm and Annette Winkelmann (eds.), *Religious Confessions and the Sciences in the Sixteenth Century* (Leiden, 2001), pp. 51–68.
Helm, Paul, 'John Calvin, the *Sensus Divinitatis* and the Noetic Effects of Sin', *International Journal for Philosophy of Religion* 43 (1998), 87–107.
Heniger, Jr., S., *Touches of Sweet Harmony: Pythagorean Cosmology and Renaissance Poetics* (San Marino, 1974).
Henry, John, 'Henry More versus Robert Boyle', in Sarah Hutton (ed.), *Henry More (1614–87): Tercentenary Essays* (Dordrecht, 1990), pp. 55–76.
Knowledge is Power (London, 2002).

Herve, J. M., *Manuale Theologiae Dogmaticae*, 4 vols. (Westminster, MD, 1943).

Heyd, Michael, 'The New Experimental Philosophy: A Manifestation of Enthusiasm or an Antidote to it?', *Minerva* 25 (1987), 423–40.

Hick, John, *Evil and the God of Love* (London, 1985).

Hill, Chrisopher, *The Collected Essays of Christopher Hill*, 3 vols. (Amherst, 1986).
Antichrist in Seventeenth Century England (London, 1971).
The English Bible and the Seventeenth-Century Revolution (Ringwood, 1994).
The World Turned Upside Down (Ringwood, 1975).

Hill, Lisa, 'The Hidden Theology of Adam Smith', *European Journal of Economic Thought* 8 (2001), 1–29.

Hirschman, Albert O., *The Passions and the Interests* (Princeton, 1997).

Hodgen, Margaret, *Early Anthropology in the Sixteenth and Seventeenth Centuries* (Philadelphia, 1964).

Hoekstra, Kinch, 'Disarming the Prophets: Thomas Hobbes and Predictive Power', *Rivista di storia della filosofia* 1 (2004), 97–153.

Hooykaas, Reijer, 'Science and Reformation', *Journal of World History* 3 (1956), 109–39.

Hotson, Howard, *Johann Heinrich Alsted 1588–1638: Between Renaissance, Reformation, and Universal Reform* (Oxford, 2000).

Howell, Kenneth J., *God's Two Books: Copernical Cosmology and Biblical Interpretation in Early Modern Science* (Notre Dame, 2002).

Huff, Toby, *The Rise of Early Modern Science: Islam, China and the West*, 2nd edn (Cambridge, 2003).

Hunter, Ian, *Rival Enlightenments: Civil and Metaphysical Philosophy in Early Modern Germany* (Cambridge, 2001).

Hunter, Michael, *Science and Society in Restoration England* (Cambridge, 1981).
The Royal Society and Its Fellows 1660–1700 (London, 1982).

Hunter, Michael and R. Lomas, *The Invisible College* (London, 2002).

Hunter, Michael and P. Wood, 'Towards Solomon's House: Rival Strategies for Reforming the Early Royal Society', in M. Hunter (ed.), *Establishing the New Science: The Experience of the Early Royal Society* (Woodbridge, 1989), pp. 185–244.

Hutton, Sarah, 'The Cambridge Platonists', in S. Nadler (ed.), *A Companion to Early Modern Philosophy* (Oxford, 2002), pp. 308–19.

Iliffe, Rob, '"The Idols of the Temple": Isaac Newton and the Private Life of Anti-Idolatry', Ph.D. dissertation, University of Cambridge, 1989.
'Abstract Considerations: Disciplines and the Incoherence of Newton's Natural Philosophy', *Studies in History and Philosophy of Science* 35A (2004), 427–54.
'Butter for Parsnips: Authorship, Audience and the Incomprehensibility of the *Principia*', in M. Biagioli and P. Galison (eds.), *Scientific Authorship: Credit and Intellectual Property in Science* (London, 2003), pp. 33–65.

Inwood, Stephen, *The Forgotten Genius: The Biography of Robert Hooke, 1635–1703* (London, 2004).

Israel, Jonathan, *Radical Enlightenment* (Oxford, 2001).
The Dutch Republic: Its Rise, Greatness, and Fall 1477–1806 (Oxford, 1995).

Jacob, Margaret C., *The Newtonians and the English Revolution, 1689–1720* (Ithaca, 1976).

James, Susan, *Passion and Action: The Emotions in Seventeenth Century Philosophy* (Oxford, 1997).

Janowski, Zbigniew, *Augustinian-Cartesian Index: Texts and Commentary* (South Bend, 2004).

   Cartesian Theodicy (Dordrecht, 2000).

Jardine, Lisa, *The Curious Life of Robert Hooke: The Man who Measured London* (San Francisco, 2004).

Jardine, Lisa and Alan Stewart, *Hostage to Fortune: The Troubled Life of Francis Bacon* (New York, 1999).

Jardine, Nicholas, 'Keeping Order in the School of Padua', in Eckhard Kessler, Daniel Di Liscia and Charlotte Methuen (eds.), *Method and Order in the Renaissance Philosophy of Nature* (Aldershot, 1997), pp. 183–209.

   The Birth of History and Philosophy of Science: Kepler's Defence of Tycho against Ursus *with Essays on its Provenance and Significance* (Cambridge, 1984).

Jedin, Hubert, *A History of the Council of Trent*, tr. Ernest Graf, 2 vols. (London, 1957–61).

Jenkins, J., 'Aquinas on the Veracity of the Intellect', *The Journal of Philosophy* 88 (1991), 623–32.

Johns, Adrian, 'The Physiology of Reading', in Marina Frasca-Spada and Nick Jardine (eds.), *Books and the Sciences in History* (Cambridge, 2000), pp. 291–314.

Jolley, Nicholas, 'Intellect and Illumination in Malebranche', *Journal of the History of Philosophy* 32 (1994), 209–24.

Jones, Jan-Erik, 'Boyle, Classification, and the Workmanship of the Understanding Thesis', *Journal of the History of Philosophy* 43 (2005), 171–83.

Jones, Matthew, 'Descartes's Geometry as Spiritual Exercise', *Critical Inquiry* 28 (2001), 40–72.

Jordan, M., 'Augustinianism', in *The Routledge Encyclopedia of Philosophy*, ed. E. Craig, 10 vols. (London, 1998), 1, 559–65.

Joy, Lynn, *Gassendi the Atomist* (Cambridge, 1987).

Kahn, Charles H., *The Art and Thought of Heraclitus* (Cambridge, 1979).

Kahn, Victoria, *Wayward Contracts: The Crisis of Political Obligation in England, 1640–1674* (Princeton, 2004).

Kassell, Lauren, 'Reading for the Philosopher's Stone', in Marina Frasca-Spada and Nick Jardine (eds.), *Books and the Sciences in History* (Cambridge, 2000), pp. 132–50.

Katz, David, *Philo-Semitism and the Readmission of the Jews to England 1603–1655* (Oxford, 1982).

Katz, J. and R. H. Weingartner (eds.), *Philosophy in the West*, tr. J. Wellmuth (New York, 1965).

Kearney, Hugh, *Scholars and Gentlemen: Universities and Society in Pre-Industrial Britain* (London, 1970).

Kelber, W., *Die Logoslehre von Heraklit bis Origines*, 2nd edn (Stuttgart, 1958).

Keller, Evelyn Fox, *Reflections on Gender and Science* (New Haven, 1985).

Klaaren, Eugene, *Religious Origins of Modern Science* (Grand Rapids, 1977).

Kleckley, Russell, 'Stealing Golden Vessels: Johannes Kepler on Worldly Knowledge and Christian Truth', Conference Paper, American Academy of Religion Annual Meeting, Denver, 17 November 2001.

Klein, J., *Francis Bacon oder die Modernisierung Englands* (Hildesheim, 1987).

Klinck, Dennis R., '*Vestigia Trinitatis* in Man and his Works in the English Renaissance', *JHI* 42 (1981), 13–27.

Kocher, P. H., 'Paracelsian Medicine in England: The First Thirty Years (ca. 1570–1600)', *Journal of the History of Medicine* 2 (1947), 451–80.

Kors, Alan, 'Skepticism and the Problem of Atheism in Early Modern France', in R. Popkin and A. Vanderjagt (eds.), *Scepticism and Irreligion in the Seventeenth and Eighteenth Centuries* (Leiden, 1993), pp. 185–215.

Koyré, Alexander, *Galileo Studies* (Hassocks, 1978).

Kraye, Jill (ed.), *Cambridge Translations of Renaissance Philosophical Texts*, 2 vols. (Cambridge, 1997).

Kretzmann, Norman, 'Infallibility, Error, Ignorance', *Canadian Journal of Philosophy*, supplementary vol. 17 (1992).

Kuhn, Albert, 'Glory or Gravity: Hutchinson vs. Newton', *JHI* 22 (1961), 303–22.

Kuiper, H., *Calvin on Common Grace* (Grand Rapids, 1930).

Kusukawa, Sachiko, *The Transformation of Natural Philosophy: The Case of Philip Melanchthon* (Cambridge, 1995).

  '*Vinculum concordiae*: Lutheran Method by Philip Melanchthon', in Eckhard Kessler, Daniel Di Liscia and Charlotte Methuen (eds.), *Method and Order in the Renaissance Philosophy of Nature* (Aldershot, 1997), pp. 337–54.

Kuyper, Abraham, *Principles of Sacred Theology* (Grand Rapids, 1980).

La Bonnardière, A.-M., *Biblia augustiniana. Le livre de la sagesse* (Paris, 1970).

Ladner, G. B., 'Erneuerung', in *Reallexikon für Antike und Christentum*, ed. Ernst Dassmann, 18 vols. (Stuttgart, 1950–), 6, 246–7.

Laird, W. R., *The Scientiae Mediae in Medieval Commentaries on Aristotle's Posterior Analytics* (Toronto, 1983).

Lamberigts, M. (ed.), *L'augustinisme à l'ancienne faculté de théologie de Louvain* (Leuven, 1994).

Landau, Iddo, 'Feminist Criticisms of Metaphors in Bacon's Philosophy of Science', *Philosophy* 73 (1998), 47–61.

Lange van Ravenswaay, J. M., *Augustinus totus noster: das Augustinverständnis bei Johannes Calvin* (Göttingen, 1990).

Laporte, Jean, *Le cœur et la raison selon Pascal* (Paris, 1950).

  Le Rationalisme de Descartes (Paris, 1950).

Larmore, Charles, 'Scepticism', in Daniel Garber and Michael Ayers (eds.), *The Cambridge History of Seventeenth-Century Philosophy*, 2 vols. (Cambridge, 1998), II, 1145–92.

Leith, John (ed.), *Creeds of the Churches* (Louisville, 1982).

Lemmi, Charles W., *The Classical Deities in Bacon: A Study of Mythological Symbolism* (Baltimore, 1930).

Lennon, Thomas M., 'Jansenism and the *Crise Pyrrhonienne*', *JHI* 38 (1977), 297–306.

'Malebranche and Method', in Steven Nadler (ed.), *Cambridge Companion to Malebranche*, pp. 8–30.

'The Cartesian Dialectic of Creation', in Daniel Garber and Michael Ayers (eds.), *The Cambridge History of Seventeenth-Century Philosophy*, 2 vols. (Cambridge, 1998), I, 331–62.

Leonard, John, 'Language and Knowledge in Paradise Lost', in Dennis Danielson (ed.), *The Cambridge Companion to Milton* (Cambridge, 1989), pp. 97–111.

Lesham, Ayval, *Newton on Mathematics and Spiritual Purity* (Dordrecht, 2003).

Lessay, Franck, 'Hobbes: une christologie politique?', *Rivista di storia della filosofia* 1 (2004), 51–72.

'Hobbes's Protestantism', in Tom Sorell (ed.), *Leviathan after 350 Years* (Oxford, 2004), pp. 265–94.

Levi, A., *French Moralists: The Theory of the Passions, 1585–1649* (Oxford, 1964).

Levison, John, *Portraits of Adam in Early Judaism: From Sirach to 2 Baruch* (Sheffield, 1988).

Lewis, Rhodri, 'John Wilkins's *Essay* (1668) and the Context of Seventeenth-century Artificial Languages in England', D.Phil. dissertation, Oxford, 2003.

Language, Mind, and Nature: Artificial Languages in England from Bacon to Locke (Cambridge, 2007).

Liébaert, Jacques, 'La Tradition Patristique jusqu'au Ve siècle', in *La Culpabilité fondamentale: Péché originel et anthroplogie moderne* (Lille, 1975), pp. 35–43.

Lindberg, David C., 'The Medieval Church Encounters the Classical Tradition', in David C. Lindberg and Ronald L. Numbers (eds.), *When Science and Christianity Meet* (Chicago, 2003), pp. 7–32.

The Beginnings of Western Science (Chicago, 1992).

Theories of Vision from Al-Kindi to Kepler (Chicago, 1976).

Little, David, *Religion, Order, and Law: A Study in Pre-Revolutionary England* (Oxford, 1970).

Loemker, L. E., 'Leibniz and the Herborn Encyclopaedists', *JHI* 22 (1961), 323–38.

Lohr, C. H., 'The Medieval Interpretation of Aristotle', in Norman Kretzmann et al. (eds.), *The Cambridge History of Later Medieval Philosophy* (Cambridge, 1988), pp. 80–98.

Lom, Petr, *The Limits of Doubt: The Moral and Political Implications of Skepticism* (Albany, NY, 2001).

Loofs, Friedrick, 'Pelagius und der pelagianische Streit', in *Realencyklopädie für protestantische Theologie und Kirche*, ed. Albert Hauck, 3rd edn, 22 vols. (Leipzig, 1896–1908), xv, 747–74.

Lorenz, Konrad, *On Aggression* (London, 1966).

Losonsky, Michael, 'Locke on Meaning and Signification', in G. A. J. Rogers (ed.), *Locke's Philosophy: Content and Context* (Oxford, 1996), pp. 123–42.

Maat, Jaap, *Philosophical Languages in the Seventeenth Century: Dalgarno, Wilkins, Leibniz* (Dordrecht, 2004).

McCasland, S. V., '"The Image of God" according to Paul', *Journal of Biblical Literature* 69 (1950), 363–5.

MacCulloch, Diarmaid, *The Reformation* (New York, 2003).

McEvoy, James, *The Philosophy of Robert Grosseteste* (Oxford, 1982).

McGuire, J. E., 'Boyle's Conception of Nature', *JHI* 33 (1972), 523–42.

'Newton's "Principles of Philosophy": An Intended Preface for the 1704 Opticks and a Related Draft Fragment', *BJHS* 5 (1970), 178–86.

McGuire J. E. and P. M. Rattansi, 'Newton and the "Pipes of Pan"', *Notes and Records of the Royal Society* 21 (1966), 108–43.

McInerny, Ralph, 'Ethics', in Norman Kretzmann and Eleonore Stump (eds.), *The Cambridge Companion to Aquinas* (Cambridge, 1993), pp. 196–216.

MacIntyre, Alasdair, *After Virtue*, 2nd edn (Notre Dame, 1984).

McMullin, Ernan, 'Conceptions of Science in the Scientific Revolution', in David Lindberg and Robert Westman (eds.), *Reappraisals of the Scientific Revolution* (Cambridge, 1990), pp. 27–92.

Maia Neto, José R., 'Academic Skepticism in Early Modern Philosophy', *JHI* 58 (1997), 199–220.

The Christianization of Pyrrhonism: Scepticism and Faith in Pascal, Kierkegaard, and Shestov (Dordrecht, 1995).

Malamud, Martha, 'Writing Original Sin', *Journal of Early Christian Studies* 10 (2002), 329–60.

Malcolm, Noel, *Aspects of Hobbes* (Oxford, 2004).

Malet, Antoni, 'Isaac Barrow on the Mathematization of Nature: Theological Voluntarism and the Rise of Geometrical Optics', *JHI* 58 (1997), 265–87.

Mamiani, M., 'The Rhetoric of Certainty: Newton's Method in Science and in the Interpretation of the Apocalypse', in M. Pera and W. R. Shea (eds.), *Persuading Science* (Canton, OH, 1991), pp. 157–72.

Mandelbrote, Scott, '"A Duty of the Greatest Moment": Isaac Newton and the Writing of Biblical Criticism', *BJHS* 26 (1993), 281–302.

'Représentations bibliques et édéniques du jardin à l'âge classique', *XVIIe siècle* 52 (2000), 645–54.

Manuel, Frank, *The Religion of Isaac Newton* (Oxford, 1974).

Manzo, Silvia, 'Holy Writ, Mythology, and the Foundations of Bacon's Principle of the Constancy of Matter', *Early Science and Medicine* 4 (1999), 115–25.

Marcus, R. A., *Saeculum: History and Society in the Theology of Augustine* (London, 1970).

'Augustine, Reason, and Illumination', in A. H. Armstrong (ed.), *The Cambridge History of Later Greek and Early Medieval Philosophy* (Cambridge, 1967), pp. 362–73.

Marrone, Steven P., *William of Auvergne and Robert Grosseteste* (Princeton, 1983).

The Light of Thy Countenance: Science and Knowledge of God in the Thirteenth Century (Leiden, 2001).

Marshall, John, 'John Locke and Latitudinarianism', in R. Kroll, R. Ashcraft, and P. Zagorin (eds.), *Philosophy, Science and Religion in England 1640–1700* (Cambridge, 1992), pp. 253–82.

John Locke: Resistance, Religion and Responsibility (Cambridge, 1994).

Martinich, A. P., *The Two Gods of Leviathan: Thomas Hobbes on Religion and Politics* (Cambridge, 1992).

Matthews, G. B., 'Post-medieval Augustinianism', in Eleonore Stump and Norman Kretzmann (eds.), *The Cambridge Companion to Augustine* (Cambridge, 2001), pp. 267–79.

Thought's Ego in Augustine and Descartes (Ithaca, 1992).

Matthews, Steven, 'Apocalypse and Experiment: The Theological Assumptions and Motivations of Francis Bacon's Instauration', Ph.D. dissertation, University of Florida, 2004.

Maurer, Armand, *Faith, Reason, and Theology* (Toronto, 1987).

Menn, Stephen, *Descartes and Augustine* (Cambridge, 1998).

Merchant, Caroline, *The Death of Nature* (San Francisco, 1980).

Merrick, J. W., *The Desacralisation of the French Monarchy in the Eighteenth Century* (Baton Rouge, 1992).

Merton, Robert K., *Science, Technology, and Society in Seventeenth-Century England* (New York, 1970).

Mesnard, Pierre, 'L'Arbre de la sagesse', *Descartes, Cahiers de Royaumont, Philosophie* II (Paris, 1957), 366–49, 350–9.

Methuen, Charlotte, '*Lex Naturae* and *Ordo Naturae* in the Thought of Philip Melanchthon', *Reformation and Renaissance Review* 3 (2000), 110–25.

Kepler's Tübingen (Aldershot, 1998).

Micklem, Nathaniel, *Reason and Revelation: A Question from Duns Scotus* (Edinburgh, 1953).

Mikkeli, Heiki, *An Aristotelian Response to Renaissance Humanism: Jacopo Zabarella on the Nature of the Arts and Sciences* (Helsinki, 1992).

Milbank, John, *Theology and Social Theory: Beyond Secular Reason* (Oxford, 1990).

Milner, Benjamin, 'Francis Bacon: The Theological Foundations of *Valerius Terminus*', *JHI* 58 (1997), 245–64.

Milton, J. R., 'Locke's Life and Times', in Vere Chappell (ed.) *The Cambridge Companion to Locke* (Cambridge, 1994), pp. 5–25.

Montagu, M. F. Ashley, 'The New Litany of "Innate Depravity", or Original Sin Revisited', in A Montagu (ed.), *Man and Aggression*, 2nd edn (New York, 1973), pp. 3–18.

Montgomery, John W., 'Cross, Constellation and Crucible: Lutheran Astrology and Alchemy in the Age of the Reformation', *Ambix* II (1963), 65–86.

Morgan, John, *Godly Learning: Puritan Attitudes towards Reason, Learning, and Education, 1560–1640* (Cambridge, 1988).

Moriarty, Michael, *Early Modern French Thought* (Oxford, 2003).

Morphos, Panos, *The Dialogues of Guy de Brués* (Baltimore, 1953).

Mulhall, Stephen, *Philosophical Myths of the Fall* (Princeton, 2005).

Mulsow, Martin, 'Ambiguities of the *Prisca Sapientia* in Late Renaissance Humanism', *JHI* 65 (2004), 1–13.

Murdoch, Brian, '*Drohtin uuerthe so!* Zur Funktionsweise der althochdeutschen Zaubersprüche', *Jahrbuch der Görres-Gesellschaft* NS 32 (1991), 11–37.

Nadler, Steven, *Arnauld and the Cartesian Philosophy of Ideas* (Princeton, 1989).

Nadler, Steven (ed.), *The Cambridge Companion to Malebranche* (Cambridge, 2000).

Nauert Jr., G., 'Magic and Scepticism in Agrippa's Thought', *JHI* 18 (1957), 161–82.

Agrippa and the Crisis of Renaissance Thought (Urbana, 1965).

Nederman, Cary J., 'Nature, Sin, and the Origins of Society: The Ciceronian Tradition in Medieval Political Thought', *JHI* 49 (1988), 3–26.

Nicolson, Marjorie, 'The Early Stage of Cartesianism in England', *Studies in Philology* 26 (1929), 356–74.

Nuovo, Victor (ed.), *John Locke: Writings on Religion* (Oxford, 2002).

Nutton, Vivian, 'Wittenberg Anatomy', in Ole Grell and Andrew Cunningham (eds.), *Medicine and the Reformation* (Cambridge, 1995).

O'Connell, R. J., 'The Plotinian Fall of the Soul in St. Augustine', *Traditio* 19 (1963), 1–35.

Augustine's Early Theory of Man (Cambridge, MA, 1968).

O'Malley, John, *Trent and All That: Renaming Catholicism in the Early Modern Era* (Cambridge, MA, 2000).

Oakley, Francis, 'Christian Theology and the Newtonian Science: The Rise of the Concept of Laws of Nature', *Church History* 30 (1961), 433–57.

Oliver, Simon, *Philosophy, God and Motion* (London, 2005).

Orcibal, Jean, *Les origines du Jansénisme II: Jean Duvergier de Haruanne, Abbé de Saint-Cyran, et son temps (1581–1638)* (Paris, 1947).

La Spiritualité de Saint-Cyran avec ses écrits de piété inédits (Paris, 1962).

Osler, Margaret, 'Divine Will and Mathematical Truths: Gassendi and Descartes on the Status of Eternal Truths', in R. Ariew and M. Grene (eds.), *Descartes and his Contemporaries* (Chicago, 1995), pp. 145–58.

'Fortune, Fate, and Divination: Gassendi's Voluntarist Theology and the Baptism of Epicureanism', in Margaret Osler (ed.), *Atoms, Pneuma, and Tranquillity: Epicurean and Stoic Themes in European Thought* (Cambridge, 1991).

'The Intellectual Sources of Robert Boyle's Philosophy of Nature', in Richard Ashcroft, Richard Kroll, and Perez Zagorin (eds.), *Philosophy, Science, and Religion, 1640–1700* (Cambridge, 1991).

Divine Will and the Mechanical Philosophy: Gassendi and Descartes on Contingency and Necessity in the Created World (Cambridge, 1994).

Otten, T., *After Innocence: Visions of the Fall in Modern Literature* (Pittsburgh, 1982).

Owens, Joseph, 'Faith, Ideas, Illumination and Experience', in Norman Kretzmann et al. (eds.), *The Cambridge History of Later Medieval Philosophy* (Cambridge, 1988), pp. 440–59.

Paganini, Gianni (ed.), *The Return of Scepticism from Hobbes and Descartes to Bayle* (Dordrecht, 2003).

Painter, Mark, *The Depravity of Wisdom: The Protestant Reformation and the Disengagement of Knowledge from Virtue in Modern Philosophy* (Aldershot, 1999).

Papageorgiou, P., 'Chrysostom and Augustine on the Sin of Adam and its Consequences', *St Vladimir's Theological Quarterly* 39 (1995), 361–78.

Park, Katherine and Eckhard Gessler, 'The Concept of Psychology', in Charles Schmitt et al. (eds.), *The Cambridge History of Renaissance Philosophy* (Cambridge, 1988), pp. 455–63.

Parker, Kim, *The Biblical Politics of John Locke* (Waterloo, Ontario, 2004).

Pasnau, Robert, 'Henry of Ghent and the Twilight of Divine Illumination', *Review of Metaphysics* 49 (1995), 49–75.

Pelikan, Jaroslav, *The Emergence of the Catholic Tradition (100–600)* (Chicago, 1971).

Penaskovic, R., 'The Fall of the Soul in Saint Augustine: A *Quaestio Disputata*', *Augustinian Studies* 17 (1986), 135–45.

Pérez-Ramos, Antonio, 'Bacon's Legacy', in Markku Peltonen (ed.), *The Cambridge Companion to Bacon* (Cambridge, 1996), pp. 311–34.

Pesic, Peter, 'Wrestling with Proteus: Francis Bacon and the "Torture" of Nature', *Isis* 90 (1999), 81–94.

Petersen, Sarah, 'The Fall and Misogyny in Justin and Clement of Alexandria', in D. Foster and P. Mozjes (eds.), *Society and Original Sin* (New York, 1985), pp. 37–51.

Pinker, Steven, *The Blank Slate: The Modern Denial of Human Nature* (London, 2002).

Pitkin, Barbara, 'The Protestant Zeno: Calvin and the Development of Melanchthon's Anthropology', *Journal of Religion* 84 (2004), 345–78.

Pollmann, K. and M. Vessey (eds.), *Augustine and the Disciplines: From Cassiciacum to Confessions* (Oxford, 2005)

Poole, William, *Milton and the Idea of the Fall* (Cambridge, 2005).

'The Divine and the Grammarian: Theological Disputes in the 17th-Century Universal Language Movement', *Historiographia Linguistica* 30 (2003), 273–300.

Popkin, Richard H., 'Magic and Radical Reformation in Agrippa of Nettesheim', *Journal of the Warburg and Courtauld Institutes* 39 (1976), 69–103.

'Scepticism and Modernity' in T. Sorell (ed.), *The Rise of Modern Philosophy: The Tension between the New and Traditional Philosophies from Machiavelli to Leibniz* (Oxford, 1993), pp. 15–32.

'Theories of Knowledge', in Charles Schmitt et al. (eds.), *The Cambridge History of Renaissance Philosophy* (Cambridge, 1988), pp. 668–84.

The History of Scepticism from Erasmus to Descartes (Assen, 1960).

The History of Scepticism from Erasmus to Spinoza (Berkeley, 1979).

The History of Scepticism from Savonarola to Bayle (Oxford, 2003).

Popkin, Richard H. and José Maia Neto (eds.), *Skepticism in Renaissance and Post-Renaissance Thought: New Interpretations* (Amherst, NY, 2003).

Popkin, Richard H. and Arjo Vanderjagt (eds.), *Scepticism and Irreligion in the Seventeenth and Eighteenth Centuries* (Leiden, 1993).

Post, G., 'The Naturalness of Society and State', in G. Post (ed.), *Studies in Medieval Legal Thought* (Princeton, 1964), pp. 494–561.

Preston, Claire, *Thomas Browne and the Writing of Early Modern Science* (Cambridge, 2005).

Pugliese, Patri, 'Robert Hooke (1635–1703)', in Brian Harrison and Colin Matthew (eds.), *Oxford Dictionary of National Biography* (Oxford, 2004).

Quinn, J. F., *The Historical Constitution of St. Bonaventure's Philosophy* (Toronto, 1973).

Rattansi, P. M., 'Voltaire and the Enlightenment Image of Newton', in H. Lloyd-Jones (ed.), *History and Imagination* (London, 1981), pp. 218–31.

Ratzsch, Del, 'Abraham Kuyper's Philosophy of Science', *Calvin Theological Journal* 27 (1992), 277–303.

Redondi, Pietro, 'From Galileo to Augustine', in Peter Machamer (ed.), *The Cambridge Companion to Galileo* (Cambridge, 1998), pp. 175–210.

Redpath, Peter, *Masquerade of the Dream Walkers: Prophetic Theology from the Cartesians to Hegel* (Amsterdam, 1998).

Reuchlin, Johannes, *On the Art of the Kabbalah*, tr. Martin and Sarah Goodman (Lincoln, NE, 1993).

Ricoeur, Paul, *The Symbolism of Evil* (Boston, 1967).

Ritschl, Albrecht, *Die christliche Lehre von der Rechtfertigung und Versöhnung*, 3 vols. (Bonn, 1882–3).

Ritter, Gerhard, 'Ein historisches Urbild zu Goethes Faust (Agrippa von Nettesheym)', *Preussische Jahrbücher* 161 (1910), 300–5.

Robbins, Lionel, *An Essay on the Nature and Significance of Economic Science*, 2nd edn (London, 1952).

Roberts, Jon H. and James Turner, *The Sacred and the Secular University* (Princeton, 2000).

Roberts, Michael, *Poetry and the Cult of the Martyrs: The* Liber Peristephanon *of Prudentius* (Ann Arbor, 1993).

Rodis Lewis, Geneviève, 'Augustinisme et Cartésianisme à Port-Royale', in E. J. Dijksterhuis (ed.), *Descartes et le Cartésianisme Hollandais* (Paris, 1950), pp. 131–82.

Rogers, G. A. J., 'Descartes and the English', in J. D. North and J. J. Roche (eds.), *The Light of Nature* (Dordrecht, 1985), pp. 281–301.

Rogers, G. A. J. (ed.), *Locke's Philosophy: Content and Context* (Oxford, 1996).

Rondet, Henri, 'Le péché originel dans la tradition: Tertullien, Clément, Origène', *Bulletin de Littérature Ecclésiastique* 67 (1966), 115–48.

   Original Sin: The Patristic and Theological Background, tr. C. Finegan (New York, 1972).

Rorty, Amélie, 'The Structure of Descartes' *Meditations*', in Amélie Rorty, *Essays on Descartes' Meditations* (Berkeley, 1986).

Rorty, Richard, *Philosophy and the Mirror of Nature* (Princeton, 1980).

Rossi, Paolo, *Francis Bacon: From Magic to Science* (Chicago, 1968).

Logic and the Art of Memory, tr. Stephen Clucas (London, 2000).

Philosophy, Technology and the Arts in the Early Modern Era (New York, 1970).

Rubidge, Bradley, 'Descartes's *Meditations* and Devotional Meditations', *JHI* 51 (1990), 27–49.

Russier, Jeanne, *La Foi selon Pascal*, 2 vols. (Paris, 1949).

Sahlins, Marshall, 'The Sadness of Sweetness: The Native Anthropology of Western Cosmology', *Current Anthropology* 37 (1996), 395–428.

Salisbury, Joyce, *The Beast Within: Animals in the Middle Ages* (London, 1994).

Salmon, Vivian (ed.), *The Works of Francis Lodwick: A Study of His Writings in the Intellectual Context of the Seventeenth Century* (London, 1972).

Saveson, J., 'Differing Reactions to Descartes among the Cambridge Platonists', *JHI* 21 (1960), 560–7.

Scattola, Merio, 'Before and After Natural Law: Models of Natural Law in Ancient and Modern Times', in Tim Hochstrasser (ed.), *Early Modern Natural Law Theories: Context and Strategies in the Early Enlightenment* (Dordrecht, 2003), pp. 1–30.

Schaff, Philip (ed.), *Creeds of Christendom*, 4th edn, 3 vols. (New York, 1919).

Schmaltz, Tad, 'Malebranche on Ideas and the Vision in God', in Steven Nadler (ed.), *The Cambridge Companion to Malebranche* (Cambridge, 2000), pp. 58–86.

Schmidt-Biggemann, Wilhelm, 'Christian Kabbala', in Alison Coudert (ed.), *The Language of Adam / Die Sprache Adams* (Wiesbaden, 1999), pp. 81–121.

Schmitt, Charles, *Cicero Scepticus: A Study of the Influence of the 'Academica' in the Renaissance* (The Hague, 1972).

'Perennial Philosophy: From Agostino Steuco to Leibniz', *JHI* 27 (1966), 505–32.

'The Rediscovery of Ancient Skepticism in Modern Times', in M. Burnyeat (ed.), *The Skeptical Tradition* (Berkeley, 1983), pp. 225–51.

Schochet, G., *Patriarchalism in Political Thought: The Authoritarian Family and Political Speculation and Attitudes Especially in Seventeenth-Century England* (Oxford, 1975).

Schouls, Peter, *Reasoned Freedom: John Locke and Enlightenment* (Ithaca, 1992).

Schrecker, P. and A. M. (eds.), *Leibniz: Monadology and Other Philosophical Essays* (Indianapolis, 1965).

Schürer, E., *The History of the Jewish People in the Age of Jesus Christ*, tr. G. Vermes et al. (Edinburgh, 1986).

Scriba, C. J., 'The Autobiography of John Wallis', *Notes and Records of the Royal Society* 25 (1970), 17–46.

Sedgwick, Alexander, *Jansenism in Seventeenth-Century France: Voices from the Wilderness* (Charlottesville, 1977).

Sepper, Dennis, 'The Texture of Thought: Why Descartes' *Meditationes* is Meditational, and Why it Matters', in Stephen Gaukroger, John Schuster, and John Sutton (eds.), *Descartes' Natural Philosophy* (London, 2000), pp. 736–50.

Serjeantson, Richard (ed.), *Generall Learning: A Seventeenth-Century Treatise on the Formation of the General Scholar*, by Meric Casaubon (Cambridge, 1999).

Seznec, Jean, *The Survival of the Pagan Gods* (New York, 1953).

Shapin, Steven, 'Descartes the Doctor: Rationalism and its Therapies', *BJHS* 33 (2000), 131–54.

    The Scientific Revolution (Chicago, 1996).

Shapin, Steven and Simon Schaffer, *Leviathan and the Air Pump: Hobbes, Boyle, and the Experimental Life* (Princeton, 1985).

Shapiro, Barbara, *Probability and Certainty in the Seventeenth-Century England* (Princeton, 1983).

Smith, George, 'The Methodology of the *Principia*', in I. Bernard Cohen and George E. Smith (eds.), *The Cambridge Companion to Newton* (Cambridge, 2002), pp. 138–73.

Smith, N., *Perfection Proclaimed: Language and Literature in English Radical Religion, 1640–1660* (Oxford, 1989).

Smith, P., *The Business of Alchemy: Science and Culture in the Holy Roman Empire* (Princeton, 1994).

Snobelen, Stephen, '"God of gods, and lord of lords": The Theology of Isaac Newton's General Scholium to the *Principia*', *Osiris* 16 (2001), 169–208.

    'Isaac Newton, Heretic: The Strategies of a Nicodemite', *BJHS* 32 (1999), 381–419.

    'Lust, Pride, and Amibition: Isaac Newton and the Devil', in James E. Force and Sarah Hutton (eds.), *Newton and Newtonianism: New Studies* (Dordrecht, 2004), pp. 155–82.

    'To Discourse of God: Isaac Newton's Heterodox Theology and his Natural Philosophy', in Paul Wood (ed.), *Science and Dissent in England, 1688–1945* (Aldershot, 2004), pp. 39–65.

    'William Whiston, Isaac Newton and the Crisis of Publicity', *Studies in History and Philosophy of Science* 35 (2004), 573–603.

Southern, R., *Robert Grosseteste: The Growth of an English Mind in Medieval Europe* (Oxford, 1986).

Spellman, W. M., *The Latitudinarians and the Church of England, 1660–1700* (Athens, GA, 1993).

    John Locke and the Problem of Depravity (Oxford, 1988).

    The Latitudinarians and the Church of England, 1660–1700 (London, 1993).

Springborg, Patricia, 'Hobbes on Religion', in Tom Sorell (ed.), *The Cambridge Companion to Hobbes* (Cambridge, 1996), pp. 346–80.

Spurr, John, 'Latitudinarianism and the Restoration Church', *The Historical Journal* 31 (1988), 61–82.

Stannard, Jerry, 'Medieval Herbals and their Development', *Clio Media* 9 (1974), 23–33.

Stark, Rodney, *For the Glory of God: How Monotheism Led to Reformations, Science, Witch-Hunts and the End of Slavery* (Princeton, 2004).

    The Victory of Reason: How Christianity Led to Freedom, Capitalism and Western Success (New York, 2005).

Steinmetz, David, *Calvin in Context* (Oxford, 1995).

Stephens, Walter, '*Livres de Haulte gresse*: Bibliographic Myth from Rabelais to Du Bartas', *MLN* 120, Supplement (2005), 60–83.

Stohrer, Walter, 'Descartes and Ignatius Loyola: La Flèche and Manresa Revisited', *Journal of the History of Philosophy* 17 (1979), 11–27.

Stone, M. W. F., 'Augustine and Medieval Philosophy', in Eleonore Stump and Norman Kretzmann (eds.), *The Cambridge Companion to Augustine* (Cambridge, 2001), pp. 253–66.

'Michael Baius (1513–1589) and the Debate on "Pure Nature": Grace and Moral Agency in Sixteenth-Century Scholasticism', in Jill Kraye and Risto Saarinen (eds.), *Moral Philosophy on the Threshold of Modernity* (Dordrecht, 2004), pp. 51–90.

Stone, Michael, *Selected Studies in Pseudepigrapha and Apocrypha with Special Reference to the Armenian Tradition* (Leiden, 1991).

The Literature of Adam and Eve (Atlanta, 1992).

Strasser, Gerhard, 'Closed and Open Languages: Samuel Hartlib's Involvement with Cryptology and Universal Languages', in Mark Greengrass, Leslie Taylor and Timothy Raylor (eds.), *Samuel Hartlib and the Universal Reformation* (Cambridge, 1994), pp. 151–61.

Strauss, Gerald, *Luther's House of Learning: Indoctrination of the Young in Reformation Germany* (Baltimore, 1978).

Strohm, Christoph, 'Zugänger zum Naturrecht bei Melanchthon', in Günter Frank (ed.), *Der Theologe Melanchthon* (Stuttgart, 2000), pp. 339–56.

Stump, Eleonore and Norman Kretzmann (eds.), *The Cambridge Companion to Augustine* (Cambridge, 2001).

Sutton, John, 'The Body and the Brain', in Stephen Gaukroger, John Schuster, and John Sutton (eds.), *Descartes' Natural Philosophy* (London, 2000), pp. 697–722.

Philosophy and Memory Traces (Cambridge, 1988).

Tennant, F. R., *The Sources of the Doctrine of the Fall and Original Sin* (New York, 1903).

Teske, R., 'St. Augustine's view of the Original Human Condition in *De Genesi contra Manichaeos*', *Augustinian Studies* 22 (1991), 141–55.

Thomson, Arthur, 'Ignace de Loyola et Descartes: L'influence des exercices spirituels sur les œuvres philosophiques de Descartes', *Archives de philosophie* 35 (1972), 61–85.

Thonnard, F.-J., 'La notion de lumière en philosophie augustinienne', *Recherches Augustiniennes*, 1962, 124–75.

Trapp, Damasius, 'Adnotationes', *Augustinianum* 5 (1965), 147–51.

Trevor-Roper, Hugh, 'Three Foreigners', in *The Crisis of the Seventeenth Century* (Indianapolis, 2001), pp. 219–71.

Tromp, Johannes, 'Cain and Abel in the Greek and Armenian/Georgian Recensions of the *Life of Adam and Eve*', in Gary Anderson, Michael Stone and Johannes Tromp (eds.), *Literature on Adam and Eve* (Leiden, 2000).

van Asselt, Willem, *The Federal Theology of Johannes Coccius (1603–1669)* (Leiden, 2001).

van der Horst, Pieter, *Japheth in the Tents of Shem: Studies on Jewish Hellenism in Antiquity* (Leuven, 2002)

van Kley, D. K., *The Religious Origins of the French Revolution: From Calvin to the Civil Constitution, 1560–1791* (New Haven, 1996).

van Til, C., *Common Grace* (Philadelphia, 1947).

Vendler, Z., 'Descartes' Exercises', *Canadian Journal of Philosophy* 19 (1989), 193–224.

Vermij, Rienk, *The Calvinist Copernicans: The Reception of the New Astronomy in the Dutch Republic* (Amsterdam, 2004).

Vessey, Mark, Karla Pollmann, and Allan D. Fitzgerald (eds.), *History, Apocalypse, and the Secular Imagination: New Essays on Augustine's City of God* (Bowling Green, OH, 1999).

Villey, Pierre, *Les Sources et l'évolution des Essais de Montaigne*, 2 vols. (Paris, 1933).

Viner, Jacob, '"Possessive Individualism" as Original Sin', *Canadian Journal of Economics and Political Science* 29 (1963), 548–59.

Voegelin, Eric, *History of Political Ideas I: Hellenism, Rome, and Early Christianity*, in *Collected Works of Eric Voegelin*, xix (Columbia, 1997).

Vollenhoven, D. H. Th., *De Noodzakelijkheid eener Christelijke Logica* (Amsterdam, 1932).

Waddell, Helen, *Beasts and Saints* (London, 1949).

Walker, D. P., *The Ancient Theology* (London, 1972).

Wallis, R. T., *Neoplatonism* (New York, 1972).

Walmsley, Peter, *Locke's Essay and the Rhetoric of Science* (Lewisburg, PA, 2003).

Warfield, Benjamin B., *Calvin and Augustine* (Philadelphia, 1956).

Waterman, Anthony, 'Economics as Theology: Adam Smith's *Wealth of Nations*', *Southern Economic Journal* 68 (2002), 907–21.

Watson, Richard A. and James E. Force, *The High Road to Pyrrhonism* (San Diego, 1980).

Weaver, David., 'From Paul to Augustine: Romans 5:12 in Early Christian Exegesis', *St. Vladimir's Theological Quarterly* 27 (1983), 187–206.

Weber, F., *System der Altsynagogalen Palästinischen Theologie* (Leipzig, 1880).

Weber, Max, *The Protestant Ethic and the Spirit of Capitalism,* tr. Talcott Parsons (New York, 1958).

Webster, Charles, 'Henry More and Descartes: Some New Sources', *BJHS* 4 (1969), 359–77.

'The Authorship and Significance of Macaria', *Past and Present* 56 (1972), 34–48.

From Paracelsus to Newton: Magic and the Making of Modern Science (Cambridge, 1982)

Samuel Hartlib and the Advancement of Learning (Cambridge, 1971).

The Great Instauration: Science, Medicine, and Reform, 1626–1660 (London, 1975); 2nd edn (Bern, 2002).

Weir, David, *The Origins of Federal Theology in Sixteenth-Century Reformation Thought* (Oxford, 1990).

Westfall, Richard S., *Never at Rest: A Biography of Isaac Newton* (Cambridge, 1983).

Westman, Robert, 'The Melanchthon Circle, Rheticus, and the Wittenberg Interpretation of the Copernican Theory', *Isis* 66 (1975), 164–93.

Whately, Richard, 'Rise, Progress, and Corruptions of Christianity', *The Encyclopaedia Britannica, or Dictionary of Arts, Sciences, and General Literature*, 8th edn (Edinburgh, 1852–60).

White, A. D., *History of the Warfare of Science with Theology in Christendom*, 2 vols. (London, 1897).

Williams, N. P., *The Ideas of the Fall and of Original Sin* (London, 1927).

Williams, Patricia, *Doing without Adam and Eve: Sociobiology and Original Sin* (Minneapolis, 2001).

Williams, Steven J., *The 'Secret of Secrets': The Scholarly Career of a pseudo-Aristotelian Text in the Latin Middle Ages* (Ann Arbor, 2003).

'Roger Bacon and his Edition of the Pseudo-Aristotelian *Secretum secretorum*', *Speculum* 69 (1994), 57–73.

Williamson, George, 'Mutability, Decay, and Seventeenth-Century Melancholy', *Journal of English Literary History* 2 (1935), 121–51.

Wingren, Gustaf, *Luther on Vocation*, tr. Carl C. Rasmussen (Philadelphia, 1957).

Wojcik, Jan, *Robert Boyle and the Limits of Reason* (Cambridge, 1997).

Wolter, Allan, 'Duns Scotus on the Necessity of Revealed Knowledge', *Franciscan Studies* 11 (1951), 231–72.

Wood, Neal, 'Tabula Rasa, Social Environmentalism, and the "English Paradigm"', *JHI* 53 (1992), 647–68.

'The Baconian Character of Locke's "Essay"', *Studies in History and Philosophy of Science* 6 (1975), 43–84.

Wood, Paul, 'Methodology and Apologetics: Thomas Sprat's *History of the Royal Society*', *BJHS* 13 (1980), 1–26.

'Science, Philosophy and the Mind', in Roy Porter (ed.), *The Cambridge History of Science*, vol. IV: *Eighteenth Century Science* (Cambridge, 2003), pp. 800–24.

Wright, A. D., *The Counter-Reformation, Catholic Europe and the Non-Christian World* (London, 1982).

Yanni, Carla, *Nature's Museums: Victorian Architecture and the Culture of Display* (Baltimore, 1999).

Yates, Frances, *Giordano Bruno and the Hermetic Tradition* (Chicago, 1991).

The Art of Memory (Chicago, 1966).

Yeo, Richard, 'Ephraim Chambers's Cyclopaedia (1728) and the Tradition of Commonplaces', *JHI* 57 (1996), 157–75.

Yolton, Jean S. (ed.), *John Locke as Translator: Three of the 'Essais' of Pierre Nicole in French and English* (Oxford, 2000).

Yolton, John, *John Locke: Problems and Perspectives* (Cambridge, 1969).

Young, Brian, 'Newtonianism and the Enthusiasm of Enlightenment', *Studies in History and Philosophy of Science* 35 (2004), 645–63.

Ziolkowski, Theodore, *The Sin of Knowledge: Ancient Themes and Modern Variations* (Princeton, 2000).

Index

Printed in the United States
145260LV00003B/53/P